Deadlock and Disillusionment

The American History Series

Abbott, Carl *Urban America in the Modern Age: 1920 to the Present*, 2d ed.

Aldridge, Daniel W. *Becoming American: The African American Quest for Civil Rights, 1861–1976*

Barkan, Elliott Robert *And Still They Come: Immigrants and American Society, 1920s to the 1990s*

Bartlett, Irving H. *The American Mind in The Mid-Nineteenth Century*, 2d ed.

Beisner, Robert L. *From the Old Diplomacy to the New, 1865–1900*, 2d ed.

Blaszczyk, Regina Lee *American Consumer Society, 1865–2005: From Hearth to HDTV*

Borden, Morton *Parties and Politics in the Early Republic, 1789–1815*

Carpenter, Roger M. *"Times Are Altered with Us": American Indians from First Contact to the New Republic*

Carter, Paul A. *The Twenties in America*, 2d ed.

Cherny, Robert W. *American Politics in the Gilded Age, 1868–1900*

Conkin, Paul K. *The New Deal*, 3d ed.

Doenecke, Justus D., and John E. Wilz *From Isolation to War, 1931–1941*, 4th ed.

Ferling, John *Struggle for a Continent: The Wars of Early America*

Ginzberg, Lori D. *Women in Antebellum Reform*

Griffin, C. S. *The Ferment of Reform, 1830–1860*

Hess, Gary R. *The United States at War, 1941–45*, 3d ed.

Iverson, Peter, and Wade Davies *"We Are Still Here": American Indians since 1890*, 2d ed.

James, D. Clayton, and Anne Sharp Wells *America and the Great War, 1914–1920*

Kraut, Alan M. *The Huddled Masses: The Immigrant in American Society, 1880–1902*, 2d ed.

Levering, Ralph B. *The Cold War: A Post-Cold War History*, 3d ed.

Link, Arthur S. and Richard L. McCormick *Progressivism*

Martin, James Kirby, and Mark Edward Lender *"A Respectable Army":*

The Military Origins of the Republic, 1763–1789, 3d ed.

McCraw, Thomas K. *American Business Since 1920: How It Worked*, 2d ed.

McMillen, Sally G. *Southern Women: Black and White in the Old South*, 2d ed.

Neu, Charles E. *America's Lost War: Vietnam, 1945–1975*

Newmyer, R. Kent *The Supreme Court under Marshall and Taney*, 2d ed.

Niven, John *The Coming of the Civil War, 1837–1861*

O'Neill, William L. *The New Left: A History*

Pastorello, Karen *The Progressives: Activism and Reform in American Society, 1893–1917*

Perman, Michael *Emancipation and Reconstruction*, 2d ed.

Porter, Glenn *The Rise of Big Business, 1860–1920*, 3d ed.

Reichard, Gary W. *Politics as Usual: The Age of Truman and Eisenhower*, 2d ed.

Reichard, Gary W. *Deadlock and Disillusionment: American Politics since 1968*

Remini, Robert V. *The Jacksonian Era*, 2d ed.

Riess, Steven A. *Sport in Industrial America, 1850–1920*, 2d ed.

Simpson, Brooks D. *America's Civil War*

Southern, David W. *The Progressive Era and Race: Reaction and Reform, 1900–1917*

Storch, Randi *Working Hard for the American Dream: Workers and Their Unions, World War I to the Present*

Turner, Elizabeth Hayes *Women and Gender in the New South, 1865–1945*

Ubbelohde, Carl *The American Colonies and the British Empire, 1607–1763*, 2d ed.

Weeks, Philip *"Farewell, My Nation": The American Indian and the United States in The Nineteenth Century*, 2d ed.

Wellock, Thomas R. *Preserving the Nation: The Conservation and Environmental Movements, 1870–2000*

Winkler, Allan M. *Home Front U.S.A.: America during World War II*, 3d ed.

Wright, Donald R. *African Americans in the Colonial Era: From African Origins through the American Revolution*, 3d ed.

Deadlock and Disillusionment

American Politics since 1968

Gary W. Reichard

WILEY Blackwell

This edition first published 2016
© 2016 John Wiley & Sons, Inc

Registered Office
John Wiley & Sons, Ltd, The Atrium, Southern Gate, Chichester, West Sussex,
PO19 8SQ, UK

Editorial Offices
350 Main Street, Malden, MA 02148-5020, USA
9600 Garsington Road, Oxford, OX4 2DQ, UK
The Atrium, Southern Gate, Chichester, West Sussex, PO19 8SQ, UK

For details of our global editorial offices, for customer services, and for
information about how to apply for permission to reuse the copyright material
in this book please see our website at www.wiley.com/wiley-blackwell.

The right of Gary W. Reichard to be identified as the author of this work has
been asserted in accordance with the UK Copyright, Designs and Patents
Act 1988.

Library of Congress Cataloging-in-Publication data applied for

9781118934340 (hardback)

9781118934357 (paperback)

A catalogue record for this book is available from the British Library.

Cover image: Getty/Juanmonino

Set in 10/13pt Meridien by SPi Global, Pondicherry, India
Printed and bound in Malaysia by Vivar Printing Sdn Bhd

1   2016

Contents

Contents

List of Illustrations

List of Illustrations

Preface

Like many books, this one took a long time—more than a decade—from conceptualization to completion. From the start, however, the working title and thesis remained unchanged. That the title *Deadlock and Disillusionment* still seems apt confirms that the interpretation that led me to propose this book to my then-publisher, Harlan Davidson, has held up over the succeeding ten years and more. Readers will judge for themselves whether they share my view, of course—but this belief has sustained me during the course of this long project.

For permitting me the luxury of this long gestation period—while I was diverted by successive administrative assignments, briefly retired, unretired, and have since been diverted again—I owe a tremendous debt of gratitude to my friend and editor, Andrew Davidson. It was Andrew who encouraged me when I suggested to him the idea of a "current political history" title for the *American History* series, to which I had earlier contributed a volume on mid-twentieth-century politics—and he stuck with me through years when surely he must have entertained doubts that the new volume would ever see the light of day. Thanks, Andrew, for your faith in my good intentions—and for your good-natured encouragement along the way. I hope you will feel at least somewhat repaid by the fact that the series, now part of John Wiley & Sons, again has a "current political history" volume.

I want to thank also four professionals whose help was invaluable in developing my manuscript into this finished work: Wiley senior project editor Julia Kirk and Emma Brown, who assisted with permissions for the images used herein; Wiley editorial assistant Maddie Koufogazos, for her great help in the later stages of the book's production, and Janet Moth, a first-rate copy-editor.

I also extend heartfelt thanks to two fine historians who took time to read the manuscript and who offered very helpful comments that allowed me to improve it. Clayton Koppes of Oberlin College, my longtime friend, read most of this book in an earlier draft and offered numerous helpful suggestions as to both content and organization. It helped that these suggestions were couched tactfully so as not to break my spirit as I worked toward completion of the project. Bill Chafe of Duke University generously agreed to serve as a reviewer of the near-final product for Wiley and he, too, offered excellent suggestions to strengthen the final product. I appreciate his careful reading of the work, as well as his willingness to allow me to acknowledge him in this public way. I apologize to both of these scholars for not taking all of their suggestions, but I hope they will recognize the specific ways in which their ideas made the book better. For any remaining weaknesses, of course, I accept full responsibility.

Finally, I want to thank my life partner and best friend, Oswaldo Pena, for his unflagging support for this project as I gave endless weekends and evenings to its completion—especially in its final stages. I might somehow have gotten to the end of the project without his unflagging support, but it certainly wouldn't have been as much fun.

Gary W. Reichard
Staten Island, NY
July 2015

Introduction: 1968—The End of an Era

Nineteen-sixty-eight was truly an *annus horribilis* in American history. Most distressing and disconcerting for the nation, two major political figures lionized by their supporters as the best hopes for achieving racial and social justice were gunned down within the short space of two months. The reverberations were drastic. The sniper shooting of 39-year-old civil rights leader Martin Luther King, Jr., in early April fanned a frenzy of frustration in heavily black urban communities across the country, producing riots in more than a hundred major cities that left thirty-nine dead and caused more than $50 million-worth of damage in already blighted neighborhoods. Two months later, Senator Robert F. Kennedy's assassination in a Los Angeles hotel on the very night of his narrow victory in the California Democratic primary seemed to deal a final, dispiriting blow to millions of Americans—especially young, idealistic anti-war protesters and impoverished African Americans and Hispanics. While not producing the level of violence that King's death had, RFK's killing seemed to end any chance that the ever-deepening divisions and climate of escalating violence in the United States

Deadlock and Disillusionment: American Politics since 1968, First Edition.
Gary W. Reichard.
© 2016 John Wiley & Sons, Inc. Published 2016 by John Wiley & Sons, Inc.

could be resolved by peaceful political means. Together, these senseless killings signaled the emptiness of political promise and an end to harmony and civility in American society. A mere two-and-a-half months after Kennedy's assassination, the bloody riots that accompanied the Democratic nominating convention in Chicago provided confirmation that American politics—indeed, American society—would never be the same.

Despair and disillusionment were manifest throughout American society in 1968. Polls showed deep pessimism across the electorate where questions of the nation's political future were concerned. At least for the previous generation and a half, since the advent of the New Deal—and largely because of it—Americans had grown comfortable in their faith that any social divisions or policy disagreements in the public sphere could be worked out via the ballot box. Voters could—and did—express their pleasure or displeasure for the governing party and then, with a mandate established at the polls, politicians could usually be trusted to work together and often across party lines to advance the public interest in directions that the majority of voters had endorsed. With the exception of the few years during which political and social harmony were riven by the stridency of McCarthyism, by and large those entrusted with the reins of power in Washington, D.C., including the leaders in both houses of Congress, had worked to find ways to compromise policy differences in the public interest, rather than concentrating on those differences.

Structurally, this political generation had been marked by orderly and civil transfers of power and a palpable sense of accountability to the public on the part of presidents and most members of Congress. Despite much gnashing of teeth among political scientists at mid-century about the lack of "a responsible party system," in fact one party or the other had held simultaneous control of both the executive and legislative branches for twenty-eight of the thirty-six years following FDR's victory in 1932. All of this—accountability, stability, public confidence in the political system, and the apparent valuing of the public interest over partisan self-interest (not to mention basic civility in the political arena)—was to change after 1968. Increasingly, the disillusionment of American voters would be obvious in their unwillingness to provide real mandates for either party. In the forty-eight-year period beginning in 1968, single-party control over the executive and legislative branches became a rare exception: in only twelve of those years were the White House and Congress controlled by the same party (the Democrats in 1977–1981, 1993–1995, and 2009–2011 and the Republicans only from 2003 to 2007). In other words, in nearly 70 percent of the twenty-three elections during this long era, the voting public consciously opted for divided—and, it could be argued, irresponsible—government. How could it not be expected that deadlock (or "gridlock," as the media more often labeled it) would be the hallmark of American politics in these years?

Other forces contributed to deadlock, as well. As several political scientists have demonstrated, party polarization, both in the electorate and in Congress, steadily intensified beginning in the early 1970s. Accompanying this trend, perhaps as a side effect of a decline of civility in American society as a whole, was a loss of "comity" in government. This was most noticeable in Congress, where traditions of respectful language and procedures had helped to maintain positive relations across party lines. All of these changes greatly reduced chances for compromise on matters of policy. The resulting inaction in turn reinforced public disillusionment with politics and government, generally. Relations between the executive and legislative branches also frayed noticeably. Beginning with the "credibility gap" that opened up under Lyndon Johnson and worsened under Richard Nixon, culminating in battles over war powers, impoundment of appropriated funds, and—ultimately—impeachment, Congress stiffened its resistance to any further strengthening of the presidency. This institutional rivalry, too, served to slow down the wheels of government.

Most of all, however, such deadlock was the result of purposeful, continual imposition by voters of "checks and balances" to limit either party's potential to govern effectively. At the same time, unrealistic as it might have been in the circumstances, the public continued to yearn for dramatic change—for a new era. Such yearning manifested itself repeatedly in presidential elections. Hopefulness for a major political turnaround was redolent in the presidential campaign themes of the era, from Nixon's "Bring Us Together Again" in 1968 to Barack Obama's "Change We Can Believe In" in 2008. This recurrent tension—the voters' almost wistful searching for dramatic, meaningful political change, followed regularly (and usually quickly) by a knee-jerk correction of course that made it impossible for either party to "go too far"— was to produce four decades and more of deadlock and disillusionment in American politics. Whether this longstanding gridlock will one day pass or represents an irreversible negative transformation in American politics remains an open question.

1

The Politics of Cynicism, 1968–1974

As 1968 dawned, no one could have predicted the political landscape that would prevail little more than a year later. President Lyndon Johnson, widely regarded as a political maestro and the recipient of landslide endorsement by the voters four years earlier, would be in lonely exile in Texas on his Johnson City ranch. Former Alabama governor George Wallace, reviled by most of the public in the early 1960s for his clenched-teeth refusal to bow to civil rights advances whose time had come, would loom as a future presidential possibility based on his strong showing as a third-party candidate in November's presidential election. Most significantly, Richard Nixon, who six years earlier had angrily announced his exit from politics, would occupy the White House. The Democrats would still control both houses of Congress, largely through inertia; but in truth, the party would lie in tatters as a result of the epic intra-party battles inside and outside the Chicago convention hall in which Hubert Humphrey secured the nomination as the Democrats' standard-bearer in August. Finally, thanks to the inroads made by both Nixon and Wallace during the bitterly contested presidential campaign, the Solid Democratic

Deadlock and Disillusionment: American Politics since 1968, First Edition.
Gary W. Reichard.
© 2016 John Wiley & Sons, Inc. Published 2016 by John Wiley & Sons, Inc.

South, which had prevailed for so many decades, would no longer be reliably Democratic.

Miseries unleashed by the Vietnam War were responsible for much of this turning inside out of American politics. But so, too, were the deep wounds inflicted by the assassinations of the Reverend Martin Luther King, Jr., and Bobby Kennedy, and the many lives lost and hopes dashed in the riot-torn spring and early summer of 1968. In a sense, Nixon's triumph in the three-cornered presidential election of 1968 served as the ultimate expression of the sense of futility that so many Americans felt. A man who owed his political ascent to his skill at "slash-and-burn" politics (witness his role in the nefarious Alger Hiss case and his 1950 campaign against the "pink lady," Helen Gahagan Douglas) had been called upon by the voters to try to bring order out of political chaos. "Bring Us Together Again"—the mythical slogan that Nixon invented and cited during his campaign—would be the theme of his inaugural speech in January 1969.

As president, Richard Nixon did anything but bring the nation together. Having successfully employed a divisive "southern strategy" to win first the Republican nomination and then the White House, he continued to encourage divisiveness in the electorate in the supposed interests of the "Silent Majority" of Americans whom he saw as aggrieved by the liberal excesses of the Great Society and hostile to the mostly youthful protesters who had taken to the streets in opposition to the Vietnam War and—sometimes—authority in general. Far more the cynical and self-interested pragmatist than the principled conservative for whom many of his supporters had hoped, Nixon carved out a mixed record in domestic policy. Having strongly implied in the 1968 campaign that he had a plan to end U.S. participation in the war in Vietnam with honor, he instead steadily escalated a damaging air war against the enemy until, four years into his presidency, he found a way to extricate U.S. troops from a losing situation.

Ultimately, Nixon was done in by the very cynicism that had propelled him into the White House and fueled his major decisions as president. Obsessed with winning re-election in

1972, distrustful of nearly everyone around him, and certain that his political critics were potential enemies of the state, he condoned illegal tactics to eliminate any and all challenges to his presidency. Then—even worse—he lied repeatedly to the American people about his role in such excesses. As a result, less than two years after having won a smashing re-election victory, he became the first U.S. president to resign from office. If the American people were "brought together" by the Nixon presidency, it was only in shared disgust and distrust for all things Washington.

The Shaping of a New Majority

Forces pointing to backlash against the national Democratic party were of nearly unprecedented proportions in 1968. First and foremost, of course, was the deep public frustration with the course and costs (in lives and dollars) of the Vietnam War, especially after the Tet offensive in February, in which the enemy caught U.S. forces by surprise. Added to this were widespread distaste and disappointment with what were seen as the excesses of President Lyndon Johnson's Great Society, especially its civil rights component. Nearly as powerful was a deepening public concern about crime in the streets and the increasing stridency and violence of protests against the war and around race issues. "In the popular mind," writes Lewis Gould in *1968: The Election that Changed America*, "the state of race relations became linked to protests against the war in Vietnam. The resulting social trauma was seen as evidence that the Johnson administration was insensitive to issues of 'law and order' and unwilling to take a tough stand against domestic dissent." Simultaneously, significant changes in the demographics of the United States had obvious political implications. The mushrooming growth and increasing political clout of the "Sunbelt," and particularly its sprawling suburbs, held great, if still incalculable, potential for upending liberal Democratic dominance.

Lyndon Johnson's vulnerabilities were so extreme by late 1967 as to invite potential challenges from within his own party. First to emerge, at the end of November, was Senator Eugene McCarthy of Minnesota, who had responded to the pleadings of anti-war activists to take up their cause (after their first choice, New York's senator Robert F. Kennedy, had declined to take the political risk). When McCarthy confounded early predictions by winning 42 percent of the Democratic vote in the March 12 New Hampshire primary (to Johnson's 49 percent), the media treated it as a defeat for the president. Four days later, a potentially more formidable challenge presented itself when the once reluctant Kennedy formally announced his own anti-war candidacy.

Johnson later claimed that he had much earlier discussed with his wife Lady Bird and his close political ally John Connally the possibility of not seeking re-election and that he had originally planned to include such an announcement in his January 1968 State of the Union address. Whether or not he had made up his mind earlier, on March 31 the president stunned the nation by announcing at the end of a televised speech on the war, "I shall not seek, and I will not accept, the nomination of my party for another term as your President."

All bets were now off as to how the Democratic race might turn out. McCarthy and Kennedy, as the only declared candidates, briefly had the contest to themselves. In late April, however, a third candidate emerged: Vice President Hubert Humphrey. As vice president, Humphrey had suffered more than a few cruel, public humiliations at the hands of Johnson, but he had remained loyal, in the hope that someday he would have his own shot at the presidency. Declaring too late to contest the two anti-war candidates in the primaries (which he would likely have lost anyway), Humphrey set to work among local and state party leaders in order to amass the necessary number of delegates for nomination.

Kennedy and McCarthy traded victories in a string of hard-fought primaries into the early summer. The June 5 California contest was critical. As the final votes were being tallied in the Golden State's primary, Kennedy's victory seemed at last to have narrowed the contest to a two-man race between himself and Humphrey. Within moments of exiting his victory celebration in a Los Angeles hotel, however, he was assassinated by a single gunman, Sirhan Sirhan. As the horror of yet another senseless assassination slowly faded in the weeks that followed, gloom and despair deepened in the Democratic party. Without the support of those who had backed Kennedy, it was impossible for McCarthy to prevail in the Democratic National Convention in Chicago, but deep and lingering animosities between the backers of the two anti-war candidates created a divide that could not be breached.

The Republican nomination contest, meanwhile, unfolded relatively smoothly. The campaign of the early front-runner, Michigan governor George Romney, had imploded in February as a result of his unfortunate comment that he had been "brain-washed" while meeting with U.S. military leaders in Vietnam. His withdrawal from the field on the eve of the important New Hampshire primary resulted in a whopping victory for Richard Nixon, who won almost 80 percent of the vote. Only two challengers remained: New York governor Nelson Rockefeller, the choice of the most moderate elements in the GOP; and a rapidly rising star on the party's right, California's recently elected governor, the telegenic former movie star Ronald Reagan. Rockefeller waited too long to declare himself a candidate and won only one primary. Reagan was another matter. Wildly popular among Republican conservatives because of his effective and loyal support for Barry Goldwater in the disastrous 1964 GOP presidential campaign, he had the additional advantage of being a fresh new face (and voice). In 1968, however, Reagan was still *too* new, and Nixon had built well. Nixon sat squarely in the driver's seat, with nearly enough pledged delegates for nomination before the Miami convention opened.

Even before the two parties could sort out their respective nomination battles, a dangerous third force had appeared in the 1968 election campaign in the person of former Alabama governor George C. Wallace. Having run surprisingly well in the 1964 Democratic primaries, the still-unrepentant segregationist was running on a new American Independent Party (AIP) ticket in '68, and his name was on the ballot in virtually every state for the November election. Though eschewing outright segregation as an objective, Wallace advocated slowing down desegregation of the nation's schools and called for stronger prosecution of the war in Vietnam, as well as forceful suppression of the growing anti-war protests. His promise to roll his limousine over the bodies of protesters who might try to get in his way captured the essence of his message. Although there was never any chance that he could win the election, it seemed possible that he could hold the balance of power in the House of Representatives, if neither major party candidate was able to win a majority in the Electoral College.

The results of the 1968 presidential election were foreshadowed by the tale of the two major party conventions. The Republicans, convening in an orderly manner in Miami in mid-August, experienced only minor drama, as the Reagan forces attempted to woo southern delegates away from the Nixon camp. They proved no match, however, for South Carolina's wily senior senator, Strom Thurmond, who helped lock up Nixon's nomination by assuring his southern colleagues that Nixon was safe on the busing issue and would be reliable in making future Supreme Court nominations. Nixon's selection of Maryland governor Spiro Agnew as his running-mate solidified his support among party conservatives, since Agnew had recently made his name as a hard-liner in response to urban rioting in his state.

The chaos at the Democrats' convention in Chicago a couple of weeks later stood in sharp contrast to Nixon's coronation in Miami. Though Humphrey's nomination was a foregone conclusion, the televised violence between protesters and Chicago police officers that unfolded immediately outside the convention hall captured the attention of millions of potential voters. In what a specially appointed presidential commission later described as a "police riot," Chicago's finest dented the heads of scores of disillusioned anti-war protesters who were demonstrating against the vice president's nomination because of his seeming complicity in the carnage in Vietnam. Humphrey's choice of Maine senator Edmund Muskie as his running-mate was credible enough, but the ticket was in tremendous trouble from the outset.

The southern strategy that had won Nixon his party's nomination was very much in evidence in the fall campaign. The Republicans' strategy matched to a tee the scenario laid out by a young Nixon campaign aide, Kevin Phillips, in his widely read 1969 book, *The Emerging Republican Majority.* Very soon, Phillips argued, American politics would be dominated by a conservative, Sunbelt-based majority made up of Roman Catholic working-class and suburban middle-class voters. This bloc should be the GOP focus in the campaign. With Wallace in the mix, moreover, Nixon could not and did not totally avoid playing the "race card." In the South, especially, his ads emphasized opposition to busing to effect school desegregation and suggested that a vote for the third-party candidate would be wasted since the "real choice" was between himself and Humphrey.

In the face of Nixon's southern strategy and Wallace's darker appeal to the more conservative elements of the traditional Democratic coalition, Humphrey was all but helpless. Finally, in late September, he broke from administration policy on the war, promising a halt to the bombing of North Vietnam by U.S. warplanes if elected—hugely irritating President Johnson in the process. As later evidence would show, however, in the final stages of the campaign Johnson became aware of outright illegal tampering by the Nixon campaign in the stalled Paris peace talks, whereby the Republican candidate's minions were attempting to persuade South Vietnamese President Nguyen Van Thieu to boycott negotiations with the promise of getting a better deal from a President Nixon. Johnson chose not to drop a bombshell on the electorate by "outing" Nixon for this violation of law, but he privately seethed and gave Humphrey an important boost just days before the election by announcing a bombing halt as well as the resumption of peace talks in Paris. This helped, but not quite enough. Though the Democrat had seemed to edge ahead in the polls on the final pre-election weekend, when the votes were tallied, Nixon had defeated him by a scant 0.7 percent, with a "mandate" of 43.4 percent of the electorate; Wallace's projected 20 percent of the vote shrank to just over 13 percent. In the all-important Electoral College, however, Nixon prevailed handily, winning 301 electoral votes to Humphrey's 191 and Wallace's 46 (all in the Deep South).

Richard Milhous Nixon was now the thirty-seventh president of the United States—on his own terms and on script. He had skillfully blended sympathy for the South's resistance to the civil rights revolution with an appeal to suburban, middle-class voters who had been turned off by the Great Society. Appealing to what he called the "Forgotten Americans," Nixon heavily emphasized the "law and order" issue, code for racial unrest in the cities, and scored heavily with white voters by doing so; a Harris poll two months before election day found that 84 percent of those responding thought a strong president could make a real difference in returning safety to the streets. He had stayed away from the Vietnam War as an issue, insisting that he did not want to undermine Johnson in his conduct of that conflict. This lack of focus on Vietnam was to have a real cost. "Precisely because the debate over the war during 1968 proved to be so meaningless," writes Walter LaFeber in *The Deadly Bet: LBJ, Vietnam, and the 1968 Election*, Nixon would be able to "continue to commit to the conflict for five more years ... ."

The overall election results suggested deadlock. Nixon's coattails were so short that neither house of Congress went Republican. He was, in fact, the first newly elected president since Zachary Taylor in 1849 to face a Congress completely in the hands of the political opposition. Even by picking up five seats in the Senate, the Republicans cut the Democratic majority only to 58-42. In the House, the GOP gained only four seats, leaving the Democratic majority at 243-192.

That the southern strategy would carry over into Nixon's presidency became clear immediately, as he announced in his inaugural address that he would seek no additional civil rights legislation, since the nation's laws had now "caught up with our consciences." Within months, Attorney General John Mitchell testified in congressional hearings against renewal of the 1965 Voting Rights Act, which the Democratic Congress renewed anyway. With greater effect, the administration intervened to temper the impact of the Supreme Court's 1968 decree in *Green v. County School Board of New Kent County* that so-called "freedom of choice" plans could no longer be used to delay desegregation of unitary school districts. In July 1969, when twenty-three Mississippi districts affected by the *Green* decision appealed for a delay, the White House issued a mixed statement. "This administration is unequivocally committed to the goal of finally ending racial discrimination in schools," read the White House release, adding that the deadlines facing the Mississippi districts might need to be extended to allow their appeal to be heard by the Supreme Court.

A key ingredient of Nixon's southern strategy during the campaign had been his oft-repeated promise to appoint conservatives to the Supreme Court. Almost immediately, he had an unprecedented opportunity to make good on this commitment by appointing two new justices. This unusual situation had resulted from a late 1968 deal between Chief Justice Earl Warren and outgoing president Lyndon Johnson that had gone sour. Fearing that the 1968 election would produce a president unlikely to appoint a chief justice sympathetic to the legacy of the liberal court he had led, Warren offered to retire as chief justice so that Johnson could elevate liberal justice Abe Fortas to the post. When Fortas's questionable business dealings and inappropriate continuing connections to the White House became issues, however, he was not only denied the chief justice position but was ultimately forced to resign from the court altogether. The result: two vacancies for Nixon to fill, including that of chief justice.

As chief justice, Nixon named Warren Burger, a respected if not overly distinguished conservative jurist from Minnesota, who was easily confirmed. To fill the second vacancy, the president wanted to appoint someone more obviously reflecting sympathy for the South. His first choice, Circuit Court judge Clement Haynsworth of South Carolina, was rejected by a bipartisan coalition in the Senate because of his failure to recuse himself from more than one case in which there had been an appearance of conflict of interest. Fighting mad, Nixon next nominated Judge G. Harrold Carswell of the Fifth Circuit Court, who lacked any obvious distinction, more than 60 percent of his opinions having been reversed by higher courts. The final straw was the revelation that several years earlier Carswell had publicly declared his belief in "white supremacy." The nomination was dead on arrival in the Senate, although the margin of defeat was only six votes. Carswell's rejection gave Nixon an opportunity to make political hay in the South. Now he could publicly identify with the "martyrdom" of the region. The day after Carswell's defeat, Nixon angrily stated that he understood "the bitter feelings of millions of Americans who live in the South about the act of regional discrimination that took place in the Senate yesterday," and pledged not to invite another such affront to the region. His next nominee, Judge Harry Blackmun from Minnesota, was confirmed easily.

Nixon did not yet control the Supreme Court, however. In October 1969, the justices spoke again on desegregation, ruling against the recalcitrant Mississippi districts in *Alexander v. Holmes County Board of Education*. In a unanimous decision, the court insisted that "effective immediately … the schools in those districts be operated on a unitary basis." Reiterating its reasoning in *Green*, the court asserted that "continued operation of segregated schools under a standard of allowing 'all deliberate speed' for desegregation is no longer constitutionally permissible." With possibilities for any further delay now ended, President Nixon finally urged compliance and courts across the South began to address the remaining instances of "dual," or segregated, districts.

An effective desegregation strategy employed by many school districts even before the *Alexander* decision was the transporting of students to schools outside their immediate neighborhood to create racially balanced schools. "Mandatory busing," unsurprisingly, was opposed by many parents, white and black alike, who feared for the safety of their children. Court challenges sprang up immediately, with most of the pressure coming from suburban white parents. The most publicized such challenge unfolded during the 1969–1970 school year in the 85,000-student Charlotte-Mecklenburg County school district in western North Carolina. In the face of this controversy, Nixon issued a statement affirming the "inviolable principle" of neighborhood schools and drawing a sharp distinction between *de facto* and *de jure* segregation. Where segregation was not the result of legal (*de jure*) segregation but rather of residential patterns, he held, "school authorities are not constitutionally required to take any positive steps to correct the imbalance."

Busing played an important part in the 1970 mid-term elections. Influenced by his conservative advisor Pat Buchanan, Nixon believed the path to firming up the "new majority" that he thought had elected him was to concentrate on social issues that could be divisive for the Democrats. To effect the strategy, Nixon unleashed Vice President Agnew as his surrogate ("Nixon's Nixon," the press dubbed him—a reference to the president's earlier role as hatchet-man for Eisenhower as his running-mate in 1952 and 1956). Agnew took up his role with zeal, spewing alliterative epithets against Democrats all across the nation, in the process coining the term "radic-libs" to paint them as being far outside the American political mainstream. Although the election results were disappointing for the GOP—a pickup of only two seats in the Senate and a loss of nine in the House—they were not bad for the party of a sitting president in off-year elections. Overall, however, the administration's strategy had some long-term costs. "The GOP's abandonment of the middle ground created an opening for a new breed of moderate Democrats," writes Matthew Lassiter in *The Silent Majority: Suburban Politics in the Sunbelt South*, "who dominated southern politics during the 1970s and assumed leadership of the national party during the 1990s."

The mid-term elections did nothing to resolve the divisive busing issue, and instead inflamed further those on either side of it. Once again, it was left to the judiciary to move the matter forward. In April 1971, the Burger Court obliged, taking up the case from Charlotte-Mecklenburg County (*Swann v. Charlotte-Mecklenburg County Board of Education*). Sweeping aside arguments that busing was difficult, awkward to implement, and contrary to the American tradition of local control of schools, the court unanimously asserted that the principle of "paired schools" and the busing of students between those schools were both constitutional and permissible as tools to redress segregation. The court explicitly acknowledged the potential difference in cases of *de jure* and *de facto* segregation and limited the scope of its decision in an important way. The *Swann* decision was far from being the final word on busing, however. "We do not reach in this case," the justices stated, "the question whether a showing that school segregation as a consequence of other types of state action, without any discriminatory action by school authorities, is a constitutional violation requiring remedial action by a school desegregation decree." Left unresolved was the question of what to do in those hundreds of school districts—largely outside the South—where "dual systems" existed solely as the result of segregated residential patterns.

Predictably, the Nixon administration responded coolly to the High Court's decision, stating simply that "it was the obligation of the local schools and district courts to carry out the mandate in *Swann*." Polls showed steadily declining public support for busing: in a November 1971 Gallup survey, 76 percent of all respondents opposed "busing of Negro and white school children from one school district to another"; among blacks, 45 percent were in support and 47 percent opposed.

Conservatism as Reform

To a degree Nixon neither expected nor desired, he was preoccupied by economic problems throughout his presidency—that is, until Watergate swamped all other issues. Lyndon Johnson's effort to afford both "guns and butter" had been only a minor issue in the 1968 election, but by the time of Nixon's inauguration in January 1969, inflation demanded attention. As Allen Matusow writes in *Nixon's Economy: Booms, Busts, Dollars, & Votes*, the new administration had two choices: pop the balloon quickly or "let the air out ... slowly." Nixon opted for the latter approach, which failed utterly. By the end of the year the nation faced steadily worsening unemployment, while inflation continued unabated—an unprecedented scenario that the media dubbed "stagflation." The administration's response was a wildly shifting series of interventions and economic controls that were inconsistent with traditional Republican policies and never comfortably embraced by Nixon himself.

As inflation continued at troublesome levels into 1970, Nixon surprised politicians and public alike by naming John Connally as his new secretary of the treasury. A former Democratic governor of Texas and longtime ally of Lyndon Johnson, Connally was perfect for the assignment and his impact on administration policy was soon apparent. In August 1971, Nixon announced a New Economic Policy (NEP) in a nationally televised speech, which included the imposition of price and wage controls for the first time since the Korean War. The NEP also included a new 10 percent "border tax" on imports and ended the longstanding convertibility of dollars into gold on the world market.

Price and wage controls proved ineffectual, however, as inflation stubbornly continued to rise. Consequently, Nixon announced Phase II of the NEP in October, extending the controls for another six months. When this extension had little impact, he simply opted for disengagement, labeling as "Phase III" the virtual suspension of all controls. Shifting focus to the problem of unemployment, which was hovering around 6 percent, the administration now took steps to ramp up federal spending.

Just as Nixon's handling of stagflation defied easy characterization, his approach to matters of social policy was difficult to pin down. In August 1969, he announced the launching of a "New Federalism," including two bold new programs, revenue sharing and an overhaul of the existing welfare system. The New Federalism never assumed coherent shape, nor did the Democratic Congress take action on either revenue sharing or the welfare reform proposal. Undaunted, and with even greater fanfare, in January 1971 Nixon reintroduced both plans, along with several others—including a bold plan for restructuring the executive branch under an even more sweeping label: "The New American Revolution." Of the administration proposals embraced in this new "reform" package, revenue sharing now seemed to have the greatest likelihood of passage. The basic idea was to substitute categorical grants to the states in six broad areas (education, urban development, transportation, job training, rural development, and law enforcement), for the vast array of narrowly defined federal grant programs that had grown up since the New Deal.

17

The concept had strong public support at the outset, but many members of Congress—liberal and conservative alike—were wary of losing control of this federal largesse. In the end, however, the State and Local Fiscal Assistance Act was enacted in June 1972, with considerable support from both parties. Initially authorized for five years, revenue sharing would remain intact into the 1980s.

The welfare reform element of the New American Revolution, the Family Assistance Plan (FAP), was an even harder sell than revenue sharing. In direct contrast to the latter program, FAP aimed to replace a number of categorical programs administered at least partly at the state level with direct federal income assistance to low-income families. The program proposed annual federal payments of $1,600 (scheduled to rise to $2,500 by 1971) to low-income families of four, coupled with a requirement that the heads of such families—excepting mothers of young children—be willing to "accept work or training." FAP drew fire from both extremes of the political spectrum in Congress. On its final run around the congressional track on the eve of the 1972 election, it was defeated mainly due to opposition from liberal Democrats, but Nixon probably did himself more damage with conservatives than with liberals in pressing for this version of welfare reform. As David Greenberg has written in *Nixon's Shadow: The History of an Image*, FAP was "the source of the right's conception of Nixon as a sellout," and "dashed [their] hopes of a Nixon-led right-wing revival."

Within twenty-five years of Nixon's presidency, observes Greenberg, "Nixon revisionism" had blossomed full-blown among historians and journalists. In these revisionist works, he notes, "Nixon appeared, improbably, as an innovator in domestic policy, an activist steward of the Great Society, the last of the big-spending liberal presidents." This view contrasted sharply with earlier assessments, which tended to view Nixon's overall impact as retrograde rather than progressive, especially when it came to matters of race and civil liberties. Notwithstanding such revisionist efforts, however, historians generally see Nixon's domestic record as centrist, ascribing much of what seemed "liberal" to his chief domestic advisor, John Ehrlichman. Matusow writes, for example, that "Nixon was neither a liberal nor the conservative of popular belief. He was a politician bent on preempting the center of American politics to build a New Majority." Stephen Hess takes a slightly different slant in *The Professor and the President: Daniel Patrick Moynihan in the Nixon White House*, suggesting that Nixon's overall domestic record was "moderate," but only "by averaging— moving sharply right, followed by moving sharply left."

There is a simpler explanation for the seemingly contradictory elements of Nixon's domestic policies: cynicism. The 3,700 hours of Nixon White House tapes that have become public over the years provide ample evidence that he had contempt for the electorate and was motivated far more often by opportunism than by anything that remotely resembled either a reformist bent or concern about the federal government's role in ensuring the "public good." Insofar as ideology mattered to him in domestic matters, Richard Nixon was a conservative. What finally motivated him in any particular situation, however, was whatever was needed to ensure his own political survival.

The Politics of War and Détente

On the day before Richard Nixon's inauguration, thousands of anti-war protesters staged a "counter-inaugural." Estimated by D.C. police at 5,000 and by organizers at 12,000, the protesters symbolically marched from the White House to the Capitol— opposite to the direction Nixon would traverse the next day. This mostly peaceful protest was followed by greater visible hostility to the new president on Inauguration Day itself. As the limousine carrying Nixon and his wife Pat passed between the crowds lining both sides of Pennsylvania Avenue, 300 to 400 militant protesters shouted obscenities and lobbed sticks, stones, bottles, and smoke bombs at the motorcade. District of Columbia police, reinforced by combat-equipped National Guardsmen and unarmed troops of the 83rd Airborne Division, arrested eighty-one protesters.

Nixon's inaugural address contrasted sharply with these scenes of contempt and hostility. In addition to promising to "consecrate"

19

his presidency to the cause of peace, he assured the nation that he was willing to listen to his critics. "We cannot learn from one another," he said in one of the most oft-quoted sentences in the address, "until we stop shouting at one another—until we speak quietly enough so that our words can be heard as well as our voices." *New York Times* columnist James Reston, no fan of Nixon's, wrote approvingly that "[t]he hawkish, combative, anti-Communist, anti-Democratic Nixon of the past was not the man on the platform today. He reached out to all the people who opposed him in the last election—progressive Democrats, the young, the blacks, the Soviets."

Figure 1.1 Nixon's "Palace Guard," H. R. "Bob" Haldeman and John R. Ehrlichman. In April 1973, both would be fired, along with White House counsel John Dean, due to fallout from the Watergate scandal. © Bettmann/CORBIS

Such optimism was grossly misplaced. Far from reaching out, Nixon surrounded himself with a "Palace Guard" in the White House, headed by the imperious H. R. (Bob) Haldeman and John Ehrlichman, that ensured minimal access to the president (and shielded him as much as possible from dissenting opinions). Within weeks of his move into the White House, Nixon was seething at congressional critics who seemed intent on challenging White House prerogatives in foreign policy. In February, Senator J. William Fulbright (D-Arkansas), chair of the Senate Foreign Relations Committee (SFRC), infuriated the president by reintroducing a resolution that would increase congressional oversight of presidential commitments abroad and establishing a subcommittee of the SFRC to monitor secret executive agreements. Nixon's national security advisor, Henry Kissinger, shared his boss's low opinion of the legislative branch as a potential partner in foreign policy-making. Together, the two became increasingly secretive and manipulative in their dealings with Congress on Vietnam, as on many other foreign policy issues.

In addition to treating his congressional critics as traitors and enemies, Nixon dramatically ratcheted up secret intelligence-gathering on foes real and imagined in the broader public. While LBJ had begun such wiretaps, the scale of illegal surveillance dwarfed earlier actions. Later, declassified records revealed that over 1500 Americans were being spied on by 1973. Even FBI director J. Edgar Hoover, no defender of civil liberties, was nervous about the sheer volume of such government eavesdropping and, had he not cooperated by dying in May 1972, would likely have been fired by an angry Nixon for obstructionism after nearly half a century in his role.

In his quest for "peace with honor," Nixon intended to continue the four-cornered Paris peace talks involving North Vietnam, the Republic of Vietnam, the National Liberation Front, and the United States, which his campaign had tried to disrupt near the end of the Johnson administration. The challenge was how to create leverage to produce progress at the negotiating table, while at the same time reducing the American military effort in order to undercut domestic opposition to the war.

"I'm not going to wind up like LBJ," he told Haldeman, "holed up in the White House afraid to show my face on the street. I'm going to stop that war. Fast." By March 1969, Nixon settled on a strategy he labeled "Vietnamization": phased withdrawals of American troops coupled with significant increases in training and equipment for the Army of the Republic of Vietnam (ARVN). Privately, he resolved to employ massive military force, as necessary, to force the North Vietnamese to agree to a settlement. In his first meeting with South Vietnam's president, at Midway Island on June 8, Thieu publicly accepted the Vietnamization strategy—although clearly without enthusiasm. Always interested in grand framing for his actions, Nixon explained to reporters in mid-July that Vietnamization was part of a broad new foreign policy approach. According to this new "Nixon Doctrine," nations that sought aid from the United States in ensuring regional security would be expected to take on greater responsibility for their own defense. At the same time, Nixon initiated the first draw-down of U.S. troops in Vietnam, announcing the withdrawal of 25,000 troops in late June.

Nixon took a surreptitious route almost immediately. In March 1969, he ordered the secret bombing of installations in North Vietnamese-controlled parts of Cambodia, directing Air Force command to falsify its logs to conceal from congressional investigators this violation of a neutral neighbor's rights. Simultaneously, he issued the North Vietnamese an ultimatum that if there were no progress in the peace talks by November, the United States would take "measures of great consequence and force." North Vietnam agreed to enter into secret talks with the United States, parallel to the official four-party negotiations, but otherwise ignored the deadline. Nixon was now boxed in. The public's patience with Vietnamization was already waning, and both doves and hawks in Congress were becoming vocal in their criticisms. The participation of an estimated twenty million people in a nationwide moratorium on October 15 reflected this growing war-weariness.

In this dicey situation, Nixon focused on shoring up support at home, announcing the withdrawal of 60,000 additional troops by mid-December and launching a public relations blitz to discredit his critics. On November 3, the president took anti-war protesters to task in a nationally televised speech, concluding his address with an appeal for support from "the great silent majority" of Americans whose voices, he argued, had not yet been heard. All of the elements of the Nixon–Kissinger strategy for achieving "peace with honor" were now in place: the imposition of Vietnamization on an unwilling Thieu; back-channel negotiations with North Vietnam, buttressed by extralegal exercises of brute force; and a public relations juggernaut to marginalize war protesters as un-American.

Nixon also sought to thin the ranks of the disaffected by ending the draft—and with it, of course, the monthly draft calls that were building anti-war sentiment among middle-class and more affluent voters. In this effort, the president enjoyed support from liberals and conservatives alike. Principled objections to conscription were reinforced by public disgust with the head of the Selective Service System, General Lewis Hershey, for his heavy-handed use of the draft to punish those who protested the war. In September 1969, Nixon fired Hershey, and three months later announced that the draft would be replaced by a lottery system based on a randomized ordering of birthdates. Following strong lobbying by the administration, Congress voted one final extension of the draft, which would expire in 1973. Nixon had achieved exactly what he wanted. The promise of transition to a professional army after the 1972 election scored political points with many voters (especially those 18- to 20-year-olds who were newly enfranchised by ratification of the Twenty-sixth Amendment in 1971), but the draft would not end so soon that it would undermine the administration's negotiating position to end the war.

Meanwhile, the political weakness of the Thieu government posed a major obstacle to achieving "peace with honor." The North Vietnamese remained obstinate in Paris, in both the official and secret negotiations, and their intransigence led a frustrated Nixon to engage in extralegal military actions that fanned the flames of the anti-war movement. Most notable—and damaging—was his decision at the end of April 1970 to launch an "incursion" (a term intended to seem somehow less aggressive than "invasion") into Cambodia.

Public outrage at the Cambodian incursion was most extreme on the nation's college and university campuses. The most violent confrontation occurred at Kent State University in Ohio, where the National Guard opened fire on a crowd of assembled students, killing four and injuring eleven others. Ten days later, at historically black Jackson State University in Mississippi, disaster struck again as two students were killed and seven were injured. By the end of spring, approximately 80 percent of the nation's colleges and universities had experienced anti-war activities of some sort, with 448 of them experiencing strikes or closure. Even in the face of these tragic events, however, the administration was not without supporters. On May 8, just four days after the Kent State shootings, approximately 200 construction workers attacked an anti-war march in New York City; ten days later, "hard-hat" rallies in support of the administration were held in numerous major cities. The administration publicly embraced such visible "patriotic support." Later in the year, a Commission on Campus Unrest appointed by Nixon strongly criticized the way in which authorities had reacted to the campus protests, judging the student deaths at Kent State and Jackson State to be "unnecessary, unwarranted, and inexcusable." Nixon privately called the report "crap."

The Cambodian operation and the events that followed heightened congressional opposition. In June, the Senate voted to repeal the 1964 Gulf of Tonkin Resolution, which had authorized the U.S. military presence in Vietnam. Two other end-the-war measures, the Cooper–Church amendment to cut off funding for military operations in Cambodia and the McGovern–Hatfield amendment calling for the withdrawal of all U.S. troops from Vietnam, failed to pass, but the administration pulled all troops out of Cambodia as they were being debated "Although Nixon escaped with his power intact," George Herring writes in *America's Longest War*, "the Cambodian venture tightened the trap he had set for himself. The domestic reaction reinforced his determination to achieve 'peace with honor' while sharply limiting his options for attaining it."

Meanwhile, the court martial of Sergeant William Calley in March 1971 for atrocities his troops had committed at My Lai three years earlier fueled yet another round of anti-war protests across the nation. Heartfelt testimony by members of Vietnam Veterans Against the War (VVAW) before the Senate Foreign Relations Committee in April and May further energized the administration's critics, culminating in the largest single anti-war demonstration yet to occur in Washington (300,000 protestors), with a companion demonstration half that size held in San Francisco. The administration responded viciously; on May Day, some 7000 protesters were rounded up and held in D.C.'s football stadium. But Nixon realized that time was running out.

The last thing the administration needed at this point was another crisis. On its face, the *New York Times*'s publication in early June of a top-secret Defense Department study of the origins of American involvement in Vietnam under previous presidents did not seem to pose any threat to the White House. Nor did Nixon initially regard it as a problem. Kissinger, however, was furious. and—knowing exactly which buttons to push—told Nixon that if he failed to take action, "It shows you're a weakling, Mr. President." Even though Nixon was not incriminated by anything in what came to be called the Pentagon Papers, the fact that a top-secret document had been leaked to the media was enough to make him responsive to Kissinger's advice. He took immediate action, securing a court order enjoining the *Times* (and by then, the *Washington Post* and *Boston Globe*) from publishing any further material from the purloined Pentagon study. On June 30, 1971, the Supreme Court ruled 6-3, in *New York Times Co. v. United States*, that this attempt to bar publication was "a flagrant, indefensible" violation of the First Amendment, and public release of the Pentagon Papers proceeded unhindered. By the end of the summer, Bantam Books had published the entire study in a best-selling paperback.

Having lost the Pentagon Papers battle, Nixon gave in to his vindictive nature, approving formation of a "Plumber's Unit" (so named because its mission was to stop leaks) to get the goods on Daniel Ellsberg, the former RAND employee who had given the Pentagon study to the *Times*. Specifically, the unit was enjoined to break into the office of Ellsberg's psychiatrist and steal his confidential medical information. The Plumbers came up with nothing for their efforts. When Ellsberg was eventually tried in May 1973 for stealing the secret documents, the judge declared a mistrial because "government agencies had taken an unprecedented series of actions" infringing on his liberties.

The revelations in the Pentagon Papers of a pattern of governmental deceit that had obscured early U.S. involvement in Vietnam further eroded support for the war. More than 70 percent of Americans now believed that it had been a mistake for the United States to have sent troops into Vietnam, and nearly 60 percent regarded the war as immoral. The administration's phased troop withdrawals helped, but one poll suggested that nearly half of those questioned felt that the pace of withdrawals was too slow. At this point, however—if not earlier—Nixon's "peace with honor" strategy was all about securing his re-election.

In late January 1972, Nixon went on television to reveal the private peace talks that had been going on for more than two years. At the same time, he pressured Thieu to consent to the public release of nine "principles" for peace that had been given to the North Vietnamese the previous fall. Thieu, however, had not seen the nine principles until then. Nixon, Kissinger, and Thieu were all aware that such a ceasefire would doom Thieu's government, and it was imperative from Nixon's point of view that this not occur until he was safely re-elected. The North Vietnamese further complicated matters for the administration by launching a massive offensive against the South at the end of March. Nixon, however, was not to be bullied. He responded by giving the go-ahead for Operation Linebacker, the most massive bombing raids yet, and for the mining of Hanoi and Haiphong harbors. These aggressive actions eventually succeeded in blunting the North Vietnamese offensive. On July 1, Nixon announced the withdrawal of an additional 20,000 troops, leaving fewer than 50,000 in the field.

Negotiations in Paris dragged on throughout election year 1972. Nixon and Kissinger held firmly to the position that the complete withdrawal of American troops depended on a final settlement that would include the return of all prisoners of war (POWs) and an internationally monitored ceasefire; nothing was said about the integrity of the Thieu regime or (as North Vietnam wanted) possibilities for a coalition government in the South. Meanwhile, the toll in lives on both sides increased steadily. As the presidential election neared, negotiations in Paris finally began to inch toward the kind of agreement for which Nixon was now willing to settle. Nixon knew, however, that more work was needed with Thieu to make sure that he would go along. To achieve that assurance, he wrote a series of secret letters to Thieu in which he promised that the United States would come to South Vietnam's aid if the North violated the terms of the proposed settlement. These letters did not become public until 1975; to that point, no one in Congress knew anything about Nixon's promise, in effect, to re-enter the Vietnam War if the accords should be violated. No matter—it is unlikely that Nixon intended to do so.

In the short run, the tactic worked. After a stumble at the bargaining table in December that led to a resumption of the American offensive (the so-called "Christmas bombing"), the North Vietnamese returned to the table. On January 23, 1973, Kissinger and North Vietnamese lead negotiator Le Duc Tho initialed a settlement, basically on the terms laid out by Nixon during the previous year. Four days later, all four parties to the formal Paris talks officially signed the accords. For the United States, at least, the Vietnam War was over.

Historians agree that the peace terms achieved in 1973 were no better than Nixon could have obtained in his first year in office. He does not seem ever to have engaged in second-guessing on this point, however. In fact, emboldened by achieving "peace with honor," he let off a fusillade at the congressional doves who had caused him so much grief for the previous four years. As reported by Larry Berman (*No Peace, No Honor: Nixon, Kissinger, and Betrayal in Vietnam*), shortly after the signing of the accords, the White House distributed a "Vietnam White Paper" to members of Congress with a message both bitter and self-congratulatory:

> For four agonizing years, Richard Nixon has stood virtually alone in the Nation's capital while little, petty men flayed him over American involvement in Indochina… . [O]ver all these years, there were the incessant attacks from the United States Congress—the low-motivated partisan thrusts from many who envied the President's office and many more who cynically molted their hawk's feathers for those of the dove… . No President has been under more constant and unremitting harassment by men who should drop to their knees each night to thank the Almighty that they do not have to make the same decisions that Richard Nixon did.

The White Paper concluded with a paean to "the millions upon millions of quite ordinary Americans—the great Silent Majority of citizens—who saw our country through a period where the shock troops of leftist public opinion daily propagandized against the President… . They were people of character and steel." For Nixon, the timing of the Vietnam peace settlement was everything. His game plan had been to end U.S. involvement in a way that would not cause problems for his re-election in 1972. Once it became clear that the Thieu regime could not be saved, it was not in Nixon's interest to have the war end too soon; the last thing he wanted was to have North Vietnam overrun the South before Americans were able to go to the polls to give him "four more years."

Had he not been saddled with the Vietnam War, Richard Nixon might have succeeded in creating a lasting legacy in international affairs; of course, absent the war, he would not likely have been elected. Certainly he wanted to be able to focus on such a grand strategy. ("If there were a way we could flush Vietnam now, flush it, get out of it in any way possible, and conduct a sensible foreign policy with the Russians and with the Chinese," White House tapes recorded him telling Kissinger in May 1972, "we ought to do it.") For most of his foreshortened presidency, however, relations with both the Soviet Union and China devolved into a "linkage" strategy, where any diplomatic breakthroughs had to be viewed within the calculus of winding down the United States' interminable involvement in Southeast Asia.

Détente with the Soviet Union was perhaps the strongest example of Nixon's *realpolitik*. His realism (and dexterity) showed in his balancing advocacy for development of a new and costly Anti-Ballistic Missile (ABM) system along with a Strategic Arms Limitation Treaty (SALT I) with the Soviets in 1972. SALT I was not an easy sell with Congress, however. As Melvin Small recounts in *The Presidency of Richard Nixon*, "[d]oves who thought that the agreement did not go far enough and hawks who felt that the Soviets had gained the most united in opposition." Success was achieved because "[t]he hawks received new arms systems and the doves the promise that the SALT process would continue."

While détente might be seen as only a gradual shift from the summitry that previous presidents had conducted, Nixon's dramatic opening up of relations with the People's Republic of China (PRC) was truly revolutionary. The same *realpolitik* was at work that underlay détente with the Soviets. Following secret negotiations conducted on his behalf by Kissinger, Nixon announced in mid-July 1971 that the first-ever presidential visit to the PRC would occur before the following spring. The visit occurred in February 1972, receiving the wall-to-wall media coverage for which Nixon had hoped. Although the joint communiqué issued by the two governments at the conclusion of the visit did not stand American policy on its ear, it came close. Recognizing the differences that separated the United States and the PRC, the communiqué pledged that neither nation would "seek hegemony" in the Asia-Pacific area. Most alarming to longtime Cold Warriors was the statement that the United States—while continuing to recognize the independence of Taiwan—would ultimately end its military presence there. Nixon had set U.S.-Chinese relations on a new path and in doing so he had accomplished the historic.

In the first decade or so after Nixon's presidency, scholars gave Nixon high marks for foreign policy, notwithstanding the ultimate outcome in Vietnam. As more documentation of the back-channel negotiations to end the war became available, however, and the costs of Nixon's relative inattention to the Middle East and parts of the developing world grew more obvious, both the objectives and achievements of Nixon–Kissinger diplomacy have fared less well with historians. There is also the matter of the way in which policy was conducted. In the introductory essay to their edited volume, *Nixon in the World*, Fredrik Logevall and Andrew Preston discuss the issue of morality in Nixon–Kissinger foreign policy. Noting that both the president and his national security advisor took an "amoral worldview" that eschewed ideology to achieve "realistic" ends, they acknowledge that critics "on both the right and the left have charged that an amoral worldview was effectively *immoral.*" Although both Nixon and Kissinger admittedly emphasized ends over means, it is impossible to overlook their constant resort to secrecy and manipulation in dealing with foreign leaders, as well as with Congress and the American public. The stunning revelations that emerged as the Watergate scandal unfolded only increased the legacy of distrust spawned by the Nixon–Kissinger approach to foreign policy.

Watergate and Its Aftermath

The scandal that ended Richard Nixon's presidency was deeply rooted in his personality—his obsessive hatred of his "enemies," paranoia about information leaks, and penchant for control—but it was also a product of the challenges of winding down American involvement in the Vietnam War and launching what seemed to be a tough re-election campaign. Historians agree that Nixon's behavior in Watergate grew directly from his desire to defend his Vietnam policies—as well as reflected his basic character. "Nixon's Watergate behavior," Keith Olson contends in *Watergate: The Presidential Scandal That Shook America*, "was not the behavior of a political aberrant; rather it was the behavior of a consummate politician.... He rose to the top, step by step, within the system and, consequently, like most presidents, reflected the political values of the system."

The Watergate break-in was part of a "dirty tricks" strategy orchestrated by the Committee to Re-elect the President (CREEP) to subvert the 1972 Democratic primaries. Since Nixon and his White House entourage believed his re-election essential to national security, it is unsurprising that they considered such nefarious operations justified, despite the enormous risks of discovery. The dirty tricks project was designed primarily to advance the prospects of Senator George McGovern, whom Nixon strategists saw as the easiest Democrat to beat in November, at the expense of the presumably more electable Edmund Muskie. After Muskie was derailed, another potential obstacle to McGovern's nomination was removed when George Wallace was forced out of the campaign in mid-May. Once again, as in 1968, violence helped to determine the outcome of a Democratic presidential nomination contest. After winning the important Florida primary and making strong showings in a number of others, Wallace appeared to be gaining momentum when, on May 15, he was struck down by a would-be assassin's bullets in a Maryland shopping center. Paralyzed by the assassination attempt, Wallace was no longer a factor in the contest for the nomination.

In addition to being aided by a dwindling field, McGovern was able to capitalize on strengths of his own. As Bruce Miroff points out in *The Liberals' Moment: The McGovern Insurgency and the Identity Crisis of the Democratic Party*, as the strongest anti-war candidate in the primaries, the South Dakota senator had inherited the support of Gene McCarthy's "middle-class and youthful antiwar activists, and the grassroots organizers who had first learned their art in his campaign," while at the same time cultivating "the Kennedy people and the Kennedy image of compassion for the poor." McGovern also benefited from the Democratic party's delegate selection reforms adopted after the 1968 convention to reduce the influence of party bosses—including the end of "winner take all" primaries. After the June 6 California primary, in which McGovern defeated Humphrey by five percentage points, the Democratic contest was effectively decided—and in precisely the way Nixon had hoped.

Unnecessary as it now was, "Operation Gemstone," CREEP's codename for an elaborate scheme of campaign subversion including a plan to bug the telephones at the Democratic National Committee headquarters, moved ahead. On the night of June 17, 1972, seven men—including two with earlier connections to the CIA—were caught by D.C. police while attempting to plant wiretaps on DNC phones. When asked about the incident the next day, John Mitchell (who had resigned as attorney general in the spring in order to head CREEP) declared that the "people involved were not operating either in our behalf or with our consent." This lie was the first of many that would ultimately be exposed in court and in the congressional Watergate hearings. No evidence exists that Nixon personally knew anything about the crime before it occurred, but by June 23 he understood that the operation had been carried out with CREEP's full knowledge. Instead of publicly repudiating those behind it, as he still could have done, he made the fateful choice to "tough it out" and conceal any administration involvement. It was this decision to cover up, not the crime itself, that led to his downfall.

The Watergate story has been recounted in scores of books, including the memoirs of several complicit White House figures, two special prosecutors, and a federal judge, as well as the works of numerous historians and journalists. The first major account, *All the President's Men*, was published in 1974 before the denouement. In it, *Washington Post* journalists Bob Woodward and Carl Bernstein presented the fruits of their investigative reporting throughout the summer and fall of 1972, which had strongly suggested connections between White House and CREEP higher-ups and the Watergate burglars. Woodward's and Bernstein's anonymous source, whom they called "Deep Throat," provided information that proved to be 100 percent accurate. (Little wonder the information was so accurate; at the time of his death nearly forty years later, "Deep Throat" was revealed to be then-deputy director of the FBI Mark Felt.)

Despite the ominous reports about possible White House complicity in Watergate, the campaign developed in a way that could not have been more advantageous to Nixon and his team.

McGovern, after winning the Democratic nomination with over 60 percent of the primary vote, experienced a disastrous convention. His acceptance speech was delayed until the wee hours of the morning, long after most TV viewers had gone to bed, and his choice for a running-mate, Senator Thomas Eagleton of Missouri, turned out to be a disaster, when it was revealed that he had undergone electroshock therapy for "depression." Within a week of his nomination, McGovern forced Eagleton off the ticket, substituting Sargent Shriver, a Kennedy in-law. The damage done by the Eagleton episode, however, could not be repaired. McGovern began the campaign approximately 30 percentage points behind Nixon, and never closed the gap. The election produced a landslide comparable to Lyndon Johnson's eight years earlier, with Nixon winning every state but one (Massachusetts); the District of Columbia also went for his opponent, leaving Nixon with 510 of 527 possible electoral votes.

For all the damage that McGovern's candidacy did to his party's chances, the reluctance of American voters to grant too much power to a single party was evident in the congressional election results. Despite the landslide for Nixon, Republicans picked up only twelve seats in the House, leaving them in the minority by 192 to 242. In the Senate, the GOP actually lost ground, as the Democrats increased their majority from 54-44 to 56-42. Nixon now confronted a Democratic-controlled Congress more liberal than before—just as the Watergate issue was about to explode.

Looking toward his second term, Nixon mused about forming a new party that would combine the Republican base with the "new majority" he imagined that he had created. He spoke frequently with Haldeman and Ehrlichman in the weeks after the election about the possibility of luring Connally into such a party, and then helping him to become president after his own term was completed. (Nixon had, in fact, seriously considered substituting Connally for Agnew on the 1972 ticket. In the end, he stuck with Agnew largely because of the vice president's value as a hatchet-man on the campaign trail.) According to Haldeman, Connally told Nixon that he thought the plan for a new party "unworkable."

Reinstalled in the White House, Nixon proceeded to act as if the election had created something of permanence on which he could build in his second term. As a first step, he designed a dramatic executive reorganization plan to centralize policy-making in the White House. As Ehrlichman explained to the *Washington Post* at the time, "There shouldn't be a lot of leeway in following the President's policies. It should be like a corporation, where the executive vice presidents ... are tied closely to the chief executive." In January, Nixon proposed a draconian budget for the next fiscal year, making it clear that if Congress should attempt to fund any of the programs for which he proposed drastic cuts or elimination, he would exercise his right to impound the appropriated funds. As Stanley Kutler notes, in *The Wars of Watergate*, "No constitutional language specified such authority." No matter. Nixon proceeded to impound billions of dollars that Congress appropriated for pollution control and other purposes.

The president and his lieutenants could not have acted with worse timing in taking these aggressive measures. The unraveling had begun. On January 8, the grand jury trial of the Watergate burglars began in Judge John Sirica's courtroom. On January 30, the jury brought in a guilty verdict against all seven defendants. Sirica, highly skeptical that the buck stopped with these seven, then exercised his power to set the date for sentencing, delaying it until March in the hope that one or more of the defendants would decide to cooperate with the court in exchange for leniency. At the beginning of February, the Senate voted unanimously to establish a Select Committee on Presidential Campaign Activities to pursue three areas of investigation: the Watergate break-in and possible cover-up; the dirty tricks that had marred the 1972 pre-convention campaign; and alleged illegalities in campaign financing. Conservative Democrat Sam Ervin (North Carolina), a recognized expert on constitutional law, was selected to chair the Watergate Committee, with moderate Republican Howard Baker of Tennessee as vice chair.

While the nation waited for the Senate committee to begin its work, a final act was played out in Judge Sirica's courtroom. On March 23, the day of sentencing, former CIA agent James

McCord, one of the seven convicted of the break-in, wrote to Sirica that the defendants had been pressured to remain silent, that the break-in had nothing to do with the CIA, and that "government officials" were involved. The judge read McCord's letter aloud in court before sentencing the burglars. Hoping to speed the unraveling of the case, he gave all seven maximum sentences but then gave them some direct advice. "I recommend your full cooperation with the grand jury and the Senate Select Committee," the judge said. "[S]hould you decide to speak freely, I would have to weigh that factor in appraising what sentences will be finally imposed … ." The lid was beginning to come off the Watergate cover-up.

For the next seventeen months, the Watergate investigation dominated the news. Even before the Senate committee began its televised hearings in May, the situation began to deteriorate for the White House. As would later be revealed, the president had been well aware of most of the details of administration involvement since June 23 of the previous year. Unaware of that fact, in mid-April Attorney General Richard Kleindienst came to the White House to deliver to Nixon what he thought would be shocking news. In addition to Mitchell, Kleindienst reported, Haldeman, Ehrlichman, White House counsel John Dean, and several CREEP officials were all deeply implicated. The attorney general advised Nixon to ask for Haldeman's and Ehrlichman's resignations, and to appoint a special prosecutor in order to blunt the congressional investigation.

Nixon badly needed a scapegoat. Looking out only for himself, he had Ehrlichman go to Mitchell to ask him to take the blame for the break-in and cover-up, but the stubborn Mitchell was unwilling to do so. The president knew, meanwhile, that Dean was talking to the prosecutors. Fearing that Dean might seek immunity by implicating others in the White House, Nixon issued a public statement in mid-April that "no individual holding, in the past or at present, a position of major importance in the Administration should be given immunity from Prosecution." As more bad news surfaced daily, prominent Republicans called for the president to appoint an independent special prosecutor.

On April 29, Nixon summoned his two loyal lieutenants, Haldeman and Ehrlichman, to ask for their resignations; Kleindienst and Dean were asked for theirs, as well. The next day, the Senate, by voice vote, approved a resolution calling for a special prosecutor. On May 17, the Senate Watergate Committee opened its televised hearings, which would span a total of fifty-three days, involving thirty-three witnesses and 237 hours of testimony. Two days later, Attorney General Elliott Richardson (who had replaced Kleindienst) appointed the eminent legal scholar Archibald Cox of Harvard University as special prosecutor. Thereafter, the Watergate Committee and two successive special prosecutors worked in parallel to piece together the sordid story of the cover-up.

Throughout May and June, testimony to Ervin and his colleagues by a parade of White House and CREEP officials built the case, brick by brick, against the president's top aides—but not yet against the president. On July 13, Haldeman's former assistant, Alexander Butterfield, unexpectedly revealed to committee staff that Nixon had installed a taping system in the Oval Office, his residence at Camp David, and the Cabinet Room. *"Everything,"* Butterfield told the stunned staffers, "was taped … as long as the President was in attendance." Nixon did everything he could over the next several months to avoid handing over the tapes, claiming executive privilege. In turn, the committee voted unanimously to subpoena them; on the same day, Judge Sirica granted Special Prosecutor Cox's request for a similar subpoena. When Nixon refused the subpoenas, asserting he would only comply under order by the Supreme Court, leading conservative Republicans publicly criticized the president for the first time. Calling Nixon's refusal a "smoke screen," Barry Goldwater asserted that the president should "come before the Senate Watergate Committee and television cameras and tell the truth." In an August 23 cover story, *Time* magazine joined the growing chorus of critics, noting that "people with nothing to hide do not hide things."

While the subpoena issue worked its way through the courts, Nixon ran into another crisis of enormous magnitude—this one involving his vice president. Largely because he had been so distrusted by Nixon and his principal aides, Vice President Agnew had been outside the loop on Watergate. He had his own serious legal problems, however. Nixon had known since April of a case against the vice president being built by federal prosecutors in Baltimore, but probably because he considered the continuing presence of the lightly regarded Agnew to be a safeguard against his own impeachment, he had not acted on the knowledge. As press reports tumbled one upon another through August and September, however, the details of the allegations emerged: Agnew was accused of taking kickbacks from construction firms while a Baltimore County supervisor in the early 1960s, and then while serving as Maryland's governor. By late September, as Jules Witcover explains in *Very Strange Bedfellows: The Short and Unhappy Marriage of Richard Nixon and Spiro Agnew*, it was clear that Nixon "wanted Agnew out, and the sooner the better." Agnew, writing self-servingly in his 1980 memoir, *Go Quietly ... or Else*, saw the whole thing as a plot by "left-wingers determined to reverse the election results by forcing Nixon out ... by a process which amounted to a coup d'etat." Their motive, Agnew asserted, was "that I was more of a conservative than [Nixon] was on domestic and foreign policy issues."

But it was Nixon, not a band of conspirators, who determined that the vice president had to go. Weary of Agnew's stubborn refusals to step down, in early October Nixon forced him to resign and take a plea bargain, The Baltimore district court, in an act of excessive leniency, fined him $10,000 and sentenced him to three years of "unsupervised probation." Utilizing the terms of the relatively new Twenty-fifth Amendment, Nixon nominated GOP House minority leader Gerald Ford to be his next vice president. The well-liked and unassuming Ford was approved 92-3 in the Senate, and 387-35 in the House.

Nixon's handling of the Agnew mess further complicated his situation with respect to the Watergate investigation. The *Wall Street Journal* expressed the hope that "Agnew's turnabout would be an inspiration" and that "President Nixon would set aside his own confrontation-prone constitutional battle and agree to release key Watergate tape recordings." Nixon, however, planned to do no such thing. Still defying the subpoenas, on October 19 he offered to have the tapes reviewed and vetted by Senator John Stennis, a staunch Mississippi conservative. Special Prosecutor Cox, however, rejected the proposal outright. The next night, in what the media dubbed the Saturday Night Massacre, not only was Cox fired, but so, too, were both Attorney General Elliott Richardson and his deputy William Ruckelshaus, both of whom had refused to comply with the president's order to remove Cox. The deed was finally done by Solicitor General Robert Bork.

The Saturday Night Massacre was a turning point. The dismissal of the special prosecutor produced a public outcry, as Nixon's approval rating for the first time slipped below 30 percent. Except for one minor blip in the next month, it would never again top that mark. Nixon attempted to salvage the situation by quickly appointing Ohio senator William Saxbe, an outspoken maverick within the GOP, as attorney general, and Bork named Leon Jaworski, a respected Texas jurist, to follow Cox as special prosecutor. But public outrage could not be so easily quelled. More dangerous for Nixon was the response in the House of Representatives, where the Judiciary Committee launched an inquiry to decide whether the president's actions constituted an impeachable offense.

The decline in Nixon's public standing as a result of the Massacre also led to a new sense of empowerment on the part of Congress in its institutional stand-off with the executive branch. The most resounding evidence of greater legislative boldness came in early November, with passage of the War Powers Resolution over the president's veto. With this action Congress vindicated those who had for so long criticized first Johnson and then Nixon for their arrogance in making war without prior congressional approval. In recognition that presidents would always need some freedom of action in dealing with crises abroad, the act set a sixty-day limit on any commitment of troops before congressional authorization would be explicitly required to maintain their presence. For a president who so jealously guarded his right to control American national security policy, Congress could hardly have inflicted a more punishing blow.

As Nixon tried to engage in more open exchanges with the press and public over the next several months, additional problems piled up. In a mid-November press conference, when asked about the seemingly low federal income taxes he had paid in 1970 and 1971, he revealed that he had taken huge tax deductions for donation of his vice-presidential papers—adding gratuitously, "I am not a crook." Much of the tax-paying American public drew the opposite conclusion. Finally, he began selectively to provide certain tapes to Judge Sirica and Jaworski—a decision that did him yet more damage. When Sirica became aware that one of the subpoenaed tapes from the critical month of June 1972 had an eighteen-minute gap in it, the media published photos of Nixon's longtime faithful secretary, Rose Mary Woods, straining to replicate the body position that would have been necessary for her to have accidentally erased that part of the tape, as Nixon had proposed by way of explanation. By January 1974, Nixon's Operation Candor was a failed experiment and he hunkered down again, trying to figure out how to satisfy the growing pressures for disclosure without giving up the rest of the tapes, which he knew could result in the end of his presidency.

The grand jury's final set of indictments, handed down on March 1, marked the beginning of the end for the Watergate drama. Four of Nixon's closest aides—Haldeman, Ehrlichman, Mitchell, and Charles Colson—were among those indicted, and rumors circulated about an "unindicted co-conspirator," whom all knew to be the president himself. Nixon's last effort to satisfy those demanding the tapes was to provide transcripts of the conversations. On April 30, he appeared once again on television, this time flanked by over 1200 pages of transcripts, which, he claimed, included everything "relevant" to the investigation. Though the House Judiciary Committee refused to accept them, the transcripts were published in newspapers across the nation and shortly thereafter in both Dell and Bantam paperbacks. If it were possible, the president's reputation fell even lower as a result of the transcripts, due to the hundreds of instances labeled "expletive deleted." Among his other failings, it was now clear that the president was given to habitual profanity, often directed toward minority groups.

By the beginning of the summer, the courts, the special prosecutor, and the House Judiciary Committee were closing the net around Nixon. In late July, the Supreme Court ruled in *U.S. v. Nixon* that the White House tapes were public property and the president had to comply with the subpoenas he had refused; by this time, the rest of the tapes hardly mattered. The House committee had prepared five articles of impeachment on the basis of what was already in the record, the first and most potent of which was for obstruction of justice. On separate votes recorded on live television over a three-day period, the committee approved three of the articles. All that remained to be determined now was *how* Nixon's presidency would end—by impeachment or by resignation. After a delegation of Republican dignitaries led by Goldwater visited Nixon in the White House in the late afternoon of August 7, giving him the depressing news that support had all but evaporated in both houses, the president made his decision. At 7:30 p.m., he informed congressional leaders of his decision to resign, and at 9 p.m., he appeared for one final time on prime-time TV, delivering the news to the American public. To the end, Nixon admitted no guilt. "I would say only that if some of my judgments were wrong—and some were wrong," he said earnestly into the cameras, "they were made in what I believed at the time to be the best interests of the nation."

When Richard and Pat Nixon left Washington, D.C., at noon on August 8, making Gerald Ford the thirty-eighth president, it could only be wondered why this superb strategist had allowed himself to be so ensnared. The White House tapes were completely responsible for his fall from power. "Without those tapes," observes Olson, "there would have been no Saturday Night Massacre, no missing conversations, no eighteen-minute erasure, and no smoking gun." Almost no one had known about their existence. Why had Nixon not simply destroyed them, and thereby had nothing to withhold when the subpoenas were issued? The answer seems inescapably simple: Nixon had created the taping system to record what he was certain would be his "historic" achievements in the White House; he had not destroyed

Figure 1.2 Richard Nixon leaving Washington immediately after becoming the only American president to resign from office. © Bettmann/ CORBIS

the tapes out of hubris, feeling certain he would be able to outsmart those who were demanding that he give them up. In the end, ironically, this president, more given to secrecy than any of his predecessors, was undone by having to reveal the details of his most private conversations in the White House. Cynicism, secretiveness, and, above all, paranoia about the enemies he vowed to bring down—these were the agents of Nixon's self-destruction.

41

Just as the Watergate crime and cover-up ruined Richard Nixon and those around him, it also gravely damaged American society. In the end, the politics of cynicism practiced by Richard Nixon produced, as John Robert Greene observes in *The Presidency of Gerald Ford*, a "citizenry made cynical about its destiny." The political costs of this cynicism would be manifest for the rest of the 1970s, making it virtually impossible for Nixon's immediate successors to heal the nation's wounds and restore positive government.

2

The Futility of Moderation, 1974–1976

"The most extraordinary thing about [Gerald] Ford's ascension to the Vice-Presidency and then the Presidency," observes Richard Reeves in his critical 1975 book, *A Ford, Not a Lincoln*, "was the lack of questioning from his peers about his abilities and capabilities." In late 1973 Ford had seemed to Republicans and Democrats alike the perfect choice to succeed Agnew as vice president, largely because of his lack of any discernible ambition for higher office and the broad consensus that he was guileless and without hidden agendas. When less than a year later Ford was sworn in as the nation's first unelected president, he again enjoyed overwhelming public support. As Lyndon Johnson's former press secretary, George Reedy, wrote in a special *Time* magazine section entitled "Where America Goes Now," it was doubtful that "ever before in history so many people wanted a politician to make it."

Ford's first official words as president brought comfort to a public battered by the storms around Nixon. "Our long national nightmare is over," he reassured the nation. "Our constitution works." The public wanted to believe this, but there had been disquieting signals during Ford's stint as vice president, as he had

Deadlock and Disillusionment: American Politics since 1968, First Edition.
Gary W. Reichard.
© 2016 John Wiley & Sons, Inc. Published 2016 by John Wiley & Sons, Inc.

continued to issue public pronouncements of support for the president even as evidence of White House culpability steadily mounted. Because of their affection for the genial Ford and their hope that he would remain free of tarnish himself, the media were largely uncritical of his statements. That it took him until almost Nixon's final days in office to begin to put any daylight between himself and the by-then disgraced president cost him little public support at the time, but when he later shocked the nation by pardoning his predecessor, the issue of his "loyalty" took on a darker aspect. No matter how likable the new chief executive and his all-American family were, the severe trauma that was Watergate would not easily be smoothed over.

The Republican right was distrustful of Ford from the outset, its resentments kindled by his selection of Nelson Rockefeller as vice president. Just six months into his presidency, a large gathering of disgruntled conservatives met at a Washington hotel to determine how to take over the party and secure the 1976 presidential nomination for one of their own; their candidate of choice was a rising political star, California governor Ronald Reagan. After failing to win over a post-Watergate Democrat-controlled Congress and having to govern by veto, Ford barely beat back Reagan's challenge for the 1976 GOP nomination, presaging the party's rightward shift four years later. Ford's luck would run out, however, in the general election. The politics of forgiveness and moderation, it turned out, were not enough to win over a disgruntled electorate.

The Politics of Forgiveness

At first, everything about the down-to-earth Ford and his attractive family was praised by the media. The new first lady, Betty, was the focus of special adulation. Her candid statements on CBS's popular *Sixty Minutes* news show that her children had probably tried marijuana and that she would not be surprised if her daughter had an affair, however, were jarring to many. Even more problematic—especially for conservatives—was Mrs. Ford's strong endorsement of the Supreme Court's January 1973 *Roe v. Wade* decision. That decision, decided 7-2 and holding that the privacy right incorporated in the Fourteenth Amendment protected a woman's right to have an abortion, had produced instant outrage on the right. Possessing more sensitive political antennae than his spouse, the president quickly remarked to the press that while his wife certainly had the right to speak her mind, "her opinions are entirely her own." Media treatment remained favorable, but the flap was a reminder of how quickly things might sour.

Ford's first actions as president were designed to heal the deep wounds that had been caused by both the Vietnam War and the prolonged Watergate crisis. A warm human being who instinctively sought harmony, he moved almost immediately to address the still painful divisions over the war. By the time he entered the White House, American military operations in Vietnam had ceased and all POWs who could be accounted for had returned home. What remained to be resolved was what to do with those young opponents of the war who had evaded the draft or deserted while in uniform. Catching even his close advisors off guard, the new president sprang a policy surprise in mid-August, announcing his intent to develop a program to offer clemency to those who had evaded the draft and/or had deserted during the recently ended war. To Ford, the distinction between clemency and amnesty was critical. While the latter equated to forgiving the crime, clemency amounted to only a lesser punishment, with the original transgression still considered to be criminal. By the time the details of Ford's plan were rolled out a month later, however, controversy over his pardon of Nixon had shoved the issue to a far back burner. Nor did the clemency program have much impact. Considered by longtime anti-war activists as unduly harsh in its requirements, the program was eventually utilized by only a small fraction of those eligible.

Whereas the clemency program caused Ford only minor political problems, his September 8 full, unconditional pardon to Richard Nixon, eliminating the possibility of his trial for obstruction of justice and other serious criminal charges, created an earthquake. In announcing the pardon, the new president told the American people that he had sought God's help in reaching his momentous decision. Emphasizing his concern for "equal justice for all Americans," he expressed his belief that it would be cruel and excessive to subject Nixon to the tortuous litigation process that would be required to determine his guilt or innocence. Taking the former president to court, said Ford, would only reignite "ugly passions" and further polarize the nation. He concluded by taking full responsibility for his decision: "I do believe that the buck stops here, that I cannot rely upon public opinion polls to tell me what is right… . I do believe, with all my heart and mind and spirit, that I, not as President but as a humble servant of God, will receive justice without mercy if I fail to show mercy."

Ford's explanation failed to convince the public. "With the stroke of a pen," writes John Robert Greene in *The Presidency of Gerald R. Ford*, the president "had destroyed his month-long honeymoon." Phone calls and telegrams to the White House, ran overwhelmingly in the negative, and Ford's approval rating sank from 71 percent to 49 percent in less than a week. The media, which had been so effusive in their praise for the first four weeks of his presidency, turned on a dime. Typical was *Newsweek*'s September 16 cover story, which lamented: "What Ford considered to be a gesture of mercy struck many as premature and certain to misfire… . By his own act, Gerald Ford had embraced the demon of Watergate."

Strong objections to Nixon's escape from the legal system were soon compounded by suspicion that Ford might have struck a "deal with the devil" in Nixon's last days in the White House, promising a pardon if Nixon would resign and give him the presidency. The truth may never be known. To the end of his life, Ford adamantly denied that he ever agreed to such a deal, or even that one was explicitly discussed. As he said at the time, his decision to pardon Nixon was an intensely personal one, made for many reasons including compassion for a defeated and apparently ailing man. "I was hearing that [Nixon] was terribly distraught," he later told journalist friend Thomas DeFrank for a volume intended to be published only after his death (it was, in 2007, with the title *Write It When I'm Gone*). "I don't know whether you could call it irrational, [but Nixon] was despondent, had an unhealthy state of mind." Ford never evinced remorse for his decision. "It was my … feeling then, just as strongly as today: I have no reservations at all," he told DeFrank. "I do feel strongly it was the right thing for the country, and whatever political consequences for me, I accepted."

The course of Ford's presidency was irrevocably altered by the pardon. Losing the adoration of the masses (and the media) was only part of the price he paid; even more damaging was the episode's impact on executive-congressional relations. As a "man of Congress," Ford had at first seemed to a battle-weary House and Senate to hold out promise of vastly improved cooperation between the two ends of Pennsylvania Avenue. After the pardon, however, scores of House members from both parties called for investigations and/or legislation so that the full stories of both Watergate and the pardon would be revealed. In mid-October Ford appeared voluntarily before the House Subcommittee on Criminal Justice to describe his conversations with Nixon and his staff prior to Nixon's resignation—the first president since Abraham Lincoln to testify before a congressional committee. This conciliatory gesture failed to heal the breach between the branches. With the 1974 mid-term congressional campaigns in full swing, partisan conflict only intensified. Congressional Democrats were not about to be denied the landslide they felt should be theirs in the wake of Watergate.

The first hostage taken by the Democratic Congress was Ford's nominee to succeed him in the vice presidency, former New York governor Nelson A. Rockefeller. Using the Twenty-fifth Amendment for a second time within the space of little more than a year, Ford had sent Rockefeller's name forward after considering only one other candidate, GOP national chairman George H. W. Bush. The president expected that Rockefeller's long record of public service would make him easily confirmable, but he was mistaken. As Laura Kalman writes in *Right Star Rising: A New Politics, 1974-1980*, Rockefeller was "a moderate not all liberal

Democrats liked, but whom all conservative Republicans absolutely detested." After weeks of grilling in both houses, he was finally confirmed by 90-7 in the Senate, but by a less overwhelming 287-128 in the House. In the lower house conservative Republicans were nearly as negatively disposed as Democrats.

The 1974 mid-term elections occurred during these protracted hearings, with predictable results. Ford worked hard to staunch GOP hemorrhaging during the campaign, but it was a lost cause. The Democrats picked up only three seats in the Senate (adding another after a special election in New Hampshire went their way, as well), increasing their total in that chamber to sixty. In the House, a bumper crop of "Watergate babies" swelled the Democratic margin to 291-144, a pickup of forty-nine seats. Believing they owed their election to disillusioned voters who wanted to see the mess cleaned up in Washington, the Democratic newcomers were intent on doing just that. Ford faced discord and potential revolt within his own party, too. As Geoffrey Kabaservice describes in *Rule and Ruin: The Downfall of Moderation and the Destruction of the Republican Party from Eisenhower to the Tea Party*, a number of conservative activists went busily about building an organizational infrastructure, including the grass-roots Conservative Caucus and think-tanks such as the Heritage Foundation, in order to neutralize moderate influence within the GOP. Ford remained mostly oblivious to these developments, fearing—according to Laura Kalman—"the left, rather than the right."

President as Political Prisoner

As 1974 came to a close, neither the divisiveness born of the Vietnam War nor the bitterness brought on by Watergate had been healed. In this unforgiving political environment, Ford had to take on a range of intractable problems, including escalating inflation, a looming recession, and growing energy problems. Lacking any mandate from the voters and confronting a Congress that had long resented usurpation of its powers by the White House, the president faced a steep uphill struggle.

The stagflation that had plagued Nixon throughout his presidency continued to bedevil Ford. During the first half of 1974, the nation had experienced its first double-digit inflation since the mid-1940s. Many economists were now predicting also a recession and rising rates of unemployment. A traditional conservative, Ford considered inflation the greater danger. In early October, he rolled out a plan calling for fiscal austerity combined with temporary tax increases, dramatizing the war against inflation by unveiling a pin emblazoned with the acronym "W.I.N.," standing for "Whip Inflation Now." A week later in Kansas City, amidst great fanfare, the president formally launched the "W.I.N." campaign, succeeding in getting over 100,000 Americans to submit "enlistment" papers for this voluntary assault on inflation. Well intentioned as it was, the campaign was soon portrayed by the media as nothing more than a publicity stunt.

Ford was quickly forced to shift gears, however, to deal with a recession that proved worse than anticipated. In his January 1975 State of the Union message, he reversed himself by advocating a tax cut rather than the tax surcharge he had proposed just a few months earlier; this loss of revenue was to be balanced by a windfall profits tax on oil companies and a sharp reduction in spending on federal programs. The administration now appeared to be irresolute, at best, in its efforts to gain control of the troublesome economy. The Democratic-controlled Congress responded by granting a tax cut nearly 40 percent greater than he had requested, while failing to effect any significant reductions in federal outlays. Grudgingly, Ford signed the bill in late March, vowing to "resist every attempt by the Congress to add another dollar to this deficit."

The nation's economic woes intensified public unhappiness with Washington, and even led to questioning of the economic system itself. Public opinion turned against federal spending for major projects and an ethos of "thinking small" increasingly supplanted traditional American assumptions of unlimited growth. Undaunted, the Democratic Congress passed an even larger tax-cut package in December, still without the offsetting spending cuts proposed by Ford. In a *pas de deux* that was to become increasingly familiar over the next year, the president vetoed the bill and Congress came back with a somewhat smaller tax reduction that he wound up signing. This unproductive pattern continued through the next year, as Ford continued to veto spending bills, including two public works bills designed to provide employment for unskilled workers. He also opposed the Democratic-sponsored Humphrey–Hawkins bill, which would have committed the federal government to take direct action to reduce unemployment to no higher than 3 percent.

The problems that strained the national economy in the 1970s also wreaked havoc at state and city levels. The most visible example was the economic crisis that hit New York City in 1975. The problems besetting the Big Apple were common across urban America: physical deterioration, a declining tax base due to outward flight by affluent, mostly white residents, and the presence of a large, relatively high-salaried public workforce the cost of whose benefits and pensions was breaking the city's budget. Not only because of its economic importance, but also due to its symbolic significance as the nation's metropolis, New York's fiscal problems found their way to Washington. When the city's mayor, Abe Beame, and New York governor Hugh Carey appealed directly to Ford for help, the president was unsympathetic. The lasting image of this interaction is the *New York Daily News*'s famous headline, "Ford to City: Drop Dead!" In December, however—forced to succumb to congressional pressure—Ford signed legislation granting New York City access to nearly $7 billion in federal loans over a three-year period. His ultimate support for the bailout afforded a ready target for Reagan and others on the right who wished to see him replaced at the top of the GOP ticket in 1976.

Energy policy was yet another battlefield on which the president and Congress contested bitterly. Ford entered the White House four months after the end of an oil embargo by the Organization of the Petroleum Exporting Countries (OPEC) that, before its end, had caused major oil shortages for American business and private consumers, It was now widely recognized that the main problem was not actual shortages, but rather the nation's growing dependence on foreign oil. Imports as a proportion of petroleum consumed in the United States had increased from 29 percent in 1972 to 38 percent two years later. If the nation failed to lessen its reliance on imports, it could be held hostage to future OPEC price hikes, or worse. Yet reducing gasoline consumption in a nation defined by its "automobile culture" would not be an easy sell. Exacerbating the problem was the fact that domestic oil producers, who benefited from continued high petroleum consumption, had a number of powerful allies in Congress, such as Democrats Russell Long of Louisiana, chair of the Senate Finance Committee, and Senator Robert Kerr of Oklahoma, himself a wealthy oilman.

The conflict over energy policy quickly became downright ugly. In January 1975, Ford outlined a comprehensive plan, including a $2-per-barrel tariff increase on imported oil to discourage consumption, a phase-out of Nixon-era price controls on oil, and economic incentives for domestic producers to increase output. His logic was that higher "prices at the pump" would reduce domestic consumption, while the price increase on imports would negate any advantage for foreign producers when domestic oil prices went up. Ford's proposal allowed Democrats to charge that he was willing to do anything, including inflicting pain on American consumers, in order to achieve his economic goals. When Congress failed to move on his proposals, he imposed a three-stage "oil import fee" by executive order. In response, congressional Democrats led successful efforts to suspend the president's authority to impose import fees for ninety days. As the impasse dragged on, Ford went on television to denounce congressional dawdling in what Yanek Mieczkowski, in *Gerald Ford and the Challenges of the 1970s*, calls "the angriest speech of [his] presidency." Twice during summer and early fall, Congress extended existing price controls over White House objections. Finally, in mid-December, with the controls about to expire and an election year dawning, Congress rolled back domestic oil prices to below-market levels and gave the president authority to effect decontrol over a forty-month period. Ford signed the Energy

Figure 2.1 Facing an emboldened post-Watergate Congress controlled by Democrats, Gerald Ford had little choice but to try to control policy through frequent exercise of his veto power. A 1975 Herblock Cartoon, © The Herb Block Foundation. Courtesy of the Library of Congress

Policy and Conservation Act (EPCA) in late December, after almost a full year of bickering.

After chafing for years under what Arthur M. Schlesinger, Jr., popularized as the "Imperial Presidency" in a 1974 book of that title, Congress was ill disposed to work with any president at the point when Ford came to the White House. It mattered little that Ford sought a partnership with Congress or that he himself had come from that body. Moreover, the president's strongly conservative bent, particularly in economic matters, virtually guaranteed that he would clash with the liberal-leaning Congress. It was not surprising, then, that during his two years in the White House, Ford had a lower degree of success with Congress than any of the post-World War II presidents who preceded him. Ironically, he received even less support in the House, where he had served for more than a quarter of a century, than in the Senate. The result for Ford was frustration, political paralysis, and an extraordinarily high number of vetoes—sixty-six in all.

For reasons that were not entirely of his own making, Gerald Ford never had a chance to heal the nation or to take charge of the political agenda on domestic issues. Rather, Ford found himself constantly on the defensive—a virtual prisoner to the resurgent post-Watergate Congress.

Détente Derailed

Nixon's efforts to blunt the effects of Watergate through displays of leadership in foreign policy had proved futile. As his fortunes plummeted during his final year in office, Congress grew bolder against the executive branch. The most potent manifestation of this counter-offensive was the War Powers Resolution, passed in the immediate aftermath of the Saturday Night Massacre. In addition, Congress sought to heighten its oversight of intelligence matters. By the time Ford entered the White House, both Democrats and Republicans were training their sights on possible CIA excesses that had been approved by out-of-control presidents. Ford also had to contend with rising criticisms in both parties about the wisdom of détente—attacks that were in part fueled by resentment of his continued reliance on Nixon's *éminence grise*, Henry Kissinger, whose arrogance had created many enemies in Congress.

The first foreign policy problem facing Ford was all too familiar. Despite the exit of U.S. troops from Vietnam, the war there had not ended. Immediately after the signing of the January 1973 peace accords, North Vietnam had launched an aggressive military offensive against the South, and within eighteen months had gained the clear military advantage. In early 1975, Ford urged Congress to appropriate $1.5 billion in military aid for South Vietnam, although perhaps he did not really want what he requested; additional American aid would only have prolonged the conflict without changing its ultimate outcome. In any event, Congress refused the request, and without further American assistance the end came swiftly for Thieu's government. On April 23, with Danang already in North Vietnamese hands, Ford proclaimed in a speech at Tulane University that the war was "finished as far as America is concerned." Within a week, the world witnessed the spectacle of the last Americans in Vietnam being evacuated from Saigon rooftops, as hundreds of South Vietnamese clamored to board the final departing U.S. helicopters. The final outcome left a very bitter taste. As Kalman writes, outright defeat after such a long, divisive, and costly war only exacerbated "cynicism about the government and the presidency in particular."

One final drama was played out in Southeast Asia before Ford could turn to other foreign policy matters. On May 12, 1975—less than two weeks after his speech at Tulane—the president received word that an American merchant ship, the *Mayaguez*, had been seized by Cambodian sailors. The next day, the ship was moved to an island approximately thirty miles from the mainland, with the fate of its thirty-nine-man crew unknown. On May 14, Ford authorized an amphibious strike on the island in order to free the crew, but the hostages had already been moved to the mainland. The loss of fifteen marines and eight helicopters in the fruitless marine landing could have dealt a disastrous blow to Ford's credibility had it not been for the Cambodians' decision to release the crew within hours of the U.S. military assault. Whatever their reasons for doing so, by this act the Cambodian captors bailed the president out politically; Ford's approval ratings shot up by 11 percent.

Scholars have differed in assessing Ford's reasons for taking such decisive military action to free the *Mayaguez* crew. Quite probably, his motives were at least partly political. With his presidency "at the nadir of its fortunes," observes John Robert Greene, "the *Mayaguez* crisis offered a timely opportunity: the Ford administration could use the situation to prove that

America—and Ford—was still tough." If that was his strategy, to a degree it worked. Moreover, liberal Democrats who had publicly counseled caution and patience in dealing with the crisis—even though they may have been right—were made to look overly timid by the quick return of the crew. Despite the positive public verdict (or perhaps because of it), the administration's precipitate action in the *Mayaguez* crisis upset many congressional leaders, who charged that Ford had failed to consult as required by the recently passed War Powers Resolution. While the crisis may have increased Ford's political capital in the short term, it also contributed to his long-term problems by strengthening Congress's determination to flex its muscles.

Ford also had to combat aggressive congressional investigations into the CIA's covert operations throughout his first full year as president. The immediate stimulus was a piece by *New York Times* investigative reporter Seymour Hersh alleging "massive" spying and illegal domestic intelligence activities by the U.S. government. Largely drawn from a top-secret, 693-page CIA internal study led by Director William Colby, Hersh's allegations were quickly picked up by other journalists and television commentators. Ford, who had known nothing of the secret study, was stunned, and moved swiftly in an effort to pre-empt potential congressional critics. On January 4, by Executive Order, he created the President's Commission on CIA Activities Within the United States, naming Vice President Rockefeller as chair.

In this political climate, however, Ford had no chance of warding off a congressional investigation. Disregarding the appointment of the blue ribbon commission, both houses quickly established special investigating committees. From the start the Senate's Select Intelligence Committee received most of the media attention, its operations dominated by its chair, Frank Church of Idaho, a liberal Democrat with presidential ambitions. Although Church assured Ford in a private White House meeting that the committee would "not be a wrecking crew," he immediately sent the White House a massive document request, including all orders and directives related to covert operations. Ford reacted defensively—as Greene puts it—attempting "to give the appearance of cooperation without actually providing the committee with any substantive documentation." In contrast, Colby chose to cooperate with the committee; in November 1975 Ford replaced him as CIA director with George H. W. Bush, who had been serving as head of the U.S. Liaison Office in China.

By far the most damning information to come before the Church Committee was hitherto unknown evidence of CIA involvement in assassination plots against several foreign leaders, including Cuba's Fidel Castro. Once this bombshell exploded, the Senate committee focused most of its attention on such plots, taking more than 8000 pages of testimony over the course of sixty days. Ford appealed to Church not to publish a report on the plots, but to no avail. After the full Senate met in secret session and opted to take no vote on whether or not to release the information, Church released it on his own authority. The report, *Alleged Assassination Plots Involving Foreign Leaders*, recounted stories of CIA complicity in no fewer than five separate assassination plots, but concluded that there was no direct evidence that American involvement had caused the death of any leader. In December 1975, the Church Committee published its full six-volume report. Among its more than ninety recommendations were proposed bans on political assassinations and efforts to subvert foreign governments.

Although many felt that the CIA probe had been compromised by Church's blatant presidential aspirations, the committee's work had important results. The most significant outcome was the establishment of permanent intelligence oversight committees in both House and Senate. The hearings also had a major impact on the balance of power between the White House and Capitol Hill. By his handling of the Church Committee, Greene writes, "Ford allowed Congress to corner the post-Watergate market on morality," with the role of moral leader "taken away from the president and assigned to Congress." For all of the aggravation the intelligence hearings caused Gerald Ford, however, they fell remarkably flat with the public. According to a Harris Poll In December 1975, a plurality of the public viewed the work of both investigating committees unfavorably. In truth, the alarming revelations about CIA excesses may have done more to increase public contempt for the political system as a whole than to provide reassurance that the separation of powers was working effectively.

Congressional criticisms of détente caused Ford as much grief as did the assault on the independence of the intelligence agencies. Despite Nixon's and Kissinger's hopes for a permanent thaw in U.S.–Soviet relations, by the time Ford became president that relationship had begun to fray badly, largely as a result of Soviet meddling in Angola and the Middle East. Nonetheless, Ford was determined to try to sustain détente by finalizing the proposed SALT II treaty and securing passage of a trade bill granting the Soviets most-favored-nation status. In November 1974 he traveled to Vladivostok to meet with Leonid Brezhnev, and returned home with a structure for an arms agreement based on the principle of equality in the number of nuclear warheads for the two nations. The growing band of détente critics in Congress, however—including hard-line anti-communist conservatives as well as liberals focused on human rights issues—had no intention of cooperating. Especially vociferous were many of Congress's most pro-Israel members, such as Senator Henry Jackson (D-Washington) and Congressman Charles Vanik (D-Ohio), who believed détente rewarded Brezhnev for supporting Israel's Arab foes and violating the rights of Soviet Jews. In late 1974, Jackson and Vanik authored a measure that made the continuation of détente contingent on the Soviet government's loosening its restrictions on Jewish emigration. Specifically, the Jackson–Vanik amendment made approval of the administration's trade bill contingent on the Soviets' promise to increase the number of exit visas for Soviet Jews who wished to emigrate.

Naïvely believing that Jackson and his supporters would cooperate on SALT II as well as on the trade bill if he could privately secure such an assurance from the Soviets, Ford persuaded Soviet foreign minister Anatoly Dobrynin to promise an increase in the number of visas for Soviet Jews, with the stipulation that the concession not be made public. When Jackson was informed of the Soviet promise by the administration, however, he leaked the news to the press, infuriating the Soviet leaders. Although the Senate then ratified the trade agreement, serious damage had been done. Ford later wrote that Jackson had "behaved like a swine" in undercutting the agreement with the Soviets, but the ambitious Democrat had accomplished what he had set out to do. In January 1975, the Soviets angrily denounced the agreement, which had been central to the Nixon–Kissinger design for détente. Meanwhile, Jackson and his allies succeeded in blocking consideration of the SALT II treaty on the Senate floor.

With détente now in tatters, Ford had to handle yet another East–West issue. The 1973 Conference on Security and Cooperation in Europe, aiming to end the divisions produced by the international agreements following World War II, had produced a document labeled "the Final Act," calling on signatory nations to cooperate in economic and scientific matters, allow freer movement of peoples, commit to peaceful dispute resolution, and accept as permanent the post-World War II boundaries in Eastern Europe. The agreement was scheduled to be signed by the thirty-three participant nations at a follow-up conference in Helsinki, Finland, in mid-summer 1975. Merely attending the conference carried political risk for Ford. Whatever the merits of the Helsinki Accords, they represented the first formal international recognition of the legitimacy of the East European "satellite" governments that had been controlled by the Soviets since the end of World War II. Conservatives charged that the agreement was a "sellout," and castigated Ford for signing it. The issue would haunt him throughout the campaign season of 1976.

Ford could not win where foreign policy was concerned. While the revival of Cold War suspicions blocked him on détente, he was also thwarted by Congress when he attempted to intervene against Soviet adventurism in Angola. There, the Soviets, along with Cuba, were strongly backing two tribally based nationalist factions jockeying for power in advance of the scheduled end of Portuguese colonial rule in November 1975. After the United States gave millions of dollars in economic aid to a rival faction, the combination of even more massive Soviet aid and Cuban troops on the ground helped to turn the tide and overwhelm the U.S.-backed forces. Again, congressional–executive conflict erupted in Washington, as Congress attached a rider to a defense appropriations bill barring any further U.S. involvement in Angola. As Greene writes, though "Kissinger and Ford had wanted to use the Angolan arena to show the world—and the U.S. Congress—that the Ford administration was still in command of its foreign policy," in the end "Congress used the Angolan affair to reassert its influence over foreign policy."

Historians have given at best a mixed verdict on Ford's foreign policy record, the consensus being that he demonstrated no particular vision in that area. Repeatedly, he was outmaneuvered by those in Congress who opposed what he set out to accomplish in the international arena. A major part of his problem, however, was that he lacked any electoral mandate whatever. Equally important was his inexperience in foreign policy. Although he agreed generally with the thrust of the Nixon–Kissinger policy of détente, writes Greene, Ford was ultimately "unable to develop a foreign policy of his own."

By 1976, so much had gone wrong for Gerald Ford that even coming close to being elected president in his own right would be a noteworthy achievement. In addition to the severe political challenges he faced after Watergate and his pardon of Nixon, he had been the target of two assassination attempts—both of them occurring in California within a single month. On September 5, 1975, while visiting Sacramento, he escaped injury or death only because the gun that Lynette "Squeaky" Fromme was holding misfired; less than three weeks later, in San Francisco, a second would-be assassin, Sarah Jane Moore, missed hitting the president with a single bullet only because a bystander saw her in time to jostle her as she took aim. Although Ford managed to survive the two attempts on his life, he did not fare as well politically.

3

Dashed Hopes, 1976–1980

The election of 1976, in the year of the nation's bicentennial, should have been a national celebration of sorts. In the acrid post-Vietnam and Watergate atmosphere, however, it proved to be almost a sullen affair. Incumbent president Gerald Ford's failure to inspire and challenger Jimmy Carter's inability to define himself produced little enthusiasm on either side, although Carter's ultimate narrow victory led at least his supporters to hope that, with Democrats back in control of the government, it would be possible to pull the nation out of the miasma created by the fall—and pardon—of Richard Nixon. Such was not to be the case.

From his first days in Washington, Carter and his Georgia aides struck virtually every wrong note possible. The new Democratic president was a highly intelligent man but knew nothing of the ways of Washington, which he had plugged as a virtue in his campaign but which made it impossible for him to govern effectively, even with his own party in control of both houses of Congress. This lack of a working relationship was the more costly because rampant inflation and a worsening energy crisis dogged him throughout his four years in office. Carter—ever the engineer

Deadlock and Disillusionment: American Politics since 1968, First Edition.
Gary W. Reichard.
© 2016 John Wiley & Sons, Inc. Published 2016 by John Wiley & Sons, Inc.

(he had graduated from U.S. Naval Academy and served as an engineer in the U.S. Navy)—tried hard to analyze and solve these problems and others—perhaps too hard, as he deluged Capitol Hill with one bill after another across a wide range of issues. In all of this, his personality and temperament were huge detriments. Humorless in public and unable and unwilling to connect with the Washington establishment, he suffered one rebuff after another from the Congress his party controlled and was increasingly ridiculed in the media. A genuine moderate on many of the most pressing social and cultural issues of the 1970s, Carter tried—with no success—to negotiate a middle course on issues such as affirmative action, abortion, and gay rights. In the context of these many setbacks on the domestic front, even the foreign policy achievements of his administration, such as the Camp David Accords and normalization of relations with the People's Republic of China, were not enough to compensate. In the end, the candidate who promised never to lie to the American people may have restored a degree of integrity to Washington, but seemed to a majority of Americans incapable of leading. By 1980, with his image as the nation's leader further eroded by the breakdown of détente with the Soviet Union and a year-long crisis created by the seizure of American hostages in Iran, Carter had the look of a one-term president. It would take only a strong Republican challenger to finish him off.

Fractured Majority

Gerald Ford's weakened position in his own party defined the themes of American politics heading into the nation's bicentennial year. In October 1975, bowing to unrest on the right, Ford initiated a conversation with Vice President Rockefeller that resulted in the latter's "voluntarily" removing himself from the GOP ticket for 1976. Jettisoning the *bête noire* of the right was not sufficient to tamp down conservative unhappiness, however. As recounted by both Laura Kalman (*Right Star Rising*) and J. Brooks Flippen (*Jimmy Carter, the Politics of Family, and the Rise of the Religious Right*), a strong backlash had built up by the mid-1970s in response to what those on the right saw as an attack on "family values." The abortion controversy, the rising force of the women's movement, an escalating divorce rate, the battle over an Equal Rights Amendment (ERA), and the budding gay rights movement all seemed to conservatives to threaten permanent rupture of the natural social order. As events would soon demonstrate, this situation not only invited a conservative challenge to Ford within the GOP but presented an opportunity for a well-positioned Democrat to cash in on the fears of religious conservatives.

The beneficiary of the conservative revolt was Ronald Reagan, who dropped his pose of disinterest, launching a series of scathing attacks on Ford and announcing that he would seek the 1976 Republican nomination. Though Reagan may have overreached by adopting too many extreme positions at once, his defeat in the New Hampshire primary by little more than 1000 votes made him a legitimate challenger. The two candidates traded victories and momentum through the rest of the primary season, with neither being able to lock up the nomination. On the eve of the GOP convention in Kansas City, Reagan sought to win the support of undecided delegates by taking the unprecedented step of naming his vice-presidential choice in advance, the moderate Senator Richard Schweicker of Pennsylvania, challenging Ford to do the same. The power of incumbency proved too much for Reagan to overcome, however. Ford won the nomination on the first ballot by just over 100 votes out of a total of 2250, and selected as his running-mate Senator Robert Dole of Kansas, who had credibility across the party's ideological spectrum. As a price of his nomination, however, Ford had to accept a "morality in foreign policy" platform plank that explicitly criticized the Helsinki Accords.

On the Democratic side, Senator Edward "Ted" Kennedy (Massachusetts) had withdrawn from the race in September 1974, leaving the nomination contest wide open. No fewer than thirteen candidates announced their candidacies prior to the primary season. Among those given little chance at the outset was former Georgia governor Jimmy Carter, an evangelical Christian and successful peanut farmer and businessman from the small town of Plains who believed that the time was right for an "anti-Washington" candidate who "would not lie" to the American people. Given the lack of a clear favorite and the complicated, fragmented process, many observers were convinced that Kennedy, or perhaps even Hubert Humphrey, would emerge as the presidential nominee from a brokered convention.

Campaigning as a centrist and Washington outsider, Carter benefited both from post-Watergate public cynicism about establishment politicians and the presence of so many liberals competing against one another in the primaries. Following surprising victories in Iowa and New Hampshire, he knocked George Wallace out of the race by winning in Florida, and by early May he was the clear front-runner for the Democratic nomination. A shocked Democratic party establishment desperately launched an ABC (Anybody But Carter) movement, but could not find a candidate. Despite pleas that he belatedly enter the race, Humphrey declined, telling his suitors "the one thing I don't need at my stage of life is to be ridiculous." Ted Kennedy, too, continued to resist overtures to reconsider. Though Carter lost five of the last nine primaries, by the end of June he had vanquished all opponents. Easily nominated on the first ballot at the party's Madison Square Garden convention in July, he chose Humphrey's protégé, Senator Walter F. Mondale of Minnesota, as his vice-presidential running-mate.

Even though the electorate knew little about his opponent, President Ford's prospects were at best shaky going into the general election campaign. In addition to carrying the heavy burden of his pardon of Nixon, he was criticized for lack of vision and his inability to work constructively with Congress. Carter made the most of these negatives, and, emphasizing his born-again Christianity, presented himself as the more virtuous of the two candidates. Hewing to the "outsider" theme, he hammered away at the corruption of the political system in Washington, temporizing on many of the tougher issues that would need to be faced if he were to win election, including the abortion issue and what to do about busing to achieve racial balance in the public schools.

Both candidates had trouble bringing their coalitions together. Carter faced the difficult task, as Flippen notes, of winning over "conservative Christians and the social liberals many of those Christians abhorred." He antagonized his evangelical Christian followers, for example, by granting an interview to *Playboy* magazine in which he spoke awkwardly of having "committed adultery in [his] heart" on many occasions. Carter also tried to channel the hard-line positions on which Reagan had scored points against Ford's détente policies, while trying at the same time to come across as "a Wilsonian moralist." The president was unable to capitalize on his opponent's weaknesses as a campaigner, however. Not only did Ford have to bear responsibility for the stubbornly sagging economy and find a way to rekindle enthusiasm among disaffected conservatives, but he had to contend with a string of inconvenient distractions, including reports of corporate gifts he had received while a member of the House and advance publication of excerpts from John Dean's tell-all Watergate memoir, *Blind Ambition*, which charged that Ford, as Speaker of the House, had tried to block a committee investigation into White House wrongdoing under Nixon.

Ford's greatest mistake in the campaign, as it turned out, was challenging Carter to engage in a series of televised debates—the first time an incumbent had done so. Running far behind his Democratic opponent, the president had judged it a gamble worth taking. Again, nearly everything went wrong for Ford that could have. In the first debate, a power shortage left the candidates standing awkwardly in front of the cameras for twenty-seven minutes before sound was restored. In the second, which was focused on foreign policy, Ford committed a gaffe that made him look totally uninformed, when he implied that the satellite nations of Eastern Europe were not under Soviet domination. Prior to the debate, voters had favored Ford on foreign policy issues by 50 to 21 percent; after the president's misstatement, that margin closed to 42 to 38 percent. "If it hadn't been for the debates," Carter later observed, "I would have lost."

The election results were extremely close, with Carter besting Ford by only 1.7 million out of 80 million votes cast. The electoral vote margin, 297-240, was the closest since before World War I. In winning all of the old Solid South and holding the heavily urban Northeast and Midwest, Carter created a mirage that he had re-established the New Deal coalition. Much of his strength in Dixie, however, was due to black voters and a surge of white evangelical Christians—the latter a phenomenon that was unlikely to recur if a future Democratic candidate were more identified with the other side of the cultural divide. Disappointed conservatives argued that if the GOP had nominated someone who could have blunted Carter's born-again appeal in the South, the election would have turned out very differently. Almost at the instant Gerald Ford lost, Ronald Reagan's political star rose.

On paper, the Democrats controlled the reins of government once again—the first time since 1968 that a single party held the presidency and both houses of Congress. The party retained commanding majorities of 61-39 in the Senate and 292-143 in the House, and Carter seemed to have a clear path to controlling the political agenda. In fact, however, as political commentator E. J. Dionne, Jr., notes in *Why Americans Hate Politics*, "It was difficult ... to interpret Carter's victory as a mandate for any policies, except for a new morality in government."

From the beginning of his presidency, Jimmy Carter was all about limits—whether related to the trappings of his office (including curtailing the playing of "Hail to the Chief") or to the reach of the United States in the world. This proved to be the wrong note for a president to strike, even in the post-Watergate era. Carter also erred in overselling himself as the ultimate honest and virtuous politician in the primaries and general election campaign. As Betty Glad writes in *Jimmy Carter: In Search of the Great White House*, "There had been a fantasy-like quality to Carter's self-presentation in the spring and summer [of 1976]. No man has the extraordinary virtue that Carter seemed to claim for himself." The immodest title of his campaign autobiography, *Why Not the Best?*, captured this self-congratulatory tendency that was to prove so problematic to Carter once in office. He might have inherited strong Democratic majorities in both houses of Congress, but he would never be able to command their loyalty.

In fact, Carter did not seem to care very much about winning over his colleagues on Capitol Hill. Burton and Scott Kaufman, in *The Presidency of James Earl Carter*, cite a post-election memo from Carter's resident pollster Pat Caddell, advising the president-elect that he should expect problems from the entrenched liberal leadership in Congress—including Kennedy, McGovern, and Morris Udall—whom the pollster labeled as being "as antiquated and anachronistic as are conservative Republicans." Carter, apparently accepting this characterization, acted accordingly, generally shunning personal interactions with them. Until dissuaded by chief domestic advisor Stuart Eizenstat, he even considered holding an initial televised "fireside chat" with the American people in advance of his first State of the Union address, which would have been an unforgivable affront to the legislative branch. For their part, congressional Democrats saw no reason to pay attention to Carter, since he had demonstrated no coattail strength in winning the White House; the average margins of victory for Democratic Senate and House candidates had exceeded Carter's by 5.4 percent and 3.7 percent, respectively. The Democratic resurgence was limited, to say the least, and Carter's relations with Congress were rocky from the start.

Carter began by addressing the still festering question of what to do about draft evaders and deserters during the Vietnam War. Whereas Ford had distinguished carefully between clemency and amnesty, Carter insisted that what was needed was a pardon. "Amnesty says what you did was right," he explained, while a pardon "says whether what you did was right or wrong, you are forgiven for it." On the day following his inauguration, he granted a full pardon to 7150 convicted draft resisters (all except those who had deserted or who had used "force or violence" in resisting); eventually, less than 10 percent of all veterans who had deserted received upgrades of their discharge. Like Ford's program, Carter's drew little praise, as the majority of the public continued to oppose such a reprieve.

Without doubt, the persistent problem of "stagflation" had helped Carter win the presidency. Focusing first on unemployment, he sent Congress a two-part stimulus package that included immediate individual and business tax cuts in the first year, to be followed by a jobs program in 1978. Liberals were dissatisfied with the proposal, believing it too modest to do any good. As the stimulus bill worked its way toward passage, Carter's political tone-deafness surfaced. In late February, he announced his intention to reduce federal spending by vetoing a number of dam and water projects that were critically important to their sponsoring legislators. He ultimately reduced the number of items on his hit list, but insisted on an overall reduction of $100 million in water projects. An administration-sponsored amendment to this effect was crushed by an almost two-to-one vote. "There is perhaps no better illustration of the president's determination to do the right thing than his actions on the water projects," writes political scientist Charles O. Jones in *The Trusteeship Presidency: Jimmy Carter and the United States Congress*. "Nor is there a more important issue for explaining the cool and cautious attitudes of congressional Democrats toward the president." The flap over the water projects came to a head in April, as both houses were nearing final action on the stimulus bill. The stimulus package as finally adopted included the originally proposed individual tax reductions and jobs program, as well as financial aid to state and local governments. In securing its passage, however, the president had severely damaged his relations with congressional Democrats.

Carter tried cautiously to address inflation in early 1978 by issuing a call for voluntary price and wage guidelines—at which both business and labor balked. By April, he had determined to assert leadership on the issue by limiting pay increases for federal workers to 5.5 percent. Six months later, he called for similar restraint in the private sector, but labor remained adamantly opposed. When AFL-CIO boss George Meany publicly criticized the White House guidelines, the thin-skinned president "banished" Meany from the White House.

Still aiming to check inflation by controlling wages, in January 1979 Carter asked Congress to adopt a Tax Incentive Plan (TIP), under which workers who settled for wage gains of no more than 5.75 percent would receive a tax rebate if inflation rose beyond 7 percent. "The proposal had a frosty reception in Congress," notes

W. Carl Biven in *Jimmy Carter's Economy: Policy in an Age of Limits*. "The administration was probably lucky that it died a quiet death, for the cost would have been high." Yet the *political* cost of Carter's failure to implement this plan was also very high—particularly when the increases in the Consumer Price Index hit double digits in 1979 and 1980. Higher food prices accounted for much of the increase, but wages were increasing faster than productivity and thus also bore some responsibility. As for productivity rates, they were unlikely to rise until improvements were made in the nation's decaying industrial infrastructure. That decay, which increasingly seemed beyond repair, was symbolized most dramatically by the downward economic spiral of the industrial Midwest, which had come to be commonly referred to as the "Rustbelt." Carter's tepid approach, consisting of repeated appeals to labor and business to "decelerate" prices and wages, with incentives for cooperation, was unequal to these daunting challenges, and managed to alienate liberals and conservatives alike.

Carter had no greater success in dealing with the energy crisis of the 1970s than had his predecessor. The nation's dependence on foreign sources of petroleum had continued to grow during Ford's presidency, reaching 50 percent by the time Carter entered the White House. The fact that oil prices were down had reduced the sense of urgency to deal with the problem, making it difficult even for skillful political leaders to make headway. Yet it was clear that the nation's natural gas reserves were insufficient to meet future domestic needs unless there were changes in patterns of usage—or additional alternative sources of energy. Carter saw clearly that a national energy policy was needed, but the task of putting such a policy in place was formidable.

In addressing these enormous challenges, Carter once again showed a stunning lack of political acumen. At the end of January 1977, in the first of his several televised fireside chats, the president announced that he had charged Energy Secretary James Schlesinger with developing a comprehensive energy policy within ninety days. Schlesinger proceeded to work in virtual isolation, not bothering to consult with the congressional leadership. Three months later, Carter, declaring that the energy

Figure 3.1 Aiming to end the "imperial presidency," Jimmy Carter rejected many of the trappings of office. As shown here, in early 1977 he delivered a televised "fireside chat" to the nation, informally attired in a cardigan sweater, asking Americans to reduce energy use by turning down their home thermostats. National Archives and Records Administration, 173549

challenges the nation faced amounted to the "moral equivalent of war," was ready to send his energy package to Congress. Clearly, any such comprehensive policy had to balance the interests of southern and western energy-producing states, represented by relatively conservative legislators, with those of northeastern high-energy-consuming states, disproportionately represented by liberal Democrats. The lack of prior consultation, therefore, was particularly problematic. Worse, the administration proposal was long and highly complex. Its 113 separate provisions included controversial items such as gasoline taxes based on consumption levels, taxes on automobiles that burned high levels of fuel, tax credits for investments in fuel efficiency in buildings, a "wellhead" tax on domestic oil, and federal control of intrastate natural gas sales. Though Speaker Tip O'Neill (Massachusetts) strongly disagreed with cramming so many controversial proposals into a single bill, he worked hard to get the bill through the House. In August, it passed—virtually intact.

In the Senate, where oil- and gas-producing interests held greater sway, the outcome was different. Leading the fight in the Senate against the administration bill was Louisiana's Russell Long, powerful chair of the Finance Committee, who viewed it as "an unmitigated disaster on the production side." In the end, the upper house adopted several of the less controversial parts of the White House bill, but rejected key elements such as the tax on "gas-guzzling" automobiles, the proposal to permit federal regulation of intrastate gas, and the proposed wellhead tax. Carter signed the badly weakened measure into law on November 9, 1978.

Disappointing as it was to the administration, the National Energy Act of 1978 represented a substantial achievement and helped to slow the nation's slide toward ever greater dependence on foreign petroleum. But, as Julian Zelizer observes in his study of Carter's presidency, *Jimmy Carter*: "The political cost of the legislation was immense. Liberal Democrats were unhappy that pricing had been deregulated. Environmental organizations were not pleased because of their opposition to promoting the development of coal and nuclear power." Moreover, after the Senate had stripped away so much of the original administration proposal, the media focused mostly on the negative, laying the blame for failure on Carter's lack of political skills.

Energy issues continued to plague Carter throughout the remainder of his term in office. He managed to obtain grudging support from Congress for a "windfall profits tax" on oil company revenues directly resulting from either decontrol or price increases due to any future OPEC embargo, but his problems were intensified by two sets of events outside his control that seemed to call into question key elements of his energy program. On March 28, 1979, a reactor at the Three Mile Island nuclear power plant in Pennsylvania leaked dangerous amounts of radiation, setting off widespread protests against the administration's encouragement of nuclear power as an alternative energy source. At about the same time, the price of gasoline again began to rise sharply, accompanied by gas shortages at filling stations and long lines of impatient motorists across the country. The shortages and high prices were mostly the delayed effect of renewed cutbacks of Iranian oil exports to the United States, but angry and frustrated American consumers tended to believe that Carter was responsible. In the wake of these developments, the president's public approval rating fell below 50 percent, where it remained for much of the rest of his term in office.

Jimmy Carter had come to the White House with a long and ambitious to-do list. High on that list were protecting the solvency of the Social Security program, instituting a national health insurance program, and reforming the welfare system. He managed to secure passage of the Social Security Amendments of 1977, reducing some benefits and raising additional revenues by correcting a technical error made five years earlier, but he failed utterly with both health insurance and welfare reform. Historians largely agree with Carter's contemporary critics that, in these policy areas as well as in economic and energy policy, his greatest mistake was trying to design comprehensive policies that, as Erwin Hargrove writes in *Jimmy Carter as President: Leadership and the Politics of the Public Good*, combined "liberal goals with tight financial limits." Perhaps a centrist Democrat more skillful in dealing with Congress could have brought it off, but the challenge was too much for Carter and his inexperienced staff.

The issue of health insurance had bedeviled Democratic presidents since Harry Truman. Carter had called during the 1976 campaign for a comprehensive, mandatory health insurance system.

Once he was in the White House, liberals—led by Kennedy and UAW president Donald Fraser—pressed for action, but Carter, lacking a plan to pay for it, backed away. "Hitherto, relations between Carter and Kennedy had been amicable," write Burton and Scott Kaufman, "but as the deadlock ... continued, they became more critical of each other." By the end of 1979, the split was all but irrevocable, and Kennedy had decided to challenge the president in the 1980 Democratic primaries.

Statistically, Carter enjoyed a fair degree of success with both the 95th and 96th Congresses. Speaker O'Neill, though often put off by Carter's lack of appreciation for how things got done on Capitol Hill, was usually helpful in keeping House Democratic troops in line. Senate majority leader Robert Byrd (West Virginia) also tried to be helpful, but Democrats in the upper house proved harder to control. The president's fiscal conservatism frequently put him at odds with the party's liberal senators—a still sizable contingent. The fight with Kennedy and others over national health insurance was an egregious example. Another case in point was the Humphrey–Hawkins bill, which many liberals considered a litmus test. After waffling on the bill, Carter wound up signing a diluted version with a weakened commitment to full employment.

Style was a major problem for Carter. Rather than attempting to smooth over differences with his party colleagues, he seemed to take pride in *not* being a party traditionalist. Temperamentally, as he acknowledged in his White House memoir, he was more at home with conservative Democrats and Republicans than with the liberal wing of his party. Both intra- and inter-party strains were exacerbated by Carter's prickly personality, which would have limited his success in working with Congress in any case. By far the greatest obstacle to a good working relationship, however, was his concept of presidential leadership, as Charles O. Jones persuasively argues in *The Trusteeship Presidency*. The "trustee" concept of leadership, Jones writes, bore within it "assumptions about the congressional capacity to govern." Congress was supposed to "support the president because he spent time on an issue, demonstrated public support, and personally avoided the strictly political (by his definition). Unfortunately for the president, this approach created a distance between him and Congress."

The prevailing mood of Congress in the late 1970s virtually ensured difficulties between the two branches. Sharp conflicts with presidents from Johnson through Ford had created a knee-jerk adversarial attitude on Capitol Hill, and the presence of large numbers of relatively new members had broken down traditional patterns of deference in both communication and interaction between the two branches. Perhaps no chief executive could have worked smoothly with Congress in these circumstances, but Carter was undoubtedly the least well suited of all modern U.S. presidents to deal with such a political landscape.

Threading the Needle

In the aftermath of Carter's election, the *New York Times* opined that his success in bringing southern white voters back into the Democratic fold gave him an opportunity to build "a viable biracial coalition" and blunt the effects of the GOP's southern strategy. When he arrived in the White House, civil rights issues, except as a subset of the broader issue of human rights, were not part of his agenda. This sharply disappointed many black leaders, as did the new president's appointment of Griffin Bell as attorney general. A longtime friend of Carter's from Georgia, Bell had evinced little enthusiasm for desegregation while on the federal bench and had a history of membership in white-only clubs. Although Carter named civil rights leader Andrew Young as U.N. ambassador and selected an attorney for the NAACP Defense Fund to head the Justice Department's Civil Rights Division, in the eyes of civil rights advocates these appointments did not compensate for concerns about Bell.

Whereas the civil rights revolution of the 1950s and 1960s had been advanced largely by the executive and legislative branches, it was clear that if the key civil rights issues of the 1970s, affirmative action and busing, were to be resolved, it would be by the courts. Only a month after Carter's inauguration, the Supreme Court

73

announced it would take up a major affirmative action case, *Bakke v. University of California*. The plaintiff, Allan Bakke, had claimed reverse discrimination at the hands of the University of California-Davis medical school based on an affirmative action admissions program that allocated a specific number of seats to "disadvantaged" students. His attorneys charged that the special category was a minority set-aside program. After considerable internal discussion about the best position to take, the administration filed a brief endorsing the principle of affirmative action but failing to distinguish it from quotas. In the end, the court split the difference, ruling for Bakke but declaring that race could be one consideration in a university's admissions decisions. Carter, like the court, was perceived as threading the needle on the issue.

On the contentious busing issue, the Supreme Court had already decided some of the most difficult issues. In *Milliken v. Bradley* (1974), the court had clarified that cross-district busing between a city and its suburbs could be justified when—and *only* when—the districts in question had engaged in *de jure* school segregation. Still, a number of cases remained where lower-level courts were under challenge after having made a determination of *de jure* segregation and ordering city- and county-wide busing plans as a remedy. The first such test presented itself to Carter's Justice Department within two months of his inauguration, when the courts took up a case involving a court-ordered busing plan for Wilmington, Delaware, and its suburbs. Yet again, the administration tried to split the difference, entering a brief supporting the court-ordered plan but arguing that the lower court had overstepped its authority in ordering that each school should include a specific percentage of black students. Carter's Justice Department consistently supported court-ordered plans in cases involving other cities, however, including Columbus and Dayton, Ohio, which were the foci of the last major busing case to be decided by the Supreme Court during the 1970s. When the court upheld both plans in July 1979, the legal parameters for mandatory busing finally seemed to be clear. The administration could claim little credit for resolving the issue, but at least it had done no harm.

In the end, Carter proved a disappointment to his African American supporters. "Blacks were hardly recompensed for their massive support of President Carter," writes Harvard Sitkoff in *The Struggle for Black Equality, 1954–1992*. Though "Carter did not seek to inflame racial antagonisms," neither did he seek "to make the perpetuation of racial inequality a central concern of Americans." Steven Lawson is only slightly more positive, acknowledging, in *Running for Freedom: Civil Rights and Black Politics since 1941*, that "[t]here were limits to what Carter could do to construct an economic foundation for racial equality," but observing that "he chose to reserve most of his moral fervor for foreign affairs, and he lacked the power of persuasion to lead Congress and the American people on a crusade toward racial equality at home."

There had been no gender gap in the 1976 election, but feminists were optimistic about Carter's presidency. Not only had the Democratic platform unqualifiedly endorsed *Roe v. Wade*, but Carter had strongly supported ratification of ERA during the campaign. The new president ran into trouble with women's rights groups almost immediately, however, when his nominee for secretary of health, education, and welfare (HEW), former LBJ aide Joseph Califano, asserted during his confirmation hearings that he would seek to ban the use of federal funds to pay for abortions—in effect, endorsing the pro-life Hyde Amendment that had been enacted by Congress the previous fall. In response to a loud outcry from the National Abortion Rights Action League (NARAL) and other women's organizations, Carter trimmed, reiterating his general support for *Roe* but going no further. His temporizing made pro-life advocates distrustful of him. The conflict between pro-life and pro-choice advocates only intensified during the remainder of Carter's presidency, growing especially bitter during the annual congressional debates over renewal of the Hyde Amendment.

ERA presented another issue on which Carter seemed to satisfy no one. In sending the proposed amendment to the states in March 1972, Congress had set a seven-year deadline for ratification. After a fast start, momentum slowed, but by

January 1977 approval was needed by only three more states to reach the required three-fourths majority. Carter and his wife Rosalynn privately pressed legislators in states that had not yet voted, but the tide had already turned; eight states quickly voted against ratification. GOP activist Phyllis Schlafly and her STOP ERA movement were particularly effective in lobbying against the proposed amendment, sending legislators home-baked apple pies to underscore the message that ERA was contrary to traditional American values. Carter succeeded in getting Congress to extend the ratification deadline to June 1982, but frustrated feminist leaders felt he was not sufficiently engaged in the escalating battle. The deadline extension proved a hollow victory, in any case. Indiana's 1978 vote in favor of ratification proved to be the last success for ERA. Not a single additional state would ratify the amendment during the next four years.

At least as divisive and problematic as ERA or abortion rights was the drive for gay rights. This movement had grown steadily in intensity in the several years following a 1969 incident known as "Stonewall"—an uprising by gays against a police contingent attempting to arrest patrons in New York City's Stonewall Bar. Carter's oft-declared commitment to human rights suggested to gay movement leaders that he would actively support their cause. In contrast, conservative Christians anticipated that the evangelical president would naturally take their side in the emerging holy war over the rights of gays and lesbians. The issue exploded within weeks of Carter's inauguration, when former beauty queen Anita Bryant launched a grass-roots movement, "Save Our Children," to repeal a recently passed Dade County, Florida, ordinance prohibiting discrimination on the basis of sexual orientation. Bryant's crusade drew support from the Reverend Jerry Falwell and other evangelical Christian leaders, as well as from prominent conservative Republicans such as Reagan and North Carolina senator Jesse Helms. In June, Dade County voters repealed the ordinance by a sizable margin but, as Kalman writes, Bryant had "galvanized the mobilization of homosexuals as well as homophobes. She had the same impact on the gay rights movement that *Roe* had on the right to life movement." Gay rights advocates, led by San Francisco activist Harvey Milk, publicly called upon the White House to support the addition of sexual orientation to the list of federal civil rights protections. Once again when confronted by extremes, Carter equivocated. When asked by the media about his position in the wake of the Dade County referendum, he replied that though he did not view homosexuality "as a threat to the family," neither did he regard it as "a normal interrelationship." When this response failed to satisfy his questioners, his exasperation was obvious. "Look," he snapped, "this is a subject I don't particularly want to involve myself in. I've got enough problems without taking on another."

The dispute over gay rights remained heated and divisive throughout Carter's presidency. In November 1978, California voters broke a string of anti-gay victories across the nation by defeating the Briggs Initiative, a proposed measure to bar gays and lesbians from teaching in the public schools. Carter's belated public statement against the initiative had the familiar result of disappointing both supporters and opponents. When, less than three weeks after Californians voted the measure down, Milk—who had been Carter's most outspoken critic among gay rights leaders—was assassinated, bitterness and disillusionment with Carter deepened within the gay community. As with feminists, Carter had alienated an increasingly active liberal voting bloc even while he simultaneously disappointed the vociferous religious right.

The 1978 mid-term elections occurred in the midst of these fierce cultural clashes. In historical context, the numerical results were not surprising, as the GOP picked up three seats in the Senate and fifteen in the House. Significantly, however, the National Right to Life Committee reported that five seats in the Senate had switched from the pro-choice column to pro-life. Many of the victorious conservative Republicans had benefited greatly from financial support by the National Conservative Political Action Committee, which had been founded only three years earlier. Though the Democrats remained firmly in control of both houses in the 96th Congress, thunderclouds were gathering. "With Carter's political coalition fracturing," writes Flippen, "the roots for a new Republican alliance had begun to grow in its place."

The Abandonment of Idealism

"Jimmy Carter entered office believing that the failure of his predecessors was moral," writes Gaddis Smith in *Morality, Reason and Power.* Accordingly, he offered "a morally responsible and farsighted vision" of American foreign policy—almost the polar opposite of the *realpolitik* approach of his Republican predecessors. In basic ways, notes Bruce Miroff in *The Liberals' Moment,* Carter's global outlook was actually "closer to McGovern's in 1972 than to those rivals of his that echoed the verities of the Cold War." Apparently hoping to invite constructive debate within his administration—and perhaps to ensure control of policy direction for himself—Carter appointed ideological near-opposites as his national security advisor and secretary of state: Zbigniew Brzezinski and Cyrus Vance, respectively. The diffident and deliberative Vance proved no match for the self-confident Brzezinski, the quintessential Cold Warrior. By the midpoint of Carter's term, Brzezinski was clearly the dominant force and—despite the president's intentions—administration policies were drifting back to familiar Cold War moorings.

To the extent that Carter presented any sort of vision for U.S. foreign policy in the 1976 campaign, it was that respect for human rights should be its guiding principle. Such a focus, he believed, would fundamentally reorient the nation from the sort of adventurism that might bring about another Vietnam, and at the same time place the United States on the side of the oppressed everywhere in the world. Settling on a uniform definition of "human rights" in a global context was difficult enough; figuring out how to center the nation's foreign policy on the concept proved to be impossible. Doing so would have required the United States to face down the Soviet Union and the People's

Republic of China for their treatment of political dissidents, as well as to intervene against repressive regimes throughout the developing world. Inevitably, therefore, Carter applied the principle selectively, eliciting criticisms from both left and right. Consequently, most studies of Carter's foreign policy, including Joshua Muravchik's *The Uncertain Crusade: Jimmy Carter and the Dilemmas of Human Rights Policy*, Scott Kaufman's *Plans Unraveled: The Foreign Policy of the Carter Administration*, and Glad's *Outsider in the White House*, have been generally critical. In the end, Muravchik concludes, "the good that the Carter policy did for the idea of human rights by broadcasting it must be weighed against the harm it did by contributing to the miasma that surrounds the term."

Despite these inconsistencies, Carter registered some significant foreign policy accomplishments during his four years in the White House. Most notable were the Camp David Accords that established a rough framework for peace in the Middle East, ratification of the Panama Canal treaties ending U.S. control of the canal, and normalization of diplomatic relations with the People's Republic of China.

Carter had a genuine interest in the Middle East, due partly to his deep religious faith. During the 1976 campaign he had seemed to embrace almost contradictory positions where Israel and Palestinian rights were concerned. While urging that Israel cede its territorial gains from the 1967 war and recognize a Palestinian state on the West Bank, he also called for "defensible" Israeli borders and opposed diplomatic recognition of the Palestinian Liberation Organization (PLO). Almost immediately after his inauguration Carter alarmed Jewish leaders by meeting with leaders from several Arab nations, including Egypt's Anwar Sadat, before talking with Israel's leadership. The path to a possible peace agreement became even more challenging in May 1977 when the Israeli elections resulted in victory for the hard-line Likud Party and the seemingly intractable Menachem Begin became prime minister. To the surprise of many, however, Carter established a personal rapport with Begin when the latter visited Washington during the summer. By late 1977, the president felt

Figure 3.2 President Carter, Egyptian leader Anwar Sadat, and Israeli prime minister Menachem Begin at the Camp David presidential retreat in March 1979, forging a framework for peace. Photo by Warren K. Leffler, Library of Congress, Prints & Photographs Division

confident that if he could bring the leaders of Israel and Egypt together, there would be a chance for progress toward peace.

The path to the eventual meeting of the three heads of state at the president's Camp David retreat required patience and careful negotiation, but in August 1978 Carter was able to announce that the gathering would occur the following month. There, the three national leaders hammered out goals for a permanent peace in the Middle East, the key ingredients of which would be Israel's withdrawal from the Sinai peninsula and Egyptian recognition of the Israeli state. On September 18, with Begin and Sadat present, Carter announced the framework to a joint session of Congress. The president's role in creating the "Spirit of Camp David" was hailed in the media, and his public approval ratings shot up from 39 percent in late July to 56 percent in mid-September.

But the Camp David Accords were a framework, not a peace agreement. Important details remained to be negotiated, which would not be simple. The accords had little support in either Israel or the Arab world. As the afterglow of Camp David faded and months passed with no progress toward peace talks, Carter again intervened personally. In early March 1979, he flew to Tel Aviv to meet with Begin, after which he carried Israel's final proposal to Sadat in Cairo. To his immense surprise, Sadat accepted the terms: return of the Sinai to Egypt, with an oil pipeline assured to Israel from the Sinai fields, and an exchange of ambassadors between the two nations. Although the status of the West Bank and Gaza remained unchanged, Begin agreed to loosen civil restraints on Palestinian settlers in those areas. A dramatic signing ceremony was held at the White House on March 26, 1979, with more than 1500 spectators in attendance. Ominously, however, the eighteen-nation Arab League announced a few days later that it did not recognize the agreement as a "final acceptable formula."

The Panama Canal issue had been brewing since 1974, when Secretary of State Kissinger had signed a "statement of principles" calling for a timetable for transfer of control of the canal and the thin strip of land known as the Canal Zone from the United States to Panama. By 1976 the canal had become a cause célèbre for Republican hawks. "When it comes to the canal," said Ronald Reagan in his race against Ford in the primaries, "we bought it, we paid for it, it's ours." This was "Carter's kind of issue," as Hargrove observes, because it offered "the opportunity to break a deadlock and also do the morally right thing." Intent on resolving the matter while his approval ratings remained high, in September 1977 Carter signed two treaties with Panama's leader, General Omar Torrijos, the first calling for American cession of the canal to Panama in 1999 and the second providing for the neutrality of the waterway and the Canal Zone thereafter.

By January, public approval of the treaties had risen from 40 percent to 57 percent, but Carter still faced the problem of winning over enough Republican votes for ratification. Senate minority leader Howard Baker and several other GOP moderates were favorably disposed, but were wary of what their support for the treaties could mean for their political survival. In the end,

Baker played a key role, working with majority leader Byrd to cobble together enough of their respective troops to produce 68-32 votes for both treaties—one vote more than the two-thirds needed for ratification.

Carter paid a high price for this victory. "While conservatives lost the ratification debate," writes Zelizer, "they exited the Senate battle with renewed energy at the grassroots level and with greater organizing strength." Moreover, public and media criticism of the treaties as reflecting "weakness" and "retreat" caused many senators of both parties who had voted for ratification to resolve not to be caught again in such a compromising position. When thirteen of the twenty treaty-supporters who were up for re-election in November either retired or were defeated, this resolve strengthened. As both Charles O. Jones and Betty Glad have observed, Carter's success with the Panama Canal treaties may, in fact, have doomed chances for ratification of the SALT II treaty, which was unfinished business from the Ford administration.

Carter had come to the White House with visions of not only completing the SALT II treaty but, as he recorded in his memoir, achieving "much larger reductions in nuclear arsenals, with exact equality between the destructive forces of the two nations." He could not have gotten off to a worse start with Soviet leader Leonid Brezhnev, however, by proposing arms reductions more extreme than those the latter had agreed to at Vladivostok. Moreover, Brezhnev saw Carter's pronouncements about human rights as an affront to Soviet sovereignty. The inexperienced Carter, as Glad writes, "failed to see that his moral abstractions were actually complicating relations with [the Soviets] and thus inhibiting his ability to secure the national security goals he sought." With negotiations stalled, in March 1978 Carter delivered a foreign policy speech at Wake Forest University laced with Cold War rhetoric, warning of the Soviets' military buildup and their "ominous inclinations." Directed primarily to the Soviets, the speech also foreshadowed a shift in Carter's focus to strengthening connections with China.

Normalization of relations between the United States and the People's Republic of China had been on the agenda since Nixon's

1972 visit. Spurred on by Brzezinski and fearing that additional delay might alienate the Chinese leadership, Carter removed a major barrier to normalization by abandoning the U.S. insistence that the two parties mutually guarantee peaceful resolution of the question of Taiwan. With that sticking point removed, the two sides entered into quiet negotiations over the conditions that had been identified in the Nixon–Mao "Shanghai Communiqué" as necessary for normalization: that the United States terminate its relations and abrogate its defense treaty with Taiwan, as well as withdraw all its military troops from the island. On December 15, the U.S. and PRC negotiators issued a joint communiqué calling for restoration of normal relations between the two nations on January 1, 1979.

It was clear that normalization was an idea whose time had come. "The serious opposition we had expected throughout our country and within Congress simply did not materialize," Carter later wrote in *Keeping Faith*. Although Goldwater, Helms, and other conservative Republican leaders sharply criticized the move (a "cowardly" act, in Goldwater's words) and some hawkish right-wing groups continued to condemn this reversal of the pro-Taiwan policies of an earlier era, a Gallup poll recorded that 57 percent of the public approved normalization, with only 23 percent opposed. As always seemed to be the case for Carter, however, he received little credit for this bold stroke; 55 percent felt Nixon had been primarily responsible. With most of the media lauding the move, Carter easily secured the necessary legislation to create a private entity, the American Institute, to serve in place of an embassy in Taiwan. On March 1, 1979, the United States and the People's Republic of China opened embassies in each other's countries.

Although Carter's more bellicose language and the opening of diplomatic relations with the People's Republic of China heightened tensions with the Soviets, both the American and Soviet leadership still hoped for a second SALT treaty. Since Vladivostok, Brezhnev had staked much of his prestige at home on achieving such an agreement. On the American side, Secretary Vance was particularly eager for resolution, warning Carter that "failure to conclude and gain approval of a SALT II Agreement would be seen as a major setback here and abroad." Accordingly, both sides made important concessions in late 1978 and early 1979 involving timetables and the exact numbers of missiles and warheads to be allowed on each side. Ultimately, the terms of the proposed agreement were generally similar to those agreed to at Vladivostok. Carter and Brezhnev signed the long-awaited SALT II treaty in Geneva on June 18, 1979.

By this time, however, Carter's saber-rattling and the U.S. defense buildup, coupled with increased Soviet adventurism abroad, particularly in Africa, had eroded both public and congressional support for another SALT agreement. In the Senate, which would have to vote on ratification, Henry Jackson had been a thorn in Carter's side all the way through the SALT negotiations, pressing for ever more restrictive provisions, and he remained a formidable foe as committee hearings opened on the treaty. The ever-caustic Jesse Helms attacked the administration's concept of "adequate verification" to ensure Soviet compliance, likening the idea to "adequate faithfulness" in a marriage. In July, beleaguered majority whip Alan Cranston (California) warned Carter that he could count on only fifty-eight positive votes— nine short of what would be required for ratification. The scenario grew worse as the hearings in the Foreign Relations and Armed Services committees ground on. Carter's lobbying efforts fell short. In November, the Foreign Relations Committee voted 9-6 in favor of ratification, but the Armed Services Committee, where the influential Sam Nunn (D-Georgia) and John Tower (R-Texas) held sway, voted 0-10 against, with seven abstentions, and issued a report labeling the proposed treaty a threat to "national security interests."

With prospects for ratification of the treaty dismal at best, the Soviets' December 1979 decision to invade Afghanistan to prop up a faltering new communist revolutionary regime "wiped out any chance for a two-thirds vote of approval," in Carter's words. Genuinely shocked, the president observed to Hamilton Jordan that this act of brutal aggression so soon after the signing of the arms control agreement in Geneva called "into question détente and the way we have been doing business with the Soviets for the past decade." In early January, he made the painful decision to abandon the SALT agreement. The epitaph for détente was formally delivered by Carter in his State of the Union address on January 23, 1980. In a speech that the press quickly labeled the "Carter Doctrine," he laid out the reasons for abandoning hope for continued negotiations. "The Soviet Union is now attempting to consolidate a strategic position that poses a grave threat to the free movement of Middle East oil," he announced.

> This situation demands careful thought, steady nerves, and reso-
> lute action, not only for this year but for many years to come… .
> Let our position be absolutely clear: An attempt by any outside
> force to gain control of the Persian Gulf region will be regarded as
> an assault on the vital interests of the United States of America,
> and such an assault will be repelled by any means necessary,
> including military force.

To the consternation of Vice President Mondale and Stuart Eizenstat, Carter also announced the resumption of Selective Service registration for males at age 18—just in case. A few days before, he had notified the International Olympic Committee that the United States would boycott the 1980 Summer Olympics, to be held in Moscow, ultimately to be joined in a boycott of the games by six other nations. Within the administration, Zbigniew Brzezinski's triumph over Vance was complete.

Carter's preoccupation with Camp David and the succeeding negotiations, as well as the hardening of U.S.–Soviet relations in late 1978 and 1979, contributed significantly to bad policy decisions in response to yet another festering crisis: the Iranian revolution. The consequence of those bad decisions would be a nearly year-long hostage crisis that ultimately helped to torpedo the president's chances for re-election in 1980.

In the time since he had come to the White House, Carter had escalated the quarter-century-long U.S. commitment to Shah Mohammad Reza Pahlavi's government in Iran. Not only had he heaped public praise on the shah on many occasions (at one point lauding his nation as "an island of stability" in the Middle East), but, over the strong objections of liberal Democrats, he had pushed through Congress legislation providing for the sale of airborne warning and controls (AWACS) aircraft to Iran, and had provided the shah with greater amounts of military assistance than had either Nixon or Ford. When the protests of radical Islamic followers of Ayatollah Ruhollah Khomeini caught fire in Iran during the final months of 1978, the shah wavered between repression and conciliation. By the end of the year, his ouster appeared inevitable. The administration had no contingency plans for a post-shah Iran. Carter continued to express support for the shah, in the process strengthening the case for Khomeini's radical followers that the "satan America" was as deserving of punishment as the shah himself.

In mid-January 1979, the shah—very ill with the malignant lymphoma which would kill him within eighteen months—ceded much of his power to a new prime minister connected with the radical faction and then left the country. Private negotiations abetted by the United States led ultimately to his resettlement in Mexico. Khomeini's triumphant return to Iran from exile signaled the death of what remained of the shah's regime. Although Carter formally recognized the new Iranian government in late February, tensions remained high around the American embassy in Tehran, with the new revolutionary regime whipping up growing anti-U.S. frenzy in the streets by its harsh denunciations. Carter's decision in mid-October to permit the shah to enter the United States on emergency medical grounds, in the face of the Iranian revolutionary government's demand for his return to Iran, was the final straw. On November 4, generalized rage turned into purposeful action, as 150 radical students stormed the embassy and kidnapped sixty-three American hostages (within two weeks the captors released thirteen women and African Americans, in a misguided effort to win support within those groups in the United States). With no viable options, Carter became a prisoner to the unfolding hostage crisis. "That story, a narrative of Americans suffering and no one willing or able to put a stop to it," writes David Farber in *Taken Hostage: The Iran Hostage Crisis and America's*

First Encounter with Radical Islam, "was the one that ultimately captured the nation in the last year of the Carter presidency."

Carter's helplessness in the Iranian hostage crisis accentuated public frustrations with his presidency. Almost nothing had turned out as he had hoped. He had not succeeded in either controlling inflation or establishing a comprehensive energy policy, and the Iranian crisis had worsened the situation by creating oil shortages and tripling gas prices during the final two years of his presidency. On a number of issues he had come into sharp conflict with his party's most powerful liberals, while at the same time sustaining heavy damage from Christian conservatives on the right. In foreign affairs, even his successes won him little credit, as his vaunted emphasis on "human rights" proved impossible to implement in any consistent way.

Having campaigned as an outsider who would cure the ills of Watergate-ravaged Washington, Carter proved to be a major disappointment to the electorate that had propelled him into the White House. In mid-July 1979—with inflation, interest rates, and public unhappiness all soaring—he delivered a much-awaited televised address in which he charged that a "crisis of confidence" was immobilizing the nation. Kevin Mattson, in *"What the Heck Are You Up to, Mr. President?" Jimmy Carter, America's "Malaise," and the Speech That Should Have Changed the Country,* analyzes how this single speech "provided a script for Carter's end." The president's objective was to call for a renewal of American idealism and belief in the nation's future, but his language was largely accusatory. Peppering his address with words such as "self-indulgence," "fragmentation," and "self-interest," Carter acknowledged that neither he nor "all the legislation in the world" could "fix what's wrong with America." "It was a speech of humility and honesty and more," writes Mattson—and it was initially well received. Within just a few days, however, Carter blindsided everyone by calling for the resignations of all members of his Cabinet, eventually replacing five. The stunning shake-up, variously labeled a "purge" and a "massacre" in the media, erased the early positive perceptions of the "crisis of confidence" address and reinforced concerns about Carter's capacity to lead the nation.

Carter's image by this time lay in total disrepair. White House communications director Gerald Rafshoon urged him to start *"looking, talking and acting more like a leader—even if it's artificial,"* including wearing dark suits for increased gravitas. Political cartoonists were having a field day, as *Washington Post* columnist Haynes Johnson wrote, having arrived at a consensus on how to portray Carter: "his figure grew smaller and smaller, his manner more and more befuddled, his gaze more frequently raised upward, as if praying for fortune or the Lord to extricate him from his problems." It seemed that Carter had indeed diminished while in the White House. Although he had focused the "crisis of confidence" speech on deficiencies in the American people's spirit, the public had come to believe that the problem was Carter himself.

4
Dogma and (More) Disappointment, 1980–1988

The magnitude of Carter's loss to Ronald Reagan in the election of 1980 and Reagan's media mastery and popularity while in the White House created a myth that the lopsided results of that election were foreordained. Forces were clearly at work that fueled growing Republican strength, but Reagan's victory was not inevitable. Despite the overwhelming problems that threatened to swamp Carter, the two candidates were locked in a tight race until the end. In the final week of the campaign, however, changing dynamics produced major shifts in voter sentiment. Nineteen-eighty, writes Andrew Busch in *Reagan's Victory: The Presidential Election of 1980 and the Rise of the Right*, "was as much a year of drastic contingencies and powerful personalities as it was one of bad underlying conditions."

Similarly, Reagan's rhetorical gifts in packaging his ideas and his penchant for announcing victory for conservative ideals created a myth that the "Reagan revolution" was a sweeping success. In substance, however, the years of his presidency disappointed the New Right in many particulars—especially in the area of social policy. At the same time, rising prosperity through

Deadlock and Disillusionment: American Politics since 1968, First Edition.
Gary W. Reichard.
© 2016 John Wiley & Sons, Inc. Published 2016 by John Wiley & Sons, Inc.

the decade led most conservatives to assume that "Reaganomics" had permanently displaced the Keynesian mantra that had ruled in Washington for half a century, but this, too, proved an exaggeration. Moreover, administration policies created huge deficits by the late 1980s. While the GOP emerged stronger and more ideologically unified from the Reagan years, the fragility of the party's hold on public affections would be demonstrated by the speed of its return to minority status in the early 1990s.

The Rise of the Right

With the odds against Carter's re-election seeming insurmountable, the 1980 Republican primary season began with a crowded field—ten candidates in all. Former president Ford, who still retained the loyalty and affection of a large swath of the Republican electorate, toyed with the idea of running but in the end decided to stay out of the race. Ronald Reagan was the clear favorite, having consistently led in GOP preference polls for the past year. The best known of the remaining candidates were former treasury secretary John Connally, Senate minority leader Howard Baker, and former CIA director and GOP national chairman, George H. W. Bush. Running far to the left of the rest of the field, Illinois congressman John Anderson also enjoyed early support, based on his record of fiscal conservatism and proclaimed commitment to "a humane approach to the issues."

The winnowing occurred quickly. By the time of the New Hampshire primary, the contest had already effectively narrowed to Reagan and Bush. Reagan's adroit handling of a snafu in a debate in the town of Nashua, during which he projected an image of being in command but also respectful of his opponents, dramatically changed the dynamic; he buried Bush by a more than two-to-one margin in a primary that had been expected to be close. By April the outcome was clear; Reagan lost five primaries (all to Bush) but otherwise swept the board. Anderson, the only "Rockefeller Republican" in the field, dropped out within weeks of losing his home state primary, announcing that he would run as an independent in the general election.

Although Reagan's nomination by the Republican convention in Detroit was a foregone conclusion, there was drama nonetheless. On the third day, rumors swirled that the nominee planned to reach out to former President Ford to join him on the ticket. When Ford publicly set conditions calling in effect for a "co-presidency," Reagan backed away from the prospective deal. The presumptive nominee then shocked the convention by announcing in a post-midnight press conference that his running-mate would be Bush, who was anathema to party conservatives, had earlier criticized Reagan for his "voodoo economics," and would clearly need to abandon his longstanding support for *Roe v. Wade* in order to accept. The choice proved to be inspired, however. With Bush's selection, writes Laura Kalman in *Right Star Rising*, "[t]he Ford and Reagan wings had come together, and veterans of the Ford administration poured into the campaign."

The ticket settled, the party then adopted its most extreme platform since 1964. In addition to calling for a constitutional amendment to ban abortion and extolling the importance of traditional family values, the platform reached to the right on economic and foreign policy, as well, embracing the controversial principles of "supply-side" economics (which purported to increase federal revenues by *lowering* tax rates) and echoing the patriotic, Cold War-inspired rhetoric of an earlier era.

In the Democratic party, a revolt had been in the works since the party's 1978 mid-term convention in Memphis, where speaker after speaker had criticized Carter administration policies. Shortly thereafter, a "dump Carter" movement was initiated by dissident liberals, who pressured Ted Kennedy to challenge the president for the 1980 nomination. In November 1979, Kennedy entered, but he stumbled badly at the starting gate, performing abysmally in a CBS interview just days before his scheduled announcement. In addition, on the very day of that disastrous interview, the story of the seizure of American hostages in Iran squashed reportage of his entry into the race. Although Carter had responded to earlier rumors of a Kennedy candidacy by asserting that he would "whip his ass," even the senator's poor start did not seem to make such an outcome likely. Adding to the president's headaches, California's quirky young governor, Jerry Brown, was also showing interest in running.

Carter opted to run a general-election-type campaign against Kennedy in the primaries, focusing on the broad question of who could best prevail in November. As Timothy Stanley notes in *Kennedy vs. Carter: The 1980 Battle for the Democratic Party's Soul*, Kennedy made a strategic error in the way he reacted to the president's tactics, "dropping his campaign's emphasis on personality … and instead running a campaign of economic protest." When the better-organized Carter won the Iowa caucuses by a two-to-one margin, Kennedy's campaign looked like a loser. The contest remained suspenseful until the president's victory in Illinois in April, which—according to political scientist Gerald Pomper in *The Election of 1980: Reports and Interpretations*—showed "that Kennedy had not revived the traditional Democratic coalition on which he had based his hopes."

It was not to be smooth sailing for Carter, however. In mid-April, without warning, Fidel Castro permitted more than 120,000 dissidents to leave Cuba for the United States in what was labeled the Mariel boatlift. Since these *Marielitos* included large numbers of criminals and mentally ill, their arrival was a formidable political problem. Carter's compassionate response, even if admirable in principle, was not popular, to say the least. Almost immediately on the heels of this public relations nightmare, a botched attempt to rescue the hostages in Iran, foiled by the crash of one of the American helicopters and the deaths of eight U.S. airmen, again illuminated the administration's powerlessness in the face of that protracted crisis. The failed rescue effort cost Carter his secretary of state, Cyrus Vance, who had been left out of the loop on this mission and resigned soon after it failed—reinforcing the public impression that the president could not control his own administration. At the convention, Carter was renominated by a two-to-one majority, but Kennedy stole the show with a blockbuster speech that ended with an unforgettable rallying cry: "the work goes on, the cause endures, the hope still lives, and the dream shall never die." The forty-minute ovation and demonstration in the aisles following his speech underscored the depth of the party's frustration with Carter.

"Even though many liberals grumbled that Jimmy Carter governed from the right, even though many conservatives grumbled that Ronald Reagan moderated his views to win," writes Gil Troy in *Morning in America: How Ronald Reagan Invented the 1980s,* "this election offered Americans a dramatic choice." The differences between the candidates grew sharper as the campaign progressed. Reagan hammered away at the administration's dismal economic record and its fecklessness in the face of the resurgent Soviet threat. Tax reduction became a particular point of emphasis, as Reagan advanced the line of the emerging supply-side economic theory. Prominent leaders of the Christian Right supported the GOP ticket with enthusiasm. Leading the pack was Jerry Falwell's Moral Majority, Inc., which, aided by other conservative religious leaders and organizations, targeted individual congressional Democrats up for re-election, grading them on widely distributed "moral report cards." The work of these Christian groups was greatly helped by the innovation of direct-mail marketing and canvassing.

Carter's situation was made even worse by John Anderson's presence in the race. Polls throughout the campaign showed the Illinois congressman holding steady at about 15 percent—a sizable showing if it were to materialize. The fact that he was more liberal than Carter on several issues suggested that his presence in the race would do more damage to the president than to Reagan. Accordingly, Carter refused to agree to a three-cornered debate proposed by the League of Women Voters, believing that such a direct confrontation would enhance Anderson's stature and credibility. When Reagan and Anderson accepted the invitation and debated with each other in late September, Carter was the big loser in terms of public relations.

With the lead shifting back and forth through September and October, Carter finally agreed to a one-on-one debate with

Reagan in Cleveland on October 28. His decision proved to be a huge mistake. Trying feverishly to negotiate an end to the hostage crisis before the election, the president was tired and haggard—and appeared as such on television screens across the nation. The polished and telegenic Reagan provided a sharp contrast, as his sunny, reassuring manner undercut the Carter campaign's efforts over many months to portray him as an over-the-hill, out-of-touch, saber-rattling extremist. Reagan delivered the *coup de grâce* in his closing statement, challenging viewers to ask themselves whether or not they felt better off than they had been four years earlier. The debate marked the turning point in the campaign.

What had been a close race turned into a rout: Reagan carried forty-four states with 489 electoral votes to Carter's 49; he also received 51 percent of the popular vote to Carter's 41 percent. Anderson fared much worse than the polls had predicted, garnering just 6.6 percent of the vote. Carter likely benefited from this shortfall. "Fear of Reagan was Anderson's undoing," writes Timothy Stanley, "causing many liberals to withdraw support and return, albeit reluctantly, to the Carter/Mondale ticket." Clearly, it was not Anderson's presence in the race that led to Reagan's landslide victory.

The Republican sweep was national in scope. Reagan's gains over the 1976 GOP vote were consistent across nearly every identifiable demographic. As Kalman recounts, "Carter ran at least 10 points behind his own 1976 performance with many voter groups: Democrats, independents, liberals, men, middle-class college graduates, blue-collar workers, union members, suburbanites, southerners (particularly white ones), westerners, Latinos, whites, Protestants (especially evangelicals), Catholics, [and] Jews." The only exceptions were black voters, whose solidarity for the Democratic ticket remained intact. As Manning Marable points out, in *Race, Reform, and Rebellion: The Second Reconstruction in Black America, 1945–1990*, however, blacks, "in spite of their revulsion against Reaganism, could not be mobilized sufficiently to accept a candidate who had done so little" for civil rights, turning out at only a 40 percent rate and perhaps costing Carter victory in more than a few southern states. The New Deal coalition had shattered. The evangelical vote broke for Reagan by as much as 60 to 80 percent; ironically, Carter's success in mobilizing such voters four years earlier probably helped to increase the magnitude of Reagan's victory.

The Reagan surge had occurred during the final days of the campaign, after most pollsters stopped sampling. The wretched state of the economy and the political fallout from the drawn-out hostage crisis clearly worked against Carter throughout the campaign—so why such dramatic change in those final few days? One explanation lies in Reagan's superior performance in the October 28 debate, which made him seem—to many, for the first time—a highly credible alternative to a president increasingly regarded as ineffectual. "Non-developments" in the hostage crisis may also have hurt Carter in the last days. Election day fell on the first anniversary of the kidnappings, and media attention to that fact was inevitable. Worse, Carter himself contributed to a heightening of expectations for a dramatic breakthrough by canceling a campaign appearance to return to D.C. over the final weekend before the election to work on a possible settlement. When nothing resulted, the public was only more frustrated with what felt like a protracted national insult. In a 1991 book, *October Surprise: America's Hostages in Iran and the Election of Ronald Reagan*, former National Security Council (NSC) staffer Gary Sick alleged that the Reagan team was responsible for this, having secretly encouraged the Iranians to delay settlement till after the election on the promise of future arms sales by a Reagan administration. An ensuing congressional investigation into this charge, however, turned up no evidence of such a reverse "October Surprise."

Despite the tendency of historians to treat 1980 as a watershed, the Reagan landslide did not represent a dramatic shift in voter sentiments. Nor did the election provide Reagan with a real mandate. As Andrew Busch points out, much of Reagan's appeal in 1980—as had been true for Carter four years earlier—was his "outsider" status; he was not the failed incumbent, nor was he associated with the accumulated ills of the past four years. Gil Troy concurs, observing:

> Not only did Reagan lack a mandate, but with all the doubts about his extremism and his intellect unanswered he entered the White House as the most unpopular president-elect in modern American history. No victorious candidate since polling began in the 1930s had such a low public-approval rating.

But the newly elected president had a much more favorable terrain on Capitol Hill than anyone had thought likely. The congressional elections produced a phenomenal pickup of twelve Senate seats by the GOP, as nearly all the liberals targeted by conservative activists went down to defeat. Included in this number were some of the best known and most powerful Democrats in the upper house, including George McGovern, Frank Church, and Birch Bayh (Indiana). Even the redoubtable Herman Talmadge (Georgia)—no liberal he—fell to an even more conservative Republican opponent. The Senate had switched from a 59-41 Democratic advantage to GOP control by 53-47. The House remained in the Democrats' hands, even though Republicans gained an impressive thirty-three seats. After four years of disappointment with one-party control in Washington, the voters had restored divided government. It was a new day, with momentum clearly on the side of Reagan and his new brand of conservatives.

Reaganomics

Economic promises were central to Reagan's campaign—and to his victory. The GOP's formula for recovery included curbing the runaway inflation and interest rates of the Carter years, reducing federal government programs, and cutting tax burdens on individuals and businesses to encourage private investment needed for economic growth. In his inauguration speech, the new president announced his intention to implement this program immediately. "In this present crisis," he famously stated early in the address,

> Government is not the solution to our problem; government is the problem... . It is time to check and reverse the growth of government which shows signs of having grown beyond the consent of the governed... . [I]t is not my intention to do away with government. It is rather to make it work—work with us, not over us; to stand by our side, not ride on our back ... .

Ever the master of symbolism, as his first act the new president froze all civilian hiring by the federal government.

Reagan laid out the administration's plan in greater detail before a joint session of Congress in mid-February. At its center was a proposal that closely tracked a 1978 bill developed by Representative Jack Kemp (R-New York) and Senator William Roth (R-Delaware), providing for $50 billion in tax cuts over a

Figure 4.1 Ronald Reagan's swearing-in, January 20, 1981. The sweeping victory of the Reagan–Bush ticket in 1980 seemed to usher in a new period of conservative dominance in American politics. Courtesy Ronald Reagan Library

three-year period. Elaborating on the supply-side reasoning underlying the measure, Reagan claimed that these reductions would produce a $500 million revenue surplus in three years. "Our aim," he explained, "is to increase our national wealth so all will have more, not just redistribute what we already have which is just sharing scarcity." At the same time, he reassured the nation that he would not touch the "social safety net" consisting of Social Security, Medicare, and Medicaid, nor would veterans' benefits or the school lunch program be harmed. Budget director David Stockman, a fiscal hawk of the first order, and Treasury Secretary Donald Regan were tasked with selling the economic plan to Congress, although the president himself also met with hundreds of legislators over the next several weeks in an effort to pitch the program. Privately, Stockman strongly urged deep budget cuts to avoid worsening the deficit.

It is unlikely that the president's economic package could have passed in Congress but for a potentially catastrophic event that gave the administration renewed momentum. On March 30, as Reagan was leaving the Washington Hilton after a speech, a would-be assassin, John Hinckley, fired off six shots at close range, hitting the president, as well as three others in his party—including press secretary James Brady. Grievously wounded, Brady suffered permanent brain damage from the incident. Reagan and the Secret Service agents who accompanied him to the hospital were initially unaware of the extent of his injuries, but doctors quickly determined that an exploding bullet which somehow failed to go off had lodged inches from the president's heart, causing major internal bleeding. A three-hour operation was successful, but it was a closer call than the public realized; the president had remained on a ventilator for eight hours following surgery and ran a high fever for nearly a week afterward. Tales of his extraordinary grace and good humor in the emergency room while awaiting life-saving surgery, however, sent his stock soaring with the American people. ("Honey, I forgot to duck," he told his wife Nancy, jokingly adding that he hoped his surgeon was a Republican.) The halo effect was immediate. Polls showed that three-fourths of those questioned now favored the administration program.

With Republicans in unanimous support, joined by more than sixty conservative Democrats (most of them so-called southern "boll weevils"), Reagan's budget measure passed the Democratic-controlled House in May; the Senate followed suit by the lopsided margin of 70-28, again with generous Democratic support. Similarly, the administration-sponsored tax overhaul passed overwhelmingly in the Senate at the end of July and, with nearly thirty Democrats rejecting Speaker Tip O'Neill's threats and cajolery, won easily in the House as well. In its final form, the Economic Recovery Tax Act (ERTA) nearly mirrored Kemp–Roth, reducing the personal income tax rate by 25 percent over three years while also decreasing the capital gains rate. Reagan was delighted with the result. His swashbuckling approach in breaking a strike by the Professional Air Traffic Controllers Organization (PATCO) a few weeks later served to confirm his new-found political invincibility.

Accompanying budget reductions on the scale that Stockman had recommended were clearly not going to materialize, however, portending possibly huge problems. The Federal Reserve Board's hard-line deflationary stance (under the leadership of Carter appointee Paul Volcker)—combined with the lack of anticipated investment in the economy by those whose taxes had been lowered—brought on a sharp and deep recession in late 1981. By December, unemployment was approaching 9 percent. If there was any good news to be had, it was that inflation was at last coming under control. As journalist Lou Cannon points out in *President Reagan: The Role of a Lifetime*, even though Reagan did not initiate the Fed's hard-line credit policy, he at least allowed Volcker the leeway to do so. That he approved was obvious when he later reappointed Volcker as chair of the Fed.

As the economy slumped, Reagan's political invincibility evaporated. His public approval ratings, which had exceeded 60 percent in the weeks following the assassination attempt, slid below 50 percent by late 1981—and continued to fall steadily over the next several months, eventually hitting a low of 37 percent in January 1983. No longer feeling constrained, the Democrats went on the offensive, hammering away at the administration on the issue of "fairness." Any economic revolution that the Republicans might have planned had been derailed. As Troy has written, the rest of the Reagan years "would be spent scrambling on the scrimmage line [that he] and his men had initially reached with breakneck speed." The parties fought more or less to a standoff in the 1982 mid-term elections. The GOP, campaigning on the insistent message, "Stay the course," retained control of the Senate by 54-46. In the House, however, Republicans lost twenty-six seats (most of those they had gained in 1980).

Though an electoral rout had been averted, all was not well with the Reagan revolution. "We can't live with outyear deficits," a worried president wrote in his diary in January 1983. "I don't care if we have to blow up the Capitol, we have to restore the economy." His concern was real—and visceral—but Reagan remained unwilling to take the drastic steps necessary to wrench the budget back into balance. The previous September, he had reluctantly signed a "corrective" tax increase that reversed some of what had been accomplished by the 1981 tax bill, closing a number of loopholes and instituting withholding on interest and dividends paid to individuals. When Stockman pressed him to take steps to address the ballooning structural deficit in the Social Security system by substantially increasing the penalty for those retiring early, however, Reagan blinked. Instead he backed a milder proposal that raised payroll taxes, gradually increased the retirement age for full benefits, and delayed costly annual COLA (cost of living adjustment) increases by six months. The bill, supported overwhelmingly in both houses, represented "a huge and enduring tax increase," as Richard Reeves notes in *President Reagan*. Deeply disappointed, Stockman wrote in his memoir, *The Inside Story of the Reagan Revolution*, that from this point forward he knew that Reagan possessed "no blueprint for radical governance."

The chances of bringing the budget into balance were further compromised by Reagan's unwavering commitment to build up American military strength. Over the first five years of his presidency, defense spending grew steadily as a share of GNP; by 1985, the Pentagon's budget was north of $250 billion—more than twice what it had been in 1980. The additional spending had an enormous budgetary impact. Despite all the promises about bringing the budget under control, annual deficits in the Reagan years ranged from $125 billion to more than $200 billion, and by 1989 the overall debt had ballooned to nearly $2.7 trillion.

By early 1983, the Federal Reserve's tight-money policies had succeeded in bringing inflation down to 2 percent and had reduced interest rates from over 20 percent to 11. At the same time, the government's deficit spending was pouring billions of dollars into the economy and—to the president's good fortune—declining oil prices provided a further economic boost. For the rest of the Reagan presidency—and, except for one brief recession, for another decade beyond—the national economy boomed. Unemployment fell to 5.4 percent, while the GNP increased at the healthy pace of about 4 percent per year. "Reagan's opponents had blamed him for the recession," writes William Pemberton in *Exit With Honor: The Life and Presidency of Ronald Reagan*, "and now had to watch helplessly as he claimed success for Reaganomics." In politics perception is reality: Reagan had ended the Carter recession.

As election year 1984 dawned, the Democrats faced a daunting task. Prosperity had returned, Reagan's approval ratings had climbed back above 50 percent, and his renomination was uncontested. In contrast, Carter's defeat had left the Democrats with no real leader, the New Deal coalition had dissolved, and there seemed no obvious path to building a majority. Former vice president Walter Mondale had the inside track for the party's presidential nomination, based on his support from the Democratic establishment. Not surprisingly, neither Kennedy nor Brown showed any interest in taking on the popular Reagan. With the Democratic nomination a prize of dubious distinction, Mondale had to contest only civil rights leader Jesse Jackson and Colorado senator Gary Hart, who had remade himself into a self-styled "New Democrat," intent on taking the party beyond interest group politics. Jackson quickly reduced his already slim prospects by making widely reported comments that were perceived as anti-semitic. He wound up winning primaries only in

D.C., Louisiana, and South Carolina. The contest was really a two-horse race. Hart prevailed throughout New England and virtually everywhere west of the Mississippi, as well as in Indiana, Michigan, and Wisconsin, but Mondale picked up endorsements from a number of unions, women's groups, and other organized bodies. By early June he had wrapped up the nomination. At the party's San Francisco convention, he generated brief excitement by selecting Representative Geraldine Ferraro of New York as his running-mate—the first woman ever to be on a major-party national ticket. By this selection, Mondale hoped to enlarge upon a gender gap that had appeared in presidential voting four years earlier. In his acceptance speech, the nominee signaled that his focus in the campaign would be on attacking Reagan's economic policies—especially the yawning deficits. "He'll raise taxes, so will I," Mondale intoned. "He won't tell you, I just did." After initially hailing the candidate for his candor, the media quickly came to the judgment that the pledge to raise taxes was a huge—probably fatal—mistake.

In fact it mattered little what Mondale promised at the Democratic convention or even during the campaign. His liberal campaign rhetoric and pessimistic message were entirely out of step with the electorate, a major part of which had decided that Reaganomics was working just fine. The president's vapid "Morning in America" theme—a reflection of the administration's lack of new ideas—resonated with a public that was relieved to see the "age of limitations" in the rear-view mirror. Moreover, the choice of Ferraro proved to be problematic, as allegations of criminal activities on her husband's part dogged the Democrats throughout the campaign. Reagan's steady lead over Mondale in the early polls into late summer widened to nearly 20 percentage points through the final two months of the campaign. In the first of two debates between the two candidates, Reagan seemed to give the Democrats an opening, appearing confused and clearly off his game on camera. Just two weeks later, however, he completely erased that negative impression by reeling off a series of smooth answers and trademark one-liners. Easily his best moment in this event, perhaps of the entire campaign, was his quip in response to a question about the possible impact of his age (73) on his ability to complete a second term. Affirming his good health and ability to meet all the rigors of the office, the president joked: "I want you to know that ... I will not make age an issue in this campaign. I am not going to exploit, for political purposes, my opponent's youth and inexperience." The burst of laughter that followed signaled to most observers the end of Mondale's quest.

On November 6, Ronald Reagan won re-election in a landslide. receiving 525 electoral votes to his opponent's 13. So-called "Reagan Democrats" were credited for the magnitude of his victory—in particular, white southerners and blue-collar workers in the Northeast and Midwest. Despite Ferraro's presence on the Democratic ticket, no gender gap was in evidence in 1984, as 55 percent of women voters cast their ballots for the president. Democrats lower down the ballot ran well ahead of their presidential nominee. Despite the presidential landslide, the Republicans actually lost a Senate seat, reducing their margin to 53-47, but picked up sixteen in the House, reducing the Democrats' margin to 253-182. The GOP saw some important moderates leave the political stage, including Howard Baker, who retired, and Charles Percy, the three-term senator from Illinois, who lost his bid for re-election. With their departure, the ideological chasm between the two parties in the Senate began to widen ominously.

Though the Democrats' criticisms of persistent deficits and the burgeoning federal debt had failed to win over the voters, the problems they identified were real. Within months of his second inauguration, Reagan found himself on the defensive against a Congress determined to bring the runaway budget under control. The effort signaled an institutional conflict as much as anything else, as GOP senators Phil Gramm (Texas) and Warren Rudman (New Hampshire) teamed up with Democrat Ernest "Fritz" Hollings (South Carolina) to craft a measure designed to reduce deficits by increasingly large amounts over a five-year period. In addition to requiring agreement between the White House and Congress on specific budget reduction targets going forward, the bill provided for automatic proportionate reductions in all programs in any year when the target was not met, with the comptroller general certifying the precise amounts of the reductions to be made. Social Security, Medicaid, veterans' pensions, and food stamps were exempted from this doomsday provision. Fearing its impact on the defense budget but bowing to the inevitable, the president signed the measure into law in December 1985. The impact of the successful congressional revolt was short-lived, however. Although the spirit of Gramm–Rudman–Hollings would dominate budget discussions on Capitol Hill for most of the next decade, the heart of the bill itself was struck down by the Supreme Court just seven months after its enactment. The provision for automatic program cuts, the court ruled, violated the separation of powers doctrine because the comptroller general, who was removable by Congress, could not exercise what was essentially an executive function.

Riding the growing wave of prosperity, Reagan paid less attention during the rest of his presidency to controlling the national debt than to putting money back into the hands of tax-payers—particularly the wealthiest ones. In 1986 he backed a second major tax reform, modeled after a flat-tax proposal that had been crafted by two Democrats, Senator Bill Bradley (New Jersey) and Representative Richard Gephardt (Missouri). Adopted with bipartisan support, the Tax Reform Act of 1986 reduced the existing tangle of tax brackets to just three, reduced the top rate from 50 percent to 33 percent, and raised the lowest from 11 to 15 percent. The tax code simplification was well received by the public, even though it was clearly most beneficial to the wealthy.

In urging reduction of the size of government, Reagan meant not only decreasing the number of federal programs but also lessening government regulation. In addition to shrinking the size of the Federal Register, the Reagan years produced significant deregulation of two major industries: automobiles and savings-and-loan banking. The loosening of environmental restrictions on domestic auto manufacturers succeeded in allowing them to compete more readily with Japanese imports. In contrast, the freeing-up of savings-and-loan operations enabled these types of banks to invest in potentially more profitable—but also much riskier—ventures. In the case of "S&Ls," the new freedom brought disaster not only to the industry itself, but to thousands of home-owners. In pressing for reduced government regulation, the Reaganites in a sense reflected the *zeitgeist* of the 1970s and 1980s. Carter, too, had advocated loosening regulation as a desirable efficiency; during his administration Congress had either reduced or eliminated federal regulation in a number of important indus-tries, including airlines, railroads, and trucking. In the Reagan years, however, as Sean Wilentz notes in *The Age of Reagan: A History, 1974–2008*, "the cause became an all-out business crusade that drew no distinctions between regulations restraining business competition and those designed to enforce laws protecting the public's health and safety."

The overall impact of Reaganomics on American society was profound. Much of the impact was not positive. While the national economy grew, the 1980s saw a widening gap between rich and poor and a near-obsession with ostentatious wealth. "For the first time in U.S. history," writes Kevin Phillips in *The Politics of Rich and Poor: Wealth and the American Electorate in the Reagan Aftermath*, "millionaires were economic nobodies as mega-wealth ballooned out of sight." Meanwhile, the other side of the picture was even more distressing, as uncounted thousands of homeless Americans, found mostly in the decaying centers of large cities but in evidence almost everywhere, reflected the downside of the economic policies of the 1980s. A distressing social selectivity seemed to be at work. As Phillips writes, "a dis-proportionate number of women, young people, blacks and Hispanics were among the decade's casualties… . Broken families and unwed teenage mothers promised further welfare genera-tions and expense." By the end of the decade, one in five American children lived in poverty, most likely in a household headed by a woman.

The economic policies of the 1980s also reinforced habits of private avarice at public expense, especially in high places. Although there have been other periods in American history when greed among public officials has been egregious—the 1880s and 1920s, for example—the Reagan years stand out as one of the worst. By the time he left the White House, more than one hundred administration officials at various levels had left office under a cloud of financial wrongdoing, including some at Cabinet level. Prominent congressional Democrats, too, were found to be on the take. The bipartisan nature of corruption helped to keep the administration from losing political ground over its numerous scandals. "Because a majority of Americans trusted Reagan more than they trusted Congress," observes Cannon, "the Democrats lacked political credibility in propounding the sleaze issue."

For all the problems that grew out of the economic policies of the Reagan years, there were also substantial achievements. Cannon, the closest journalistic observer of Reagan and his politics throughout the latter's career, concludes that his "economic policy was better than it looked when he left office." Economic historian Robert Collins agrees, observing in *Transforming America: Politics and Culture during the Reagan Years* that "the fundamental statistics of the economy's performance during the Reagan years were impressive." For good or ill, as Cannon contends, the president himself played the central role in achieving these overall economic outcomes, even if he generally relied on underlings to implement his ideals.

Reagan's policies slowed only slightly the decades-long growth of "social safety net" programs and government regulation. This was not surprising, since Reagan never wanted to destroy that safety net. Rather, he may have sought to do too much. As president, Cannon writes, Reagan "always wanted government to provide more services than he was willing to finance... . He was a guns-and-butter president, favoring both a military buildup and continuation of the welfare state created by the New Deal." Reagan himself emphasized that he never intended to abolish social welfare. "The press is dying to paint me as ... trying to undo the New Deal," he wrote in his diary in early 1982. "I remind them that I voted for F.D.R. 4 times. I'm trying to undo the 'Great Society.'" As Cannon observes, Reagan "never once came close to submitting a budget to Congress that provided the revenues to pay for the government programs he thought necessary."

Culture Wars and Party Politics

Ronald Reagan was not the kind of politician that the Religious Right would normally have supported. He had migrated from small-town Illinois to the ultimate sin city, Hollywood, before World War II and had spent a quarter-century there before being elected governor of California in 1966. Divorced before marrying starlet Nancy Davis in 1952 and estranged from two of his children, he could hardly be considered a paragon of family values. Moreover, in 1978 he had weighed in against California's controversial Briggs Initiative, which would have barred gays and lesbians from teaching in the public schools. Nonetheless, once it became clear that Reagan would be the 1980 GOP nominee, Christian conservatives enthusiastically flocked to his standard. Reagan repaid the Religious Right for its support by repeatedly asserting his opposition to abortion, his support for prayer in public schools, and his commitment to traditional family values— even while he remained personally aloof from the movement itself. Most important for conservative Christians, writes Daniel Williams in *God's Own Party: The Making of the Christian Right*, Reagan "endorsed the movement's attempt to bring religion into politics."

Although Reagan never lost sight of the need to cultivate social conservatives, he did not always deliver for them. An especially important issue for the Christian Right was protection of family values. "In the second half of the 1970s," writes Robert Self in *All in the Family: The Realignment of American Democracy Since the 1960s*, the Religious Right had "created a furor over the state of the American family without precedent in the twentieth century," raising "the specter of family breakdown as national ruination." Accordingly, pro-family conservatives introduced legislation immediately after Reagan's inauguration, labeled the Family Protection Act, that attempted to strengthen parental rights, end a number of federal education programs, and defund abortion counseling, as well as bar federal funding for organizations "advocating homosexuality as a lifestyle" and/or undermining "the role of women as it has historically been understood." The sweeping nature of the proposal opened it to ridicule by its opponents and made it vulnerable to criticism on many fronts. With neither Reagan nor his staff exerting any effort on its behalf, it failed to reach the floor of either house.

The "right-to-life" cause, however, received greater attention and support from the newly elected president. Reagan strongly opposed abortion on demand ("how anyone could deny that the fetus is a living human being is beyond me," he wrote in his diary after viewing a demonstration ultrasound that anti-abortion activists had brought to a White House meeting). He gave early and visible support to Senate conservatives in their efforts to address the issue. Senators Jesse Helms of North Carolina and Orrin Hatch of Utah, respectively, introduced the most promising proposals. Helms's measure, preferred by anti-abortion activists, defined human life as starting at conception and guaranteed Fourteenth Amendment protections to the human fetus, thereby making abortion a criminal offense. Hatch's approach was a con-stitutional amendment that would undo *Roe v. Wade*, turning abortion back to the states to control. Both proposals were stalled by a filibuster led by liberal GOP senator Robert Packwood (Oregon) until Reagan intervened by pressing majority leader Baker and other powerful Republicans to vote for cloture. He racked up points with the Religious Right by lobbying for adoption of Helms's bill, but the effort did not succeed. A cloture vote to bring Helms's measure to the floor then fell ten votes short, and it was finally tabled by a vote of 47-46. Social conservatives were deeply disappointed with the result, but Reagan may not have been surprised at the outcome. With polls showing that popular support for abortion on demand was on the increase during the early 1980s, he expended little effort during the rest of his presidency to secure adoption of an anti-abortion amendment.

On a third priority of the Christian Right—prayer in the public schools—Reagan's approach was again more show than substance. The larger issue of religion's place in American society had been important to conservative Christians since at least the early 1950s, when William F. Buckley had published *God and Man at Yale*. As Robert Self recounts, Buckley's charge was essentially that "[s]tateism and atheism ... had replaced virtue and individualism as core values in Yale's curriculum," and that American culture, generally, faced the same threat. A series of Supreme Court rulings, observes Self, had further heightened "Christian fears of an intrusive secular state." Especially repellent to conservatives were court decisions in the early 1960s that had banned both public prayer and the reading of the Bible in public schools and other public places. These fears and resentments, heightened by battles over abortion, ERA, and gay rights, fueled the new evangelical political fervor into which first Carter, and then Reagan, tapped. After Reagan was re-elected and foreign policy and national security issues took center stage, however, the issues dearest to the hearts of Christian conservatives moved to the periphery of the administration's agenda.

It could not have been predicted when Ronald Reagan took office that the gay rights revolution would emerge as a major political issue. It did so because of a frightening, usually fatal new disease, Acquired Immune Deficiency Syndrome (AIDS), which appeared for the first time in 1981. So strong was the public and media fixation on this scourge that the surgeon general, C. Everett Koop, labeled it as the defining issue in the cultural wars of the 1980s. "AIDS pitted the politics of the gay revolution of the seventies against the politics of the Reagan revolution," he wrote in his autobiography, *Koop: The Memoirs of America's Family Doctor.* For too long, Reagan remained aloof from the crisis, unwilling to confront the "gay plague" directly. Koop, who argued from the beginning for aggressive government education about sex practices that led to AIDS, was initially frozen out of administration policy decisions about how to deal with the epidemic. "If ever there was a public in need of education and straight talk about AIDS, it was the American people," he wrote. "But for an astonishing five and a half years I was completely cut off" from the issue. Not until fall 1985, after the death of Hollywood acquaintance Rock Hudson from the disease, did the president even utter the word "AIDS" in public.

Though Reagan resisted pressure from rabid conservatives that he denounce homosexuality, he maintained distance from the gay community. He never tried to discuss the health crisis with representatives from gay and lesbian organizations—which, of course, were well positioned to help fight the battle. Meanwhile, the Christian Right vilified gays as the cause of the new illness, rather than its victims, and called for draconian schemes up to and including quarantining the infected. "The poor homosexuals," railed conservative commentator Pat Buchanan, "they have declared war upon nature, and now nature is exacting its awful retribution."

Within the administration, Koop applied increasing pressure on Reagan to do something. In October 1986, the surgeon general issued a report predicting 180,000 deaths from AIDS over the next five years if nothing was done, and calling for abstinence, monogamy, and condoms as the antidotes to the epidemic. At his wife's urging, Reagan finally delivered a major address on AIDS at a May 1987 fundraiser to fight the disease. Instead of making the kind of frank speech that Koop had been urging, however, the president avoided mentioning the types of sexual practices by which the disease was transmitted, instead merely calling for testing and falling back on platitudes such as "AIDS affects all of us." Frustrated, the Democratic-controlled Congress took the initiative by setting aside $20 million for Koop to prepare an AIDS mailer to be sent to every American household; the educational piece was delivered to 107 million households in May 1988—the largest government mailing in history.

By the time Reagan left office, over 82,000 AIDS cases had been confirmed in the United States and more than half that number had died, mostly gay males; the Centers for Disease Control estimated that the number of infected probably numbered ten times those reported. Unraveling the mysteries of the Human Immunodeficiency Virus (HIV) that was found to be responsible for AIDS would have taken years in any case (the first effective drugs for treatment were not discovered for nearly another decade), but there can be no doubt that the lack of leadership from the White House delayed progress unnecessarily. "The absence of presidential leadership and the silence of the national political class," writes Robert Self, "permitted the consolidation of what can only be called a poisonous homophobia." It also likely contributed to thousands of deaths that could have been prevented.

Issues of race and civil rights were also divisive in the Reagan years, although they created political fault lines different from those arising over conflicts about family values, abortion, and gay rights. During the 1980 campaign, Reagan had mostly avoided race issues, instead employing coded language that appealed to disaffected whites, including attacks on "welfare queens" who he said took advantage of government aid programs that were supported by middle-class (i.e., white) tax dollars. After receiving less than 10 percent of the black vote in the election, Reagan felt free to follow his "small government" instincts where civil rights issues were concerned. Though he was not motivated by racism, his policies advanced the southern strategy at least as effectively as Nixon's had.

The backgrounds of Reagan's appointees to positions directly involved with race issues accurately reflected his policy inclinations. W. Bradford Reynolds, a corporate attorney who served as assistant attorney general for civil rights, brought to his post—in political scientist Robert Detlefsen's words in *Civil Rights Under Reagan*—"a principled agenda for reformulating civil rights policy" in a conservative direction. Clarence Pendleton and Clarence Thomas, appointed to head the Civil Rights Commission and Equal Employment Opportunity Commission (EEOC), respectively, were both outspoken black foes of affirmative action. Each of these key administration figures would play a significant role in reversing the role of the federal government as a defender and advocate of hiring preferences for underrepresented minorities.

Under Reynolds's guidance, the Justice Department filed a number of suits with the Supreme Court challenging affirmative action programs. Though none was successful, Reagan's success in installing a new conservative majority on the federal bench ultimately produced judicial decisions that severely damaged such programs. Also important in shifting the playing field back in the direction of supposedly "color-blind" approaches favored by white opponents of affirmative action were significant budget

111

cuts to the two agencies that had most strongly backed affirmative action programs, the EEOC and the Office of Federal Contract Compliance Programs (OFCCP) in the Department of Labor. By peeling off its two most liberal members, Reagan also managed to de-fang the Civil Rights Commission, which had been a persistent advocate for the civil rights lobby in the 1970s.

These assaults on affirmative action successfully branded the GOP as the defender of white voters who objected to federal policies they perceived as "pro-minority." Yet the administration's efforts did not uproot the vast array of affirmative action programs that had become institutionalized in the private sector since their inception two decades earlier. They were simply too entrenched. As John Diggins notes in *Ronald Reagan: Fate, Freedom, and the Making of History*, by the 1980s "American firms and schools of business [had] professionalized the field of employment relations with new offices of 'human resources,' which made racial hiring as legitimate as health care and pension benefits." Reagan was thus able to score political points with his voter base without fundamentally altering employment strategies with which even many conservative businessmen had made peace.

Busing also remained a point of contention among both blacks and whites in the Reagan years. The president did not take on the issue directly, but Reynolds led administration efforts to undo the results of court decisions of the late 1970s. In *Washington v. Seattle School District No. 1*, he challenged an appeals court decision that had overturned a voter-approved initiative barring busing to achieve racial balance in Washington state's public schools. But the accumulated weight of judicial precedent on the subject was by then too strong. When the Supreme Court upheld the lower court's decision in 1982, the game was over—even for the Reagan administration. As Detlefsen observes, this verdict clearly and finally demonstrated the High Court's "commitment to the integrationist ideal" and busing became, in effect, "irreversible public policy."

The action that most clearly reflected the Reagan administration's desire to turn back the clock on the civil rights revolution was its effort to block renewal of the Voting Rights Act in 1982.

The Justice Department took aim in particular at the provision in the 1965 act that required "pre-clearance" of any proposed changes in election procedures in all precincts (mostly southern) where racial discrimination had previously been legally sanctioned. It quickly became clear that efforts to block renewal of the law would prove futile, as civil rights forces rallied and pressed legislators to strengthen key provisions. Facing inevitable defeat, the administration quietly withdrew its opposition and went along with renewal of the act.

Historians differ in their assessments of Reagan's civil rights record, ranging from Manning Marable's charge that the president "was aggressively hostile to blacks" to Gil Troy's more nuanced interpretation that the "assault on the civil rights agenda was more rhetorical than real," and was hemmed in by "Reagan's inherent caution when governing." Though not a racist, Reagan clearly harbored old-fashioned ideas where race issues were concerned. He either could not understand or refused to understand why government intervention was necessary to protect the rights of non-whites, and why such intervention could not be entirely withdrawn. There were also political reasons for Reagan to take negative positions on civil rights issues while he was in the White House. As Sean Wilentz observes, "While earning the enmity of civil rights advocates and black voters, the administration signaled to the new southern Republicans and the 'Reagan Democrats' its militant opposition to civil rights laws that they felt threatened their social and economic status."

Reagan's race policies may have been less to blame for the worsening of black–white relations in the 1980s than broader social and economic forces. As Marable points out, the progress that had been made in desegregating American society by the 1980s, especially when coupled with the widening gap between rich and poor during the decade, did more damage to blacks than any of the administration's efforts to undo affirmative action, busing, or federal enforcement of anti-discrimination laws. Desegregation, with its benefits for the black professional and middle classes, Marable writes, "frequently meant the geographical as well as cultural separation of the black middle class from the working-class and low-income African-American population, which was still largely confined to the ghetto." Consequently, "[i]n large cities ... the environment turned increasingly ugly," as drug use and violence exploded. In turn, as "the specter of the black criminal was popularized in the media and the political arena, government leaders were pressured to adopt more severe measures to ensure law and order." An overt southern strategy was no longer necessary to attract disaffected whites to the party that could most effectively distance itself from these urban (read, racial) dysfunctions.

On another emerging issue related to racial and ethnic differences, the political calculus differed sharply from that on civil rights issues. Immigration—both legal and illegal—had become a rising public concern as a result of the heavy flow of Southeast Asian and Central American refugees into the country, Castro's dumping of the *Marielitos* onto United States shores, and the indeterminate numbers of undocumented immigrants steadily entering the nation, mostly from Mexico. Estimates of the numbers of illegal residents in the U.S. by the mid-1980s ranged wildly, with the consensus placing the total at around eleven or twelve million. Large numbers of voters in both parties, particularly in the Southwest, were critical of what they saw as lax federal enforcement of the nation's border controls and immigration laws. Unions and the nation's African American community were especially unhappy with the sharp competition for jobs these newcomers posed. On the other hand, business interests, particularly "agribusiness," were interested in growing this cheap labor supply. Hoping to find an acceptable compromise, Reagan appointed a bipartisan Commission on Immigration Reform, chaired by former Notre Dame president Father Theodore Hesburgh, to devise a solution.

The resulting legislation, the Immigration Reform and Control Act, passed with bipartisan support and was signed into law in November 1986. The legislation straddled the problem by providing for amnesty for undocumented immigrants who could prove that they had resided continuously in the country since 1982 (presumably about three million), while at the same time stiffening penalties for those who knowingly employed undocumented workers. To ensure legal hiring practices, employers were required to have all employees complete a new government form (the I-9) certifying that they could work legally in the United States. When Reagan signed the bill, he recorded in his diary: "It's high time we regained control of our borders & this bill will do that." Even those who supported the measure, however, knew it fell far short of solving the problem. Not only was it unclear how future illegal entry into the nation could be stemmed, but the law said nothing about what to do with the some nine million undocumented individuals who did not qualify for amnesty. The "immigration question" would continue to fester, for future presidents and legislators to handle (or not).

Reagan tried during his second term to maintain control over the direction of policy related to social and economic issues, but an increasingly assertive Congress made that difficult. As he increasingly came to be regarded as a lame duck, Democrats vociferously attacked administration economic policies, calling attention to mounting deficits, the widening income gap in the country, and a worsening negative trade balance. Perhaps most problematic for sustaining the Reagan revolution was that, aside from the tax revision plan, the White House cupboard was bare of ideas in his second term. The 1986 mid-term elections only made matters worse for the administration. Benefiting from the voter weariness that inevitably sets in with a second-term president, the Democrats padded their majority in the House by five seats and took control of the Senate by 55 to 45, with a net gain of eight. Ominously for the Republicans, six freshman GOP senators who had been elected with Reagan in 1980 were turned out of office.

If the conservative revolution ran aground on Capitol Hill during the second half of the 1980s, however, it was alive and well in the judiciary. During his eight years in the White House, Reagan had the good fortune to be able to appoint a new chief justice to the Supreme Court and replace two retiring justices. His first selection for the court in 1981, Sandra Day O'Connor—the first woman ever to serve as a Supreme Court justice—was a disappointment to anti-abortion activists, but was otherwise a solid conservative. Five years later, Reagan's nomination of sitting justice William Rehnquist to succeed the retiring Warren Burger as chief justice drew substantial opposition. As Cannon notes, the thirty-three votes against Rehnquist (all Democrats) represented the highest vote against any successful court nominee in the twentieth century. To fill Rehnquist's slot, Reagan chose another strongly conservative jurist, Antonin Scalia. Aside from his ideological credentials, Scalia had the additional virtue—from the perspective of social conservatives—of being only 50 years old and likely to serve for decades.

Reagan's next court nominee—to fill the seat of retiring moderate justice Lewis Powell in July 1987—proved to be the most controversial of all. Robert Bork, who had done Nixon's dirty work by firing Special Prosecutor Archibald Cox in the "Saturday Night Massacre," was a provocatively conservative jurist from the time Reagan had named him to the U.S. Court of Appeals for the District of Columbia in 1982. His nomination for the High Court awakened fierce opposition from the two most influential Democrats on the Senate Judiciary Committee, Ted Kennedy and Joseph Biden (Delaware). While Nixon's two southern nominees, Haynsworth and Carswell, had run into similar buzz-saws nearly two decades earlier, "[t]he battle over Bork was different," as Cannon notes, "because it challenged his opinions, not his legal qualifications or personal integrity." Such polarization over a Supreme Court nomination had not erupted since Herbert Hoover's day. Bork's pugnacious demeanor in his confirmation hearings made the opposition's job easy. In October, he was rejected by a vote of 42 in favor, 58 opposed; six moderate Republicans joined virtually all of the chamber's Democrats in the negative column. After Reagan's next nominee for the seat had to withdraw because of youthful indiscretions with marijuana, he finally settled on Judge Anthony Kennedy from California, a conservative of more moderate stripe than either Scalia or Bork. Kennedy was unanimously confirmed, and a new *de facto* conservative majority was in place. The fight over Bork had a lasting impact on the process of confirming Supreme Court nominations.

Though Kennedy had made it through easily, as Lou and Carl Cannon write in *Reagan's Disciple: George W. Bush's Troubled Quest for a Presidential Legacy*, "[a]fter Bork, both sides were spoiling for a fight," and future presidents of both parties would find it far more difficult to get bipartisan support for their High Court nominees.

Most historians see Reagan, in Troy's words, "as more of a compromiser than a revolutionary on social issues." Despite the limits on his personal commitment to positions on the far right, however, the years of his presidency witnessed an escalation in polarization between the two major parties, as well as within the broader public, on cultural issues. Surprisingly, while Reagan remained popular until the end of his presidency, polls showed that a growing plurality of Americans opposed his stated views on such issues as abortion rights and affirmative action. For all of the later lionization of Reagan as the architect of a conservative revolution in the 1980s, the evidence points to the contrary.

Reagan's World

In matters of foreign policy, Reagan's best and worst qualities were fully on display. He was steadfast in his commitment to ending the nuclear arms race and ridding the world of the threat of nuclear annihilation. He also brought with him to the White House clearly formed ideas about how to deal with the Soviet Union. In challenging Ford for the 1976 GOP nomination, he had strongly criticized détente. In Reagan's view, as James Mann explains in *The Rebellion of Ronald Reagan: A History of the End of the Cold War*, the Soviets were not simply a rival superpower with whom the United States should seek peaceful coexistence, but a "repressive and repugnant" state whose end was inevitable. Since the Cold War was essentially a competition between two economic systems, "it was conceivable that one side might fail." That there were discernible signs of economic decay in the Soviet Union confirmed in his mind that such failure could occur soon.

By the 1980s, however, the United States faced a complicated array of world issues unrelated to the bipolar Cold War competition. Directing American foreign policy, therefore, required nimbleness and breadth of focus. Reagan lacked both the necessary knowledge about other parts of the world and the level of interest needed for such leadership. Nor was he inclined to explore options when crises arose, instead often displaying the same certitude that characterized his approach to Cold War issues. "Reagan's intuitive decisions were almost always reactive," notes Cannon, adding that he "rarely solicited policy options during his eight years in office. In fact, he so rarely made inquiries of his staff about anything that the exceptions were always notable." Although Reagan characteristically took an active role in National Security Council and National Security Planning Group (NSPG) meetings and prided himself on being the one who made key decisions, the outcomes of those discussions did not always reflect careful deliberation.

Reagan's lack of interest in detail was a major problem, since he often left it to others to implement whatever decisions were reached and rarely requested much follow-up. He possessed other personality quirks, too, that contributed to disorder in the White House inner sanctum. As diplomatic historian Melvyn Leffler writes in *For the Soul of Mankind: The United States, the Soviet Union, and the Cold War,* "The president's style of decision making, his aloofness, his aversion to conflict, his disdain for facts and detail, and his penchant for ideological verbiage contributed greatly to [that] disorder." Such dysfunction was intensified by the fact that members of the senior staff frequently disagreed with one another about basic objectives. Throughout Reagan's presidency, his national security team was split between hardline ideologues such as CIA director William Casey, Secretary of Defense Casper Weinberger, and U.N. ambassador Jeane Kirkpatrick on the one hand, and more pragmatic "accommodationists" like Vice President Bush, Secretary of State George Schulz, and top presidential aides Michael Deaver and James Baker on the other. Moreover, unprecedented turnover in the key position of national security advisor also produced major discontinuities; in Reagan's eight years in the White House, six different men held this key position.

Reagan was definitely most comfortable when dealing with the familiar issues of the Cold War. As a proponent of containment, he resolved from the outset to exert steady pressure on the Soviets, but to do it indirectly by providing aid and equipment to regional "surrogates" whenever possible. This approach was later labeled the "Reagan Doctrine." Exhibit A was Central America, where Reagan sought to reverse what he regarded to be Carter's wrongheaded decision to support left-leaning governments that had displaced U.S.-friendly dictatorships. Believing it essential to halt this "red tide," Reagan embraced a strategy of backing indigenous insurgents ("contras") against the Sandinistas in Nicaragua, signing a National Security Defense Directive (NSDD 17) in 1982 that provided funding to set up a 500-man force to destabilize that government. When the administration took a more direct approach in the case of Guatemala, selling military equipment to the repressive right-wing government, Congress reacted emphatically. In December 1982, by a vote of 411-0, the House adopted the Boland Amendment, banning military assistance to the contras. Covert U.S. aid continued to flow to the contras, however, despite the fact that in late 1984 the House passed another, broader ban (Boland II) that also outlawed nonmilitary support for the anti-communist fighters.

In another theater in the western hemisphere, Reagan acted more overtly, but with no greater regard for congressional prerogative. In late October 1983, a pro-communist coup toppled an only slightly less left-leaning government on the tiny Caribbean island of Grenada. Citing potential danger to some 800 American medical students on the island, and without bothering to negotiate or consult with Congress, the administration launched an amphibious and air attack. Reagan's cavalier disregard of Congress in the case of Grenada was the more egregious given its timing.

Less than two weeks before the invasion the president had signed into law a joint resolution authorizing the presence of U.S. troops in strife-torn Lebanon for up to eighteen months but requiring consultation by the White House for any extension beyond that time. By the time Congress had passed the resolution, U.S. troops had been involved in that nation for over a year. The background was complicated and multi-layered. In June 1982, Israel had intervened militarily in Lebanon, laying siege to Beirut with the objective of trapping, then expelling, forces loyal to the Palestinian Liberation Organization (PLO). As Israeli attacks on the city's Muslim neighborhoods became more deadly by mid-August, Reagan intervened, warning Israeli prime minister Begin that if the attacks persisted, the entire U.S.–Israeli relationship could be called into question. Relenting, Begin reached an agreement with PLO leader Yasser Arafat that the remaining Palestinian forces could depart peaceably from Beirut. Reagan dispatched a contingent of 1400 Marines to help oversee the removal, withdrawing them in early September when the last of the PLO fighters left. Continued strife, however, led to the return of 1200 U.S. troops as part of a multinational peacekeeping force. As the U.S. military presence turned into a months-long occupation, deadly conflict occurred. In April 1983, a suicide bombing of the American embassy in Beirut took sixty-three American and Lebanese lives. The Marine contingent then hunkered down in Beirut Airport—an inviting target for further terrorist attacks as the military conflict widened. Though some in the administration worried about "mission creep," on September 10 President Reagan signed a directive committing "to restore the sovereignty of the Government of Lebanon throughout its territory." As the Marines were increasingly drawn into ground skirmishes, Congress passed a joint resolution authorizing the continued military presence in Lebanon. The decisive roll calls in both houses were strongly partisan: 54-46 in the Senate, with only two Democrats in support, and 253-156 in the House, with Republicans overwhelmingly in favor and Democrats almost evenly divided.

On the morning of October 23, hours after Reagan had made the decision to invade Grenada, he learned that a second deadly strike on Americans had occurred in Lebanon—a suicide bombing of the U.S. barracks at Beirut Airport. Initial reports were that over 100 Marines had been killed; the final figure was 240. In the face of this catastrophic loss of American lives, the success of the

Grenada operation launched the next day was critical. Direct engagement on the island resulted in nineteen U.S. deaths and over 100 wounded, with about three times that number of casualties on the other side, but the coup was aborted. Wrapped in red, white, and blue by the administration, the quick triumph produced a 15 percent surge in Reagan's public approval. Though Congress had been bypassed, there was little it could do to object.

Victory in a lopsided battle on a tiny Caribbean island could hardly serve as an antidote for the tragedy in Lebanon. Moreover, the suicide bombing at Beirut airport underscored the irresolution of the policy underlying the Marines' presence there. Congressional reaction was muted, although one Democratic senator remarked bitterly, "One day we've got the numbers of Marine deaths which shocked us all, the next day we find we're invading Grenada. Are we looking for a war we can win?" As Reagan struggled over how to respond to the carnage in Lebanon, his advisors argued among themselves. With CIA intelligence reports suggesting Iranian involvement, both CIA director Casey and George Shultz pressed for military retaliation. Reagan resisted their entreaties on the basis that there was no clear evidence indicating who was responsible. Media coverage of the Lebanon catastrophe was largely critical of the administration's policy—or lack of same—in sending the troops there in the first place. An early February Gallup poll recorded that 58 percent favored withdrawal of U.S. troops and only 28 percent approved the way Reagan was handling the crisis. On February 10, the president pulled the remaining Marines out of Lebanon. The whole sad business reflected the administration's lack of a thought-out policy in deploying the Marines in the first place.

The Grenada and Lebanon involvements were just sideshows for the administration; the real focus, from the start, was on U.S.–Soviet relations. Reagan's basic strategy for winning the Cold War was to exert pressure on the Soviets in every way possible. He took every opportunity to speak out against the Kremlin and its repressive ways, especially when his verbal attacks might encourage dissidents in regions under Soviet domination. Such an occasion presented itself in December 1981, when a strike by the Polish labor union Solidarity widened into a challenge to the country's communist regime. When the Polish government imposed martial law to try to break the will of the strikers, Reagan penned a personal letter to Soviet leader Leonid Brezhnev in which he warned darkly that "[t]he United States cannot accept suppression of the Polish peoples... . [We] will have no choice but to take concrete measures affecting the full range of our relationship." As the government crackdown continued in Poland, Reagan imposed only mild economic sanctions, but in February he directed the CIA to provide aid and intelligence to Solidarity; this assistance would continue throughout the decade.

Reagan's overarching objective was to achieve the elimination of nuclear weapons altogether. This commitment was rooted in deep personal conviction, reinforced by his sitting through five days of war games in March 1982 that "produced" a direct Soviet attack on Washington, D.C., and the death of the U.S. president. Reagan spoke frequently, both privately and publicly, about the unwinnable nature of nuclear war, since millions would die on both sides and there would be no habitable land left. The fact that a highly vocal nuclear freeze movement had emerged in the United States in the early 1980s encouraged him to press forward with the idea. That movement took on renewed momentum in November 1983, after the airing by ABC of *The Day After*, a terrifying post-nuclear television movie set in Lawrence, Kansas. Reagan watched the show, along with an estimated 100 million other viewers. "It's very effective & left me greatly depressed," he wrote in his diary after viewing the show. "Whether it will be of help to the 'anti-nukes' or not, I can't say. My own reaction was one of our having to do all that we can to have a deterrent & to see there is never a nuclear war."

As part of his strategy to end the possibility of a nuclear cataclysm, Reagan had earlier called for development of a nuclear defense shield: the Strategic Defense Initiative, or SDI. "What if we tell the world we want to protect our people, not avenge them," he speculated in his diary—"that we're going to embark on a program of research to come up with a defensive weapon that could make nuclear weapons obsolete?" The idea, dubbed

"Star Wars" by the media, failed to gain traction, despite Reagan's persistent efforts to sell it to Congress and the American public. Scientific consensus held that a dependable anti-missile defense shield was not yet—if ever—achievable, and critics suggested that the far-fetched concept was a product of Reagan's tendency to confuse fact with fiction. Some even suggested that it came out of his exposure to science fiction fantasies during his early movie career.

The SDI concept obviously worried the Soviet leadership, however, and was probably as important a factor in bringing them to the negotiating table as was the general U.S. defense buildup. Yuri Andropov, who had succeeded Brezhnev as Soviet General Secretary upon the latter's death in November 1982, warned gravely that such a deterrent would start the world down "an extremely dangerous path." His successors, first Konstantin Chernenko and later Mikhail Gorbachev, would take the same view, voicing the suspicion that the United States' real motivation was to be in a position to launch a first strike without fear of retaliation. None of Reagan's writings or speeches suggest that this was the case. Rather, on several occasions he proposed that whichever side developed such a deterrent shield should share it immediately with the other. The legacy of mistrust was too long and too deep, however, for the Soviets to consider this a serious suggestion.

Reagan's aggressive approach during his first three years in the White House produced "one of the chilliest periods in U.S.–Soviet relations since the onset of the Cold War," in Lou Cannon's words. Tensions between the two superpowers approached perilously near flashpoint on at least two occasions in late 1983. On September 1, Soviet warplanes shot down a Korean Airlines passenger jet (KAL 007) over the Soviet Union. All 269 passengers and crew were killed—among them sixty-one Americans, including Georgia congressman Lawrence McDonald. The Kremlin asserted that the plane had knowingly violated Soviet airspace and had continued on its path even after receiving official warning, and claimed, more improbably, that the Soviet fighter pilot believed the 747 jet to be an American spy-plane. Reagan condemned the attack in the harshest terms, calling it "an act of barbarism, born of a society which wantonly disregards individual rights and the value of human life," but he did not take the drastic actions that many feared and anticipated. Yet another near-miss occurred later the same month, when Soviet intelligence misinterpreted a joint U.S.–NATO war simulation to be the beginning of a first strike against the USSR. Only after placing their own nuclear fighters on combat alert did the Soviets realize their mistake and call off the alert.

Reagan took a markedly less belligerent tone beginning in early 1984, increasingly emphasizing the need for a negotiated end to the nuclear arms race. His tactical shift may have reflected a realization of how close the two sides had come to war, or his sense that the U.S. defense buildup had reached the critical mass needed to convince the Soviets they could not win it or, more likely, both. Too, significant leadership changes had occurred in the Kremlin, as 54-year-old Mikhail Gorbachev came to power after a succession of older, more rigid leaders. As Mann explains, "Gorbachev represented a new generation of Soviet leaders. They were known as *shestidesyatnaki*, Russian for 'men of the sixties.' They had come of age in ... the brief period of Nikita Khrushchev's challenge to orthodox Stalinism." Gorbachev quickly confirmed expectations that he represented something new, announcing the need for monumental changes in Soviet political and economic life: *glasnost* ("transparency") and *perestroika* ("restructuring" to allow workers more participation in management and greater autonomy for economic enterprise, generally).

This unlikely relationship between the septuagenarian U.S. president and the young Soviet leader was to change history. Convinced that Gorbachev was worth courting, Reagan extended a personal invitation for him to visit Washington at his earliest convenience. Their first meeting occurred on neutral ground in Geneva, Switzerland, in November, where Gorbachev made clear that he could not agree to arms reductions so long as Reagan pursued SDI. Importantly, the two leaders agreed to hold two more summits and to remain in communication about the range of nuclear issues on the table. Conservative Republicans distrusted

Gorbachev and worried about the president's eager embrace of the unknown new leader, but the American public felt differently. A CBS News poll after Reagan's return from Geneva in November showed that 83 percent of those questioned approved of the summit, with nearly half believing Gorbachev to be "a new kind of Soviet leader." Communications between the two heads of state were frequent and cordial in the months after their first meeting. Gorbachev proposed that the next summit be one-on-one, and occur in either London or Iceland. Reagan

Figure 4.2 Reagan forged a strong personal relationship with reform-minded Soviet leader Mikhail Gorbachev that produced historic arms reduction agreements at a succession of summit meetings. The two leaders are shown here at the breakthrough Reykjavik, Iceland, summit in October 1986. © Martin Athenstaedt/dpa/CORBIS

readily agreed and the meeting was scheduled for October 11 and 12, 1986, in Reykjavik.

The Reykjavik summit was amazing—as much for what it nearly accomplished as for how quickly hopes for a breathtaking settlement were dashed. In their opening meeting, Gorbachev proposed that the two sides reduce strategic arms by 50 percent and completely eliminate all medium-range missiles. Not to be outdone, Reagan countered with a proposal to demolish *all* nuclear weapons over a prescribed period of time. The two sides reached tentative agreement on mutual withdrawal of all missiles from Europe (the "zero-zero option" that Reagan had been seeking). Gorbachev expressed willingness to sign off on the whole package—but only if the United States ceased to pursue SDI. At that point, Reagan angrily broke off the talks and the two parted icily (fittingly enough, given the setting). Still, Reykjavik was a highly significant event. "At the time," writes James Mann, the summit "was widely perceived as a failure. In retrospect, it was a turning point in the Cold War standoff over nuclear weapons.... Each side had seen how far the other would be willing to go." In the United States, a familiar dynamic appeared: hard-line Cold Warriors condemned the Soviets' intransigence while the public at large approved what had happened at Reykjavik. White House pollster Richard Wirthlin told the president that his approval rating had leapt to a record high 73 percent.

Nothing is secure in politics, however. Almost immediately, the president's fortunes entered free-fall. His problems, which came to the fore just weeks after the Reykjavik summit, had nothing to do with Gorbachev, SDI, or the nuclear arms race. Rather, it involved a messy business of questionable constitutionality that was the product of the administration's muddled policy in the Middle East and its clandestine program of assistance to anti-leftist forces in Central America. The so-called Iran-Contra affair began with revelation by a Lebanese newspaper on November 3 that Reagan's former national security advisor, Bud McFarlane, had visited Iran to arrange for the United States to provide missiles and other military hardware in exchange for Iranian help in securing the release of five American hostages being held by the Islamist militant group (and now political party) Hezbollah in Lebanon. Reagan settled on a variation of the "stonewalling" technique made famous by an earlier Republican president, issuing a simple, technically true but misleading statement: "Our policy of not meeting concessions to terrorists remains intact." In a televised speech to the nation, he assured millions of viewers that "We did not—repeat did not—trade weapons or anything else for hostages, nor will we." For once, his magic failed. An ABC News poll the morning after the speech revealed that fewer than one-fourth of the public believed the official explanation that the arms were being shipped to Iran simply "to improve relations" with that nation. Pressed further on the subject in a press conference a week later, Reagan made a number of misstatements about the numbers and types of arms that were involved, and falsely (or erroneously) denied that Israel had been involved in the transaction.

The arms-for-hostages story was damaging enough in its own right, but there was more. When, at Reagan's request, Attorney General Ed Meese conducted an internal investigation of the issues, he discovered that Israel had been selling the arms to Iran at a price billions of dollars greater than the price the Israelis had paid to the United States, and that the overage had been deposited in numbered Swiss bank accounts from which Contra leaders were drawing funds to support their efforts against leftists in Nicaragua and El Salvador. The illegal operation was being overseen by National Security Advisor John Poindexter's aide, Colonel Oliver North. On November 23, the attorney general notified Reagan of this highly problematic state of affairs. North got to work immediately, enlisting his secretary and others in the shredding of documents that would uncover the trail of secret deals and actions.

The familiar question of "What did the president know and when did he know it?" now arose, and continued to dog Reagan until the end of his presidency. At certain points in his diary entries, Reagan registered genuine surprise at revelations that unfolded in the course of discussions with his advisors and ensuing formal investigations of Iran-Contra. On the other hand, an earlier entry on December 5, 1985, is disturbing. Describing a briefing on the Lebanon hostage issue in the NSC earlier that day, he wrote: "Subject was our undercover effort to free our 5 hostages held by terrorists in Lebanon. It is a complex undertaking with only a few of us in on it. I won't even write in the diary what we're up to." In the end, however, Reagan's apparent confusion and contradictory statements seemed believable enough, in the eyes of many, that he was able to work his way through it with only non-mortal political wounds. Poindexter, North, and—eventually—Chief of Staff Donald Regan were not so fortunate. The former two were gone from the administration within two days of Meese's revelations to Reagan in November, and Regan was forced out the following February.

It was not entirely inappropriate that Regan became one of the sacrificial lambs of the Iran-Contra episode. Although he certainly was not the architect of the policy decisions involved, his ineptitude as chief of staff, argumentative personality, and lack of connection with Congress—not to mention with Nancy Reagan, now more fiercely protective of her husband than ever—clearly contributed to the White House's clumsy handling of the fall-out from the scandal. Had the president not agreed to a bizarre job-swap suggested by then-treasury secretary Regan and then-chief of staff James Baker in January 1985, the smooth and cautious Baker would still have been in a position to exercise wise influence as the plot unfolded.

The general plot of the Watergate cover-up and exposé was replicated as the Iran-Contra drama, frequently referred to in the press as "Irangate," played itself out. A day after Poindexter's briefing to the full National Security Policy Group, Reagan appointed a three-person review commission, headed by former GOP senator John Tower, and called for appointment of a special counsel, as well. Within days, both houses of Congress announced plans to set up select investigating committees. By early December, the president's approval rating had slipped from the lofty levels achieved after Reykjavik to about 40 percent. The 1986 congressional elections had occurred the day after the initial story appeared on McFarlane's trip to Iran, but the strong Democratic showing at the polls was related more to the voter fatigue that marks the final mid-term election of a two-term president than to Iran-Contra. In any case, with Democrats now firmly in control of both houses, the outlook for the administration in the upcoming hearings appeared problematic.

That the Iran-Contra mess ended differently from Watergate was largely due to Reagan's reservoir of good will and popularity, but a more important factor may have been the broadening suspicion that he was no longer able to function at 100 percent mental capacity and thus might have forgotten facts that he once knew about the whole seamy operation. Though not an attractive tradeoff, seeming to fall asleep at the wheel was far less damaging to Reagan than possible culpability for unconstitutional operations and lying under oath. It was also helpful to him that the Tower Commission, before which he reversed his testimony, reported its conclusions in late February 1987, before congressional hearings could get traction. The commission concluded that the president "should have insured that the N.S.C. system did not fail him," but that the whole operation was probably the creation of CIA director William Casey, rather than the White House. Because Casey had suffered a massive stroke the previous December that left him comatose until his death the following May, this contention would never be proved or disproved—and there was, in fact, logic to support such a conclusion. Reagan was largely exonerated in the commission's report, though the portrayal of his lax oversight was not flattering. In a final address to the American people on the subject a week after the report's release, the president was far from contrite. Though he accepted "full responsibility" for the episode, he acknowledged no wrongdoing where his testimony was concerned. "A few months ago," he said, "I told the American people I did not trade arms for hostages. My heart and my best intentions still tell me that's true, but the facts and the evidence tell me it is not."

The congressional hearings had little effect on the Reagan presidency. The questioning of some 500 witnesses over forty days dominated the headlines but, with the president seemingly exonerated, the hearings failed to draw millions to the television screen, as in Watergate days. Moreover, the square-jawed, tele-genic North, testifying in full uniform replete with battle ribbons, emerged as a media hero (an image he would later parlay into an unsuccessful run for the Senate from Virginia). "North dominated the committees," writes Malcolm Byrne in *Iran-Contra: Reagan's Scandal and the Unchecked Abuse of Presidential Power*. His testimony marked "the turning point." In the end, both committees divided along party lines. The Democratic majority reports cast blame directly on the president and charged that the diversion of aid to the Contras was a clear violation of the Boland Amendment. The fact that the Republican minority dissented in each case made the outcome appear to be just another partisan exercise.

Figure 4.3   Oliver North, one of the major perpetrators of the secret arms-for-hostages deal known as the Iran-Contra scandal, testifying before the special congressional committee investigating the matter. © Bettmann/CORBIS

Neither the media nor the public had much stomach for pressing the case further, even though many claimed that the administration's infractions may actually have been more serious than those comprised by Watergate. It was the special investigator, Lawrence Walsh, laboring quietly for a number of years, who produced the only convictions of the main perpetrators—though successful appeals and pardons by Reagan's Republican successor would neutralize most of those convictions. Iran-Contra had a lasting impact, however. As Will Bunch writes in *Tear Down this Myth: How the Reagan Legacy Has Distorted Our Politics and Haunts Our Future* "[t]he scandal, not only weakened Reagan's presidency when it happened, but it arguably undermined the respect of future presidents for the Constitution because he essentially got away with it."

Reagan still had the actor's gift of timing—and in the most important way possible. The popping of the Iran-Contra balloon in early 1987 allowed him to move front-and-center again with Mikhail Gorbachev to finish what the two had begun at Reykjavik. For reasons of his own, Gorbachev told Reagan in February 1987 that he would no longer insist that the United States abandon the SDI concept as a precondition for a nuclear arms settlement. Reagan immediately dispatched Shultz to Moscow to finalize negotiations on the Intermediate-Range Nuclear Forces (INF) Treaty that had been discussed at the Iceland summit.

Even while working to conclude the INF Treaty, Reagan was not about to reduce pressures on the Soviets when there was a chance to support uprisings of those under communist rule. A perfect such opportunity presented itself in June 1987, when he had the opportunity to speak to hundreds of thousands in West Berlin. With the Brandenburg Gate as his backdrop, Reagan knew that his words could be heard by the citizens of East Berlin just across the Wall. He was speaking to Berliners on both sides, to his critics at home, and directly to Gorbachev when he uttered his famous public challenge to the Soviet leader: "General Secretary Gorbachev," he said, hitting a number of key themes at once, "if you seek peace, if you seek prosperity for the Soviet Union and Eastern Europe, if you seek liberalization: Come here to this gate! ... Mr. Gorbachev, tear down this wall!"

For all its bravado, the Berlin speech did not interrupt momentum toward finalization of the INF Treaty and the promised third summit between Reagan and Gorbachev. That meeting was set for early December in Washington. The American political landscape was a consideration, as 1988 presidential politics were already heating up. While every prospective Democratic candidate supported the proposed INF Treaty, all but two of the Republicans who wanted to succeed Reagan were openly opposed. Only Vice President Bush was supportive; Senator Robert Dole (Kansas) had not yet taken a position. Just prior to Gorbachev's scheduled arrival, the president went on a public relations offensive, touting the treaty strongly in a nationally televised interview. The Soviet leader arrived on December 7 to great fanfare, as "Gorby fever" captured Washington. At 1:45 p.m. the next day, the two leaders sat down to affix their signatures to the treaty, which implemented "zero-zero" by eliminating all short- and intermediate-range missiles from Europe.

The task of securing ratification—in an election year, no less— lay ahead. It was important that this happen as quickly as possible, since Reagan and Gorbachev had agreed to meet again in Moscow in May to exchange ratification documents. Once presidential jockeying in both parties began in earnest, the task would become even more difficult. The far right was bitterly scornful of the treaty. Howard Phillips, chair of the Conservative Caucus, branded Reagan "a useful idiot for Soviet propaganda," and a group of right-wing leaders announced formation of an Anti-Appeasement Alliance to fight the treaty. In the Senate, Jesse Helms and Dan Quayle (Indiana) were the most persistently troublesome, posing objection upon objection. With Shultz doing much of the work, the administration peeled off just enough Republican votes to secure ratification. On May 27, after several conservative amendments had been defeated, the Senate ratified the treaty by a final vote of 93 to 5. Five days later, In Moscow, the two leaders issued a joint statement affirming the final agreement. The Moscow Summit, as Wilentz writes, "was the capstone of Reagan's presidency.... Not incidentally, it dissipated the ignominy left over from Iran-Contra, and it began a rise in public approval that peaked during his last days in office." Reagan had secured his legacy.

Some scholars and analysts have contended that Reagan was primarily responsible for ending the Cold War, arguing that his get-tough policy, insistence on Soviet accountability, and commitment to a rapid defense buildup based on expensive modern technologies finally brought the Soviet leadership to the realization that the Cold War was an unwinnable contest. It is important to note, however, that what Mann calls Reagan's "zigzag approach to Soviet policy" did not seem to be getting the United States very far until Gorbachev assumed power in the Soviet Union. Probably, as Gorbachev contended years later, Soviet domestic politics played a greater role in determining his actions than did Reagan's threats. Some also hold that it was more specifically Reagan's dogged commitment to develop SDI that drove the Soviets to abandon an arms race they could no longer afford; by 1987, however, the fallout from Iran-Contra had so undermined Reagan's control of the congressional agenda that funding the nuclear defense shield was no longer a possibility. If Gorbachev had not been motivated by Soviet political and economic considerations, he could have decided to wait Reagan out.

Reagan deserves credit, however, for his willingness and ability to negotiate successfully with the wily Soviet leader. He "struck just the right balance with Gorbachev," writes Gil Troy, "resolute enough not to be underestimated, and flexible enough to encourage Gorbachev's revolution." Leffler paints a more nuanced picture, writing that Reagan "was often short on facts and devoid of knowledge… . But he was no pushover. He was calculating, competitive, tough-minded, and disciplined. He instinctively grasped the rhythm of negotiations." Gorbachev represented a unique opportunity to negotiate a new relationship, and Reagan had the ability to act on that opportunity.

As president, Ronald Reagan stood astride the 1980s to a degree not seen in American politics since Dwight Eisenhower's persona had defined the 1950s. Yet much of his seeming political dominance was illusory. Remarkably effective when addressing the broader public, he never mastered the political environment within the Beltway. Rather, the administration's few but significant policy victories in the first year or so of his presidency created a mystique of control. In that first year, Reagan's major proposals related to taxes, defense, and expenditure reductions won nearly unanimous support from congressional Republicans, as well as the backing of sizable numbers of "boll weevil" Democrats. Thereafter, however, his success rate on Capitol Hill tailed off to mediocre, at best. Contrary to popular mythology, his congressional support scores were lower than those of Nixon, Ford, or Carter. Reagan's optimism and deft public relations skills, however, made him seem a winner even when he was not. Even while Congress was overriding veto after veto in the last two years of his presidency, in the eyes of a substantial part of the public he retained the image of a president in control.

Five years after leaving the White House, Reagan wrote a poignant public letter acknowledging that he had been diagnosed with Alzheimer's disease. The news was greeted with sadness and sympathy across the nation; also, however, it provided an explanation for erratic behaviors during his final few years in office that had led some at the time to wonder whether Reagan was fully attentive to complicated matters of state. Reagan's biographers tend to agree that he was characteristically "remote and disengaged," in the words of Lou Cannon. He tended to drift at times from the main points of conversation, sometimes interjecting anecdotes that, though perhaps humorous, were unrelated to the subject under discussion. In the final two years of his presidency, these tendencies were more noticeable. His at times confused responses during the Iran-Contra crisis seem to be most easily explained by the fact that he was already losing focus because of the onset of that dread disease. It will never be known whether or not, or to what degree, Reagan as president was experiencing such symptoms, although more than one geriatric specialist came forward after he announced his illness to offer the opinion that this had likely been the case.

After all the difficulties created by the Iran-Contra revelations, Reagan left the Washington stage to sustained applause in January

1989. It is not clear, however, precisely what his revived approval ratings signified. Will Bunch, in his strongly critical *Tear Down This Myth*, likens Reagan's popularity at the end of his presidency to a "relief rally—relief that a personally likable president who'd shown severe signs of aging and drift had made it successfully all the way through eight years." Aside from the all-important breakthrough in U.S.–Soviet relations, actual achievements by the administration were few. Nor had public opinion moved rightward on most issues during his presidency. For all the appeal of Ronald Reagan's personality, the concept of a "Reagan revolution" that would control American politics for the next generation is a much-exaggerated myth.

5

Squandering the Inheritance, 1988–1992

Ronald Reagan's easy style, charm, and personal charisma allowed him to retain the affection of the public to the end of his presidency, but his vice president and chosen successor, George H. W. Bush, was a different kind of animal. Lacking the magnetism of Reagan, Bush started off the 1988 campaign well behind his Democratic rival. Only by resorting to hardball politics that included barely disguised appeals to white racism and attacks on his opponent's patriotism did Bush manage to turn his political fortunes around and, eventually, win the election handily. Having promised a "kinder, gentler" regime than the Reagan years, Bush immediately ran into trouble with the Democratic-controlled Congress. In many ways, the new president was the victim of his predecessor's policies; the deficits that had piled up from eight years of Reaganomics-in-action constrained Bush from taking any "kinder, gentler" initiatives and, most problematically, eventually forced him to approve a tax increase he had sworn before the 1988 GOP convention that he would never permit. Breaking his famous "read my lips" pledge damaged him mortally with the Republican right.

Deadlock and Disillusionment: American Politics since 1968, First Edition.
Gary W. Reichard.
© 2016 John Wiley & Sons, Inc. Published 2016 by John Wiley & Sons, Inc.

Still, Bush enjoyed unprecedented opportunities and great successes in the realm of foreign policy that had the potential to salvage his presidency and win him a second term. The fall of the Berlin Wall in 1989 and demise of the Soviet Union just two years later made him the American Chief Executive who presided over the end of the Cold War. Moreover, he earned astronomical public approval ratings in early 1991 following the brief, gloriously successful Gulf War against Iraq. The fact that he and Secretary of State James Baker had almost unilaterally put together a coalition of nations to fight (or at least support) that war made him seem a world leader of great stature. Briefly—despite the breaking of his no-taxes pledge—it looked as if Bush might be unbeatable in his race for re-election. The sputtering economy, however, refused to turn upward in time to relieve him of the issue in the 1992 campaign. In the face of this economic downturn, Bush's nearly palpable dislike for dealing with domestic issues made him politically vulnerable to a degree unimaginable in the palmy days after the Gulf War victory. The Democrats, intent on reclaiming power in the wake of what they regarded as the obvious failure of Reagan's entire domestic agenda, were eager to pounce.

Succession by Hardball

Although they had begun as distrustful rivals, Reagan and his vice president developed a mutually beneficial partnership once in office. Ruminating in his diary after having been asked in 1984 whether he planned to be neutral in the 1988 GOP contest, Reagan wrote: "this will be a tough one for me. I've always believed the party should choose the nominee but when the time comes I'm afraid my heart will be with George Bush if he makes the run." It was widely assumed that the vice president would indeed run. Never fully trusted by the Religious Right, he knew that his unswerving loyalty to Reagan would be an asset in that event, and took care never to breach the president's trust even when, as in the case of Reagan's optimism about Gorbachev, he strongly disagreed with him on policy. Remaining quietly loyal was a small price to pay, even on matters of foreign policy where he—correctly—believed himself better qualified than the president.

Being closely identified with the so-called "Reagan revolution" also had its downside. Not only were the investigations into Iran-Contra dominating the news and the staggering costs of the administration's economic policies becoming more and more obvious, but, as E. J. Dionne observes in *Why Americans Hate Politics*, "the conservative experiment was exhausted and the conservative coalition increasingly unstable." Bush faced the tricky challenge of taking up Reagan's mantle while at the same time carving out a distinctive political identity somehow different from the president's. Having morphed from moderate to conservative in 1980 when he joined Reagan on the ticket, he had to decide how far he should move back toward the middle after making it through the GOP primary thicket. He also needed to convince voters that he was big enough to fill Reagan's cowboy boots. The "wimp factor," as *Newsweek* uncharitably labeled it in a cover story on Bush's announcement of his candidacy in November 1987, would dog him throughout the primary and general election campaigns. His determination to overcome such criticism contributed importantly to his decision to adopt the advice of his top campaign strategists, Lee Atwater and Roger Ailes, and—against his better instincts—"go negative" in order to win first the nomination and then the election itself.

The sorting out among the GOP candidates occurred with unexpected speed. Finishes far back in the field in Iowa ended the candidacies of the most conservative contenders, former Delaware governor Pete DuPont and Jack Kemp, leaving a three-man race among Bush, televangelist Pat Robertson, and Senate minority leader Bob Dole. Bush's disappointing third-place finish in Iowa—well behind the regional favorite Dole—made it imperative that he win the next-up New Hampshire primary. He did so convincingly, largely by finding the right buttons to push with Dole, causing the latter to show (inevitably) the irascible side that was his greatest political liability. "Tell him to stop lying about my record," Dole growled when NBC news anchor Tom Brokaw asked him after the primary what advice he had for Bush. The response cemented a public impression that the senator was an angry man who might not be able to remain objective in a crisis. After Bush won a crushing victory in South Carolina and took all sixteen primaries on Super Tuesday, the contest was effectively over. Dole folded his tent after losing in Illinois, allowing Bush to clinch the nomination in late April.

The Democrats had been left in depression and disarray by the shellacking they took in 1984. Retaking the Senate two years later had helped their mood but not their sense of direction for the future. In their 1986 book, *Right Turn: The Decline of the Democrats and the Future of American Politics*, political scientist Thomas Ferguson and sociologist Joel Rogers hyperbolically summed up the conventional wisdom at the time about the changed political scene, observing: "the policy initiatives of the Reagan Administration announce the end of the New Deal era." This offered the Democrats an opportunity, in their view, since poll results increasingly indicated that public attitudes on a range of social issues were actually moving away from the GOP's stated positions. "America's transit to a new, center-right party system," they wrote, "does not imply that Republicans will dominate that system in the way the Democrats dominated the New Deal party system."

The general contours of this analysis underlay the efforts of a number of Democrats, mostly from the South and West, to create a different public philosophy for their party. In February 1985, Virginia governor Chuck Robb, Tennessee senator Al Gore, Georgia senator Sam Nunn, former Arizona governor Bruce Babbitt, Representative Richard Gephardt, and a number of other prominent self-styled New Democrats, announced the formation of the Democratic Leadership Council (DLC). The DLC was to be independent of the Democratic National Committee (DNC), so that it could exercise influence unaffected by the traditional interest groups that had come to dominate the party's message and organization. The goal, as described by Kenneth Baer in *Reinventing Democrats: The Politics of Liberalism from Reagan to Clinton*, "was to forge a new electoral coalition among moderate and 'populist' southerners and westerners, plus the 'so-called neo-liberals' in other parts of the country, around 'ideas, not constituency groups.'"

Looking to 1988, it seemed likely that some sort of New Democrat would emerge as the party's nominee. Arguably the two strongest possible Democratic candidates, traditional liberals Ted Kennedy and New York's governor, Mario Cuomo, had long since taken themselves out of the race, but it would not be an easy path for whomever won the nomination. Jesse Jackson, who epitomized the party's interest-group structure and mocked the DLC as "Democrats for the Leisure Class," was back to make another run, this time with a broader multiracial coalition than he had been able to knit together in 1984. The front-runner among the other declared candidates, Gary Hart, saw his candidacy implode in early 1987 when the media exposed him in a dalliance aboard a yacht appropriately named *Monkey Business.* Among the remaining aspirants, those considered to have the best chance were two other liberals, House majority leader Dick Gephardt and Illinois senator Paul Simon, and Massachusetts governor Michael Dukakis, more of a technocrat than an ideologue.

The Democratic contest unfolded in parallel fashion to that of the GOP: the Iowa caucuses reduced the field dramatically, New Hampshire reordered the survivors to the great disadvantage of the Iowa winner, and Super Sunday's results left only two contestants standing. As Bush had done on the Republican side, Dukakis made New Hampshire his springboard, all but polishing off Gephardt and Simon. The only one of the candidates to have designed an all-states approach, the Massachusetts governor then bested Gore and Jackson on Super Tuesday, taking eight states, including the big prizes of the day, Texas and Florida. Following Dukakis's triumphs in Wisconsin, Pennsylvania, and New York, the Democratic contest was effectively settled. There was an unspoken problem in the results, however. "The perception of Dukakis as a vote-getting powerhouse was growing, write Jack Germond and Jules Witcover in *Whose Broad Stripes and Bright Stars? The Trivial Pursuit of the Presidency 1988,* but "little was being said about how much of his vote was anti-black, or more precisely anti-Jackson."

With both nominations decided, Bush and Dukakis were effectively running against each other from May on—with the Democrat enjoying a double-digit lead in the polls. What amounted to a too-early beginning of the general election campaign—especially with two such relatively colorless candidates—contributed to a sense of ennui in the electorate that would be reflected in an extremely low turnout in November. The two party conventions, however, provided brief excitement and—in the case of the Republicans—a surprising choice of running-mate.

Meeting in Atlanta in June, the Democrats tried to paper over differences between the party's liberals—especially Jackson—and the New Democrats who had pressed unsuccessfully for a different kind of platform. The result was a document only one-tenth as long as the one which Mondale had ridden to defeat, but including all of the traditional appeals to interest groups. Dukakis's choice of Texas senator Lloyd Bentsen as his running-mate was popular both inside and outside the convention hall. A courtly and intelligent legislator with few if any enemies, Bentsen was also a member of the DLC. The unquestioned high point of the convention—in terms of partisanship and entertainment—was future Texas governor Ann Richards's soaring and searing keynote, lampooning Bush as having been "born with a silver foot in his mouth." Her speech brought the highly partisan house down, but set an antagonistic tone that the Bush camp would meet in spades. Jackson's speech, too, was brutal toward the Republicans, as he referred sarcastically to the Reagan years as "midnight in America." Entertaining it all may have been, but as Troy writes, "[b]y painting the Reagan years in such stark terms," the Democrats "risked losing the millions of Americans who were only mildly displeased or actually more comfortable" at the end of Reagan's presidency.

The GOP convention, held in New Orleans a month later, moved Bush ahead of Dukakis in the polls for the first time—a lead he never relinquished. Primarily responsible was the candidate's acceptance speech, which journalists and historians agree was by far the best of his career. Its most memorable lines, so effective in the campaign, would later contribute to the demise of Bush's presidency. "The Congress will push me to raise taxes," he told his increasingly excited audience, "and I'll say no, and they'll push, and I'll say no, and they'll push again. And all I can say to them is: read my lips. No new taxes." Bush's surprise selection of Indiana's junior senator, the young and untested Dan Quayle, as his running-mate, on the other hand, was not so well received. Despite the Bush team's attempts to coach Quayle through the campaign, he frequently came off as callow and uninformed, and was decimated by Bentsen in the single vice-presidential debate of the campaign. Worse, the Bush team discovered only after Quayle had been added to the ticket that he had possibly used influence to get into the Indiana National Guard rather than serving in Vietnam. According to Herbert Parmet, who had access to Bush's unpublished diary in writing his biography, *George Bush: The Life of a Lone Star Yankee*, less than a year later Bush privately recorded of his vice presidential selection, "it was my decision, and I blew it, but I'm not about to say that I blew it."

Even before his convention performance, Bush had begun to gain on Dukakis, largely by caving in to Atwater's insistence that the only way to win was by attacking his Democratic foe hard and continuously. His relentless assault got more intense as the campaign progressed. Going after Dukakis for having vetoed a Massachusetts bill that would have required teachers to lead their students in the Pledge of Allegiance, Bush virtually appropriated the American flag as his campaign's symbol. Even more damaging to Dukakis were the Bush campaign's "Willie Horton" ads, featuring a felon of that name—who happened to be black. Horton, serving time for first-degree murder, had been granted a weekend furlough under a state program supported by Dukakis, during which he was arrested for kidnapping and assault in Maryland. The GOP ads implied permissiveness and worse on Dukakis's part for allowing a convicted murderer to run free, although Massachusetts was just one of many states that had such a furlough program. Throughout the campaign Bush hammered away at Dukakis for not owning up to his liberalism, taunting him by referring only to the "L-word." The GOP campaign took a heavy toll. Ever the unemotional, legalistic debater, Dukakis never managed to counter the GOP assault effectively. That cold detachment undid him in his televised debates with Bush.

The Republican victory was sweeping—especially in the Electoral College, where Bush prevailed by 426 to 111. While Dukakis improved upon Mondale's dismal showing four years earlier, winning just under 46 percent of the popular vote, his reach was limited. He won only in reliably Democratic states and in D.C., failing to take any of the battleground states. Analyzing the results, political scientist Marvin Wattenberg, in *The Rise of Candidate-Centered Politics: Presidential Elections of the 1980s*, sees the election as a "retrospective" judgment—"an after-the-fact mandate for the Reagan revolution." Yet Bush's victory carried no mandate; Democrats actually picked up a small number of seats in both the House and Senate and most of the prominent liberal Democrats running for re-election were victorious. Still, most observers agreed that, as Kenneth Baer observes, "[t]he 1988 election confirmed the progressive weakening—even the slow death—of the New Deal coalition." A steep turnout decline among black voters was especially damaging to Dukakis in the South and the large industrial cities of the North. The 50.1 percent voter turnout was the lowest since the election of Calvin Coolidge in 1924.

An obvious conclusion to be drawn from this decline in participation is that voters were unenthusiastic about both presidential candidates and turned off by the nastiness of the "soundbite" campaign. "Bush's election," write Germond and Witcover, "was confirmation that the era of the campaign professional had reached maturation," and ruthless hired guns like Atwater and Ailes would be a key part of national politics going forward. This was a formula for heightened partisanship and bitterness in elections to come, as well as in governing the nation after the dust settled. The voters also showed that they were ambivalent about the direction they hoped the country would take in the next four years; estimates placed the percentage of those who split their tickets at 45 percent.

The Bills Come Due

Time's post-election cover story on the "Outlook for the Bush Years" was subtitled "Reaganism Without Ideology, Persistence Without Brilliance—and Serious Trouble with Congress." The magazine's prediction was sound. Though Bush had made the necessary adjustments to serve Reagan loyally, he had never won over the "movement conservatives" who combined social conservatism with a reflexive aversion to taxes. Moreover, Bush possessed neither the star-power nor the communication skills of his predecessor, a major reason why he was criticized from the beginning for lacking "vision." Of *Time*'s three predictions, however, the one that proved most accurate was that the new president would have to do nearly continuous battle with Congress.

"The mantra within the Bush camp," writes Timothy Naftali in his brief overview, *George H. W. Bush*, "was that this friendly takeover had to be understood as Bush I and not Reagan III." As hard as Bush had had to work to carve out his own identity while appealing to Reagan's voter base, he faced an even greater challenge in defining a unique approach to governing after his eight years as part of the Reagan administration. He set about the task in his inaugural address. Repeatedly using the phrase "a new breeze is blowing" during his address, the forty-first president made clear his intent to distinguish his policies from those of the fortieth. Media reaction was mostly generous and favorable. "[I]f George Bush signaled anything by proclaiming a 'new breeze,'" wrote *Time*, it was "a move away from the Reagan era's tacit approval of selfishness, an end to the glorification of greed."

The formal transition was bumpy. The vetting of potential Cabinet members and other appointees was headed by a group dubbed the "Scrub Team" for the zealousness of its background investigations, particularly to find evidence of loyalty to Bush rather than Reagan. The president's eldest son, George W., played the key role in this process. The new president also brought in perhaps his oldest and closest friend, James Baker, to be secretary of state, and cleaned house in the White House inner sanctum, bringing in the abrasive duo of New Hampshire governor John

Sununu as chief of staff and former deputy treasury secretary Richard Darman as head of the Office of Management and Budget. Another longtime friend, Brent Scowcroft, became national security advisor. The appointment of Scowcroft, a frequent critic of Reagan's foreign policy—especially toward the Soviet Union—signaled that Bush intended a break from his predecessor's foreign policy.

In his inaugural address, speaking directly to the congressional leaders present, the new president proclaimed the onset of "the age of the offered hand." Indeed, George H. W. Bush seemed temperamentally well suited to work with the opposition, but there were forces at work at the end of the late 1980s that worked against him. "Congress and the Democratic majority with which Bush would have to deal was a more formidable force than his Republican predecessors had faced," writes political scientist Barbara Sinclair in Michael Nelson and Barbara Perry's edited collection, *41: Inside the Presidency of George H. W. Bush*. In support of this generalization, Sinclair cites the expansion of congressional staff, rule changes that reduced committee autonomy and strengthened the role of party leaders, and greater party cohesion among Democrats. Bush also encountered substantial practical hurdles in trying to roll out any kind of agenda for consideration by Congress. One, an imbroglio over his nomination of former senator John Tower to be secretary of defense, was of his own making. The other issues that hijacked the administration's agenda from the outset were carryover problems over which he had no control: the roiling mess that was the nation's savings-and-loan banking system and the bloated federal deficits that had grown out of Reaganomics.

In some ways, Bush's virtues proved to be failings, in terms of his working productively within the political system. Loyal and trusting to a fault, he found it difficult to turn away from any friend in need—even if that need could do damage to Bush himself. Such a case was his ill-fated nomination of Tower to head the Defense Department. Well qualified on paper, having served as chair of the Senate Armed Services Committee, the imperious Tower was widely disliked and was renowned for his heavy drinking and womanizing. These issues combined to do him in. On March 9, after more than five weeks of rancorous partisan exchange, Tower's nomination was turned down on an almost straight party-line vote—the first rejection of a Cabinet nomination since 1959. Bush recovered quickly, persuading Congressman Dick Cheney of Wyoming (who had served as Ford's chief of staff) to take the position. Though Cheney was unanimously confirmed, the Tower fiasco had done serious damage.

By 1989, the rapidly worsening situation in the savings-and-loan industry could not be ignored by either the administration or Congress. There was no way out but to throw federal money— massive amounts of it—at the problem in order to stop the hemorrhaging. The crisis had grown from the passage of legislation in 1982 allowing S&Ls to expand their investments into business and commercial real estate. In the go-go atmosphere of the 1980s, this had led banks down the path of irresponsible speculative investments designed to keep their cashflow adequate to support the costs of generous interest rates with which they had lured depositors. By mid-decade, the industry had begun to self-destruct, as hundreds of banks failed across the nation. To avert the system's complete collapse and the near-certain recession that would follow, the administration and Congress agreed on a bail-out originally totaling $50 billion, to be administered by the Federal Deposit Insurance Corporation (FDIC); the total would eventually exceed three times that amount. There was collateral political damage from the S&L crisis, as well. The successful jockeying for special favor by influential S&L executive Charles Keating resulted in the Senate Ethics Committee's reprimand of Alan Cranston (California), who had to step down as Democratic whip, as well as lesser sanctions for four others: Democrats Dennis DeConcini (New Mexico), John Glenn (Ohio), and Donald Riegle (Michigan), and Republican John McCain (Arizona).

Dealing with the S&L crisis not only took up valuable time at the outset of the Bush presidency, but caused the government to bleed money at the worst possible time. The all-consuming problem facing Bush as he entered the White House was the enormous budget deficit that had resulted from the specious supply-side formula during the eight years of the Reagan administration. Bush papered over the problem in his first budget (FY 1990), securing passage for a plan that optimistically forecast a reduced deficit and promised unspecified reductions and revenue increases. Neither the reductions nor the increases materialized, and by 1990, as Sinclair writes, "a minimalist deal was no longer a viable option." Darman had been quietly telling Bush for several months that tax increases of some kind would be needed to close the deficit. Confronted by bad choices in every direction, the president tried to approach "the budget emergency as if it were a foreign policy problem," writes Naftali. "His instinct was to reach out to fellow leaders and work the issue"—in secret, if possible. Thus was born the "summit" strategy: to work privately with the congressional leadership to hammer out a deal.

To provide political cover, a budget deal would need support from majorities on both sides of the aisle. Bush proceeded under the optimistic assumption that this would be possible, vastly underestimating the anti-tax fervor in Republican ranks— particularly in the House. In June, he agreed to a request from Senate majority leader George Mitchell (Maine) that increased taxes at least be on the table for discussion. This was a huge tactical error; at the least, the president should have held that card to his vest until a deal had been struck. As the summit negotiators secretly developed their plan through the summer, they packaged hefty gasoline taxes with major cuts in domestic spending, including reductions in Medicare and other entitlements sacrosanct to liberal Democrats; the administration also abandoned a capital gains tax reduction it had been pushing. When the proposal was daylighted in the fall, the impossibility of achieving bipartisan consensus was immediately evident. A large segment of the president's own party, vociferously led by firebrand Representative Newt Gingrich (Georgia), spoke out against the plan, while on the Democratic side, opposition to the Medicare cuts caused major defections. When the bill came up for a vote in the House, it was opposed by majorities in both parties and went down to defeat, 179-254. Bush's approach had failed utterly; perhaps worse, as

Parmet observes, "[i]n a day when 'taking the pledge' against further taxation was rapidly supplanting anticommunism as the rallying point for conservatives, the administration's initiative appeared as an incredible betrayal."

With the compromise plan dead and his Republican troops in revolt, Bush lost all leverage with the Democratic Congress in the construction of an alternative plan. The result was a bill devised largely along lines favored by the Democratic leadership, substituting higher tax rates on wealthier taxpayers for the gasoline tax while reducing the cuts to Medicare. The bill passed, predictably drawing most of its support from Democrats. In the House, 88 percent of the Democrats voted in favor, while 85 percent of the Republicans voted no. A final insult to Bush was Gingrich's vengeful refusal to appear behind him in the ceremonial signing of the budget bill in the White House garden. The whole exercise proved a disaster for the president, with long-lasting repercussions.

The timing of the administration's defeat on the budget bill was perfect for Democrats, coming as it did right before the 1990 mid-term elections. Sensing potential disaster for the GOP, Ed Rollins, co-chairman of the Republican National Committee, urged the party's congressional candidates to run against the president's position on the tax issue—a move that got him fired at Bush's insistence after the election. It was too late for the Republicans to reframe their campaign, however, and the party lost further ground in both houses: the Democrats picked up one additional Senate seat and seven in the House (the GOP lost an additional Senate seat the following year, when Senator John Heinz of Pennsylvania was killed in an airplane crash and was succeeded by Democrat Harris Wofford). The Democrats' showing restored their strength in Congress almost to post-Watergate levels, ensuring that Bush's next two years would be a severe political challenge.

Politically costly as it was to Bush, the 1990 budget deal failed to solve the problem. By 1991, the long-feared recession was well underway, with rising interest rates strongly inhibiting economic growth. By mid-year, unemployment had risen to 7.8 percent, the highest rate since the recession of the early

Reagan years. Ominously, polls showed that most Americans saw themselves as economically worse off than they had been the year before. A particularly damaging political consequence of the continuing deficit problem was the forced closure of more than twenty military bases. Although Defense Secretary Cheney wisely punted the initial recommendations to a special commission, the administration could not escape responsibility for the final decisions. The closures included seven bases in California and three in Texas—states that were absolutely critical to Bush's chances for re-election.

The huge deficit and related downturn colored virtually all decisions on domestic policy for the rest of Bush's term in office. In alluding to his desire for a "kinder, gentler" society in his inaugural address, he had laid out some of his general domestic policy objectives. Unfortunately, however, meaningful action on these issues would require major federal spending. A case in point was education reform. The administration's full education proposal, "America 2000," rolled out in spring 1991, was disappointingly modest. As John Robert Greene writes in *The Presidency of George Bush*, the plan "placed the burden of school improvement squarely on the backs of the localities," requesting no funds to restore the funding cuts of the Reagan years, urging voluntary tests to measure school success, and calling upon the nation's businesses to raise the money necessary to establish "break the mold" schools. The administration then actually cut education funding in its FY 1992 budget, with Secretary of Education Lamar Alexander hitting the road to serve as a super-salesman on behalf of the program.

The two most important domestic policy accomplishments during Bush's presidency were restoration of the Clean Air Act of 1970 and passage of the Americans with Disabilities Act. Renewal of the Clean Air Act, which Congress had been kicking down the road ever since its expiration in 1981, required the balancing of sharply conflicting interests. As political scientist Paul Quirk explains in his essay in *The Bush Presidency: First Appraisals*, reduction of urban smog and toxic pollution called for control of auto emissions and limitations on manufacturers of chemicals and other similar products, while addressing the menacing effects of acid rain required placing limits on industrial furnace emissions. In this instance, Bush's penchant for high-level, private negotiations—which had failed miserably in the case of the budget negotiations—served all parties well. The Clean Air Act Amendments became law in fall 1990, along the general lines proposed by the administration. Crediting the president for his leadership in this effort, Greene observes that he was more proactive in protecting the environment than any previous president with the exception of Teddy Roosevelt.

The legislation that became the Americans with Disabilities Act (ADA), as Parmet notes, represented Bush's "clearest push toward a 'kinder and gentler society.'" A rarity during his presidency, the bill swept through Congress with strong bipartisan support. Essentially extending language similar to the 1964 Civil Rights Act to those with disabilities, the act mandated improved access to transportation services for the disabled and required the Federal Communications Commission (FCC) to ensure equivalent services for those with speech and hearing deficiencies. ADA also explicitly covered those struggling with AIDS. Another 1990 measure, the Ryan White Comprehensive AIDS Resources Emergency Act, named for an Indiana teenager who had died of the disease after contracting HIV from a transfusion, provided more specific benefits for low-income victims of the dread disease, funding a "payer of last resort" insurance program for AIDS victims who lacked insurance or were underinsured. These enactments represented a distinct advance from the policies of the Reagan years.

On the issue of reproductive rights, there was evidence that Bush's conversion to a pro-life stance in 1980 had been genuine. The administration filed an amicus brief in *Webster v. Reproductive Health Services of Missouri*, seeking to have the Supreme Court overturn *Roe v. Wade*. While the court stopped short of an outright reversal, it gave the states power to set additional restrictions on women's access to abortion. Bush then announced his support for an anti-abortion amendment to the Constitution, which— given the composition of Congress—had zero chance of passage.

He was able to hold the line, however, against a number of bills passed by Congress that would have interfered with restrictions being imposed by some states on women's right to choose abortion. None of his ten vetoes of abortion-related bills was overridden. Other than standing firm against expanded abortion rights, however, Bush did little to mollify the Christian Right— and he lacked Reagan's rhetorical gifts to persuade them otherwise. As Daniel Williams states in *God's Own Party*: "The Bush administration turned out to be even worse for their cause than they expected." Pat Robertson spoke for the most outraged among conservative Christians, writing in his 1991 book—ironically titled *The New World Order*—that Bush seemed to be "unwittingly carrying out the mission … of a tightly knit cabal whose goal is … a new world order for the human race under the domination of Lucifer and his followers."

Not surprisingly, the state of race relations in the United States was still somewhat raw when Bush assumed office. Poll results indicated that while whites generally believed the situation to have improved in the late 1980s, black respondents said they had gotten worse. As on the abortion issue, a Supreme Court decision catalyzed a renewal of conflict. In a 1990 case, *Wards Cove Packing Co. v. Atonio*, the court, in effect, abolished the right of plaintiffs to sue employers on grounds of discrimination based on the "non-representative" composition of their workforce. When the Democratic-controlled Congress attempted to reverse the results of the decision, Bush labeled its effort a "quota bill" and responded with a veto. Many Republicans picked up on the issue in their congressional campaigns—most notably Jesse Helms, who used it successfully against his opponent Harvey Gantt, the black mayor of Charlotte. Renewed partisan strife over issues of race suggested that 1992 might see a replay of the "Willie Horton" strategy by the GOP.

In the summer of 1991, the racial atmosphere was further exacerbated by Bush's nomination of a conservative black former member of the Reagan administration, Clarence Thomas, to fill the Supreme Court seat of the retiring civil rights icon, Justice Thurgood Marshall. The president had considered naming

Thomas when presented with his first chance to make a court appointment two years earlier, but, recognizing that his lack of experience on the bench at that time might make confirmation difficult, had opted for a moderate New Hampshire judge, David Souter. Souter had quickly disappointed the extreme right with his down-the-middle views. With Marshall's retirement, Thomas seemed the perfect choice for Republicans, since there was an unspoken expectation that this particular seat on the court would remain "black," and his tenure as head of the EEOC under Reagan had been marked by lack of sympathy for affirmative action and even minority rights, generally. Just as Thomas's nomination was being reported out, a young female law professor—also black—lobbed a hand grenade into the Judiciary Committee. Anita Hill, who had worked with Thomas during his EEOC days, raised embarrassingly explicit charges of sexual harassment against the would-be justice, turning the reconvened hearings into a lurid daily soap opera, which millions of Americans viewed on live television. Bush's nominee now pulled the "race card" of all race cards, fending off Hill's charges with accusations of his own. He aimed his fire at the all-white-male Judiciary Committee, claiming that he was being victimized as an "uppity black" and being "lynched" for his judicial views. Both media and public opinion were divided over Hill's charges, which may actually have worked to Thomas's advantage by drawing attention away from justifiable questions that had arisen about his judicial fitness for the bench. Sent forward by the Judiciary Committee on a divided committee vote, his nomination was confirmed by the full Senate by 52 to 48, with only eleven Democrats voting aye. Thomas's appointment advanced Bush's goal of ensuring that the court's major cases would be decided by a conservative majority.

Timothy Naftali titles his first chapter on Bush's presidency, "Cleaning Up Reagan's Mess." Perhaps Bush's biggest such challenge was to find a way to pay the overdue bills from the Reagan years. "It was almost as if Reagan had set a trap with his supply-side profligacy," writes Sean Wilentz in *The Age of Reagan*, "presiding over what looked like good times with the bill falling due when he left office." Much as Gerald Ford had, Bush began his presidency hoping for bipartisan cooperation with Congress to address these issues. It was not to be. With Reagan out of the picture, the energized Democratic leaders in both House and Senate flexed their muscles and challenged Bush at virtually every turn. Bush ended up by trying to control the direction of domestic policy by frequent resort to his veto power—again, as Ford had done. But Bush also had trouble holding his own party in line. While he tacked to the right on some issues, such as abortion and civil rights, he was never accepted as a "real" conservative by the Christian Right or by movement conservatives like Newt Gingrich. His greatest shortcoming may have been that he was not Ronald Reagan. He "lacked the political skills," writes Donald Critchlow, in *The Conservative Ascendancy*, "to satisfy the right wing while appealing to the general electorate."

New World (Dis)Order

Although Bush had remained loyal to Reagan's foreign policy while vice president, he took pains to emphasize differences between the two in his 1988 campaign. This was especially the case in U.S.–Soviet relations, as he implied that on his watch the United States would be more cautious, waiting for evidence of actual change in Soviet actions, rather than accepting promises at face value. As James Mann writes in *The Rebellion of Ronald Reagan*, these campaign statements "were not merely an election tactic.... . Bush had moved in the opposite direction from Reagan, becoming more hard-nosed toward Moscow as the president was becoming more conciliatory." Once elected, the forty-first president surrounded himself with like-minded "realists": Baker at the State Department and Scowcroft as national security advisor—both longtime, trusted friends—as well as Cheney at Defense and Colin Powell as chief of the joint chiefs of staff. These were men of practical experience, cold-eyed about how much "the enemy" could be trusted to change. The bench was strong

Figure 5.1 The first President George Bush was well served by a strong national security team, but his "right-hand man" throughout his administration was Secretary of State James Baker, shown here with Bush conferring at the Conference on Security and Cooperation in Europe Plenary in November 1990. George Bush Presidential Library and Museum

behind these top advisors, as well—especially in Scowcroft's shop; his deputy, Robert Gates, had served as CIA director, while his Soviet affairs specialist was a bright young academic from Stanford University, Condoleezza Rice.

Bush had an opportunity to meet with Gorbachev while still president-elect, accompanying Reagan and Secretary of State Shultz on a cruise with the Soviet premier in New York Harbor in December 1988. The meeting did not go well. When Bush asked Gorbachev what U.S. investors might look forward to if *perestroika* succeeded, the Soviet leader's almost testy response was "Even Jesus Christ couldn't answer that question." As Naftali writes, Gorbachev "left New York wondering whether Bush was a closet hawk," puzzled because he had just given a speech at the United Nations in which he had announced a reduction of a half-million troops from the Soviet military, as well as the withdrawal of six armored divisions from the East European satellite nations.

154

Once in the White House, Bush struck a tone very different from Reagan, opting to wait out developments in the new Soviet Union in the belief that its economic erosion would give the United States an opportunity to strike better deals down the road. Nominally a period of "strategic review," this "pause" (or *pauza*, as the Soviets called it) lasted through half of Bush's first year in the White House. "The so-called strategic review was neither truly strategic nor a proper review," wrote Baker in his memoir, *The Politics of Diplomacy*, adding that "much of the review was run by Reagan administration holdovers." During the *pauza*, Bush sought no high-level meetings or additional negotiations, although in May he proposed for future discussion a Conventional Forces in Europe (CFE) agreement calling for substantial troop reductions in both NATO and Warsaw Pact forces. As the *pauza* dragged on, the administration was hammered from both right and left for its indecision; liberals were especially critical of Bush's unresponsiveness to Gorbachev.

With U.S.–Soviet relations on hold, Bush demonstrated his realist approach, as well as his desire to restore bipartisanship to foreign policy, by moving decisively to address the political fallout from Reagan's support for the Nicaraguan contras. Powerful Senate Democrats, including Joe Biden, John Kerry (Massachusetts), and Christopher Dodd (Connecticut), evidenced willingness to work with the administration to heal partisan wounds around the issue. In March 1989, Bush asked Congress to embrace a plan for peace that had been developed two years earlier by regional leaders, whereby the United States would provide only humanitarian support to the contras in return for the Sandinista government's promise to hold free elections early in 1990. Though the administration's strategy angered the far right, it succeeded. The bill authorizing humanitarian aid passed with a strong bipartisan majority, and in March 1990, Nicaraguan elections resulted in the defeat of the Sandinistas and the ouster of President Daniel Ortega. The Central American boil, as Baker labeled it in his memoir, had been lanced.

A second nagging Central American problem confronting Bush when he entered the White House was the growing intransigence of Panamanian strongman Manuel Noriega in the face of U.S. demands that he stop the illicit drug trade funneling through his nation into North America. The Reagan administration had secured Noriega's indictment in the United States on drug charges, but had taken no further steps against him. When Noriega ignored election results that produced victory for the opposition party, Bush realized that he would have to be forcibly removed from power. Sending 2,000 troops to the Canal Zone, he called upon the joint chiefs of staff to devise a plan for military intervention to overthrow Noriega and bring him back to the United States to face trial. After a poorly organized internal coup attempt against the dictator failed in October 1989, Bush decided to put the military plan into action at the first visible provocation. His opportunity came in mid-December, when Panamanian Defense Force (PDF) troops shot and killed an American military officer, brutally beat another, and sexually assaulted the second officer's wife. The next day, the president gave the go-ahead for Operation Just Cause, which was set into motion shortly after midnight on December 20. Involving more than 25,000 troops and 300 aircraft and attack helicopters, the operation succeeded within hours. The swift victory left no opportunity for objections from Congress—especially when polls indicated 80 percent approval of Bush's action. Brought to the United States to stand trial, Noriega was convicted and imprisoned for drug trafficking, money laundering, and racketeering. Although the new Panamanian government proved little better than Noriega's, the invasion dramatized Bush's willingness to engage U.S. military might when he felt it was justified.

Just as events in Central America presented a distraction from U.S.–Soviet relations, so too did a horrendous event that played out in Beijing in early June 1989. After nearly two months of demonstrations by students and other protesters calling for democratic reform, the Chinese leadership sent armed troops into Tiananmen Square in the heart of the capital to disperse the huge throng. The scene, televised worldwide, was horrendous, as was the death toll: estimates of casualties varied wildly, from the Chinese government's reported 300 to more reliable estimates from the Chinese Red Cross and other observers that ranged from 2500 to 5000. Bush immediately denounced the brutality, and then anguished over how, or if, to respond to it. Ultimately, both he and Scowcroft decided that, as the latter put it in their joint memoir, *A World Transformed*, the U.S. "had too much invested in the China situation to throw it away with one stroke." After calling his old friend, former Chinese leader Deng Xiaoping, and sending Scowcroft on a secret mission to communicate the United States' strong disappointment with the government's handling of the protests, Bush limited his response to merely holding up loans to the People's Republic from the World Bank.

There was strong pressure in Congress, on both sides of the aisle, for the administration to do more, but Bush remained adamant. In late 1989, both houses unanimously passed a measure, sponsored by and named for Representative Nancy Pelosi (D-California), to extend sanctions on the Chinese in a number of directions. Bush vetoed the bill and then, against overwhelming odds, engaged in a fierce campaign to win the votes necessary in the Senate to avoid override. In what may have been his most impressive feat working with the Democratic-controlled Congress, he prevailed in the struggle by turning around thirty-seven votes. Bush's judgment in this instance proved to be sound. His secret, back-channel communications, followed by a diplomatic mission in December, produced at least some liberalization of the PRC government's stance toward the dissenters, and by May of 1990 the United States extended China's most-favored-nation trade status.

As Hal Brands writes in *From Berlin to Baghdad: America's Search for Purpose in the Post-Cold War World*, events following Tiananmen Square clearly demonstrated that Bush "was more enthusiastic about improving relations with China than with the Soviet Union." Indeed, adds Brands, the president may have wanted to ensure "that the United States remained ahead of Moscow in forging positive ties with China." The events also moved Bush, however, to consider more deeply the possible ramifications of remaining aloof from the rising political agitation in the Soviet-dominated East European nations—especially Poland, which had overturned its communist government virtually at the same time as the massacre in Tiananmen Square. As riotous crowds took to the streets in other East European capitals in the following weeks, Bush grew increasingly worried about how the Soviets might react. His visits to Poland and Hungary on the way to a G7 economic summit in July convinced him to break the *pauza* and seek his first summit with Gorbachev in order to forestall potentially catastrophic conflicts in the satellite states. In October, the president announced that the two leaders would meet on the island of Malta two months later. This was a momentous decision on Bush's part.

Before the two heads of state could convene, the situation in both the Soviet Union and its satellite nations changed dramatically. In late summer, Latvia had joined Estonia in declaring independence from the Soviet Union. With protests continuing throughout Eastern Europe, Gorbachev strongly believed that the only way the communist governments in those states could be preserved was through political liberalization, such as he was attempting through *perestroika* in the Soviet Union. Moreover, his problems at home made it difficult for him to offer military assistance to besieged satellite governments. While visiting East Berlin in October, the Soviet leader hedged his support of the extreme hard-line East German ruler Erich Honecker, asserting that East German policy was made "not in Moscow, but in Berlin." Less than a week later, Honecker was out and the chain of events leading to the destruction of the Berlin Wall on November 9 was set in motion. No other single event could have symbolized so powerfully the end of the Cold War as the fall of the Wall. By the end of December, communist governments in Yugoslavia, Bulgaria, and Czechoslovakia had fallen peacefully, and Rumania's dictator Nicolae Ceauşescu and his wife had been executed by firing squad.

The Malta summit marked a dramatic change in Bush's stance toward his Soviet counterpart in the face of the latter's crumbling power base in Moscow. "I will seek to avoid doing anything that would damage your position in the world," he told Gorbachev during the summit. It was clear, however, that the balance of power between the two superpowers had shifted dramatically by this time. Now convinced that it was safer to back the leader he knew than to risk what might follow, Bush adhered to his strategy even when Gorbachev took steps in March 1990 to block Lithuania's efforts to break away from the Soviet Union. In doing so, he raised the ire of the political right, as reflected in columnist George Will's acid comment that "Bushism is Reaganism minus the passion for freedom." Even Richard Nixon got into the act, penning a critical op-ed piece in the *New York Times* (of all places). Bush's policy paid immediate dividends, however, as he secured Gorbachev's acquiescence to a vote on German reunification in March 1990, and a few months later, to Germany's joining the NATO alliance.

Both Greene and Parmet credit Bush with "managing" the relationship with Gorbachev so that the changes in Eastern Europe—particularly the peaceful reunification of Germany—could occur so smoothly. This is a justifiable verdict. White House Chief of Staff John Sununu's later comments in an oral history interview—intended to apply to Bush's overall approach to the ending of the Cold War—seem on target as a description of the president's tactics in relation to these world-shaking events in East Europe. "Bush's handling put just enough tension on the line," observed Sununu. "You know, it's like catching a 10-pound bass on a 3-lb. line, you've got to keep the tension [just right].... He handled it exactly right and that was the art at the time ... ."

While a number of things seemed to be going right for Bush in the realm of foreign policy, in the Middle East problems stemming from Reagan's clandestine policies came home to roost, with the emergence of Saddam Hussein as an overt threat to regional stability. In the interest of maintaining the balance of power in the region, the Reagan administration had supported Iraq in its decade-long war with Iran, providing Saddam with billions of dollars in armaments and cash even while secretly selling arms to Iran to raise funds to supply the contras. This massive American support kept Iraq from losing the war, but the result was a bloody, hard-fought draw between the two nations that left both economically devastated. Saddam Hussein had accumulated debts totaling $80 billion, much of which was owed to Iraq's neighbors in the region, and with oil prices declining sharply, there was no source of revenue to pay those obligations.

The end of the Iran–Iraq war in August 1988—followed almost immediately by Saddam's brutal use of chemical weapons to subdue Iraq's restive Kurdish minority—pointed to the need for reassessment of U.S. commitment to the ruthless dictator. In Congress, there was strong and growing bipartisan support for cutting off American aid and trade credits, as well as imposing harsh economic sanctions on Iraq, to forestall the possibility of U.S. dollars being used to increase Saddam's stockpile of traditional and perhaps even nuclear arms. If Bush seriously considered any change in policy on Iraq, it was not apparent. In late June 1989, he secretly signed off on NSD-26, a directive that called for continued political and economic "incentives" to encourage Saddam to play a more constructive role in the region. In late 1989 Congress passed legislation calling for sanctions on Iraq, but the president pocket-vetoed the measure. The same scenario would be repeated a year later. With so much at stake, broader congressional-executive consultation would have been appropriate and helpful to the president, especially in view of the military conflict that lay down the road. But Bush, as former acting general counsel to the U.S. House of Representatives Charles Tiefer writes in *The Semi-Sovereign Presidency: The Bush Administration's Strategy for Governing Without Congress*, "conducted foreign policy toward Iraq as he liked, based on his personal hopes of a positive relationship with an unpopular leader without regard to the contrary view of the public and Congress."

On the evening of August 1, 1990, the White House received reports that Saddam's troops, which had been massing on Kuwait's border, had invaded the small, relatively helpless neighboring state. The following morning, the UN Security Council adopted Resolution 660, condemning the invasion and threatening economic sanctions if Iraqi troops were not withdrawn. By the time the resolution passed, however, the 120,000-strong invasion force had completely subdued Kuwait, seizing its rich oil fields. Bush responded by moving American warships into the

Persian Gulf and freezing all Iraqi and Kuwaiti assets in the United States. Branding the invasion an act of "naked aggression," the president gave no initial indication of possible military action, but he contacted Gorbachev immediately to press the Soviet leader to join him in issuing a statement condemning the takeover. Gorbachev, though staggering under an economic crisis at home and beleaguered by hard-line critics in the Kremlin, agreed to do so in hopes of remaining relevant in the international arena.

As Tiefer points out, if Bush's continuing "secret courtship" of Saddam Hussein had been more widely known at the time, the Iraqi invasion would almost certainly have created political headaches for the administration. In the circumstances, however, Congress more or less closed ranks with the president. Tellingly, Bush and Scowcroft say nothing about the administration's pre-invasion Iraqi policy in the long discussion of the buildup to the Gulf War in their joint memoir, *A World Transformed.*

Upon his return to Washington on August 5 from a previously scheduled meeting with British prime minister Margaret Thatcher, Bush announced his resolve to take action. As a first step, Bush had already decided, again without consulting with Congress, to send Defense Secretary Cheney to seek King Fahd's permission to deploy a U.S. force of 100,000 on Saudi Arabian soil in order to deter Saddam from continuing his aggression into that oil-rich nation. To the surprise of Bush and Cheney, the Saudi monarch quickly agreed. In a televised address on August 8, Bush informed the nation of the deployment, soon to be code-named Operation Desert Shield. Seeking to shore up support from the American public and potential international partners in the event U.S. military action ensued, Bush and Scowcroft coined a catchphrase designed to underscore the grave importance of thwarting Iraq's aggression. Speaking to a joint session of Congress in early September, the president rolled out the new phrase, "the New World Order." The lofty label seems to have been created as much to cover the administration's flanks against critics at home as for any other reason. "There may have been a geopolitical component," writes Hal Brands, "but at its heart, the notion was a domestic political creation."

161

Acting under UN Resolution 660, Bush was committed to ensuring that any military action against Saddam Hussein would come from a multinational coalition, not the United States alone. The administration's diplomacy, carried out by Secretary of State Baker on a whirlwind tour of world capitals, was hugely successful in raising money for the military exercise and firming up commitment among coalition partners. By October, there were over 400,000 troops, representing thirty-six nations, in the region; almost half of this force were U.S. troops. This was a tremendous diplomatic accomplishment on the part of Bush and Baker, and helped greatly on Capitol Hill. Both houses of Congress overwhelmingly passed resolutions approving the American deployment, but at the same time asserting the legislative branch's right to authorize such a massive assignment of troops abroad.

With coalition troops in place, reports of Iraqi atrocities in Kuwait—whether accurate or not—convinced Bush that military action would probably be needed to force Saddam Hussein to give up his conquest. "We must get this over with," he wrote in his diary in mid-October. "The longer it goes, the longer the erosion [of support.] I think we can draw a line in the sand." Accordingly, he asked Powell to have the commanding general in the Central Theatre of Operations, General Norman Schwarzkopf, draw up plans for an offensive to drive out the Iraqi occupying forces. After the plan was presented to the NSC on October 30, Scowcroft, Cheney, and Powell advised the president that a doubling of U.S. forces would be necessary. Resolved to go ahead with the operation, the president assured them that the Pentagon would receive "whatever it needed." Although Bush had consulted earlier the same day with the congressional leadership, he had not raised the question of a possible military offensive. Now, with the mid-term congressional elections just days away, he held back from making any announcement of an imminent troop buildup. The elections, as *Congressional Quarterly* noted, "unfolded in a curious vacuum from the crisis brewing in the Persian Gulf." On November 8, the elections behind him, Bush announced that American forces in

Saudi Arabia would be increased from 230,000 to more than 500,000. His approval rating, which had been 75 percent in August, dropped to 50 percent after the announcement.

Bush's action dramatically altered the political situation at home. "The news of the troop increase, particularly its size," he wrote later, "whipped up a new outcry in Congress and furious attacks on me that I had changed policy and decided to go to war without consultation." Since the 101st Congress had adjourned *sine die* before the elections, both Democratic and Republican leaders, including the ranking Republican on the Senate Foreign Relations Committee, Richard Lugar (Indiana), now called for a special session so that Bush could explain his plans and objectives. The administration resisted such entreaties, as Scowcroft later wrote, for fear that if Congress were to insist on taking up a resolution approving military action and it were to fail, "it would undermine not only our credibility and our political leadership of the coalition, but also the international efforts to reverse the invasion." As leading Democrats such as Senate majority leader Mitchell and House leaders Tom Foley (Washington) and Richard Gephardt pressed the administration to allow time for the sanctions to work on Iraq and the Senate Armed Services Committee held hearings on the wisdom of military action, Bush and Baker worked successfully to get the UN Security Council to authorize the use of force if Iraq did not withdraw from Kuwait by January 15, 1991. The Soviets supported the resolution, with only Cuba and Yemen voting no and China abstaining. Going to the UN was a masterstroke. "Although we didn't realize it at the time," wrote Bush in *A World Transformed*, the UN resolution "changed the debate with Congress, creating a context for the use of force which helped bring it aboard." The Security Council resolution also helped with U.S. popular opinion. A January 4 ABC–*Washington Post* poll indicated that 66 percent now approved Bush's handling of the Gulf crisis.

In further preparation for an offensive against Saddam, Bush extended one final offer to negotiate, proposing a meeting between Baker and Iraqi foreign minister Tariq Aziz, which occurred in Geneva just days before the January 15 deadline set by the UN. At the meeting, however, Baker simply handed Aziz a letter from Bush addressed to Saddam that described the dire consequences if Iraq failed to meet the UN-imposed deadline. Aziz responded, "We accept war."

On the day before the Baker–Aziz meeting, Bush had asked the new Congress to pass a resolution supporting "the use of all necessary means to implement UN Security Council 678," in effect authorizing U.S. military action if Iraq failed to meet the UN's deadline. On January 12, companion authorizing resolutions came up for votes in both houses, but not before Democrat-sponsored measures to extend sanctions and to require explicit congressional authorization for actual engagement of U.S. forces in hostilities, respectively, were debated and defeated. The final votes for passage of the Gulf War resolution, as the matching House and Senate bills were collectively dubbed, were 250-183 in the House and 52-47 in the Senate. Like all other presidents following passage of the 1973 War Powers Resolution, Bush rejected the constitutionality of that statute, but he felt he had to take the gamble of asking Congress to support U.S. military action before the fact. He had won big. "I felt the heavy weight that I might be faced with impeachment lifted from my shoulders as I heard the results," he later wrote.

Operation Desert Storm commenced on January 17, 1991, beginning as an aerial bombardment of Iraqi positions in Kuwait, as well as targets in Iraq itself. Millions of Americans sat transfixed in front of their television sets, watching live coverage of the air war by the Cable News Network (CNN) and the three major networks. For more than a month, Apache attack helicopters and Stealth bombers rained down destruction on Iraq's radar stations, suspected military installations and production centers, and other military and governmental targets in Baghdad. Bush had hoped that the air attacks alone might lead to Iraqi withdrawal from Kuwait, and to Saddam's overthrow at home, as well. When neither occurred after a month of furious attacks, he grew impatient to put Schwarzkopf's invasion game plan into action. Even Saddam's belated announcement in mid-February that he was ready to comply with the UN's initial Resolution

660 and withdraw from Kuwait was not enough to dissuade Bush, who told Cheney to press on with the strategy. On February 25, Bush gave the go-ahead for ground operations to begin. The invasion force, including some 85,000 U.S. Marines enjoying extensive air cover, was almost instantaneously successful, reaching Kuwait City before Saddam could even get reinforcements there. The negative side of this instant success, however, was that most of the Iraqi forces remained outside of what had been envisioned as a kind of pincers operation designed to encircle and capture them. For the next couple of days, coalition forces mercilessly bombed the vastly outmanned, retreating Iraqi forces as they made their way home.

Concerned not to have U.S. forces perceived as butchers, Bush worried about how far to proceed with the war now that Saddam's forces had been driven from Kuwait, and what terms to set as the basis for a ceasefire. "How do we quit?" he asked himself in his diary on February 26. "How do we get them to lay down their arms?" Bush had hoped all along that the war would lead to Saddam's ouster, but by his own people rather than at the hands of coalition forces. To make that a war aim at this point seemed out of the question. On February 27, just two days after the beginning of the ground war, the president decided to end the assault at midnight, as most of the Republican Guard made it back to Iraq. Kuwait was liberated, and with a loss of fewer than 150 American lives and only 87 lives among the remaining coalition forces. "By God," Bush declared, "we've kicked the Vietnam syndrome once and for all."

Bush was criticized at the time for allowing Saddam to continue in power instead of hunting him down, and for allowing so many Iraqi forces to return home. The second-guessing escalated dramatically a decade later, after the horrific attacks by Islamic militants on the World Trade Center. Colin Powell's explanation for the decision to end the war with Saddam still in power is persuasive. "What tends to be forgotten," he writes in *My American Journey*, "is that while the United States led the way, we were heading an *international* coalition carrying out a clearly defined UN mission. That mission was accomplished." He adds: "From the geopolitical standpoint, the coalition, particularly the Arab states, never wanted Iraq invaded and dismembered."

If one of Bush's goals had been to shake off "the Vietnam syndrome," in some ways he succeeded. The coalition's blitzkrieg victory in the Gulf War set off a near-orgy of patriotism in the United States, complete with parades and a new anthem of sorts, country music singer Lee Greenwood's *God Bless the U.S.A.* Democrats who had opposed the military action were now as enthusiastic in victory as their GOP colleagues, sporting flag pins on their lapels and, of course, joining in honoring the returning veterans for their sacrifice and stunning victory. In the general public celebration, Bush's approval ratings, so mercurial in the year leading up to the war, hit historic highs. But as is usually the case, the euphoria was misplaced. As Marvin and Deborah Kalb point out in *Haunting Legacy*, despite Bush's hopeful pronouncement, "the ghost of Vietnam" had not been extinguished; it was to rise "again and again to haunt official consideration of American intervention" by later presidents in other international conflicts. Moreover, not only did the brutal Saddam Hussein remain entrenched in Iraq, but as Brands reflects, "the mere fact that the conflict had occurred meant that the post-Cold War world was likely to be an unfriendly place for some time to come."

Events in the former Soviet satellite nations reinforced the sense that the end of the Cold War did not equate to the coming of world peace. In January 1991, Soviet troops intervened in Latvia and Lithuania, presaging a possible crackdown on the independence movements there. Bush and Scowcroft avoided any overt reaction, concerned—as they later explained—that intervention "might bolster the hard-liners around Gorbachev" and lead to his removal. Indeed, keeping Gorbachev in power increasingly became the administration's controlling objective in dealing with the Kremlin. Events, however, soon outran that strategy. Struggling to maintain control of the government and viability for the Soviet Union itself in the face of the revolutions across Eastern Europe, Gorbachev slated a nationwide referendum in mid-March 1991 on a proposed Union Treaty that would transform the USSR from a centralized union into a federation of semi-autonomous states. Nine republics, including Russia, voted in favor of the treaty, but, troublingly, six others boycotted the referendum. Moreover, Russia's flamboyant and ambitious leader, Boris Yeltsin—while nominally supporting Gorbachev's efforts—exhibited clear designs on greater power for himself and for Russia within the federation. It was downhill for Gorbachev from that point forward. In late April he met with leaders of the nine republics that had approved the federation, getting their agreement to work together to address the nation's problems, but at the cost of their increased role in government decision-making. In June, seven of the republics reached agreement on a revised Union Treaty that further decentralized the central government's powers.

The demise of the Soviet Union was underway. As the end neared, Gorbachev managed to occupy center stage with Bush one more time, meeting with him in Moscow for the signing of the Strategic Arms Reduction Treaty (START 1) on August 1. The culmination of the arms-reduction efforts begun by Reagan and Gorbachev in what was beginning to seem a long-ago period in U.S.–Soviet relations, START 1 produced huge reductions in inter-continental and sea-launched ballistic missiles, as well as airborne nuclear arms. While Bush was in the Soviet Union for the signing, erosion of that country's economy and governmental authority was in evidence everywhere. The president and his inner circle understood that Gorbachev's political end was likely, but he continued to give public support to his Soviet counterpart. Speaking to the Ukrainian Supreme Soviet on his way home from the treaty-signing, Bush delivered what seemed an ambivalent message to those within the Soviet Union who sought greater independence. In what was derided by critics as his "chicken Kiev" speech, he told his audience:

> [F]reedom is not the same as independence. Americans will not support those who seek independence in order to replace a far-off tyranny with a local despotism. They will not aid those who promote a suicidal nationalism based on ethnic hatred.

Events accelerated rapidly after Bush's return to the United States. In mid-August, a group of Kremlin hard-liners pulled off what looked to be a successful coup to remove Gorbachev from power while the latter was vacationing in the Crimea. Aided by immediate strong opposition to the coup from Yeltsin and his backers, the embattled Soviet leader managed to wrest back control from the conspirators, whom he then sent to prison. He paid a high price for Yeltsin's support, however, having to agree to resign as leader of the Soviet Communist Party, as well as replace his cabinet with a committee headed by one of the Russian president's closest political allies. The outcome, as the *New York Times* reported on August 24, represented "a virtually complete surrender by … Gorbachev to the liberal and democratic forces who had defied the coup and rescued him." Over the next few months, several of the constituent republics declared independence from the new federation; on December 8, a new Commonwealth of Independent States was formed. Yeltsin then set to work "assiduously to complete the dismantling of the USSR," writes Scowcroft, adding that "[i]t was painful to watch [him] rip the Soviet Union brick by brick away from Gorbachev, and then transfer most of them to Russia." By Christmas, Gorbachev had resigned and the Soviet Union was no more.

Bush never doubted the correctness of sticking with Gorbachev, rather than offering encouragement and support to Yeltsin and his democratic followers. In the wake of the failed August coup, he wrote in his diary that "If we had pulled the rug out from under Gorbachev and swung toward Yeltsin you'd have seen a military crackdown far in excess of the ugliness that's taking place now." There were reasons beyond the geopolitical for his steadfastness, as well. As historians have noted, Bush was inherently cautious and conservative, always preferring the stability of the known over the unknown. Too, he had bonded personally with Gorbachev, whose support during the Gulf War he greatly appreciated. If Bush's refusal to switch allegiances before Gorbachev's fall is understandable, however, his reluctance to provide significant aid to prop up Yeltsin and the new Russian government afterward is questionable. In February 1992, former president Nixon weighed in on the matter, charging publicly that the administration's response to Yeltsin's request for financial aid was "pathetically inadequate." Similarly, Bush seemed to lack vision for how to deal with post-Soviet problems in Eastern Europe. By July 1991, it was already clear that Yugoslavia was on the brink of civil war. Acknowledging the fact in his diary, Bush wrote: "This is one where I've told our top people, 'We don't want to put a dog in this fight.'" He added: "This concept that we have to work out every problem, everywhere in the world, is crazy." It seemed unlikely, however, that, having won the Cold War, the United States could enjoy the luxury of standing aside while the sorting out went forward.

In *The Presidency of George Bush*, John Robert Greene offers a generally favorable view of Bush's foreign policy, adding that "[f]undamental to his diplomacy was an improved relationship with the Soviet Union that led to the New World Order that he later claimed as his chief legacy." This assessment gives far more credit to Bush than seems warranted. He did not set out to establish an "improved relationship with the Soviet Union." In fact, the *pauza* during the first six months of his presidency reflected a greater distrust for Gorbachev than was harbored by his predecessor, and it ended—without the reflective analysis that had been promised—only because Bush feared what an isolated Gorbachev might do in response to the growing unrest in the Soviet Union's East European satellites. Moreover, as Jeffrey Engel observes in his essay in *41: Inside the Presidency of George H. W. Bush*, because of his inherent caution in the face of change, Bush "still rebuffed the idea that the Cold War was over" even after the Berlin Wall came down. "In truth," Engel writes, "he simply did not know what would come next. If the Cold War was over, what was America's global vision?" Bush never developed such a vision, preferring to deal with the here-and-now.

Greene's observation about Bush's having helped to create a New World Order is also overly generous. Bush did not even begin using that phrase until September 1990, and then only in the context of his need to garner support for a probable military response to Saddam Hussein's aggression in the Middle East.

Thereafter, he spoke of it more and more frequently, perhaps even believing that a new international system was rising from the rubble of the Cold War. While it is undeniable that much was new about the world during Bush's presidency, it seems a misnomer to have characterized such events as a new order. In fact, international affairs in those years could hardly have been more *dis*ordered. By the time Bush left the White House in January 1993, it was clear that old certainties in U.S. policy had not been replaced by new ones. Indeed, the new world appeared more unpredictable and perhaps even more dangerous than it had been during the Cold War. Nor did Bush himself appear to subscribe to the concept of a New World Order after the Gulf War was over. As Hal Brands writes, "[i]n several instances, Bush showed a marked lack of enthusiasm for intervention in conflicts that appeared to be ideal test cases for the New World Order, instead choosing to stay on the sidelines when vital interests were not at stake." Yugoslavia was one such test case; Haiti and Somalia were two others.

Whatever the limitations of Bush's cautious approach in foreign affairs, it is indisputable that he enjoyed the challenges of diplomacy far more than dealing with social and economic issues at home. "There's a story in one of the papers saying that I am more comfortable with foreign affairs," he wrote in his diary in October 1990, "and that is absolutely true. Because I don't like the deficiencies [*sic*] of the domestic, political scene." This overt preference made him an easy target for criticism. Typical was a Herblock cartoon that appeared in the *Washington Post* while the president was abroad for the signing of START 1 in late July 1991. Beneath a large placard carrying the message "Welcome to the U.S.A., George Bush—Have a Nice Visit," one would-be greeter turns and says to another, "Remember, he's not making the trip to our country to hear about our problems." As Bush neared the end of four years in office, facing the challenge of a re-election campaign with the U.S. economy in deep trouble, this cartoon seemed to say it all.

6

The Deepening Divide, 1992–2000

By 1992, nearly a decade of conflict between Republican presidents and Democratic Congresses had fostered twin dysfunctions: the conservative–liberal divide had grown ever sharper, while increasing numbers of voters were turned off altogether by politics and politicians. These phenomena made for slippery political terrain in a presidential election year. The problems facing each of the two parties differed sharply. For Democrats, the challenge was to carve out a new identity for a party whose message the voters had rejected in three consecutive presidential elections. The task for President Bush, who had neither resolved nor even fully faced the overwhelming problems left by his White House predecessor, was to persuade voters that he would somehow do so in a second term.

Bill Clinton's emergence as the candidate to beat in the Democratic primaries, and the resilience he demonstrated in winning the nomination, seemed to signal a new, energetic liberal era. The first "baby boomer" to occupy the White House, Clinton breathed new life into his party, but was not trusted by congressional Democrats—especially liberals. Moreover, serious missteps in his first two years in the White House dissipated public support

Deadlock and Disillusionment: American Politics since 1968, First Edition.
Gary W. Reichard.
© 2016 John Wiley & Sons, Inc. Published 2016 by John Wiley & Sons, Inc.

and allowed the GOP to recapture both houses of Congress. He would have to contend with a Republican Congress for the rest of his presidency. Perhaps the canniest politician to occupy the White House since FDR, Clinton was largely up to the challenge of dealing with divided government. House Republicans in particular attempted to thwart him at every turn, but their obstructionist tactics blew up in their faces, resulting in Clinton's easily winning re-election in 1996. Almost as soon as he was re-elected, however, unfolding scandals demanded his attention and impaired his ability to initiate change.

Even after revelation of a lurid White House sex escapade led to his impeachment by the House, the ever-resilient Clinton managed to keep his balance. With the public solidly behind him, the Senate turned back the articles of impeachment and Clinton rode out the rest of his term, helped by a wave of almost unprecedented prosperity. Despite all, he left the White House with an approval rating reminiscent of that of the famously popular Dwight Eisenhower four decades earlier. Clinton's personal popularity could not, however, mask the deep interparty divide that had opened wider during his presidency. It seemed inevitable that the 2000 election would be bitterly contested, whoever the candidates might be.

The Illusion of Liberal Revival

George Bush's victory in 1988 had strengthened the resolve of the New Democrats, exemplified by the Democratic Leadership Conference (DLC), to take over the party and choose the nominee for 1992. To win back Reagan Democrats, the party's message had to change. The DLC's first step was to identify a potential standard-bearer to carry this new agenda to the voters in 1992. They found a taker in Bill Clinton, the governor of Arkansas. For the ambitious Clinton, it was a good arrangement. He inherited a national staff, as well as access to an aggressive public relations operation, nearly two years before the 1992 primary season. On October 3, 1991, he announced his candidacy for the Democratic nomination.

The rest of the uninspiring Democratic field had already taken shape, including former senator Paul Tsongas of Massachusetts, former governor Jerry Brown of California, Governor Douglas Wilder of Virginia, and Senators Tom Harkin of Iowa and Bob Kerrey of Nebraska. Some of the strongest potential candidates (notably Mario Cuomo, Jesse Jackson, and Senator Bill Bradley of New Jersey) had opted out early, perhaps discouraged by President Bush's high approval ratings in the wake of the Gulf War triumph. Wilder's withdrawal in early January cleared Clinton's path in an important way, since now no black challenger could keep him from scoring big with black voters, as he had done in winning four gubernatorial elections in Arkansas.

The New Hampshire primary was critical for Clinton, as the acknowledged front-runner. His most dangerous challenger was Tsongas, who was expected to do well since he came from a neighboring state. Before Granite State voters could cast their ballots, Clinton suffered two body blows that threatened to knock him from the lead to oblivion. The first occurred in January, in the form of a salacious article in a supermarket tabloid dredging up a story from his Arkansas days about an affair with sometime night-club singer Gennifer Flowers. This was not the first time Clinton's private behavior had come under scrutiny. Experienced in fending off such stories from their Little Rock days, the candidate and his wife Hillary Rodham Clinton immediately went on the offensive, appearing on a special edition of the popular TV news show *Sixty Minutes*, to tell the American public that, though their marriage had not been without troubles, they remained deeply committed to one another. "Brilliantly," writes William Chafe in *Bill and Hillary: The Politics of the Personal*, "the Clintons had simultaneously exposed their emotional souls, defended their family's sanctity, and turned a debilitating personal weakness into a political strength." Overnight polls showed 80 percent of the public wanted Clinton to stay in the race.

Three weeks later—just days before the primary—another potentially devastating story appeared—this time in the *Wall Street Journal*. Focused on Clinton's draft history, the new account discussed a letter he had written in 1969, just after implementation of the draft lottery, resigning an ROTC slot he had sought in order to avoid the possibility of being drafted for service in Vietnam. Perhaps the most damning part of the report was that his belated willingness to risk being drafted had come only after his birthday had been assigned number 311 in the draft lottery—well below the threshold number for young men to be called in the subsequent year. There was nothing to be done to make this problem disappear; the candidate simply redoubled his campaign efforts, relying on charisma to push the story off the front pages.

Clinton's tireless efforts in the final days before the primary could not bring victory out of the ashes, but he finished a healthy second to Tsongas, earning him a nickname: "the Comeback Kid." After he swept every state except Massachusetts and Rhode Island on Super Tuesday, only Jerry Brown stood in the way of his nomination; he lost no major state the rest of the way, even becoming the first candidate ever to beat a Brown (Jerry or his father, Pat) in a California primary.

Having dispatched his Democratic rivals for the right to challenge the incumbent president, Clinton now faced another formidable obstacle: an unpredictable independent candidate. On the day Clinton won the California primary, the headlines glossed over his clinching the nomination to focus instead on polls showing Texas multimillionaire Ross Perot running ahead of both him and President Bush. Supremely self-confident and disdainful of what he claimed was a broken political system in Washington, Perot had announced in February that he would run as an independent if his supporters could get his name on the ballot in every state. His supporters did exactly that. Perot's support grew quickly, but his overbearing persona brought on problems. By July, he began to slip in the polls, with Bush taking a slight lead in the three-cornered race.

The Democratic convention afforded Clinton the chance to build momentum, and he seized the opportunity. Keeping firm control of the proceedings, he created a picture of a unified party and burnished his image via an emotional seventeen-minute film, "The Man from Hope," reminding voters that he had grown up in poverty in rural Arkansas, the son of a hard-working single

mother. His surprising selection of Tennessee senator Al Gore—
another moderate New Democrat in his mid-forties—was well
received, creating visible excitement in the convention hall.
Unexpectedly, on the day of Clinton's nomination, the ever-
inscrutable Perot folded up his candidacy, citing the "revitalization
of the Democratic party" as the main reason. Clinton blazed
ahead of Bush in the polls, opening up a double-digit lead after
having trailed all spring.

In contrast to Clinton's single-minded pursuit of his party's
nomination, the man who occupied the White House showed
little enthusiasm for the prospect of another national campaign.
Always thin-skinned, Bush had taken umbrage at sniping from
political opponents and media pundits after the glory of the Gulf
War victory had ebbed. In March 1991, he confided to his eldest
son, George W., that he was even unsure about running for re-
election. Although he soon pulled out of that funk, Bush delayed
putting in place any kind of re-election machinery until virtually
the eve of the primary season. As political scientist Hugh Heclo
observes in his essay in *41: Inside the Presidency of George H. W. Bush*,
the president's campaign organization "was by all accounts
languid, bordering on the comatose." The architect of his 1988
victory, the late Lee Atwater, was very much missed.

Even a superior campaign organization would have been
challenged by the problems weighing George Bush down in early
1992. By far his biggest problem was the economy. Layoffs were
increasing dramatically as 1991 ended, hitting white-collar as
well as blue-collar Americans. The huge budget deficit, with its
likely impact on interest rates, worried economists and voters
alike. Moreover, as Perot's popularity made clear, government
itself was seen as a huge problem—and Bush was the current
steward. The fact that the president appeared oblivious to the
rising tide of woe made matters even worse. Although forecasts
by the White House economic team suggested that recovery was
on the way (which it would be, by the third quarter of 1992),
Bush hurt his cause by failing to confront the issue head-on.

There was no chance that the president could be denied his
party's nomination, but to his conservative critics it looked as if

he could be roughed up and perhaps pushed rightward. The most strident of these was Pat Buchanan, who had been clobbering "King George" for more than a year from his pundit's perch on CNN's popular *Crossfire* talk show. Buchanan announced his candidacy for the Republican nomination in late 1991, and—with little money on hand, but plenty of vitriol—took off on the primary campaign trail against the president. After winning a respectable 36 percent of the New Hampshire vote, Buchanan lost nearly every remaining contest lopsidedly, but he remained a carping presence into the early summer and secured a prime-time role at the GOP convention as well as major platform concessions.

The Republican convention contrasted sharply with Clinton's coronation exercise in New York. Buchanan was the headliner on opening night and, as Geoffrey Kabaservice writes in *Rule and Ruin*, "declared a religious and cultural war against Democrats, feminists, and homosexuals," describing the Democratic ticket as "the most pro-gay and pro-lesbian ticket in history." On the second night, Marilyn Quayle, wife of the vice president, delivered a hard-edged address on family and traditional values. The GOP platform also reflected the values of the party's conservative right. Bush's acceptance speech did nothing to mitigate the convention's overall angry tone. Some party moderates were disgusted. "You don't build majorities by excluding whole groups of people," Senator Richard Lugar of Indiana told reporters, "and you don't have to be nasty to be conservative. … It is not a winning message."

That comment proved prophetic for Bush, who had to run on a platform far more extreme than his own views. In contrast to the pinched message of the GOP, Clinton and the Democrats were working to expand their party's reach into the broader electorate. The Clinton–Gore campaign manifesto, *Putting People First*, adhered closely to the New Democrat message, even while the two telegenic young running-mates held steady to "traditional liberal commitments" on social issues such as abortion rights. The contrast between the two campaigns, reinforced by the continuing economic recession, kept Clinton comfortably ahead of Bush in the polls going into the fall.

The election scenario was scrambled once again on October 1, however, when Perot surprisingly announced that he was re-entering the race. The polls immediately put him in double digits again. His re-entry complicated matters for Bush far more than for Clinton. The president had agreed only belatedly in late September to debate his Democratic challenger. Perot's re-emergence presented a dilemma. If the president now agreed to three-cornered debates, he would almost certainly be attacked on stage by both the other candidates. On the other hand, he needed to do something to change the dynamics of the race. In early October Bush relented, and three presidential debates were crammed into little more than a week between October 11 and 19. The gamble failed. Perot picked up little additional support from the debates, but Clinton gained substantially. The final Gallup poll before the election showed Clinton in the lead with 44 percent, followed by Bush at 36 percent, and Perot at 14.

The polls proved to be almost spot-on. Clinton's margin of victory in the popular vote was 43 percent to the president's 38 percent, and Perot's 19 percent. In the Electoral College, the result was a landslide: 370 electoral votes in the Democratic column and 168 for the president, with Perot not carrying a single state. After Bush's concession speech, the young president-elect and his wife appeared before a raucous band of supporters in Little Rock to launch the new era of change, dancing exuberantly on stage to their signature campaign song, Fleetwood Mac's "Don't Stop (Thinking About Tomorrow)."

There was reason for Clinton supporters to hope that a transformation had occurred. For the first time in nearly a generation, voter turnout had increased, with 55 percent of eligible voters coming to the polls. Moreover, Clinton's victory was national in scope. He carried all eleven states in the Northeast (and D.C.), six southern and border states, seven in the Midwest and Plains regions, and eight in the West. While the victor's big-tent strategy was effective in winning back large numbers of Reagan Democrats—particularly in the South and Midwest—the ticket also did well with traditional Democratic constituencies such as low-income voters, blacks, Hispanics, and those with lower levels of education. The gender gap that had appeared in 1988 widened further; Clinton's margin among women voters was 5 percent higher than among men (46 to 41 percent). Perot's impact turned out to be party-neutral. Polls indicated that he drew support in nearly equal measure from both of the other candidates.

Whatever enthusiasm for change the Clinton–Gore victory demonstrated, it did not translate to the races for Congress. Clinton had virtually no coattails to help Democrats down-ticket. In the Senate the party balance remained exactly the same, while the GOP actually picked up nine seats in the House. The so-called "Year of the Woman Candidate," however, increased the number of female House members from twenty-eight to forty-seven and women senators from two to six. Perhaps most significantly, for the first time since Reagan's first term, a single party controlled both the White House and Capitol Hill.

Optimism ran high after Clinton's victory. The new president gave a soaring Inaugural Address, evoking memories of JFK with his call for "a season of service" from young Americans. "Our democracy must be not only the envy of the world, but the engine of our own renewal," he said. "And so today, we pledge an end to the era of deadlock and drift." Within a few weeks, however, the new administration was foundering. It was immediately evident that the Democratic majorities in Congress did not represent automatic support for the new president. Moreover, the president's personal preoccupation with the vetting and selecting of Cabinet appointees during the transition period had left him no time to construct a meaningful legislative agenda.

Compounding Clinton's problem was that in his first post-election press conference, he gave a too-definitive affirmative response when asked whether he intended to act on his campaign promise to permit gays and lesbians to serve openly in the military. What had been just one of many campaign commitments was suddenly elevated to seem the administration's top legislative priority. Since no groundwork had been laid on this issue with the top military leadership or key congressional leaders, the repercussions were predictably disastrous. Clinton's effort to find a middle way on the gays-in-the-military issue failed utterly.

A few days before his inauguration, he worked with incoming defense secretary Les Aspin to craft a compromise whereby he would ask the military to cease asking potential recruits about their sexual orientation while the administration worked with the service branches to construct a more lenient policy. When members of the joint chiefs learned of the plan, they demanded an immediate audience with the president. Of greater concern, Georgia Democrat Sam Nunn, the powerful chair of the Senate Armed Services Committee, made it clear that he opposed ending the ban. Clinton was reduced to announcing, with Nunn by his side, that he would defer action on the issue for six months to allow time for study. In the meantime, the military would stop asking questions about sexual orientation, though service personnel found to be gay could still be discharged.

The issue rumbled along for nearly six months, finally being resolved in July by Clinton's announcement of what came to be known as "don't ask, don't tell"—approximately what JCS chief Colin Powell had proposed at the uncomfortable January meeting. Under the new policy, if a serviceman or -woman did not verbally acknowledge his or her homosexuality, the military would take no action. Deeply disappointing to Clinton's gay and lesbian supporters was the provision that any service member who either acknowledged same-sex attraction or was outed as such would be presumed likely to act on those tendencies and thus be subject to discharge. Given the strong hostility of the military leadership and the lack of public support, it seems unlikely that there was anything Clinton could have done to achieve a better outcome in the early 1990s.

"It's the economy, stupid!" was not just Clinton's campaign mantra; repairing the economy was his chief focus from the moment he entered the White House. In trying to develop an approach for reviving the economy, however, the new president confronted the dilemma of how to deal with the mountain of debt from more than a decade of Reaganomics. Meaningful action would require taxation—but what kind, and of whom? As a New Democrat, Clinton appreciated the need to rein in government programs and government spending in order to reduce the yawning deficit, but at the same time he wanted to extend portions of the government safety net for the poor and middle-class. To counter the GOP's likely obstructionism, Democratic unity would be imperative—but that was unlikely.

The protracted debate over development of a budget package eventually took a toll on Clinton's patience, while projecting a public image of the president as indecisive. The plan that he presented to Congress included an array of controversial provisions. The proposal included increases in selected social safety net programs, but the projected deficit reductions were twice the size of new spending. The administration's package gave almost every faction something to dislike. By late August, the White House had ginned up enough votes to produce a tie, so that Vice President Gore could cast the tie-breaking vote. Clinton was elated with the budget victory, proclaiming when he received word of the Senate vote: "What we heard tonight at the other end of Pennsylvania Avenue was the sound of gridlock breaking … ." Given that not a single Republican had voted for the measure, this was a gross exaggeration.

Although the budget struggle turned out positively for the administration, its other first-year policy initiative, health-care reform, ended disastrously and did substantial damage to the administration in the process. Throughout the 1992 campaign, Clinton had emphasized the need to address the plight of the 38 million Americans who lacked health insurance, as well as to contain rapidly escalating health-care costs. As president, he appointed the First Lady to lead a task force charged to develop the specific plan. This turned out to be a huge tactical error. Brilliant and ambitious, Hillary Rodham Clinton was a divisive figure—admired by feminists and liberals, but distrusted by conservatives as an elitist who was intent on pressing a radically liberal agenda. She had further ruffled feathers by insisting on an office in the West Wing (unprecedented for a First Lady) and limiting the access of the White House press corps. Her appointment to such a high-profile assignment in the first weeks of the new administration fueled the suspicion of critics that the Clintons intended a co-presidency, in which she, rather than the man who had been elected, would control the direction of domestic policy.

Figure 6.1 Bill and Hillary Clinton were the first couple to occupy the White House where the First Lady was a true partner in policy-making. Her most controversial role occurred in the first year of Clinton's presidency, when she headed a White House task force charged to develop a sweeping health-care plan that never became law. © Wally McNamee/CORBIS

Hillary Clinton's performance as co-chair of the task force initially won positive reviews, but her penchant for secrecy and unwillingness to compromise were soon in evidence. Months of behind-closed-doors hearings eroded public support for the task force and its planning process. The panel's proposal, announced in late July, placed responsibility on large employers to insure their employees, provided for federal subsidies to insure the poor, capped the cost of health insurance premiums, and called for state-level "health care alliances" that would bundle enrollments and serve as intermediaries with hospitals and other providers to keep down costs.

Before the health reform plan could gain any momentum, the administration's attention had been diverted to the nagging budget negotiations. Consequently, the White House had no time to educate the public about the complex proposal. On September 22,

Clinton finally unveiled the plan in a passionate speech to Congress, complete with a large red, white, and blue Health Security card as a prop; five weeks later, the health security bill— all 1342 pages of it—was delivered to Capitol Hill. Polls reflected that 60 percent of the public supported health-care reform in principle, but also that the details of the administration plan were not understood. "Not only was health reform forced to wait until after the budget passed Congress," writes Theda Skocpol in *Boomerang: Health Care Reform and the Turn Against Government*, "the delay greatly reduced prospects for congressional, press, and public understanding of the ... plan." As a result, "both health reform and the President himself lost credibility with the public and Congress."

By the end of the year, health-care reform was in deep trouble. The interests opposed to the plan—health insurers, the pharmaceutical industry, big corporations that would have to provide the bulk of the resources for their employees' coverage, and even smaller businesses that feared that their obligations might increase over time—flooded the airwaves with ads designed to fan fears about rising costs and red tape. "Ambitiously launched but poorly explained," writes Skocpol, "Health Security gave antigovernment conservatives exactly the target they were looking for—a proposed federal initiative that could be portrayed as threatening to the American middle class."

As the anti-health plan barrage grew in intensity and Hillary Clinton pressed her husband to resist suggestions for compromise from moderate Democrats, GOP leaders sensed an issue that could bring the party victory in the mid-term elections and pressured party members not to offer any suggestions to shape a more acceptable framework. Polls now showed that more Americans opposed health-care reform than supported it; Clinton's approach had failed totally. "By substituting regulation for revenues the Clinton team hoped to make the health plan palatable," write James MacGregor Burns and Georgia Sorensen in *Dead Center: Clinton-Gore Leadership and the Perils of Moderation.* "The tactic proved worse than useless." The death knell came in late summer when Senate majority leader George Mitchell told the president that there would be no health reform passed by the 103rd Congress. Furious with the Democratic congressional leadership for giving up, Hillary Clinton wanted to take the bill to the floor anyway, thereby forcing Republicans to take a stand and then face the consequences with the voters. This the president was unwilling to do. "The more cautious strategy won out," Hillary wrote later in her memoir, *Living History*, "and health care faded with barely a whimper."

Observers later speculated about whether Clinton could have secured passage of a more moderate health-care measure, perhaps one centered on an individual mandate concept. This seems unlikely, even if the president had been willing to resist his wife's urgings to stand firm for universal coverage. As David Bennett writes in *Bill Clinton: Building a Bridge to the New Millennium*, "a minimal program with thin and dubious financing would have failed to excite passionate supporters, would have stimulated vociferous resistance by liberals in the House, and probably would have faced the same kind of opposition by conservatives opposed to any plan." In any case, the final results could hardly have been worse for Clinton. With just three months remaining until the mid-term elections, as William Berman concludes in *From the Center to the Edge: The Politics & Policies of the Clinton Presidency*, the health-care proposal had "become a millstone around the neck of the Democratic Party."

As the elections approached, the administration could point to a few positive achievements. One was the budget bill, though its implications for future deficit reduction were not yet fully appreciated. Clinton had also made good use of his first opportunity to fill a seat on the Supreme Court in mid-1993, gaining easy Senate confirmation for respected District of Columbia Circuit Court judge Ruth Bader Ginsburg. Her appointment to replace the conservative Byron "Whizzer" White moved the court to the left and added a second female justice. Substantive legislative achievements included the creation of a national service program, AmeriCorps, and passage of both a crime control bill and the Brady Handgun Violence Prevention Act. The crime bill was popular for its addition of 100,000 community-based policemen in the streets of America's towns and cities, but it also included a ban on assault weapons that, coupled with the background checks and five-day waiting period for the purchase of handguns that were required by the Brady bill, galvanized the powerful National Rifle Association (NRA) in opposition to Clinton and the Democrats.

Although Clinton's policies were liberal enough to re-energize the Republican right, they frustrated liberals in his own party. An example was his welfare reform proposal. Acting on his campaign promise to "end welfare as we know it," Clinton proposed to convert welfare to "workfare" and impose a five-year lifetime limit on individual welfare recipients. Carrying a $9 billion price tag for workforce training, the bill never even made it to committee hearings. Even more costly to Democratic unity was Clinton's embrace of the North American Free Trade Agreement (NAFTA), which the Bush administration had negotiated but which required legislative approval before it could be implemented. Clinton was committed to the principle of free trade but knew that organized labor viewed the agreement between Canada, Mexico, and the United States as a job-killer for Americans. In this instance, he was greatly aided by public support from former presidents Ford, Carter, and Bush, who flanked him on stage as he made his case for the treaty in September 1993. It passed the House in mid-November by a vote of 234-200, with only 100 Democrats voting in favor. In the Senate, the battle lines were similar, as nearly equal numbers of Republicans and Democrats joined together to produce a 61-38 affirmative vote. Clinton signed NAFTA into law on December 8, 1993—a victory for the president, but at considerable cost to his relations with labor leaders and party liberals.

Clinton carried other heavy baggage into the mid-term elections, as well. In March 1993, the Justice Department had decided to end federal law enforcement officers' siege of the compound of David Koresh and his Branch Davidian followers—suspected of weapons violations for the large cache of guns they had amassed—opting instead to launch a raid on the buildings. Attorney General Janet Reno later noted that she had asked Clinton to authorize the siege because of reports that David Koresh was sexually abusing some of the women, including minors, among his followers.

Soon after the raid commenced, everything went terribly wrong. After releasing some of the children, Koresh and his remaining followers set fire to their compound, with the result that eighty cult members—including twenty-five children—died. In the anger and confusion that followed, Reno responded to press inquiries before Clinton did, creating the false impression that he was unwilling to take responsibility for the incident. "I was furious at myself," Clinton wrote in his memoirs, "first for agreeing to the raid against my better judgment, then for delaying a public acknowledgment of responsibility for it."

Far more damaging to the White House were investigations of both Clintons that had begun almost as soon as they moved into the White House. One centered on Hillary Clinton's abrupt dismissal of the head of the White House travel office (which handled arrangements for the White House press corps), along with six colleagues, for alleged mismanagement. The First Lady's precipitate action before allowing time for the accused to respond to her concerns led to criticism of her imperious manner and—more damagingly—to accusations that the dismissals were part of a plot to redirect White House travel business to a longtime Clinton friend. "Travelgate," as it was instantly labeled by the media, amounted to nothing substantive, but turned out to be the first in a long succession of scandals—real and invented—that would plague the Clinton White House. Much more serious was the fallout from the July 1993 suicide of Assistant White House Counsel Vince Foster, an associate of the First Lady's in Little Rock's Rose law firm and one of her closest friends. In Washington, Foster was the guardian of most of the Clintons' financial records. It was ultimately determined that his suicide was what it seemed—the final act of a desperately unhappy person—but before its resolution the incident invited an irresistible new line of attack for the Clintons' detractors. The most vitriolic anti-Clinton radio and TV commentators even suggested that the president and/or First Lady might have had something to do with Foster's death; such conspiracy theorists also relentlessly raised the suspicion that the death was connected to what Foster might have known about the Clintons' possible malfeasance in an Arkansas land deal known as Whitewater.

Whitewater had flared briefly as an issue during the 1992 campaign, but had faded after an audit revealed the Clintons had lost serious money by investing in the property. Near the end of 1993, the issue emerged again as part of an investigation into the financial conduct of the Clintons' longtime friend, banker Jim McDougal. The couple was alleged to have used influence in securing loans for McDougal. Still raw from the charges that had been flung at them in connection with Foster's death and nervous about what their private papers might contain about her possible conflict-of-interest violations at the Rose law firm, Hillary persuaded the president to tough it out and refuse to supply the requested files. This stance predictably encouraged their attackers. In January, the president reluctantly asked Attorney General Reno to appoint an independent investigator—another tactical error. Neither the appointment of New York attorney Robert Fiske in that capacity nor Fiske's conclusion in June that the Clintons had done nothing illegal could quiet media speculation about possible malfeasance by one or both of the Clintons. In August, the outlook for the administration grew darker when a three-judge panel of the D.C. Circuit Court of Appeals charged with appointing independent counsels replaced Fiske with Kenneth Starr, claiming that since Fiske had been appointed by Clinton's attorney general, he had a conflict of interest. The fact that Starr had served as Bush's solicitor general and had a history of association with conservative organizations made him at least equally susceptible to a charge of conflict of interest, but from the opposite direction. Nonetheless, Starr was authorized to begin the entire investigation anew, ensuring that Whitewater would have a long life during Clinton's presidency.

Most of Bill Clinton's problems in his first two years in the White House stemmed from the health-care fiasco and the unfolding Whitewater drama. Both of these sets of problems had gone wrong largely due to his deference to Hillary in matters of strategy (and, in the case of health care, substance as well). This pattern of deference, as Chafe argues, reflected a "personal partnership the president and First Lady had negotiated in their political lives," which was a direct result of Clinton's often reckless extramarital exploits as governor. Hillary's bailout of her husband on the eve of the New Hampshire primary had been the most recent evidence of her part of the bargain; it would not be the last. "[B]y making himself eternally indebted to Hillary for forgiving his infidelities," observes Chafe, Clinton had put himself in the position of having to yield influence to her whenever she held strong opinions on policy and tactical matters. Her no-compromise stance and penchant for secrecy in connection with both health-care planning and Whitewater had produced demonstrably negative consequences. An important question, going forward, was whether the first couple would continue this pattern and risk a downward spiral of a presidency that had begun with such high hopes.

Amidst the troubles, the familiar issue of Clinton's pre-presidential sexual improprieties once again reared its head—this time in the form of a renewed allegation by nightclub dancer Paula Jones that, while governor, he had made inappropriate advances toward her that amounted to sexual harassment. Given what was known about his past, the three-year-old case represented a believable scenario—one more problem that had to be dealt with in mid-term election season. Jones's allegations ultimately became an even greater headache for the president. As was already beginning to be clear, the pattern of scandals stealing headlines from positive accomplishments would be a constant throughout Clinton's presidency. "In Clinton's world," wrote George Stephanopoulos in *All Too Human: A Political Education*, years after serving as Clinton's White House communications director, "good news rarely arrived without a shady companion."

The Politics of Triangulation

Having arrived in the White House with the intention of moving the New Democrat agenda, Clinton knew he would have to count on support from the moderate wing of the GOP. The Republicans' utter refusal to cooperate from the outset, however, laid waste to such hopes, leading to months of conflict and little legislative progress. The personification of Republican negativism was House

GOP minority whip Newt Gingrich, whose rise had been propelled by his no-holds-barred, hyperbolic style and willingness to attack anyone in his way. Nominally the number two Republican in the House behind moderate minority leader Bob Michel of Illinois, Gingrich had taken over as chief strategist for the new, younger conservative House members who favored unrestricted warfare against the Democrats. Senate majority leader Dole was instinctively more pragmatic but, with presidential ambitions of his own, was intent on carving out points of difference from the president and his policies. In addition to facing this stone wall of opposition on the other side of the aisle in both houses, the administration was under sustained heavy assault by a battalion of right-wing radio and television talk show hosts, whose main objective seemed to be to fuel public anger. Gingrich and his followers hoped to draw on such right-wing fury to ensure that the GOP would take control of Congress in the 1994 mid-term elections.

The Democrats appeared increasingly vulnerable, as accumulating problems sank Clinton's approval ratings to 40 percent by late spring of 1994. Aiming to turn the elections into a referendum on the administration, Gingrich heaped abuse on the president, deriding him as the most far-left president of the twentieth century. In late September, to dramatize the GOP's rejection of the administration and all it stood for, Gingrich gathered 350 of his colleagues for a flamboyant spectacle on the Capitol steps: the ceremonial signing of a "Contract with America," which would be the GOP's platform for the congressional elections. "The ceremony, like the contract itself, was designed for the media" writes Steven Gillon in *The Pact: Bill Clinton, Newt Gingrich, and the Rivalry that Defined a Generation*. Social wedge issues were absent from the document, which focused instead on traditional conservative issues such as balancing the budget, cutting social services, and reducing the size and power of the federal government.

The GOP strategy succeeded brilliantly, as the party captured both houses of Congress for the first time in four decades. The Senate, which had been controlled by the Democrats 56-44, shifted to a Republican majority of 52-48. As further evidence of the scope of the disaster, two sitting Democrats, Richard Shelby of Alabama and Ben Nighthorse Campbell of Colorado, changed their party allegiance, padding the GOP majority to 54-46. The overall shift of ten seats in the Senate was seismic—nearly equaling the Republican sweep in 1980. Results in the House were even more dramatic: a pickup of fifty-four seats by the GOP, surpassing in magnitude the influx of Democrat "Watergate babies" after Nixon's resignation in 1974. Even worse, from the perspective of the White House, Congressman Michel's retirement meant that Gingrich would be elevated to the position of Speaker in the 104th Congress. The anti-Clinton tide surged everywhere, knocking out Democratic superstars such as Governors Mario Cuomo of New York and Ann Richards of Texas (who lost to former president Bush's son, George W.), and ousting the Speaker of the House, Tom Foley. A particularly notable result of the elections was the GOP's showing in the South. While that region had become increasingly reliable for Republicans at the presidential level since Nixon's initial election, only one southern state had a GOP-majority House delegation going into the 1994 elections; now seven southern states had Republican majorities, reflecting a profound political change that would grow more pronounced in subsequent elections. The Christian Coalition played an important role in producing these results. One exit poll indicated that more than 20 percent of voters identified as evangelicals or born-again Christians, three-fourths of whom had voted for GOP candidates. "Gods, gays, guns, and Clinton" seemed to explain the anti-Democrat tide.

Shell-shocked, Clinton privately expressed the hope that Gingrich and his troops might misread the results as a mandate for extremism and therefore overreach. The stinging defeat led the president to question his fundamental leadership style and strategy and whether or not he had the right people in place to help him negotiate the new political terrain. Not only did the opposition now control both houses, but the defeat of so many southern moderates had shifted the center of gravity among congressional Democrats farther to the left. Even prior to the election, Clinton had felt it necessary to reach out to an old political advisor from

Arkansas days, Dick Morris, to help him to figure out how to improve his position. The First Lady, discouraged and chastened by the bitter experiences of the first two years in the White House, concurred. Attempting to recover from the electoral disaster, Clinton drew increasingly close to Morris. The consultant had a well-deserved reputation for a big ego, hardheadedness, and callousness as a political operative. As Stephanopoulos put it, Morris was "the dark Buddha whose belly Clinton rubbed in desperate times"—and these were desperate times.

Morris was certain of what Clinton should do. Trying to split the difference between the positions of the two parties had not worked, he pointed out; with the GOP emboldened by victory and the Democratic caucus tilting further to the left, maintaining that failed strategy would be disastrous. His advice was to "triangulate"—that is, seek to create policy positions separate from those of the two parties in congress that were not simply compromises. In doing so, Morris argued, the president should co-opt the most popular elements of the Republican program, such as reducing the deficit, the size of government, and the scope of regulation, and meld them with ideas appealing to traditional Democratic constituencies—such as social services, affirmative action, and concern for the environment.

Clinton bought the idea, rolling out his new strategy in his 1995 State of the Union Address. The speech ran for an hour and a half—the longest such address in history. In it, he returned to the core ideas he had promulgated before his election: smaller government, tax reductions, and elimination of the deficit. The speech was a tremendous success—interrupted almost a hundred times by applause—and, despite its length, praised by the media. Gingrich and his Republican colleagues still had the momentum, however. Following through on his boast that the House would vote on all ten items in the Contract within a hundred days, the new Speaker whipped seven of them through by early April.

At this point, Clinton was aided by an otherwise terrible event: the bombing of the Alfred P. Murrah Federal Building in Oklahoma City, which killed 168 and injured nearly 700 more. Clinton went on the air immediately to denounce the act of terrorism and promise that "we will find the people who did this." For once he got lucky; within hours, the bomber, an anti-government militiaman named Timothy McVeigh, was captured after having been pulled over for a minor traffic infraction not far from Oklahoma City. Two accomplices were arrested shortly afterward. At the memorial held for the bombing victims, Clinton delivered an inspiring sermon-like address that underscored his skill as "comforter-in-chief" in time of crisis. Polls reflected 84 percent approval of his handling of the nerve-shattering events of the week. Taking advantage of the opening, the president delivered a follow-up address in Minneapolis in which he denounced "those loud and angry voices in America today whose sole goal seems to be to keep some people as paranoid as possible and the rest of us torn up and upset with each other." His words could have applied as much to politicians and media hate-mongers who fed on conflict as to the violence-prone militia members so recently in the news.

By Memorial Day, Clinton had resolved to reclaim the initiative—starting with the budget issue. As part of the Contract with America, Gingrich had been pushing for a budget that would lead to a zero deficit in seven years, requiring painful cuts in programs such as Medicare and Medicaid, while granting tax reductions to higher-income taxpayers. This GOP budget, rather than the proposal submitted by the White House, became the center of political discussion. Putting the triangulation strategy into action, Clinton quickly submitted a plan that would also achieve a balanced budget, but in ten years rather than the GOP's seven, substituting a middle-class tax cut for the reduction proposed for upper-income taxpayers, and providing for lesser cuts in Medicare, Medicaid, and other popular programs that would be hammered by the GOP plan. Congressional Democrats howled, but polls showed strong public approval of the White House's offer of a credible alternative to the Republican plan.

Gingrich was confident that he could force acceptance of the GOP plan by threatening a government shutdown when the budget expired. The impasse continued into the fall. Clinton, banking on the likelihood that the public would not accept drastic

191

cuts in basic social services, never wavered. With supreme confidence, the Republican House leadership continued to assume that the White House would cave when the final continuing resolution expired in mid-November. Senate majority leader Dole was a dissenter, fearing potential negative consequences for the GOP in 1996, when he might challenge Clinton for the White House, but he could get nowhere with his party colleagues. The Speaker's House lieutenants, majority leader Dick Armey and whip Tom DeLay, both tough-talking Texans, were even more intransigent than the Speaker. A last-ditch White House meeting as the clock ticked down on November 13 ended badly—and the government was temporarily closed for business.

The advantage had clearly shifted to Clinton. Emboldened by the failure of his party's scorched earth approach, Dole began to work seriously with the White House on a compromise. These efforts were sufficiently promising that on November 19 Congress passed another continuing resolution, reopening government and providing a second window of time to achieve final agreement. With polls now reflecting strong public opposition to a shutdown, even Gingrich was ready to deal, but his hard-line lieutenants and the rebellious GOP freshmen stubbornly resisted. Talks bogged down again, and in mid-December, "non-essential" federal offices closed down.

The outcome of the budget standoff was now inevitable—and no one knew that more surely than the veteran Dole. When New Year's Eve negotiations proved fruitless, he announced that Senate Republicans would vote with the Democrats to end the shutdown. On January 2, the Senate passed a measure to fund the government for another ten days; the chastened House then voted an even longer extension to permit final negotiations. After a few more weeks of haggling, the battle was over. Gingrich's arrogance had trumped common sense and created a turning point that no one could have predicted two months earlier.

Although the budget battle was his most important victory-by-triangulation, Clinton enjoyed additional political wins in 1995, as well. In addition to vetoing a bill banning late-term abortions, he successfully pushed a grab-bag of measures that had broad public support, including bills giving the government greater control over tobacco advertising, raising the minimum wage, providing tax credits for child adoption, and allowing employees to carry their health insurance with them when changing jobs. Most valuable politically, perhaps, the president crafted an artful approach to the knotty problem of affirmative action, once again a divisive social issue. With 1996 presidential politics increasingly the context, all likely Republican hopefuls were staking out positions in opposition to "racial preferences." Speaking in July at the National Archives, Clinton delivered one of his patented blockbuster speeches. The issue, he said, was essentially how to continue successfully on "America's rocky but fundamentally righteous journey to close the gap between the ideals enshrined in these treasures here ... and the reality of our daily lives." Affirmative action might present difficult choices, he held, but the right answer was to "mend it, don't end it." The phrase became a White House byword, reaffirming the Democratic party's commitment to the principle while allowing room for judges and legislators to negotiate the details. By finding a path through this thicket, the president likely averted the possibility of an independent candidacy by Jesse Jackson in 1996 that could have been ruinous for him.

Almost miraculously, Clinton now had reason for optimism as he looked toward the 1996 election. The outcome of the budget showdown had largely neutralized Gingrich and his rowdy troops and, combined with the president's deft handling of other issues, produced strong public approval ratings at just the right time. Moreover, in November former JCS chairman Colin Powell, whose enormous popularity would have made him a formidable opponent, announced that he would not seek the presidency.

Dark clouds were gathering as well, however. It was becoming clear that Kenneth Starr, the court-appointed special investigator into the Whitewater miasma, would be less an open-minded fact-gatherer than an aggressive prosecutor. Although the White House had continued to deflect subpoenas for documents related to the land deal, pressures for their release grew inexorably. In December 1995, Hillary Clinton made an awkward admission that the subpoenaed records had suddenly been found in a "storage closet," and they were subsequently turned over to Starr and his staff. As the Whitewater inquiry continued, Republicans in Congress ramped up investigations of administration activities on other fronts, including the long-simmering Travelgate episode and other, mostly minor issues. The Contract with America having failed as a long-term strategy, it appeared that an investigative strategy might be the GOP's tactic of choice for 1996.

Going on the offensive, Clinton used his 1996 State of the Union Address as a springboard for his upcoming re-election campaign. "The era of big government is over," he proclaimed to the amazement of many, including especially his Democratic colleagues in Congress. In the remainder of the address, however, he signaled a continuing commitment to activist government for the "right" reasons, emphasizing issues related to family values, but couched differently from the way Christian conservatives had defined them.

At least two candidates, Dole and Senator Phil Gramm of Texas, seemed to have the high profile and fund-raising capacity to get off to a quick start in the 1996 GOP primary contests. Dole had steadily polled ahead of all other GOP rivals by a margin of at least 40 percent throughout 1995; late in the year he decided to make the race. Gramm began in a much weaker position, enjoying strong name recognition but lacking the ability to connect with everyday voters. Several other potential candidates—including Jack Kemp, Dick Cheney, and Dan Quayle—removed themselves from the race early. Other possibilities were longshots, at best: Buchanan, who had demonstrated no capacity to attract supporters beyond the extreme right; Senator Lamar Alexander of Tennessee, who had served as Bush's first secretary of education but lacked a national following; and millionaire businessman Steve Forbes, a political neophyte who jumped into the race with an anti-establishment appeal similar to Perot's in 1992—though possessed of a much warmer demeanor. Forbes was willing to spend $25 million of his own money to bankroll his candidacy, which centered almost exclusively on his proposal for a flat tax to replace the nation's complex graduated income tax structure.

As in 1992, Dole won the Iowa caucuses, driving Gramm out of the race, and moved hopefully to New Hampshire. Once again, however, the Granite State threw Dole for a loop, as Buchanan edged him out there. Forbes, though barely cracking double digits, enjoyed a tremendous press, appearing in late January on the covers of both *Time* and *Newsweek*. His Pied Piper-like promise of the flat tax as panacea so worried the others that they sharply escalated the level of negativism in their advertisements. These concerted attacks took a heavy toll on Forbes, whose poll numbers began a steady decline. When Dole won South Carolina handily and then swept fifteen states in the early weeks of March, the nomination was his.

Once again the general election campaign began much too early. Running way behind the president in the polls, Dole announced in mid-May that he would resign from the Senate so that he could devote full attention to his campaign—with "nothing to fall back on but the judgment of the people of the United States and nowhere to go but the White House or home." Any benefit he derived from this dramatic gesture was canceled out, however, by his consistent gaffes on the campaign trail. At one point, he seemed to challenge the scientific consensus that smoking was addictive; soon after, he suggested that the head of the National Association for the Advancement of Colored People (NAACP) was "trying to set him up" by inviting him to address the group at its national convention. On the positive side, Dole's selection of Jack Kemp as his running-mate was applauded within the party. Like Bush before him, however, Dole found it difficult to negotiate hot-button issues such as abortion. While he did not repeat Bush's mistake of allowing the party's right fringe to dominate the GOP convention in San Diego, his acceptance speech set a distinctly backward-looking tone, as he linked Clinton with a "baby boomer elite who never grew up, never did anything real, never sacrificed, never suffered, never learned," and concluded by promising to build a bridge back to a "better past of tranquility, faith, and confidence in the nation."

As might have been expected from Clinton's triangulation approach, the bills that found their way into law during election season reflected no consistent ideology. Most pleasing to the right was the Defense of Marriage Act (DOMA), defining marriage as a union between a man and a woman and permitting states not to recognize same-sex marriages performed in another state, for which even Democrats voted two-to-one in favor. Though criticizing the measure as "divisive and unnecessary," Clinton signed it into law. Recognizing that this harsh legislation had alienated liberal Democrats as well as the party's gay and lesbian constituency, Clinton worked with Ted Kennedy—unsuccessfully—to try to secure passage of a proposed Employment Non-Discrimination Act (ENDA) to extend non-discrimination protection to cover sexual orientation.

A second bill enacted during the heat of the 1996 presidential campaign, the cumbersomely named Personal Responsibility and Work Opportunity Reconciliation Act, was far more beneficial politically to Clinton than DOMA. A major Clinton campaign promise in 1992, welfare reform had been delayed by the administration's decision—most unwise, in retrospect—to concentrate first on health care. The president was now intent on achieving welfare reform legislation before the election. By late July, a bill had been worked out. Although Clinton was unhappy with some of its provisions, such as denial of food stamps and medical care to future legal immigrants, he knew that time was running out and so signaled that the bill would still achieve his goal of "ending welfare as we know it." Republicans in both houses supported the bill almost unanimously, with Democrats closely divided. As signed into law in August, the bill ended the Aid to Families with Dependent Children (AFDC) program, which served approximately 1.5 million children, replacing it with a Temporary Assistance to Needy Families (TANF) program, capped at five years per family. Central to the reform was the requirement that adult recipients seek work within two years. Unpopular as it was with liberals, welfare reform proved to be a quick success: aided by the prosperity of the late 1990s, welfare rolls would shrink by 60 percent, from 14.1 million to just under 6 million and child poverty would also decrease. After passage of the measure, the GOP looked for other ways to cooperate with the White House, hoping to shed the onus of obstructionism. "Implicit in the newly cooperative Republican strategy," observes John Harris in *The Survivor: Bill Clinton in the White House*, "was that legislators were giving up on [Dole] ... and looking out for themselves."

By the end of summer, it was clear that Dole could not close Clinton's double-digit lead in the polls. The ever-erratic Perot had also again entered the field as an independent candidate, carrying the banner of a new Reform party, but this time generated little enthusiasm. Despite his solid lead, Clinton campaigned energetically, honing his centrist message while drawing sharp distinctions between his party and the GOP on vital issues such as social security, Medicare, Medicaid, support for education, and environmental protection. Dole, frustrated at trailing an opponent whom he considered to have serious character flaws, became more and more intemperate, taking to shouting during his speeches, "Where's the outrage? Wake up, America!" As the contest entered its final stages, Clinton turned his attention to key congressional races, hoping to help the Democrats regain control of Congress.

The election results were strikingly similar to those of four years earlier. Clinton won the Electoral College by 379-159, losing only three states he had carried the first time (Colorado, Georgia, and Montana) and winning two that he had lost (Arizona and Florida). The popular vote, too, was similar to 1992: Clinton fell short of a majority, winning just over 49 percent, but he received 3 million more votes than he had won against Bush; Dole received almost exactly the same number of votes as Bush had (just under 41 percent), while Perot received only about 40 percent of his 1992 vote. Clinton again ran up his highest margins among lower-income voters, blacks, Hispanics, Catholics, and Jews, as well as with those with both less than a high-school education and more than a college education. Disturbingly, turnout was dramatically lower than in recent elections—the second lowest in modern times, at 49 percent of eligible voters. The very low turnout among Democratic voters likely accounted for Clinton's falling short of the double-digit margin of victory that had been predicted. Dole's showing would have been worse, but for revelations of Democratic campaign fund-raising irregularities in the final days of the campaign.

The congressional elections were disappointing to Clinton, however. The GOP held on to its majorities in both houses, picking up two seats in the Senate to increase its majority to 55-45, and losing only three in the House, leaving the party with a majority of 227-206 (with two independents). In the House, the "southernization" of the GOP was almost complete; after the 1996 elections all but two former Confederate states (Texas and Virginia) had Republican-dominated delegations.

Although Clinton saw his re-election as public endorsement of New Democrat principles and confirmation of his triangulation strategy, he was only partly right. Exit polls on election day recorded that 55 percent believed the country was moving in the right direction, but the outlook was not entirely positive. The temporary pragmatism of congressional Republicans seeking to re-establish their credibility had allowed legislative progress in late 1996, but Dole's crushing defeat increased disaffection on the right. "[H]aving swallowed their pride and followed ... Dole in order to win," wrote Wilson Carey McWilliams in Pomper's post-election volume, *The Election of 1996: Reports and Interpretations*, "social conservatives were forced to endure a humiliating combination of neglect and defeat." He added: "They conclude that, all things being equal, Republicans cannot defeat Democrats in an election that turns on economics and government programs. ... [T]hey argue for the need to *define* campaigns in terms of social and moral issues."

Even in victory, Clinton pledged that he would work cooperatively with the opposition-controlled Congress. "The American people returned to office a president of one party and a Congress of another," he said in his second Inaugural Address. "Surely they did not do that to advance the politics of petty bickering and extreme partisanship they plainly deplore. No, they call on us to be repairers of the breach." In his 1997 State of the Union message, the president called for only minor initiatives: enlargement of Head Start, public education reform, and expansion of NAFTA.

On Capitol Hill, a sobered Gingrich seemed inclined to take a similar tack, as he fought back a potential coup attempt by the party's most conservative House members and then pulled his GOP troops into civilized negotiations with the White House on the fiscal 1998 budget.

The ensuing budget discussions differed dramatically from those two years earlier. As Harris writes, there was an "understanding that differences were going to be split—no 'train wrecks' this time." On August 5, with a beaming Gingrich standing over his shoulder, Clinton signed the fiscal 1998 budget bill into law, including the largest tax cut since the 1980s but also modest increases in spending for education and children's health. Once again, however, Clinton's practical approach alienated a significant segment of his party's left; House majority leader Gephardt was joined by about 40 percent of House Democrats in voting no on the compromise budget.

As Gillon observes in *The Pact*, the bipartisan cooperation that produced the 1998 budget agreement might well have been the first of several "grand bargains" if Clinton and Gingrich had been able to control events. The strength of the economy was a great advantage; annual economic growth stood at more than 4 percent, unemployment was less than 5 percent, and the deficit was disappearing faster than anyone had predicted. Clinton, however, was under intense pressure from Special Investigator Starr and his minions, who seemed intent on expanding the boundaries of the Whitewater investigation, and Gingrich lacked the control over his colleagues that he had once possessed. As Gillon writes, the Speaker "now viewed himself more as a reformer than a revolutionary"—a position that Armey, DeLay, and other vociferous conservatives did not share. Their loyalty to Gingrich was at best suspect. The bruises Clinton had inflicted on his party's liberal wing were also a growing problem. When the White House moved to expand free trade beyond NAFTA by pushing for fast-track legislation that would limit Congress to only a yes-no vote on any proposed executive trade agreement, Gephardt and his liberal followers joined with conservative Republicans to block the measure.

Undaunted, Clinton and Gingrich continued to lay private plans—unbeknownst at the time even to Vice President Gore—to establish a centrist coalition that could enact major revisions of Social Security and Medicare. This most unlikely partnership, had it succeeded, might have produced a political transformation. The two leaders shared the belief, according to Gillon, that if "they could create an enduring legislative majority that could address real problems ... [t]he American public would reward them for their success, creating an incentive for other political leaders to reject partisanship and participate in a bipartisan coalition." In mid-January 1998, however, as they were still shaping these ambitious plans, the *Washington Post* published a front-page story about the president's alleged misdeeds with a young White House intern. Hopes for bipartisan cooperation evaporated, as the president was forced into a fight for his political life.

Quest for a Post-Cold War Foreign Policy

"No other modern American president inherited a stronger, safer international position than Bill Clinton," writes foreign policy specialist William Hyland in *Clinton's World: Remaking American Foreign Policy*. With the end of the Cold War and dissolution of the Soviet Union, the United States stood unchallenged as the world's only superpower. In the 1992 campaign, Clinton had criticized President Bush's conduct of foreign affairs only at a general level, focusing on the president's passivity in the face of human rights abuses in such places as Somalia and Haiti and Bush's failure to assert a vision for the post-Cold War world.

When Clinton entered the White House, the world's lone superpower did indeed lack vision and purpose in its foreign policy. The basic challenge was to define the nation's interests clearly in this new world, and to lead the American people to implement the policies needed to advance those interests. Clinton was not dealing with a *tabula rasa*, however; there were controlling parameters. "Isolationism was never a viable alternative," Hyland writes. "The real debate was between two categories of international Realists: between those who conceived the national interest in broadly traditional terms—to protect the nation's territory, wealth, and access to necessary goods—and those who would pursue policies of disinterested globalism." Clinton seemed certain to choose "globalism," a phrase that implied a commitment to worldwide economic interconnectedness in an increasingly democratic and market-oriented international environment.

Clinton's greatest challenge in foreign policy was that there was no longer a Cold War on which the public could focus. In the absence of a clear and present enemy, the electorate seemed to have lost interest in foreign policy altogether. Even when the president became convinced that something had to be done on the world stage, the American people were hard to convince, if they were willing to pay attention at all. His attempts to handle three major crises inherited from the Bush years—in Somalia, Haiti, and Bosnia—revealed how difficult it was to engage the public behind meaningful U.S. involvement abroad, especially if it might require sacrifice or military action.

Somalia presented an ugly problem for the incoming administration. Bush's commitment of 20,000 U.S. troops to a UN peacekeeping effort in late 1992 left Clinton with no attractive options. The Senate approved a non-binding resolution in early February 1993 approving the mission but also explicitly referencing the timelines set by the War Powers Resolution. Senate Democratic majority leader Mitchell observed tartly that "UN Security Council resolutions are no substitute for congressional authorization." Clinton, not interested in a showdown over war powers in a conflict to which he did not assign high priority, committed immediately to reduce U.S. forces to 4500 by spring. Even this troop reduction was insufficient to ward off Republican criticisms of the administration for its flouting of the War Powers Resolution, however. By early summer, the role of the UN mission was clearly shifting from humanitarian relief to quasi-combatant. The costs of this "mission creep" became clear in early October, when a botched effort to capture Somalian warlord Mohamad Farah Aidid in the capital city of Mogadishu failed disastrously, with two U.S. Black Hawk helicopters being shot down, eighteen American soldiers killed, and dozens wounded. Televised images of the body of a slain U.S. soldier being dragged through the streets of Mogadishu produced anger and revulsion in Congress as well as among the broader public, increasing pressure on the administration to find an honorable way out of the deepening mess.

Clinton now "felt trapped between ... bad options," as Stephanopoulos later wrote in his memoir, either "accepting failure by abandoning an ill-conceived operation, or avenging [U.S.] losses by going in with 'decisive force.'..." With polls showing that less than a third of American voters supported keeping U.S. troops in Somalia, the president announced a temporary buildup of some 1700 additional forces but set a deadline of March 1994 for withdrawal. The difficulty in exiting from Somalia made him averse to becoming further involved in Africa; he refused even to consider intervening in Rwanda, despite an estimated 800,000 deaths there at the hands of Hutu extremists. Responding to press questions about U.S. intentions in the face of this genocide, Clinton explained, "there is a political and military element to this" that outsiders could not successfully address.

A humanitarian crisis in Haiti proved equally frustrating. There, the democratically elected government of Jean-Bertrand Aristide had been overthrown by a junta headed by General Raoul Cédras. Reportedly, at least 4000 of Aristide's followers had been killed, and more than 50,000 had attempted to flee to the United States. In the 1992 campaign, Clinton had criticized Bush for his failure to respond to the crisis, but once in the White House he, too, resisted the potential influx of hundreds of thousands of Haitians onto Florida's shores. A settlement was struck with Cédras in July whereby he promised to give up the reins of power and allow Aristide's return. In September the UN voted to send in 1200 advisors to safeguard the transition, with the United States to furnish half. With the military situation rapidly worsening in however, Congress was not about to give Clinton any leeway in Haiti. A resolution by Majority Leader Mitchell calling for prior approval of any military operations on the island passed by a vote of 98-2.

Matters were further complicated when Cédras reneged on his promise and allowed an angry mob to block a group of American and Canadian engineers as they tried to disembark at Port-au-Prince. Clinton was now caught between opposing forces at home; members of the Congressional Black Caucus pressed hard for intervention to permit Aristide's return and calm the crisis, while Republican leaders remained opposed to any U.S. involvement. When the UN authorized the use of force to break the impasse, Senators Dole and Judd Gregg (R-New Hampshire) secured unanimous approval of a resolution stating that the UN measure could not substitute for an explicit authorization required by the War Powers Resolution. Boxed in, Clinton coupled threats of military intervention with negotiations, sending Colin Powell, Senator Sam Nunn, and former president Jimmy Carter to negotiate a peaceful resolution of the crisis. "Luckily for him," writes Hal Brands in *From Berlin to Baghdad,* "the negotiations succeeded"—but only in the final moments, as U.S. planes were in the air on the way to an attack on the Haitian government's strongholds. Cédras departed and Aristide returned. U.S. troops remained on the island as part of a UN peacekeeping force until 1996.

In *Clinton's Wars: The Constitution, Congress, and War Powers,* political scientist Ryan Hendrickson argues that the congressional–executive face-offs over Somalia and Haiti reflected congressional "deference" to "presidential unilateralism." This seems off the mark. In refusing to acknowledge the authority of Congress to require advance authorization for the use of U.S. troops, Clinton was acting consistently with every other post-War Powers Resolution president. Far from being compliant, both Republicans and Democrats in Congress (Mitchell, for example) tried to exercise vigilance about the possible use of troops in the two crises. True, the possibility existed that Clinton would deploy U.S. forces without congressional authorization, but in both instances he pulled back, mostly because of the threat of congressional opposition.

Whereas Somalia and Haiti presented unpleasant choices, events in Bosnia posed a major conundrum. As polls showed, the American public wanted the United States to stay out of the raging conflagration created by Serbian president Slobodan

Milosevic's "ethnic cleansing" campaign against non-Serbs in Yugoslavia. Special targets were the Muslim populations of the breakaway republic of Bosnia and, later on, Kosovo in the northern part of Serbia itself. "Bosnia," writes journalist Richard Sale in *Clinton's Secret Wars: The Evolution of a Commander in Chief*, "incessantly posed the unavoidable and fundamental question of what sort of principles were to prevail in the world and to what extent the United States would act to establish their supremacy."

By 1993, the UN Security Council had established an arms embargo on all of Yugoslavia, with greater impact on Bosnian Muslims than on Serbian forces. The UN had also authorized the employment of "all measures necessary" to allow for the delivery of humanitarian aid. Although Congress had earlier authorized President Bush to lift the arms embargo on the Bosnians, he had not acted. During the 1992 campaign, Clinton had proposed a policy of "lift and strike"—that is, ending the embargo on Bosnia and Croatia (also under attack by Serbia) and threatening the use of NATO airpower to push back Serbian aggression. Once in office, however, he was sobered by the strong reservations of holdover JCS chief Colin Powell, who warned that the use of airpower could replicate the nation's disastrous experience in Vietnam.

Following up on his campaign promises, however, Clinton undertook to provide up to 25,000 U.S. troops as part of a multilateral peacekeeping force in Bosnia in the hope that a peace agreement could be reached. With National Security Advisor Tony Lake, Secretary of State Warren Christopher, and UN Ambassador Madeleine Albright all pushing for a firm response, but public opinion reflecting little enthusiasm for intervention, Clinton wobbled. He decided to go ahead with the "lift and strike" plan, but only if leading NATO partners would support it. When Christopher met individually with the major European heads of state to get their agreement, however, he was uniformly rebuffed. Chastened, the president backed down.

In February 1994, a deadly Serbian air attack on an open market in the Bosnian capital of Sarajevo motivated Clinton to try again to formulate a coordinated response. This time, he managed to persuade his NATO counterparts to support "pinprick" air strikes against Serbia, but these failed to end the fighting. Almost certainly, the administration's perceived indecisiveness in the face of the ever-deepening crisis contributed to the sweeping Republican victories in the 1994 mid-term elections. In turn, those election results further complicated matters for the White House, as the arch-conservative Jesse Helms took over as chair of the Senate Foreign Relations Committee.

Inside the administration, Clinton was under increasing pressure to take decisive steps to end the Bosnian crisis. Finally, in mid-July 1995, Milosevic committed an atrocity of such magnitude that Clinton determined to take the lead in shaping a NATO response. Following revelations of the cold-blooded execution and mass burial of 8000 Muslim men and boys in the small mountain town of Srebrenica, the president approved an "endgame" strategy that proposed the use of air strikes on Serb positions to force Milosevic to negotiate a settlement. Assistant Secretary of State Richard Holbrooke was dispatched to Europe with the task of selling the plan to NATO allies.

Clinton was now dealing from a stronger hand. The Srebrenica massacre had pushed American public opinion in the direction of supporting U.S. involvement in Bosnia, and Dole had orchestrated Senate passage of another resolution calling for the lifting of the Bosnian arms embargo. In late August, Milosevic ensured the success of Holbrooke's mission with NATO allies by carrying out yet another heavy shelling of Sarajevo. The NATO response, Operation Deliberate Force, consisting of 3500 bombing sorties on Serb positions, finally broke the back of Serbian aggression. In early September, Milosevic entered into talks involving Croatia and Bosnia-Herzegovina, setting a blueprint for the peaceful partitioning of the territories with guarantees of protection for all minority peoples. Final peace terms were to be negotiated in late October in Dayton, Ohio. The resulting Dayton Accords, closely patterned on these agreements, were hammered out over a period of three weeks. Clinton then informed Congress of his plan to deploy 20,000 U.S. troops to Bosnia to ensure the peace. In an effort to avert a congressional revolt, he promised that the troops would be home in one year.

There was no way, however, that Clinton could make good on his guarantee that U.S. troops could be withdrawn within a year, and in fact that proved impossible. "From 1993 to 1995, Clinton faced attacks over his inaction in Bosnia," Hal Brands writes. "[B]y 1996 and 1997, he was under fire for considering extending the intervention past the originally prescribed one year." By 1998, House conservatives went on the attack, but were unable to pass a resolution calling for total withdrawal; the troops remained in place, as did the tenuous agreement reached at Dayton.

Problems flared anew in the region when Milosevic turned on another Muslim minority, the Albanian Kosovars. Using "scorched-earth" tactics, Serb forces displaced almost a third of a million Kosovars from their homes, creating yet another major humanitarian crisis. As the atrocities of the Bosnian crisis played out anew, Clinton reacted boldly, threatening air strikes without the cover of a UN authorizing resolution and before securing NATO approval of such an action. By the end of January 1999, he had obtained both. A peace agreement seemed imminent in mid-March, but no sooner had it been signed than Milosevic unleashed another crushing attack on the rebel Kosovo Liberation Army. In response, NATO—with the United States again in the lead—launched what could only be called a full-scale air war on Serbia.

By this time, the president was mired in serious problems at home, stemming from yet another sex scandal, layered on top of the lingering Whitewater investigation. Congressional Republicans, emboldened by the president's deteriorating political position, unleashed a fusillade against the escalation of commitments in the Balkans—even charging that—in a deceptive maneuver modeled on a 1997 movie, *Wag the Dog*—the air strikes represented a cynical effort to divert public attention from White House scandals. Clinton, with backing from influential Senate Republicans, managed to avert passage of a resolution calling for an end to U.S. involvement, even though the House—by a tie vote—rejected a measure authorizing the military action.

When NATO airstrikes took out the Serbian power grid, Milosevic finally agreed to accept increased autonomy for Kosovo.

Russian leader Boris Yeltsin's withdrawal of support for Serbia provided the critical leverage. As Marvin and Deborah Kalb record in *Haunting Legacy*, Secretary of State Madeleine Albright later observed that if Milosevic had not conceded by winter, Clinton would have had to consider "going it alone" in Kosovo. Fortunately, he did not have to confront that stark choice. Within a year, Milosevic's government had been overthrown. Indicted as a war criminal by the International War Crimes Tribunal, the Serbian strongman would be arrested by UN forces in 2001 and later die in prison while awaiting prosecution for his crimes.

There are valid grounds to question the constitutionality of Clinton's actions in the Kosovo crisis. "The distinctive feature of Clinton's military action in Yugoslavia lay in its raw violation of the fundamental requirement of the war clause," writes David Adler in his co-edited book (with Michael Genovese), *The Presidency & the Law: The Clinton Legacy*. This "'presidential war' … marked the first time in our history that a president waged war in the face of a direct congressional refusal to authorize the war." Yet neither chamber chose to challenge the executive branch directly. Clinton's actions in Kosovo were certainly bold—but probably no more an explicit violation of war powers than Reagan's actions in Lebanon and Grenada. The unenforceability of the War Powers Resolution was once again laid bare.

Helpful intervention by Russian president Boris Yeltsin in the Kosovo negotiations represented repayment to Clinton for the latter's steadfast support of his regime from the time he entered the White House. The choice about how to deal with the new Russian government was anything but clear-cut after the implosion of the Soviet Union. Bolstered by private advice from former president Nixon and urged on by Christopher and chief Russian specialist Strobe Talbott, Clinton decided early on that the only way to bring political stability to Russia was to assist in its economic recovery. Though polls showed three-fourths of American voters opposed sending additional aid to Russia, the White House moved decisively, pressing Congress to approve $1.6 billion in direct aid to the Yeltsin government; eventually, the total approached $4 billion.

Sticking with Yeltsin posed major challenges for Clinton, as the Russian leader struggled to consolidate his authority in Moscow. In October 1993, an uprising orchestrated by ex-communists and right-wing extremists in the Duma nearly led Yeltsin to dissolve that legislative body, an action that would have presented Clinton with a dilemma of major proportions. Though that crisis was averted, in December the same opposition forces won a majority of the popular vote in the Russian parliamentary elections—in effect, a negative referendum on Yeltsin's regime. Clinton may have borne some responsibility for these results, as his push for inclusion of a number of newly liberated East European nations in NATO added to Yeltsin's troubles at home.

Despite these obstacles, the friendship between Clinton and Yeltsin strengthened as they negotiated their respective domestic challenges and attempted to resolve the instability that had resulted from the breakup of the Soviet Union. As the Dayton Accords were being hammered out in October 1995, the two leaders conducted a highly successful mini-summit on the grounds of FDR's estate and museum in Hyde Park, New York, which ended—remarkably—with Yeltsin agreeing that Russia would participate in the UN peacekeeping force in Bosnia. Receiving almost as much media attention as this breakthrough agreement was an alcohol-induced wisecrack by Yeltsin to the assembled reporters that they were "a disaster"—a comment that doubled Clinton over with laughter, rendering him incapable of comment for a few moments.

The Hyde Park agreement was hugely important in advancing Clinton's objective of a democratized and unified post-Cold War Europe. But maintaining the partnership with Yeltsin also forced Clinton into some uncomfortable choices that cost him at home—most notably when the Russian leader, in order to win respect from his jingoistic rivals in Moscow, ordered the bombing of rebellious Chechnyan forces, beginning a long and bloody civil war in that embattled region. As Clinton remained on the sidelines, unwilling to denounce the brutality in Chechnya, Republican detractors attacked him for his inconsistency in refusing to condemn actions that looked very much like what was going on in Yugoslavia. The relationship with Yeltsin continued to pay off for Clinton, however. After both leaders had been safely re-elected, they met in person again in Helsinki in March 1997 to discuss the vision of a "free, peaceful, undivided Europe," symbolized by an expanded NATO that would provide security across the continent. Two months later, the unimaginable happened, when NATO granted Russia a "consultative" voice in its policy decisions. In late summer, it was announced that former Soviet satellite states Poland, Hungary, and the Czech Republic would become members of NATO; a few months later, Clinton privately assured the leaders of Latvia, Lithuania, and Estonia that their nations, too, could eventually join NATO, but only after he and Yeltsin had left office.

These dramatic geopolitical changes produced domestic criticism from both left and right. A number of leading Democrats charged that administration policies could unnecessarily antagonize Russia, while conservative Republicans led by Helms railed against the "mongrelization" of NATO by adding former satellite nations. This odd coalition succeeded in passing a measure mandating a three-year waiting period for new members of NATO. Meanwhile, increasing instability in the Russian economy and Yeltsin's failing health raised questions about the long-term viability of Clinton's adventurous partnership with his Russian counterpart. Despite the lack of unanimity at home, as Hyland observes, "[t]he Clinton achievement most likely to define his legacy was the expansion of NATO," significant in that it "marked the end of any temptation toward a new disengagement from Europe." There was nothing Clinton could do, however, to ensure stability in post-Cold War Russia. The accession to power in Russia of Vladimir Putin, a former leader of the Soviet KGB, in 2000, raised the specter of a dramatic reversal of the U.S.–Russian rapprochement.

Having entered the White House focused on economic issues and domestic policy, Clinton was compelled to spend a substantial amount of his time and attention on foreign policy and national security concerns. In addition to the crises in Somalia, Haiti, and Yugoslavia, and the challenge of dealing with post-Soviet Russia, the administration undertook to lead peacemaking efforts in both the Israeli–Palestinian morass (unsuccessful) and in Northern Ireland (somewhat more successful). He also had to respond to ominous new challenges in the Middle East. In February 1993, the nation was stunned by a terrifying attack on U.S. soil: the attempted destruction of the North Tower of the World Trade Center by a truck bomb detonated in an underground parking garage. Although the death toll was only six, more than 1000 were injured. The bombing was quickly traced to a band of Islamic extremists, six of whom were later brought to trial and convicted. Two months after the World Trade Center bombing, Kuwaiti officials uncovered an assassination plot aimed at former president Bush days before his scheduled visit to that country. When it was ascertained that the Iraqi Intelligence Service was behind the plot, Clinton retaliated swiftly against Saddam Hussein, ordering missile attacks on a number of Iraqi military and government targets. Notifying Congress only after the fact, he justified his action on the basis of the "self-defense" provisions included in Article 51 of the UN Charter. As Adler writes, however, the circumstances "did not satisfy the Article 51 criterion ... . The armed attack had ceased, and there was no immediate threat of a renewed attack."

Conflict with Iraq continued throughout Clinton's years in the White House, stemming largely from Saddam Hussein's frequent violations of "no-fly zones" over parts of Iraq and his refusal to cooperate with UN inspections of Iraqi weapons arsenals, as well as his repeated brutalities directed at Kurdish and Shiite domestic foes of his Sunni-dominated Baathist regime. On at least five occasions between 1993 and 2000, the administration launched unauthorized air strikes in Iraq. The most damaging of these reprisals, Operation Desert Fox, occurred in December 1998, with more than 600 bombing assaults on over 100 targets. By this time, Hussein's actions had produced a surge of support in the United States for "regime change" in Iraq, resulting in Congress's passage of the Iraq Liberation Act.

August 1998 saw another horrific attack on American lives and property by terrorist forces—this time on the U.S. embassies in Kenya and Tanzania. The precision of the attacks was as alarming as the scale of destruction, as the two suicide bombings occurred almost simultaneously. Within days, CIA director George Tenet informed Clinton that the attacks had been orchestrated by al-Qaeda, an extremist Islamic terrorist group born out of the resistance to Soviet aggression in Afghanistan a decade before, which drew much of its funding from a virulently anti-American Saudi, Osama bin Laden. Again without seeking either congressional authorization or a UN resolution, Clinton ordered missile strikes on suspected al-Qaeda weapons caches in the Sudan and on a remote outpost in Afghanistan where U.S. intelligence suspected bin Laden would be meeting with other top al-Qaeda operatives. The attacks, though largely ineffectual, were supported by more than 70 percent of Americans. The administration also increased the size and role of its relatively new counterterrorism program. From this time forward, writes Sale, Osama bin Laden "never left Clinton's mind, right up to the end of his presidency."

Clinton received relatively little credit for his conduct of foreign policy at the time he left office. Nearly all who have written about his administration agree that when he entered the White House he was both less interested and less skillful in dealing with foreign policy than he was in domestic matters. The disagreements come in evaluating his handling of complex world events after those first bumpy years. Hal Brands asserts that the "lack of a moral center" in the Clinton administration's policies made it legitimately vulnerable to attacks from Helms and others on the Republican right. As a result of this standoff with the GOP, he contends, by the end of Clinton's second term, "congressional influence in foreign policy was at a 25-year high." In view of the fruits of Clinton's sustained, successful partnership with Yeltsin, his aggressive leadership of the multilateral intervention in Yugoslavia, and especially his successful orchestration of NATO expansion, such a verdict seems off the mark. Clinton did not shrink from reacting to threats, as well as opportunities, abroad, even in the most difficult year of his presidency when facing impeachment. In fact, as political scientists Ryan Hendrickson and David Adler both strongly assert, he was more likely to push the boundaries of executive authority in foreign policy than any of his immediate predecessors. Brands also criticizes Clinton for failing to develop an overarching approach to world affairs. "The problem with Clinton's foreign policy," he states, "was not his specific initiatives but his inability to manage their intersection." But where, precisely, were such points of "intersection"? True, Clinton may not have been able to chart a single path through the many, varied crises of the post-Cold War decade, but neither did his detractors have a coherent plan. A fairer appraisal is that of Sale, who argues that Clinton did, in fact, adhere to a basic global strategy. "To begin with," he writes, "Clinton from the first resisted any American retreat into isolationism after the end of the Cold War." Nor did he let others hijack his essentially multilateral agenda. By the beginning of his second term, adds Sale, Clinton

> had learned to impose his own personality on … crises, stamping his own imprint on them, and not only author his own major decisions but make them stick. … [He] was able to explain to his public why it would benefit the people and make more secure American national interests, and he was persuasive in gaining at least temporary support among a mainly indifferent public.

Crises of the Clinton Presidency

Attacks from the right on both Bill and Hillary Clinton were relentless from their first days in the White House. The First Lady's influence within the administration in the first two years fueled such attacks. The president's outflanking of the GOP following the party's smashing victory in the 1994 mid-term elections, capped by his easy re-election, served only to inflame partisan hostility toward him. Such outrage was not only political, but moral. Many of Clinton's foes, especially in the media, considered him terminally flawed—a womanizer and congenital liar who was willing to say or do anything in order to stay in power. Paula Jones's sexual harassment case and the lingering

Whitewater investigation represented possibilities for damaging the president, perhaps fatally, yet neither one seemed to gain early traction. A Supreme Court decision on May 27, 1997, however, changed the playing field entirely, setting in motion a chain of events that would nearly force Clinton from office.

In that critical decision, *Jones v. Clinton*, the court ruled that a sitting president was not immune from civil suits arising from actions taken before assuming office and unrelated to the conduct of that office. As a consequence, Clinton could be required to testify in response to Jones's allegations that while governor he had subjected her to unwanted sexual attention and that, when she refused to cooperate, she suffered employment discrimination in her state job. Jones had neither lost her job nor been denied raises after the alleged encounter, but the case represented a huge potential embarrassment for the president in that it would almost certainly lead to prosecutorial rummaging into his pre-White House sex life. Clinton's lawyers had earlier offered Jones a settlement of $700,000, but she had refused it unless a public apology were forthcoming; this the president had not been willing to give. Now, trapped by the Supreme Court decision, he would have to answer whatever questions Jones's attorneys might pose about his reckless indiscretions.

The vast extent of the danger was soon clear. As Jones's lawyers prepared their case, they received information from a Pentagon employee, Linda Tripp, that Clinton had had a recent affair with her young co-worker, Monica Lewinsky, while the latter had been serving as a White House intern. When Jones's lawyers subpoenaed Lewinsky in mid-December to give a deposition the following month, she chose to file an affidavit instead. On January 7, she submitted her statement, denying any sexual involvement with the president. Lewinsky's affidavit became an immediate problem for Clinton, as Tripp had been secretly taping her phone calls with Lewinsky in which the latter had gone into the details of her relationship with the president, and the older woman had turned these tapes over to the Jones legal team. Clear evidence therefore existed that Lewinsky had lied in her affidavit, and Clinton's possible culpability in advising her to submit the false statement became a serious charge against him. Although Jones's legal team was primarily interested in the pattern of sexual misconduct on the president's part that the affair reflected, at least one of her lawyers decided that Starr's Whitewater investigation team might be able to make use of the information connecting Clinton to a more serious crime: obstruction of justice.

Starr, whose animosity toward Clinton had deepened as he dug into the Whitewater case, jumped on the new lead immediately. The president was scheduled for deposition in the Jones case on January 17. Thinking it likely that Clinton would repeat the falsehoods in Lewinsky's affidavit, Starr sought authorization from Attorney General Reno to expand his own investigation to include possible obstruction of justice, perjury, and witness tampering on the president's part in the Lewinsky matter. Although Reno could have denied this bold request, she did not want to appear to be stonewalling. Within twenty-four hours, Starr had his fishing license to go after the president.

In his deposition, Clinton essentially repeated Lewinsky's story, denying that a physical relationship had existed between the two. The president well knew the probing questions about the alleged Lewinsky affair spelled trouble. He also had another problem, this one closer to home. Up until this point, Hillary Clinton had known nothing about what had transpired between her husband and Lewinsky. On the morning of January 21, she—along with the rest of the country—learned about the alleged affair when the *Washington Post* broke the story. Trusting her husband, who assured her it was a lie—and true to the terms of the long-established partnership the couple had developed—the First Lady once again came to his rescue. Appearing on NBC's *Today* show a few days later, she angrily characterized the story as a fabrication cooked up by a "vast right-wing conspiracy, that has been conspiring against my husband since the day he announced for president." His wife's public support was crucial to Clinton's chances to escape unscathed, as polls showed an immediate uptick in his approval ratings. A majority of Americans believed that if the president had indeed had an affair with Lewinsky, it should be considered a private matter and had no bearing on his ability to run the country.

The president's battle for survival was just beginning, and would drag on for months. Yet life in the Oval Office went on, as Clinton had to continue to deal with problems at home and abroad. "I was compelled as never before to live parallel lives," he wrote in his memoirs, "except that this time the darkest part of my inner life was in full view." The president continued in a state of denial until August, by which time Starr and his team were ready to question him before a grand jury. Possibly worse than having to face the jury, as Clinton prepared his testimony he knew he had to let Hillary know that he would be giving testimony different from his statements of January—in other words, that he had lied to her earlier. As both he and she indicate in their respective memoirs, the First Lady was furious—and stayed that way, at least in private, for weeks.

On August 17, Clinton testified from the White House, his responses televised to the courtroom in which the grand jury sat. By this time, Lewinsky had signed an immunity agreement with Starr and had provided a detailed accounting of ten encounters with the president over a span of sixteen months, even supplying graphic physical evidence in the form of a stained dress. Trapped, Clinton for the first time admitted in his testimony that "inappropriate sexual contact" had occurred, but stubbornly refused to concede most of the investigators' specific points. He had no choice but to hang tough in his testimony, since admitting to the intimate acts that Lewinsky had described to Starr's lawyers would be tantamount to confessing that he had committed perjury in his deposition in the Jones case.

Clinton's grand jury testimony marked the low point for him in his struggle with Starr and congressional Republicans. That night, he "explained" the change in his testimony in a nationally televised speech that was part apology but also part condemnation of his prosecutors. "It is time to stop the pursuit of personal destruction and the prying into private lives and get on with our national life," he proclaimed defiantly at the conclusion of his address. Overnight polls indicated that the president's speech had mollified a public that wanted to get the Lewinsky mess behind it as soon as possible. Congressional Republicans, however, were howling for the president's scalp. More problematically, many Democrats also seemed displeased with what they saw as insufficient contrition on Clinton's part. As the president worked to avert a rebellion within the Cabinet and to regain the loyalty of his party comrades in Congress, the White House defense team unleashed a barrage of criticism of Starr, claiming that the investigator had been blatantly biased from the beginning.

The president's efforts to paint Starr and the Republicans as the villains in the piece provoked a degree of overreach he may not have foreseen. On September 10, the House released the entire 445-page independent counsel's report, replete with lurid details of Clinton's physical relationship with Lewinsky, that many felt was unnecessarily salacious—even pornographic. "If shifting the political balance was the object, it became clear within days the opposition had failed," writes Harris. "Polls showed ... disdain for the effort to humiliate [the president]." Instead of retracting their claws, however, the GOP leaders in the House redoubled their commitment to "get" Clinton. Though the White House was clearly willing to settle for a vote of censure, the Republican leadership wanted more; nothing short of impeachment would do. Clinton further benefited when his videotaped deposition before the grand jury was shown on network television in late September. Humiliating as were the details revealed in his testimony, the inquisitorial aspects of the exercise—questions coming at the president from a faceless voice—created sympathy, rather than condemnation. "The reaction of many viewers was that the subjection of a President ... to this unprecedented humiliation rite in a 'stadium' of millions was punishment enough," writes Richard Posner in his authoritative *An Affair of State: The Investigation, Impeachment, and Trial of President Clinton*, "and that impeachment and conviction would constitute a gratuitous anticlimax." Impeachment, in fact, now seemed to most Americans to be just one more partisan attack on the White House, rather than a legitimate constitutional process.

By training their sights on removing Clinton, the GOP hoped to produce massive gains in the 1998 mid-term congressional elections. The strategy completely backfired, as the relentless hammering of the president instead buttressed support for him among Democrats and even independents who had previously been critical of his behavior. The result was slight Republican losses at the polls, almost unheard of in a sixth-year mid-term election. The GOP margin in the Senate remained unchanged at 55-45, while the party lost four seats in the House, reducing its majority to 223-211. Gingrich actually paid a higher price than Clinton from the events of the fall. Facing a revolt in the GOP caucus for having mismanaged the fall campaign, he announced his resignation as Speaker; the following January, he resigned from the House altogether.

With the elections behind him, Clinton dropped any pretense of contrition and went into full battle-mode. On November 19, his attorneys reached a settlement with Paula Jones, paying her $850,000 to drop her suit. Encouraged by polls that showed little public support for impeachment, the president resolved to fight to the end. By mid-December, the House was ready to vote on four articles of impeachment that had been passed on a straight party-line vote by the Judiciary Committee. The first two focused on perjury in the president's testimony in the Paula Jones case and his deposition to the grand jury, while the third charged him with obstruction of justice for coaching Lewinsky and the fourth alleged that he had willfully misled the public and abused executive privilege in defending against the Starr investigation. With Gingrich sidelined, leadership of the GOP forces fell largely to the troika of Henry Hyde (Illinois), chair of the Judiciary Committee, Dick Armey, and Tom DeLay. Along the way, the intensity of the partisan fight had ended the career of GOP Speaker-elect Robert Livingston (Louisiana), whose own past extramarital affairs were exploited by incensed Democrats, leading him to resign before even being formally anointed Speaker.

On December 19, the first act of the drama closed: on almost straight party-line votes, Clinton was impeached on two of the four charges, by votes of 228-206 on the charge of perjury before the grand jury and 221-212 on obstruction of justice. Although Clinton may have originally held out a hope that none of the articles would pass, the partisan shape of the final votes helped

Figure 6.2 One of the most resilient public figures of his—or any other—generation, Bill Clinton survived impeachment and left office two years later with a higher than 60 percent approval rating. Here, Clinton supporters are shown demonstrating against impeachment in December 1998. © Najlah Feanny/CORBIS SABA

his cause, solidifying the public image that the whole exercise was political rather than constitutional. Still, the outcome of the Senate trial could not be assumed. Senators in both parties, not relishing the obligation to take up a case for which much of the general public had lost respect, mostly avoided public comment. It was hard for even the president's strongest defenders to deny that he had committed perjury; the question was whether or not that offense, in this instance, rose to a level that demanded his removal from office—or whether, even if it did, the public cared.

Senate deliberations began immediately after the new Congress assembled in January, and lasted for more than a month. As Posner writes, the proceedings were "[t]runcated and anticlimactic—indeed, a parody of legal justice." Both sides simply wanted the trial to be over. The president's lawyers urged that no witnesses be called, and that the case be decided on the basis of the written record alone. In the end, they nearly got their way, although Lewinsky and two others were deposed and videotaped excerpts were included in the Senate's deliberations. The unorthodoxy of the White House lawyers' approach—as well as their recognition that the case was not likely to be decided on its legal merits—was evidenced by their decision to have the president's friend, the folksy former senator from Clinton's home state, Dale Bumpers, give the closing "argument."

With a two-thirds vote necessary to convict, the outcome of the Senate trial was obvious before the votes were taken. Leaks to the media made clear that the pro-impeachment forces would fall far short. "The most serious procedural failure was the failure to impose a gag rule," writes Posner. "As a result, the normal order of a trial—hearing, then verdict—was reversed, just as Alice's trial in *Alice in Wonderland*." The denouement came on February 12, when the Senate rejected the perjury charge in the Lewinsky case by a vote of 45-55, and the obstruction of justice article on a 50-50 tie vote. As in the House, the vote was highly partisan; all forty-five Democrats voted to acquit on both measures, joined by ten Republicans on the first charge and five on the second.

Clinton's victory in the face of the tawdry Lewinsky scandal produced another significant outcome—this one involving Hillary Rodham Clinton. Not only did her steadfast loyalty to her now-exposed philandering husband make her a martyred heroine of sorts, but her actions had profound implications, as well, for the First Couple's relationship and for her own possible political future. As Chafe observes, Hillary's "decision to rescue Bill ... represented her liberation from him" in an important way. "Her sacrifice for Bill opened the door to freedom for herself," he adds. "When she closed the door on the option of leaving Bill in 1998, she opened the door to becoming a powerful politician in her own right."

Like most observers at the time, scholars who have studied the Clinton impeachment agree that crimes were committed—certainly, at least, perjury. There is also general agreement with the Senate verdict that these crimes did not justify the president's removal from office. Moreover, a strong argument can be made that, compared to the violations of basic constitutional principles in the Iran-Contra episode, Clinton's legal transgressions were minor and innocuous.

The impeachment struggle, however, intensified the increasingly bitter party warfare of the 1990s, touching off a *kulturkampf*, in Posner's phrase, in which each side came to regard the other as not only reprehensible but even illegitimate, when it came to governing. "Clinton's opponents on the Right," Posner continues, "were so odious to the Left that many on the Left, including a number of prominent intellectuals, denied (or evaded the issue of) his guilt, while Clinton himself ... became for many on the Right the preeminent symbol of all they hate." Despite having to spend a full year of his second term fighting simply to stay in office, Clinton ended his presidency more popular than ever, with higher public approval ratings than any president in the previous half-century. He achieved this largely by means of intelligence, political savvy, flexibility, and a capacity for reinventing himself. As Richard Reeves wrote, in *Running in Place*, in the year Clinton sought re-election, he was "a compleat democrat, ever ready to change course to tack with the opinion of the great American public." Clinton's changes of direction reflected more than mere instinct or opportunism, however. Genuinely committed to the "third way" he had espoused in his first campaign, he adopted change as a strategy—and that strategy succeeded in frustrating, even if not defeating, his Republican foes throughout his eight years in office.

Bill Clinton may have outfoxed his opponents by surviving impeachment and remaining popular with the American public, but he did not succeed in his quest to solidify the future of his party. Although he "erased Democratic vulnerability on a number of issues," writes Gillon, he left behind "a new fault line on questions of morality and personal integrity." Moreover, the impeachment struggle had deepened the bitterness between the parties, adding "partisan fuel to the generational divide, [and] making any consensus unlikely for the foreseeable future." This was the unhappy context for the election of 2000.

7

The Politics of Polarization, 2000–2008

Despite having received only a minority of the votes cast in 2000 and being awarded the presidency by a partisan majority on the Supreme Court, George W. Bush initially set out to govern as if he had obtained a clear majority. How this would have turned out absent the destruction of the two World Trade Center towers on September 11, 2001, is hard to imagine. The attacks on the Twin Towers converted him into a "war president" who could and did evoke that image to bring Congress into line on policies favored by the administration. Awful as it was, the disastrous event gave Bush an enormous opportunity to be a "uniter"—but he failed to capitalize on that opportunity. In fact, far from being the unifying president he had promised to be during the campaign, he quickly became a more divisive figure than any previous modern president.

The "war on terrorism" that Bush and Cheney launched in the wake of 9/11 began as a campaign to track down and eradicate al-Qaeda leader Osama bin Laden but quickly morphed into a poorly (critics said, dishonestly) justified war to oust Iraqi leader Saddam Hussein. It also formed the context for most of Bush's

Deadlock and Disillusionment: American Politics since 1968, First Edition.
Gary W. Reichard.
© 2016 John Wiley & Sons, Inc. Published 2016 by John Wiley & Sons, Inc.

important decisions and actions during the remainder of his two terms in the White House. Indeed, Bush seemed to interpret the initial rallying of the American people to a patriotic cause, as well as his narrow re-election victory in 2004, as mandates not only to continue the war on terrorism but to push for changes sought by his conservative political base. This misreading, coupled with the military morass that soon developed in Iraq, led to a precipitous decline in his and his party's political fortunes. The air of certainty he projected in connection with policies that were increasingly unpopular exacerbated the problem. The consequence was a sweeping Democratic victory in the 2006 mid-term elections and, two years later, the election of Barack Obama as the forty-fourth president of the United States.

Ultimate Deadlock: *Bush v. Gore*

Despite the misadventures that weakened Bill Clinton's presidency near its end, the Democrats enjoyed significant advantages going into the 2000 election season. The economy was booming, Clinton was enjoying strong approval ratings, and Vice President Al Gore had the president's unequivocal backing as the party's standard-bearer. Although during the impeachment battle the media had identified at least six potential challengers to Gore, all but one—former senator Bill Bradley of New Jersey—had dropped out of contention by fall 1999. In contrast, the GOP carried the heavy baggage of its failed, seemingly vindictive impeachment strategy. Moreover, it appeared that there could be as many as ten candidates in the Republican field, threatening a blood-letting that could further damage the party's chances of success in 2000.

Money speaks in American politics, and it brought quick resolution to the Republican nomination contest. The 2000 primary calendar was even more strongly front-loaded than four years earlier. More than ever before, therefore, the advantage would go to those who were well funded and best organized. In the Republican party, the clear beneficiary was George W. Bush, son of the forty-first president and recently re-elected as governor of Texas with more than 60 percent of the vote (including a 40 percent share of the Hispanic vote). With the help of Texas oil money, Bush had built up a massive war chest by mid-1999—almost two times the combined amount that had been raised by all other Republicans interested in the nomination. By fall, six of the GOP aspirants had dropped from the field. Pat Buchanan, giving up his quest to wrench the party to the extreme right, announced that he was no longer a Republican and opted to take over Ross Perot's Reform party as his vehicle for 2000. This mass exodus left Bush with only two legitimate challengers: millionaire Steve Forbes, back for another run after his quixotic 1996 campaign, and Arizona's senior senator, John McCain, a former Vietnam POW widely regarded as a party renegade. Forbes, unable to reignite any meaningful support, was out of the race by February. Only McCain stood between Bush and the nomination.

Bush's massive funding advantage allowed him to employ a "fifty-state" strategy from the beginning of the primary season, which promised to serve him well in the general election campaign. McCain, in contrast, had to roll the dice on three states, hoping to upset the favorite early and move on from there. His best chance was in New Hampshire; from there, he hoped that by winning the South Carolina and California primaries, he could demonstrate a national appeal that would bring him the necessary financial backing to win the nomination. After Bush predictably won the Iowa caucuses, McCain won a resounding victory in New Hampshire by out-hustling the Texas governor and holding over 100 town hall meetings. His eighteen-point margin of victory suggested that, despite his unpopularity with the GOP establishment for backing campaign spending reform, he might be able to derail his lavishly funded opponent. This was a chimera. With the help of a number of far-right groups, the Bush campaign buried McCain by attacking him for his stands on abortion, the tobacco industry, and taxes—as well as planting (or at least not speaking out against) false rumors that he had fathered a mixed-race child out of wedlock.

When these tactics produced victory for Bush in the Palmetto State, McCain was finished. The Arizonan did not attempt to disguise his bitterness at the end; rumors persisted long after the election that he did not in fact vote for his rival.

The Democratic primary campaign was also brief. As the more liberal candidate and the only practical alternative to Gore, Bradley appeared strong for a time in 1999. The former senator's aloofness and tendency to extreme wonkiness, however, quickly eroded both media and voter support, and he got no closer to the front-runner in national polls than 15 to 25 percent as the primary season opened. After Gore won the Iowa caucuses and took the New Hampshire primary, he was unstoppable. Bradley withdrew on March 9, coincidentally the same day that McCain left the GOP field. The frontloading of primaries in both parties had once again set up a greatly prolonged general election campaign.

The relative weakness and disorganization of Gore's campaign allowed Bush to open up a lead by April that he was to hold until the Democratic convention in August. The Republican candidate also enjoyed an all-important edge in media attention. "From the primaries until the end of the Democratic convention," wrote political scientist Marjorie Randon Hershey in Gerald Pomper's post-election volume, *The Election of 2000*, "George W. Bush had the look, and the coverage of a hands-down winner." The fifty-state strategy of the spring was clearly paying off. So, too, was Bush's decision to soften his party's edges with the electorate by running as a "compassionate conservative." His selection of his father's secretary of defense, Dick Cheney, as his running-mate was unexpected and certainly not consistent with fashioning a more compassionate Republican approach, but Cheney's position on the ticket provided reassurance for many who were concerned about Bush the younger's total lack of foreign policy experience. The GOP convention during the first week of August reinforced Bush's intended message while keeping the party's base on board. As political scientist Gary Jacobson writes in *A Divider, Not a Uniter: George W. Bush and the American People*, the first day of the conclave "verged on self-parody," featuring "a parade of speeches delivered almost exclusively by women, children, and minorities."

The platform, in contrast, firmly embraced the positions of the party's right on wedge issues such as abortion, gay rights, gun control, and affirmative action.

The Democrats' convention in Los Angeles two weeks later reflected Gore's tactical challenges, as the first two nights focused on the Clinton and Kennedy legends, respectively. Hoping to win over moderates and independents, the vice president badly needed to carve out an individual persona for the campaign. His choice of Connecticut senator Joe Lieberman, one of the party's earliest and strongest critics of Clinton's involvement with Monica Lewinsky, as a running-mate was widely hailed—not least because Lieberman was the first Jew ever on a major party presidential ticket. Gore outdid himself in his acceptance speech, channeling the economic populism that had long been one of the Democrats' winning suits and coming across as one who could lead in his own right. Consequently, he enjoyed a sizable bounce from the proceedings, eradicating Bush's 15-plus percentage-point pre-convention lead.

Both candidates' campaigns were defined by the way they handled the "Clinton factor." In a sense, Bush chose to emulate Clinton, reaching toward the center by stressing the moderation of his views. "Just as Clinton had sought to shift the Democratic party away from its liberal, soft-on-crime, weak-on-defense, pro-welfare identity," writes Peter Baker in *Days of Fire: Bush and Cheney in the White House*, "Bush was now trying to redefine the Republican Party, sanding off the harsher edges of the Gingrich revolution." Specifically, he championed education reform, as well as a pragmatic approach on immigration, and touted his record of bipartisan cooperation with a Democratic legislature as governor of Texas. Gore, on the other hand, still resentful of being misled by Clinton during the Lewinsky scandal, failed to stress his connection with the administration's sterling economic record. Instead, the vice president in effect opted to go it alone, giving up his trump card and turning the election, as Pomper wrote, into "a contest between two individuals and their personal programs."

Gore's go-it-alone strategy did not serve him well, since the public viewed Bush as by far the more affable of the two candidates. Unfortunately for Gore, the likability gap showed clearly in the presidential debates—especially the first one, in which, already suspect for his elitist, know-it-all demeanor, he was caught on camera several times grimacing and sighing while listening to Bush's responses to the interlocutors' questions. Though the vice president did well in the two subsequent debates, he never recovered the ground he lost by this initial debate performance. Even the last-minute revelation of Bush's arrest for drunk driving many years before could not undo the damage. The two candidates arrived at election day tied in the polls.

Voter turnout was low—about 51 percent, only a slight uptick from four years before. Subsequent analyses revealed that this low voter participation hurt Gore more than Bush—and that Democratic losses were primarily due to the vice president's failure to concentrate his efforts on bringing loyal Democrats to the polls. The significance of his strategic error in distancing himself from Clinton was evident as the votes were counted on election night. As the TV networks filled in their election maps, it became clear that Bush had won eleven states that Clinton had carried four years earlier, shockingly including Clinton's home state of Arkansas and Gore's Tennessee. As ballots were tallied through election night, the plotline became increasingly dramatic, with the outcome resting on the tally in one final swing state: Florida. Just before nine o'clock, each of the news channels called Florida for Gore; shortly thereafter, however, one by one, they retracted the call and then, with Fox News in the lead, awarded the state and the presidential election to Bush, who appeared to have an insurmountable, even if minuscule, lead of 1700 popular votes in the Sunshine State. Gore, believing like other viewers that the call was final, then telephoned Bush to concede. Within an hour or so, however—with the totals shifting as the counting continued—he called back to tell a nonplussed Bush that he was withdrawing his concession. Bush was more than miffed, and the two had a briefly unpleasant exchange on the phone. The outcome was now up in the air, as reports streamed in about irregularities of various sorts in several Florida counties, most of which had been expected to go for Gore.

As Americans awoke the next day to an unresolved election, the Bush and Gore teams plotted their strategies for getting to endgame. Gore, behind in the official tally, believed he had been robbed. Problems in the Florida vote count abounded—almost entirely in populous southeastern counties that were Democratic strongholds, including Palm Beach, Broward, and Miami-Dade. Most striking was the situation in Palm Beach County, home to hundreds of thousands of elderly Democratic voters, where, inexplicably, Buchanan had received over 3000 votes, well over his totals anywhere else in the state. As quickly became clear from complaints from aggrieved voters, the problem stemmed from a "butterfly ballot" devised by the county elections supervisor that positioned punch marks in an array confusing to the county's huge senior citizen electorate, leading them to cast their votes mistakenly for the arch-conservative Buchanan. Belatedly recognizing their error, huge numbers of these voters had then punched a second hole for Gore, causing their ballots to be thrown out as "over-votes." In the other two counties that were Gore strongholds, there was an opposite problem: "under-votes" that were not counted because the holes that voters punched did not entirely remove the pieces of ballot ("chads") in order that their votes could be machine-tabulated. Even more egregious, though somewhat more difficult to prove, were reports from all across the state that thousands of voters had been disfranchised by various means, including incorrect purging of names from voter rolls, the moving of polling places without adequate advance notice, and lack of support for non-English-speaking voters—all of which had disproportionately disadvantaged minority voters.

Under Florida election law, the closeness of the initial tabulation triggered an automatic recount, which began immediately. Unfortunately for Gore, however, a simple recount could not correct the errors and injustices that had caused the rejection of alleged over- and under-votes and that had cost him so dearly. While the second canvass tightened the distance separating the two candidates, the vice president still trailed. The machinations of Florida's Republican secretary of state, Katherine Harris, co-chair of the Florida Bush campaign, made things even worse for the

Democrats, as she interpreted state election law to require the final count to be certified within a week of the election—leaving no time for anything but a mechanical recount. In announcing her decision, she ignored a provision in Florida's election law stipulating that no vote should "be declared invalid or void if there is a clear indication of the intent of the voter." Gore forces maintained, with reason, that both the "over-votes" in Palm Beach County and the "under-votes" in Broward and Miami-Dade represented cases where there was potentially clear indication of intent.

At this point, the outcome of the 2000 presidential election became the province of the courts, rather than the electorate, and the partisanship of the judicial system was alarmingly revealed. To begin, the Florida Supreme Court—all of whose members had been appointed by Democratic governors—came to Gore's rescue, staying Secretary of State Harris from certifying the results of the recount (which appeared to sustain Bush's victory, but with a reduced total of fewer than 1000 votes). Instead, the court required a statewide manual recount to resolve the issue of the contested under- and over-votes. Complicating matters, however, was its insistence that the recount be completed within five days, by 5 p.m. on Sunday, November 26—a deadline that was to prove impossible for the board of elections in the state's most populous county to meet. On Saturday, one day before the Florida Supreme Court's deadline, the Miami-Dade election commissioner stopped the recount, announcing that it could not be completed by the prescribed deadline. The results of the foreshortened recount left Bush in front by 537 votes—less than one-hundredth of 1 percent of the total Florida vote. When the Gore campaign appealed on the grounds that the deadline had disadvantaged its candidate, the Democrat-friendly state Supreme Court ordered yet another recount—this time of all rejected "under-votes"—with a directive to election officials to pay attention to "voter intent." Thus commenced a drama, televised daily across the nation, of Florida's local election officials painstakingly examining ballots with "hanging chads" to determine whether or not they should be counted.

As Bush's margin shrank to approximately 150 votes, with the prospect that it might disappear altogether, his campaign team took the case to the U.S. Supreme Court for resolution. It was not a sure thing that the High Court would accept the case, given the longstanding principle that states were the arbiters of their own election laws. The Rehnquist Court, however—with its usually reliable conservative majority—took the case. On the night of December 12, the court spoke, issuing a 7-2 majority opinion to the effect that the recount process was too erratic and varied across the state to guarantee "equal protection" to all voters. More important, it also issued a 5-4 ruling that the recount be stopped because it could not be completed in time to meet the Florida statutory deadline of December 12 for certification of the state's electoral vote. In fact, the binding nature of that statutory requirement was debatable, but the court had ruled. Thirty-six days after election day, the justices had anointed a winner: Bush received Florida's 25 electoral votes and, with them, defeated Al Gore by 271-267 in the Electoral College.

At the time, Democrats expressed outrage at the court's action, assigning clearly partisan motives to its conservative, Republican-appointed majority. GOP spokespersons, on the other hand, citing the equally partisan-seeming rulings of the Florida Supreme Court, contended that the High Court's intervention had been the only way to resolve the controversy. Scholars and legal experts have also clashed in their assessments of the court's ruling. Legal scholar Robert Post, a contributor to Bruce Ackerman's edited volume, *Bush v. Gore: The Question of Legitimacy*, holds that "[t]he Court's declared concern with the unequal treatment of punched ballots loses all conviction in the face of [its] manifest indifference to the much larger disparity in the treatment of ballots as between different Florida counties." But what was the remedy for dealing with pre-existing differences in county election laws across the Sunshine State, which in fact existed in nearly every state? As Reagan's former solicitor general, Charles Fried, observes, also in Ackerman's volume:

> True it is that the methods of [vote] tabulation in our country vary from state to state and even precinct to precinct. But these differences are ordained before any particular election is held, and,

existing ex ante, they do not systematically disfavor any candidate or group of voters. The Florida court by contrast set in motion a system of disparities *after* the election had been held, when it was known just what depended on every subjective judgment, every change of standard from one moment to the next in counting ballots.

Although there continues to be disagreement among experts on such details of the *Bush v. Gore* decision, most of the constitutional law scholars who contributed to the Ackerman volume—reflecting a cross-section of ideology—tend to agree on two crucial points: (1) the Supreme Court should not have intervened until Congress had either counted the electoral votes in January or, in the manner of the disputed Hayes–Tilden election of 1876, established a mechanism for resolving the dispute; and (2) in any case, the court's decision to honor the debatable Florida law requiring early certification of the vote by December 12 and to stop the hand recount aimed at honoring "voter intent" was wrong-headed, in that it had the effect of denying "equal protection under the law" to those whose votes had been "over-" or "under-" counted.

Whether right or wrong, the court's intervention in the 2000 election sullied the body's reputation for apolitical neutrality. In his dissent from the majority opinion, Justice Stephen Breyer put it well. "Although we may never know with complete certainty the identity of the winner of this year's Presidential election," he wrote, "the identity of the loser is perfectly clear. It is the Nation's confidence in the judge as an impartial guardian of the rule of law." The underlying illogic of the majority opinion strongly suggested that it was grounded more in partisan motives than constitutional principles. Polls in the wake of the Supreme Court verdict revealed that only a slim majority of the electorate as a whole believed that Bush had really won. Those same polls, however, showed that three-fourths of all voters accepted George W. Bush as the legitimate president. Gore's gracious concession speech following the court's opinion was a big help in that regard.

The 2000 election should never have been so close as to require recounts or court cases. Prior to the election, writes Thomas Edsall in *Building Red America: The New Conservative Coalition and the Drive for Permanent Power*, "every predictive model suggested that Al Gore should win decisively, with the economy strong, the deficit gone, and ... Clinton continuing to be popular with the electorate. These economic and political science models predicted Gore would receive from 53 to 60 percent of the vote." What had gone wrong? True, Gore had won the popular vote—but only by 0.5 of 1 percent. One factor that clearly benefited Bush was Buchanan's decision not to contest the GOP nomination. This allowed the Religious Right more easily to support the party's nominee, who, despite his overt appeals to centrist voters, spoke proudly of his rebirth as a Christian. Gore, on the other hand, by failing to take advantage of the economic record of the Clinton–Gore administration and by keeping the popular president out of the campaign until its last, desperate days, blew his chance to hold the Clinton coalition together. His wooden public persona and perceived elitism made matters even worse, especially in states like Tennessee and Arkansas, where voters had responded so well to the president's folksiness on the campaign trail. It is also possible, as Pomper suggested in *The Election of 2000*, that the scandals of the Clinton administration may have rubbed off on Gore, even though voters approved of Clinton's handling of the presidency. Finally, at least in key states where the vote was close (certainly including Florida), the presence on the ballot of Green party candidate Ralph Nader cut into Gore's vote, and could have been the deciding factor in allowing Bush to achieve ultimate victory. Fearing the "Nader factor," near the end of the campaign Gore supporters in some states had attempted to use the Internet—an important force in a presidential election for the first time—to arrange "vote trades" between Gore supporters in states where the outcome was unlikely to be close and Nader supporters in toss-up states where the Green party threatened to tilt the state toward Bush. The idea was to help Nader secure at least 5 percent of the nationwide vote so that he would automatically be eligible for the ballot four years later, while at the same time concentrating Gore's vote in the states that mattered most. "The [web]sites generated a lot of media interest and a lot of 'hits,'" wrote Marjorie Randon Hersey in her essay in Pomper's post-election volume, after the election, "though there is no way to know how many of these trades were actually carried out."

Although both Bush and Gore had focused their campaigns on winning over centrists and independents, the ultimate shapes of the two parties' coalitions diverged even more sharply than they had in the previous two elections. Clinton's sixty-point-plus personal approval ratings masked deep, bitter cultural divisions that had been exploited by the GOP and exacerbated by mostly conservative court decisions during the years of his presidency. It proved impossible to make the election about the political center. "Not only two candidates, but virtually two nations confronted each other in the election of 2000," wrote Pomper. His analysis showed that, in addition to the largest gender gap that had yet been recorded, the election results showed increased partisan polarization between rich and poor (14 percentage points), single vs. married voters (13 points), gays and straights (23 points), non-believers and churchgoers (25 points), and—especially— blacks and whites (a whopping 48 points). Moreover, added Pomper, "the parties' supporters had become philosophically coherent. ... Fewer than one of every thirteen Republicans considered themselves liberals, and fewer than one in eight Democrats were conservatives."

While the election was not a repudiation of Clinton, the results suggested that the Republicans' "scorched earth" tactics during the preceding decade had not hurt them with the electorate. The Democrats managed to pick up four Senate seats, but the resulting 50-50 balance in the upper house left Vice President Cheney with the deciding vote. Among new Democratic faces in the Senate were three women: by far the highest-profile of these was First Lady Hillary Rodham Clinton, who won the seat of retiring New York Democrat Daniel Patrick Moynihan. The total number of women in the upper house increased to thirteen. In the House, the Republican margin declined only minutely, from 223-211 to 221-212, with two independents caucusing with the

Democrats. The GOP's showing in House races had clearly benefited from redistricting in several Republican-controlled states that had dramatically increased the number of the party's "safe" seats. For the first time since Dwight Eisenhower's first two years in the White House nearly a half-century earlier, the GOP controlled the White House and both houses of Congress.

The outlook for interparty cooperation as Bush took the oath of office was bleak. As Jacobson observes, by the turn of the new century both political leaders and the electorate had "become increasingly divided along party lines by political issues and ideology." Even inter-regional cooperation seemed to be threatened, as the electoral map showed increasingly heavy majorities for each of the two parties clustered in defined regions. Bush carried thirty states encompassing virtually the entire interior portion of the country—Red America—while Gore carried twenty on the two coasts and the populous upper Midwest, along with the District of Columbia—Blue America. Most Democrats may have grudgingly accepted Bush as the nation's president, but they were bitter about the way his victory had been achieved. In turn, wrote E. J. Dionne in *Why Americans Hate Politics*, that anger provoked a "furious counterreaction" on the right that threatened to play out over the next four years.

The Politics of Anti-terrorism

One casualty of the protracted struggle over the 2000 election was the time available to plan for the incoming administration. With only thirty-eight days between the Supreme Court's decision and Inauguration Day, the Bush team did not have the luxury of careful vetting and weighing of alternative appointees to the Cabinet. The president-elect relied heavily on Cheney for advice on the composition of the national security team, and ratified the vice president's choices of several prominent "neoconservatives" (proponents of an aggressive U.S. posture in the post-Cold War world) to the most important positions. These included, most notably, super-hawk Paul Wolfowitz as deputy secretary of defense under Donald Rumsfeld, another Cheney recommendation. Rumsfeld, though not usually included by the media as one of the "neocons," nonetheless brought to the defense post (which he had held twenty-five years earlier under Ford) a tough-mindedness that squared well with Cheney's worldview. Another key appointee, National Security Advisor Condoleezza Rice, was a Bush intimate rather than a Cheney sidekick, but she, too, was a hardheaded pragmatist. The outlier on the team was Secretary of State Colin Powell, important to the new president because of his popularity and credibility with media and public alike, but unlikely to wield great influence in this cold-eyed circle. "Vulcans," several of these incoming advisors had nicknamed themselves while still advisors to candidate Bush. The name "captured perfectly the image the Bush foreign policy sought to convey," writes James Mann in *Rise of the Vulcans: The History of Bush's War Cabinet*, "a sense of power, toughness, reliance, and durability."

Bush did not come to the White House with clearly defined objectives where American foreign policy was concerned. During the campaign, he had criticized Clinton's tendency to multilateralism and frequent resort to the UN as justification for U.S. actions, but he had not suggested how his approach might differ from that of his Democratic predecessor. An early indication came in March 2001, however, when he exerted his executive authority to renounce the Kyoto climate change treaty that Clinton had signed but not referred to the Senate for ratification. Bush's reneging on Kyoto implied disdain for multilateral agreements and a worrisome propensity to "go it alone" where world problems were concerned.

One point on which the Bush security team agreed was that Clinton had seemed obsessed with al-Qaeda, the Islamic terrorist faction responsible for the bombings of the World Trade Center in 1993 and the American embassies in Kenya and Tanzania in 1998. Within days of Bush's inauguration, Richard Clarke, who had served as counter-terrorism coordinator under Clinton and been retained in his position by Rice, tried to convince the new administration that al-Qaeda was indeed an imminent threat.

Specifically, Clarke urged Rice—without success—to convene a Cabinet-level review of the dangers posed by the radical Islamist group. The administration's dismissal of Clarke's warnings appears damning in retrospect, though it must be recognized that Clarke had been focused on al-Qaeda and its destructive potential for years. In contrast, the Bush team had barely settled in, and was trying to assess where the primary security concerns of the United States lay. Not until September 4, 2001, did Clarke's entreaties bear fruit in the form of a meeting of the "principals" (Cabinet-level national security personnel) to okay a plan to focus on al-Qaeda as a major threat to U.S. security.

Exactly one week after that meeting, the folly of ignoring Clarke's earlier warnings became clear. Bush was in a Tampa, Florida, elementary-school classroom on the morning of September 11 when two hijacked airliners struck the World Trade Center towers and a third plowed into the Pentagon. A fourth hijacked plane crashed in Pennsylvania, due to the heroic efforts of the passengers aboard, all of whom perished. Although the president's televised reactions were criticized as too blasé as he made his way out of the classroom, his reaction was visceral. "My blood was boiling," he wrote in his memoir. "We were going to find out who did this, and kick their ass." In his speech to the nation that evening, he was less than articulate, uttering jarring, wooden phrases such as "These acts shattered steel but they cannot dent the steel of American resolve." But in the next few days, he was at his best. Visiting the scene of the destruction and speaking movingly to rescue workers just two days after the attacks, Bush created a powerful image of on-the-ground leadership that drove his approval ratings through the roof.

The president's otherwise undistinguished speech on the night of 9/11 contained one sentence that transformed American foreign policy and foreshadowed a military involvement that would dominate the next decade and more. "We will make no distinction," he declared, "between the terrorists who committed these acts and those who harbored them." With this assertion, the president served notice that no government or power that condoned, or appeared to condone, the terrorist acts of 9/11

Figure 7.1 President Bush rallied the nation after the horrendous attack on the World Trade Center buildings on 9/11 by visiting the site and speaking to the firefighters and other rescue workers within days of the attack. © WIN MCNAMEE/Reuters/CORBIS

would be safe from American retribution. As soon became clear, Saddam Hussein's Iraq was directly in the president's—and Vice President Cheney's—sights at the time he made this pronouncement, even though there was no evidence that Saddam had either helped or shielded the terrorists.

Bush also moved quickly to beef up the country's capacity to deal with threats to its security, setting up an Office of Homeland Security in the White House, with Pennsylvania governor Tom Ridge as its head. Simultaneously and surreptitiously, the administration decided to bypass the 1978 Foreign Intelligence Surveillance Act (FISA), which had been adopted in the wake of the Church Committee's findings, by permitting surveillance of private e-mail and telephone communications without prior permission from the FISA court. At a Cabinet meeting on September 17, the president directed Attorney General John Ashcroft, FBI director Robert Mueller, and CIA director George

Tenet to coordinate domestic plans for homeland defense, and delegated Secretary of State Powell to issue an ultimatum to the Taliban in Afghanistan to cease their protection of al-Qaeda terrorists. Rumsfeld was requested to develop military plans to seek out the perpetrators of the 9/11 disaster. On the evening of September 20, Bush delivered a nationally televised speech to a joint session of Congress that hit every note with perfect pitch. "I will not yield. I will not rest," said the president in Churchillian cadence. "I will not relent in waging this struggle for freedom and security for the American people." In a way no one could have predicted, George W. Bush had become the president of all the people; his opportunities for leadership seemed limitless.

Acting quickly, Bush's team pulled together a broad policy directive, NSPD 9 ("Defeating the Terrorist Threat to the United States"), that, in Hal Brands's phrase in *From Berlin to Baghdad*, "opened the door to a virtually unbounded notion of antiterrorism." As Bush worked to rally public support for whatever steps might be needed abroad, the administration consulted with congressional leaders to secure legislation to deal with the aftermath of the attack. Cheney played a major role, pressing for support on the basis of "evidence" of questionable veracity. In addition to allegations that Hussein was building a stockpile of enriched uranium to produce nuclear weapons, according to Barton Gellman in his Pulitzer Prize-winning *Angler: The Cheney Vice Presidency*, Cheney shared an unverified claim that the Iraqis were readying drones with poisonous chemicals to be deployed using electronic maps of the eastern United States. On September 14, Congress passed with only a single dissenting vote (Democratic representative Barbara Lee from Oakland) a resolution authorizing Bush "to use all necessary and appropriate force against the nations, organizations, or people that he determines planned, authorized, committed, or aided the terrorist attacks." The administration had tried to secure even more open-ended authorization than it received, as Charlie Savage recounts in *Takeover: The Return of the Imperial Presidency and the Subversion of American Democracy*. Its last-minute efforts to widen its authority to secure authorization to use such force against enemies within the United States had been rejected by Senate Democratic majority leader Tom Daschle. Had this effort succeeded, Bush would have been legally empowered to conduct the war on terrorism at home. When the White House pushed also for restoration of aid to Pakistan and other questionable "allies" in the fight against terrorism, concerns voiced by a few leading Democrats were swept aside. "All of the legislation," GOP senator Mitch McConnell (Kentucky) declared, "has to be viewed through the prism of the situation we find ourselves in."

In the wake of 9/11, the American public was unnerved, not knowing what to expect next, or where it might occur. This widespread angst was exacerbated in mid-October, when letters containing deadly anthrax spores, mailed from a common location (Trenton, New Jersey) and marked "9-11-01" were found in mail delivered to several highly placed public officials and the offices of the three major television networks. The mystery of the anthrax letters was never solved, though investigators concluded that they were almost certainly of domestic origin. "We believed more attacks were coming, but we didn't know when, where, or from whom," Bush wrote in his memoir. "Striking the right balance between alerting and alarming the public remained a challenge … ."

As Savage observes, "[t]he Bush-Cheney administration seized the atmosphere of emergency and uncertainty that followed 9/11 to dramatically expand the zone of secrecy surrounding the executive branch"—an end to which they had already been committed. Just days after the attacks, Cheney had signaled in an appearance on *Meet the Press* that the administration was probably going to have to work on the "dark side" to be effective against its enemies. In late October, the White House secured easy passage of its signature legislation for the war on terrorism: the clumsily named-after-the-fact U.S.A. PATRIOT Act (for which a title was concocted specifically to spell out the acronym). Adopted by a vote of 98-1 in the Senate and 357-66 in the House, the act legalized the broad surveillance procedures that the administration had already implemented in defiance of existing law, allowing domestic eavesdropping for the purpose of gathering foreign intelligence, loosening the rules for the granting of warrants for wiretapping by the FISA court, and requiring telephone companies and e-mail providers to disclose electronic communications upon request by law enforcement agencies. Though initially supported by the vast majority of congressional Democrats, once in operation the law became a favorite target for anti-administration critics as an unconstitutional infringement of civil rights.

Two additional pieces of legislation in the months after 9/11 completed the domestic underpinnings of the war on terrorism: one established a federal Transportation Security Administration (TSA) to replace the private corps of baggage screeners in American airports; the second, the Homeland Security Act, was a far-reaching law enacted only after the administration had used it as a hammer in the 2002 mid-term elections. The latter act supplanted the White House Office of the same name and brought under a new Cabinet-level department a number of agencies previously housed in other departments. These included the Secret Service, U.S. Coast Guard, and Immigration and Naturalization Services (INS), which was renamed Immigration and Customs Enforcement (ICE). The act also established a color-coded Homeland Security Advisory System, which quickly came to be a pervasive part of American life; green (low threat) and blue (guarded) advisories were hardly seen in the early years after 9/11; more common, depending on the level of "chatter" being picked up by U.S. intelligence, were yellow (elevated) and orange (high). This situation would change over time, as the nation's nerves quieted.

By the time these statutes were enacted, Bush had already used the authority he had been granted by Congress to launch a massive air war in Afghanistan, where Osama bin Laden was in hiding, protected by the Taliban government. Having assembled a multilateral "coalition of the willing" drawn largely, but not exclusively, from among NATO allies, on October 7 Bush announced the onset of Operation Enduring Freedom. The waves of battering air strikes, aimed at suspected al-Qaeda training camps and Taliban military installations, succeeded with breathtaking speed reminiscent of the Gulf War. Within five weeks, they had wreaked sufficient damage that the anti-Taliban Northern Alliance was in control of the Afghan capital, Kabul. Taliban control of the country had been broken, sharply reducing the likelihood of official protection for bin Laden and his al-Qaeda followers. Important questions remained, however: how could stability be assured in Afghanistan and what role would the United States have to play in the effort? Moreover, bin Laden had not been found. Bush, already planning by this time to extend the military campaign into Iraq, opted to rely on Afghan forces to continue the quest for the terrorist mastermind. The gamble failed, and in December bin Laden slipped out of his hiding place in the Tora Bora mountains undetected.

Bush's plans to widen military action beyond Afghanistan became clear to all in his February 2002 State of the Union Address. Labeling the rogue nations of Iran, North Korea, and Iraq an "Axis of Evil," the president purposely blurred the line between governments harboring the terrorist faction responsible for 9/11 and those that posed danger because they possessed or might develop "weapons of mass destruction" (soon to be shorthanded as WMD) that could be used by terrorists. "By seeking weapons of mass destruction, these regimes pose a grave and growing danger," he said, invoking the hyperbolic rhetoric he had employed so effectively in the immediate aftermath of 9/11. "[T]he price of indifference would be catastrophic." As usual, Cheney's influence was at work in the "Axis of Evil" pronouncement. "Speechwriters recall little if any input from Cheney on the 'axis of evil' passage," writes Gellman. "But the strategic concept belonged to the vice president." In any case, the leap of logic tying the 9/11 terrorists to these rogue regimes was a considerable one, and for the first time congressional Democrats began openly to question Bush's broad intentions in the war on terrorism.

Critics were justified in their concern that the administration might use the blank check that Congress had written a few months earlier to carry out military operations of its own design and, at the same time, seek political gain from public apprehension about terrorism. In January, a story leaked that

Karl Rove had told the Republican National Committee annual meeting that the GOP could "go to the American people on this issue of winning the war," adding that the voters "trust the Republican party to do a better job of protecting and strengthening America's military might and thereby protecting America." Within weeks, political unity was clearly fraying. By May, several leading Democrats were on the attack, charging that the administration was keeping Congress in the dark about its intentions and, more improbably, that the president might have known in advance about the impending 9/11 attacks and done nothing in response. New York's junior senator, Hillary Clinton, was as outspoken as anyone on the issue, waving a copy of the *New York Post* with the headline, "Bush Knew" as she spoke on the Senate floor in mid-May. Scenting blood, the Democrats called for a "broad public inquiry" into what the government knew—and when.

Bipartisan congressional interest in a full-scale investigation into the background of the 9/11 attacks led to an announcement in February 2002 of a joint inquiry by the House and Senate Intelligence Committees. The souring of inter-party relations in the following months, however—coupled with signs that the White House did not intend to cooperate fully—escalated calls for an independent commission, to which each political party would appoint an equal number of members. Pressure in the media, as well as from the families who had lost loved ones on 9/11, ultimately overcame White House resistance to such an inquiry, and in late November 2002 Bush signed into law a bill establishing the ten-member 9/11 Commission. With former GOP governor Thomas Kean as chair and former Democratic congressman Lee Hamilton as vice chair, the commission was given broad subpoena powers and access to classified intelligence documents. The study was expected to take eighteen months to complete.

Though Bush had moved first against Afghanistan after 9/11, from the outset he was making plans to move against Saddam Hussein, Convinced that the Iraqi leader was providing (or planning to provide) WMDs to al-Qaeda, he was also eager to correct what he saw as his father's mistake of not having taken the Gulf War to its conclusion—though he never publicly criticized that decision. The possibility of "regime change" in Iraq had in fact been discussed inside the White House soon after George W's inauguration, well before 9/11. Cheney and Rumsfeld both strongly supported aggressive action, motivated more by geopolitical than ideological considerations. On the very day of the attacks on the World Trade Center, Rumsfeld brought up the idea of retaliating against Hussein. Bush needed little persuasion. In late December, he asked General Tommy Franks, head of the U.S. Central Command, for a briefing on what would be required for a successful assault on Iraq. Franks's estimate of 145,000 to 275,000 U.S. troops did not discourage the president, who asked him to develop a specific strategy. Meanwhile, intelligence efforts turned up no hard evidence of connections between the Hussein government and al-Qaeda operatives.

The administration now put on a full-court press to make the case for Saddam Hussein's culpability in the 9/11 attacks. "We are hunting down al-Qaeda one by one," the president assured Congress in September 2002, long after bin Laden had escaped from his Afghanistan redoubt. "The biggest threat, however, is Saddam Hussein and his weapons of mass destruction." The White House message received total buy-in from the GOP congressional leadership, despite there being zero evidence of any connection between Hussein and al-Qaeda. "There is no doubt that Iraq supports and harbors these terrorists who wish harm to the United States," said GOP House Speaker Dennis Hastert in October 2002. "Is there a direction connection between Iraq and al-Qaeda? The president thinks so." The administration repeatedly asserted the charge that the Iraqi regime had nuclear weapons and was committed to sharing them with terrorists endangering the United States. As early as his 2002 State of the Union Address, Bush had specifically cited intelligence reports that the Iraqi government had purchased enriched uranium in Africa that, he suggested, could only be for purposes of producing WMDs. Though that claim would ultimately be discredited by a first-hand participant, former ambassador Joseph Wilson, it helped for the moment to silence administration critics.

The Democrats were without an effective strategy in the face of administration claims of intelligence supporting the need for regime change in Iraq. Concerned about the 2002 mid-term elections, congressional Democrats, even though suspicious of the administration's arguments, had to walk a cautious line. Making the most of its advantage, just weeks before the mid-term elections the White House sought congressional authorization to take all necessary steps against Iraq. The resolution passed easily—by 296-133 in the House and 77-23 in the Senate. In the end, Democrats were almost evenly split on the measure. "The numbers were inflated by those with presidential ambitions," Lou and Carl Cannon write in *Reagan's Disciple: George W. Bush's Troubled Quest for a Presidential Legacy*, "but who nonetheless expressed misgivings about the invasion."

Bush campaigned aggressively for GOP candidates in the 2002 mid-term elections, visiting almost every state in which there was a possibility of Republican victory; the president of all the people had become the Republican-in-chief. The administration's aggressive efforts succeeded in the face of a demoralized opposition, as the GOP picked up two Senate seats and six seats in the House. Not since 1934 had the president's party gained seats in both houses in a mid-term election. The results did not signify national unity, however, so much as an increasingly deep partisan divide. "Bush's near universal approval ratings among Republicans, his energetic fund-raising and frenzied last-minute campaigning in competitive states, combined with effective Republican grass-roots drives to get out the vote," writes Jacobson, "put Republicans over the top." The election "was won by mobilizing the base rather than broadening the party's appeal." Significantly—and White House political strategists would not miss the lesson for 2004—Republican victories had been mostly fueled by Christian conservatives, who turned out in large numbers and voted enthusiastically for their patriotic president. "It might be said that the last vestiges of 9/11 bipartisanship effectively ended that [election day] evening," concludes Robert Draper in *Dead Certain: The Presidency of George W. Bush*.

As part of his strategy to force Saddam Hussein from power, Bush had been pressing the UN to insist on carrying out the weapons inspections it had ordered earlier. He minced no words in addressing the annual meeting of delegates in early September. "Are Security Council resolutions to be honored and enforced, or cast aside without consequences? Will the United Nations serve the purpose of its founding, or will it be irrelevant?" On November 8, just after the U.S. congressional elections, the Security Council issued a new, stronger resolution on Iraqi arms inspections, promising "serious consequences" if the Iraqi ruler failed to comply. Convinced that the UN meant business this time, Saddam yielded. In late November, UN arms inspectors entered Iraq. The Bush administration moved ahead with plans for regime change in Iraq anyway, beginning a buildup of American forces in the Gulf region that would total approximately 250,000 by early 2003. On February 5, Secretary of State Powell—the most widely credible member of Bush's National Security team—delivered an impassioned address to the Security Council, asserting there was "irrefutable evidence" that Iraq was producing WMDs, even though he apparently still harbored personal doubts about such claims. When that body turned down a motion to issue an ultimatum to Saddam, Bush decided to go it alone. On March 17, he laid down the gauntlet, telling the Iraqi leader to step down from power or face imminent attack.

Powell's speech had more impact on the American public than on his UN audience, with polls indicating that more than 80 percent of Americans now accepted the WMD argument. On the other hand, there were sharp partisan differences over what should be done. Almost two-thirds of those who identified as Democrats and nearly as many independents responded that the United States should "wait and give the United Nations inspectors more time," while only 30 percent of Republicans favored delaying military action. Lacking counter-evidence to oppose the administration's claims, Congress had little option but to go along. According to Bob Woodward in *Plan of Attack: The Definitive Account of the Decision to Invade Iraq*, following a briefing of congressional leaders by Rice on the administration's plans to move against Saddam, GOP senator John Warner of Virginia remarked to her: "You got to do this and I'll support you. ... But I sure hope you find weapons of mass destruction because if you don't you may have a big problem."

The U.S. bombardment of Iraq that began on March 19, 2003, had immediate results. By the second week of April, troops on the ground, including those from the "coalition of the willing," succeeded in taking Basra, Baghdad, and Kirkuk in the north. With victory—whatever that might entail—seeming inevitable, Bush, arrived on the deck of the aircraft carrier *Abraham Lincoln*, stepping out of the fixed-wing navy fighter that had transported him wearing a naval flight suit. After he had changed into a business suit and tie, he proceeded to proclaim success to the American people in a televised address live from the deck of the ship. While his words acknowledged that Operation Iraqi Freedom was but one battle in an "ongoing war," the red, white, and blue banner that served as his backdrop, proclaiming "MISSION ACCOMPLISHED," was the lasting image from the news clip. In his memoirs, Bush explained that the banner had been "intended as a tribute to the folks aboard the *Lincoln*," but to the world it looked differently. The president's speech and its setting, writes Draper, "evoked images of the morally unambiguous Second World War."

The "shock and awe" unleashed on Iraq by the U.S. military in the spring of 2003, however, proved anything but decisive. Saddam had fled Baghdad, leaving a power void; bringing order to the headless country was another matter altogether. In early May, Bush dispatched a *de facto* government to Iraq, the Coalition Provisional Authority. The newly installed regime, headed by former U.S. ambassador (to the Netherlands) Paul Bremer, immediately committed a huge tactical error that would come back to haunt the occupying forces. Although the coalition's message to Saddam Hussein's Baathist party followers had been that if they refused to take up arms against the coalition invasion they would be permitted to remain in place, the opposite happened. As described by Richard Clarke in his memoir, *Against All Enemies: Inside America's War on Terror*, now "the U.S. had another message: 'You're all fired.'" Since joining the Baathist party had been mandatory for Iraqis who wished to hold government positions under Saddam, Clarke notes, "[b]y dismissing them all ... there were suddenly no experienced managers." A second important miscue by Bremer was his decision to divert electricity from Baghdad to the countryside, which had the effect of plunging the capital into near-economic chaos and periodic darkness. In addition, the provisional government ordered the dissolution of the Iraqi army, leaving thousands of armed young Iraqis with neither gainful employment nor any stake in helping to maintain public order.

As the situation steadily deteriorated in post-invasion Iraq, the Bush administration launched a concerted propaganda campaign at home. Its aim was to convince the public that the president had been right to suspect that Hussein was developing WMDs, despite former ambassador Wilson's July 2003 refutation of the Niger uranium deal on which the claim was based. Democrats jumped on Wilson's revelations, calling loudly and insistently for an investigation into both the substance of the administration's claim and its continued misrepresentations after learning the truth about the "uranium deal." Cheney's office took the lead in harassing and trying to discredit Wilson. As was discovered much later, his chief of staff, Scooter Libby, was responsible for "outing" Wilson's wife, Valerie Plame, as an undercover CIA agent, in direct violation of federal law forbidding such disclosure. CIA director Tenet dutifully tried to accept blame for the revelation, but the Democrats were unconvinced and the partisan atmosphere grew more heated as election year 2004 approached. There was trouble within GOP congressional ranks, as well, as a small group of powerful Republican senators broke with the administration over whether a requested $18.6 million for Iraqi reconstruction should be a grant or a loan. Even the capture of Saddam Hussein in December 2003 did little to improve the worsening atmosphere for the White House; within weeks of the capture, Bush's approval ratings had fallen back into the high 40s.

The administration's public relations hit a low point in spring 2004, with the revelation of the inhumane and at times pornographic humiliation of captured Iraqis at the hands of

U.S. service personnel at the prison in Abu Ghraib, outside Baghdad. So severe was the political fallout when these human rights violations surfaced that Bush, as he later recounted, considered sacrificing Donald Rumsfeld as an act of White House contrition. "I knew it would send a powerful signal to replace the leader of the Pentagon after such a grave mistake," Bush wrote in his memoir. The problem was, however, that "[t]here was no obvious replacement." Behind the scenes, there was even more trouble for Bush, though the public as a whole remained unaware of it until it came out in Senate testimony three years later. In early March, while Attorney General Ashcroft was hospitalized and in a critical condition, Cheney and his staff attempted to coerce him into re-certifying the warrantless domestic surveillance program so it could be re-authorized by the president (as it had been regularly since 2001). When Deputy Attorney General James Comey, to whom Ashcroft had temporarily shifted his authority, adamantly refused to sign, Cheney tried to get Bush to re-authorize the illegal program anyway. Only the threat of mass resignations by Comey, FBI director Mueller, and other Department of Justice personnel caused Bush to step back from the brink, averting a public relations calamity. "Had he not done so, political advisors said," writes Gellman in *Angler*, "his first term would have been his last, and a Watergate-style backlash, shackling future presidents with new restraints, would have been hard to prevent."

Adding to the administration's woes in the spring of 2004 was the hype surrounding Michael Moore's box-office blockbuster, *Fahrenheit 9/11*, a scathing—if questionably documented—cinematic indictment of Bush's Iraq policies. In this environment, the White House's propaganda campaign of the previous several months came under renewed criticism from the left. "Republicans' faith was barely shaken" by these events and revelations, writes Jacobson, "while the proportion of Democrats who thought the president was 'honest and trustworthy' fell … to less than 30 percent in polls taken in 2004." It looked increasingly as if Bush would follow in his father's footsteps as a one-term president.

Imagined Mandate

Since George W. Bush had promised to be a "uniter" and had won the presidency only after the Supreme Court intervened, it was initially expected that he would hew to a moderate course in the White House. Whatever his own predilections might have been, however, Rove and his other political handlers persuaded him that the better course was to play to his conservative base. Even before the election had been settled, pollster Matthew Dowd had presented Rove (and Bush) with poll data purportedly showing that the so-called "swing vote" had shrunk to an almost negligible size in presidential elections—from about 22 percent in 1980 to only 6 or 7 percent in 2000. That being the case, he argued, it made more sense for Bush to strengthen his hold on the GOP base, intensifying its loyalty and ensuring its heavy turnout the next time around. The day after the Supreme Court made Bush president, vice president-elect Cheney delivered this harsh message to the party's remaining moderate senators, the so-called "Wednesday Group." As recorded by Lincoln Chafee (Rhode Island), a charter member of the group, Cheney's message sounded "a clashist approach on every issue, big and small," indicating that "any attempt at consensus would be a sign of weakness." Recounting the shocking meeting later in his memoir, *Against the Tide: How a Compliant Congress Empowered a Reckless President,* Chafee wrote that if Cheney meant what he said, "the president-elect would not only reignite the partisanship of the Clinton-Gingrich era but would make it even more toxic."

Bush wasted no time after his inauguration before demonstrating that the "compassionate conservatism" of the campaign was more rhetorical than real. His first executive actions signaled combativeness, including not only rejection of the Kyoto Treaty, but the reopening of federally owned land to commercial use, the easing of air and water pollution standards, and a near-ban on the use of federal money for organizations advocating abortions. The appointment of two high-profile anti-abortion Cabinet members, John Ashcroft as attorney general and Tommy

Thompson as secretary of health and human services, as well as the establishment of a new White House office for faith-based initiatives, provided indisputable evidence of the new president's intention to play to his conservative supporters. Six months into his presidency, Bush announced his decision not to permit federal funds to be used for stem cell research—a position that brought on intense criticism from the scientific community. In style, too, he was combative and uncompromising. "Bush's idea of legislative leadership, by his own and others' descriptions," wrote Jacobson in 2007, "is to stake out a firm position right at his own ideal point … defend it against all objections, pursue it with focus and tenacity, and compromise only at the last minute and the smallest extent possible to gain the victory."

All of this was on full display in the first legislative fight of the Bush presidency, over the White House's tax reduction proposal. Although there were signs that the long-running boom of the 1990s was weakening, the new president was intent on returning much of the large Clinton-era budget surplus to taxpayers. Repeating the supply-side nostrum that the cuts would provide a stimulus to the economy and avert recession, he proposed a whopping $1.6 trillion in tax cuts over ten years. "The tax cut plan was … a defining test for the new president," writes Baker in *Days of Fire*. "Never far from his mind was his father's read-my-lips reversal." The White House's no-compromise posture proved extremely costly; after rejecting the pleas of party moderates to reduce the cuts in order to spare popular and needed programs such as special education, Bush was shocked in late May when moderate Republican senator Jim Jeffords of Vermont announced that he was switching parties. The 50-50 balance that had made Vice President Cheney the deciding vote in the Senate after the 2000 election was suddenly gone; the Democrats were again in control. The White House eventually had to give ground in the tax cut battle, accepting a bill reducing taxes by $1.35 trillion over ten years. The measure then passed easily in both houses, and Bush signed it into law in 2001, with a ten-year sunset clause unless it were specifically renewed.

Bush did reach across the party aisle on the issue of education reform, on which he had focused in the 2000 campaign. Making a tactical decision to break with the conservatives on school vouchers, he decided to work with Senator Ted Kennedy to craft a national education policy that would hold schools accountable based on student test results. What bound Bush and Kennedy together was not so much agreement about standardized testing, but a common commitment to closing the "achievement gap" between white students and students of color. With Kennedy's help and cooperation between GOP House Education Committee chairman John Boehner (Ohio) and ranking Democrat George Miller (California), a bill was crafted and passed by March. The "No Child Left Behind" law would prove to be one of Bush's most lasting policy legacies. A second White House measure to achieve passage with a degree of bipartisan support was a proposal to establish a prescription drug benefit for seniors who opted for private health plans rather than Medicare. Amended in the lower house to include also pre-tax health savings accounts (HSAs) to pay for medical expenses, the bill was signed into law by the president in December 2003. These two successful bipartisan ventures, however, did not serve as a basis for others. Increasingly focused on the war on terrorism and the war in Iraq, Bush gave little attention to domestic issues during the remainder of his first term.

Not only were some of the president's controversial executive actions deeply unpopular with a large segment of the electorate, but publication of Bob Woodward's best-selling *Plan of Attack* in April—harshly critical of the administration's failure to consider any options other than war in Iraq—had intensified public concern about how the White House was carrying out the war on terrorism. Gearing up for re-election, Bush and his advisors aimed at making the 2004 election "a choice—not a referendum." The best approach seemed to be to draw as stark a contrast as possible between the president—as the decisive, patriotic commander-in-chief at a time of grave national peril—and whomever the Democrats might choose to nominate.

Like Richard Nixon in 1972, Bush fervently hoped his opponent in 2004 would be the early Democratic front-runner and most extreme anti-war critic—in this case, Vermont governor Howard Dean. While Dean's at times shrill denunciations of the war appealed to the most liberal segments of the electorate, particularly the young, they did not seem a likely recipe for success with the broader public in the wake of 9/11. Moderate Democrats, desperate to oust Bush from the White House, were increasingly intent on selecting the nominee with the best chance of defeating the president. Nearly all other likely aspirants for the nomination—Senators Joe Lieberman, John Edwards (North Carolina), and John Kerry (Massachusetts), and Representative Richard Gephardt—had voted for the Iraq war authorization, in a way neutralizing the anti-war issue among them. After a brief boomlet for former NATO commander General Wesley Clark, Kerry, who was a decorated Vietnam War veteran, rose to the top as the most credible of these converted anti-war critics.

As in 2000, the Democratic contest sorted out quickly. Making an all-out effort in Iowa that included special appeals to veterans, Kerry knocked off both Dean and Gephardt, who had been expected to do well there. Dean lost any chance of going further into the campaign by self-immolating on television as the Iowa returns came in, emitting what the media described as a "primal scream" in his concession speech (which was seen by millions of viewers thereafter on YouTube). Kerry, after carrying his neighboring state of New Hampshire by 82 percent soon after, quickly became an inevitability, clinching the nomination in early March. Briefly, the presumptive nominee tried to lure Bush's old GOP rival, John McCain, to be his running-mate on an "all-veteran" ticket that might prove impossible for Bush to defeat. McCain, however—even if still resentful of the Bush campaign's dirty tricks four years earlier—could not be won over. Kerry eventually chose one of his primary foes who had almost blatantly campaigned for the second spot, the telegenic young North Carolina senator, John Edwards. Although Kerry did not announce Edwards's selection until the eve of the Democratic convention in July, as Evan Thomas and his *Newsweek* colleagues wrote in their post-election analysis, *Election 2004: How Bush Won and What You Can Expect in the Future*, the North Carolinan "was everywhere that spring campaigning for Kerry, especially in the closely contested border states." Once again, in what was coming to be the norm, the general election campaign began months before the party nominations were officially decided by the national conventions.

Bush's decision to focus on solidifying his conservative base ensured that he faced no competition at all from within his party, and he was thus able to launch his campaign against Kerry as soon as the Democrats' choice was clear. The White House strategy, pure Rove, was to continue to build that base, while portraying Kerry as an effete, typical Northeastern liberal (who spoke French, even!), out of step with mainstream American values. At the same time, the Bush campaign's focus would remain more squarely on the war on terrorism than on defending the increasingly troubling military stalemate in Iraq. In such a campaign, reopening the cultural divide on social issues also seemed attractive. "Rove had never stopped campaigning since the 2000 squeaker," wrote Thomas et al. "[H]e had been building the Republican base, the vast Red State army of evangelicals; flag-waving small-town and rural American Dreamers; 60s-hating, pro-death penalty, anti-gay marriage social conservatives; Big Donors—the new Republican majority ... ." Thus, the uniter of 2000 morphed into the candidate of Red America, hoping to triumph on the basis of social and cultural divisions that largely coincided with opposing views on the rectitude of the Iraq war.

One issue that highlighted the cynicism of Bush's re-election campaign was that of same-sex marriage. The matter had been brought to the political fore by a June 2003 Supreme Court decision, *Lawrence v. Texas*, outlawing state anti-sodomy laws, and—five months later—a Massachusetts Supreme Judicial Court ruling in *Goodridge v. Department of Health* that explicitly approved gay and lesbian marriage in that state (fortuitously for Bush, Kerry's home state). For all his public professions of born-again Christianity, Bush had never before been known for whipping up cultural intolerance for campaign purposes. Rather, his "instinct on gay-rights issues," writes David Frum in *The Right Man: An*

Inside Account of the Bush White House, had been "clear and emphatic: *Do not touch them!*" In the wake of the *Lawrence* and *Goodridge* cases, however, and facing the challenge of a decorated war veteran who might be able to pierce his commander-in-chief's armor, Bush gave in. In February 2004, he announced his support for a constitutional amendment that would ban same-sex marriage throughout the United States, thereby legitimizing the Religious Right's increasingly vituperative campaign for such an amendment and encouraging its efforts to place anti-same-sex-marriage initiatives before voters in several states. The proposed constitutional amendment predictably stalled in the Senate, but anti-same-sex-marriage measures appeared on the ballot in eleven states in the fall.

Kerry's veteran status had probably helped him secure the Democratic nomination, but it caused him grief in the general campaign. Even before his formal nomination in July, a group of fellow "swift-boat" veterans with whom he had served in Vietnam three decades before became agitated as a result of publication of an admiring campaign biography, Douglas Brinkley's *Tour of Duty: John Kerry and the Vietnam War*. In the minds of these fellow veterans, the book was marred by factual errors and seemed to glorify Kerry's exploits while demeaning those of others, including his commanding officer at the time. The group of some 300 anti-Kerry veterans caused tremendous problems for him, enlisting right-wing muckraker Jerome Corsi to produce a vituperative counter-volume, *Unfit for Command: Swift Boat Veterans Speak Out Against John Kerry*, while coordinating with individuals loosely connected to the Bush campaign. Following the Democratic convention in Boston, from which Kerry received a mild bounce, the self-styled Swift Boat Veterans for Truth went into full battle mode, flooding the airwaves with a well-financed television ad campaign in the first weeks of August. Fox News gave their efforts a major boost by running approximately 150 news stories that featured the ad. On August 19, Kerry issued a belated response undercutting most of the claims in the attack ad, but by then it had taken on a life of its own. Allegations that Karl Rove had masterminded the entire campaign were false, but the *New York Times* identified an attorney directly involved in the Bush re-election campaign as a co-conspirator just prior to the GOP convention.

Perhaps because of the diminishing size of a truly undecided bloc, it is unlikely that the campaign changed many voters' minds. Kerry proved to be a fairly ineffectual campaigner on the stump, often appearing to over-intellectualize and disdaining the time-honored formula of shaping a single, memorable theme and repeating it in every appearance. Although he tried to make Iraq the key issue of the campaign, his earlier vote in support of the authorizing resolution diminished the impact of his attacks, and a clumsy remark early in the campaign season that he had been for a key measure before he was against it played into the Bush campaign strategy of portraying him as a waffler. Kerry was far the better debater, however, and he trounced Bush in the first of the three scheduled presidential debates, with the president appearing "whiny and wriggly as a spoiled child" and Kerry appearing "Presidential," in Thomas's phrasing. The candidates performed equally well in the remaining two televised confrontations, however, and after Cheney overpowered the naive-seeming Edwards in the vice-presidential faceoff, the series of debates as a whole amounted to a draw. As election day neared, the presidential contest was too close to call. Even a pre-election surprise videotape released by bin Laden, aimed at bringing about Bush's defeat, failed to move the needle from the almost even split in the electorate tracked by the polls.

Unimaginably, the election's outcome was as close as the 2000 cliffhanger had been—though it would be resolved much more quickly. Again, Americans woke up the next morning not knowing who had been elected president. This time it was Ohio, not Florida, on which the final electoral result depended. Early exit polls that had pointed to a Kerry victory in the Buckeye State were contradicted as the votes there were tallied. Once again, as in Florida four years earlier, disquieting stories circulated about irregularities in many local polling places that had disproportionately disfranchised young and minority voters. Though such patterns were disturbing, the statewide results were definitive enough by midday that Kerry formally conceded. This time, at least there was a clear-cut overall winner. In an election marked by an extraordinarily high turnout (60.1 percent of eligible voters), Bush received 50.7 percent of the popular vote and Kerry, 48.3 percent; the president's margin of victory in the Electoral College was 286-251. Notably, Bush won fewer votes from independents than Kerry—the first victorious candidate since Kennedy for whom that was the case, notes Jacobson.

The 2004 congressional elections, too, turned out well for the administration, as the GOP gained four seats in the Senate (winning all five seats in the South that were up for election), and increased its majority in the House by three seats. The most notable Democratic loser was Senate minority leader Tom Daschle, while the newcomer who captured the most attention was Barack Obama, a state legislator who swept to a landslide victory for the vacant Illinois Senate seat after having electrified the 2004 Democratic convention with a keynote speech extolling the possibilities for a more unified nation.

The 2004 outcome, as Jacobson notes, represented the narrowest re-election margin for any sitting president in history. The unprecedented amounts of money spent on the two campaigns—an astonishing $847 million combined, representing nearly twice the amount spent by the two contenders in 2000—had produced a disquieting result. The candidates had succeeded in mobilizing their respective bases, and now the distance between them seemed greater than ever. In particular, religion seemed once again an especially divisive force in the electorate. The state referenda on same-sex marriage brought huge numbers of conservative Christians and Catholic voters to the polls, in fact probably accounting for Bush's victory in the decisive state of Ohio. Religiosity—that is, the strength of one's religious beliefs— seemed to be a factor across the board. According to a pre-election ABC/*Washington Post* poll, within both parties the strength of a voter's religiosity was strongly correlated with degree of support for Bush and his conduct of the war in Iraq. In such a close election, however, almost any issue might be labeled as decisive. It is possible, for example, that the Swift Boat campaign and its ubiquitous advertisements were the key, dissuading enough Democrats and independents from voting for Kerry to allow Bush to win narrow re-election.

Seemingly oblivious to the implications of his narrow margin of victory, as in 2001 Bush chose to regard the electoral result as a mandate to move full speed ahead with his personal agenda. In his first post-election press conference, he laid out an ambitious conservative roadmap for his second term, declaring to startled reporters: "I earned capital in the campaign, and now I intend to spend it." Planned administration initiatives included not only removing the sunset clause on the 2001 tax cuts and passing tax "simplification" including pro-business provisions, but even tampering with the third rail of American politics, Social Security. Draper sees logic at work on Bush's part, noting: "No Child Left Behind, tax cuts, the Patriot Act, Homeland Security, authorization to invade Iraq, Medicare, prescription drugs, supplemental war funding—the White House had always gotten what it wanted. And that was before November 2004. Bush was stronger than ever." If Bush saw it that way, however, he was misreading the election's outcome. More on target is Jacobson's observation: "If 'political capital' means popular support that can be drawn upon to win legislative victories, Bush's was in a currency honored only in Republican territory."

Within three months of his second inauguration, Bush took on the most divisive item on his agenda, Social Security reform. The boldest part of his plan was an option for younger members of the workforce to invest part of their Social Security taxes in private retirement accounts from which they might expect to earn a better return. GOP legislators had been wary of the president's wading into this issue, already worrying about its impact on the next mid-term elections. Democrats were adamantly opposed from the outset. The president pushed hard for his package over the next few months, but—with few congressional allies willing to risk their necks by supporting the measure—it made little headway against the entrenched Democratic opposition. By fall, Social Security reform was dead in the water. In his memoir, the usually non-introspective Bush noted ruefully that he "may have misread the electoral mandate by pushing for an issue on which there had been little bipartisan agreement." As Lou and Carl Cannon observe, however, it may actually have been Bush's own personal unpopularity at that point more than the unattractiveness of the "privatization" option that did his plan in. "Features of [the] proposed reform, notably private accounts," they write, "enjoyed broad public support until they were paired with the name Bush—then the bottom fell out."

What had happened to render Bush capital-less so soon after his re-election? The continuing morass in Iraq was a major part of the explanation; nothing had improved on the ground by late 2005, nor was the political situation there becoming more stable. As the numbers of dead and wounded U.S. troops continued to climb, the administration attempted to avoid publicizing such casualties, even disallowing the televising of images of the caskets of deceased service members returning to the United States. At least equally damaging to Bush's credibility as a leader, however, was the administration's perceived incompetence in the face of the devastation of New Orleans by Hurricane Katrina at the end of August. With death tolls approaching 2000 and scores of thousands more (mostly black) residents in need of shelter and housing, the president delayed for four days before even visiting the city and, even as the Federal Emergency Management Agency (FEMA) was delivering too little, too late, he bestowed praise on the agency's obviously struggling director, Michael Brown, for "doing a heckuva job." The statement, writes Douglas Brinkley in *The Great Deluge: Hurricane Katrina, New Orleans, and the Mississippi Gulf Coast*, "became emblematic of the President's ignorance about the situation and his tendency to take a casual attitude toward it." As the city continued to reel, Bush's tone-deafness seemed to know no bounds. Although there had been widespread specula-tion about the weakness of the city's levees for days as Katrina had gained force and headed to New Orleans and the president had been briefed accordingly by the director of the National Hurricane Center, a few days after the storm he inexplicably told news anchor Diane Sawyer on *Good Morning America*: "I don't think anybody expected the breach of the levees." By his demeanor on the show, Brinkley observes, "[t]he President came across ... as remote, unable to articulate the comforting words [needed] to rally the nation in its hour of peril." The media were unforgiving in covering these developments and in their characterization of the president's inept response. Slowly, the relief effort improved, but neither the city of New Orleans nor Bush's political fortunes would ever fully recover from this disaster. "The administration's buffoonish response to Hurricane Katrina," writes Geoffrey Kabaservice in *Rule and Ruin*, "reinforced the perception that conservatives undervalued competence in government and didn't care about poor and minority Americans." Bush had few answers at the time, but in his memoir he reflected painfully: "I faced a lot of criticism as president. ... But the suggestion that I was a racist because of the response to Katrina represented an all-time low."

Bush's plummeting popularity beginning late in the first year of his second term pretty much ended any chance for the second-term agenda he imagined in the afterglow of his re-election. There was no prospect of his making the 2001 tax cuts permanent, though they would at least remain on the books till their scheduled ten-year expiration. Perhaps making a strategic decision to back off the hard-edged positions he had advanced, he made an effort to secure meaningful immigration reform in May 2006, presenting his proposal in a nationally televised speech— "the first-ever primetime presidential address on immigration," as he noted in his memoir. Similar in approach to the Immigration Reform and Control Act of twenty years earlier, Bush's plan included strengthened border protection, stricter enforcement of rules for businesses employing immigrant workers, a special temporary worker program, and—as the centerpiece—a path to citizenship for undocumented immigrants if certain requirements were met, including that they learn English. With the help of Ted Kennedy and Arizona's two GOP senators, John McCain and Jon Kyl, Bush managed to get the measure through the Senate twice—in 2006 and again in 2007. The more conservative House, however, remained opposed. Moreover, by 2007, conservative talk-show hosts had made opposition to immigration reform a major cause, fueling public anger on the right and making any further attempts at such legislation not worth the price for moderate legislators. "If I had it to do over again," wrote Bush in *Decision Points*, "I would have pushed for immigration reform, rather than Social Security as the first major initiative of my second term." That he did not, of course, was due to his erroneous belief that his political "capital" after re-election made such strategic choices unnecessary.

Perhaps George W. Bush's most lasting conservative legacy was his impact on the federal judiciary. Congressional Democrats gave him a hard time on his nominations to lesser federal courts from the outset, blocking many of them by filibuster even while the GOP controlled the upper house. Still, eight years of appointments allowed him to have a cumulative impact on the ideological direction of the lower courts, as is true for any two-term president. Most significant, however, was the decisive change on the Supreme Court that he managed to effect. Uncertain as to whether he would have an opportunity to replace any members of the court while in the White House, Bush wanted to be ready in case he would. He established a staunchly conservative vetting team, chaired by Cheney and including Rove, Ashcroft, White House counsel Alberto Gonzalez, Cheney's aide Scooter Libby, and White House chief of staff Andrew Card. Opportunity came in 2005, when Justice O'Connor, a moderate "swing" vote on the court, announced her retirement in order to care for her ailing husband. Intent on finding a relatively young justice whose influence on the court would be lasting, Bush settled quickly on 50-year-old John Roberts, a conservative of keen intellect and impeccable credentials. A District of Columbia Court of Appeals judge, Roberts had served as Rehnquist's clerk before joining the Reagan administration, during which he served in the White House counsel's office; he had later served as deputy solicitor general under the first Bush. His nomination was well received. Before his confirmation hearings could even begin, however, the ailing chief justice, William Rehnquist, died, creating yet a second court vacancy—including, of course, the most important one. Seeing the smooth confirmation path ahead for Roberts, Bush switched his nomination to be a replacement for the chief justice and moved to fill O'Connor's seat with another woman, White House counsel Harriet Miers. Unfortunately for the president, Miers's candidacy ran into immediate trouble because of her lack of judicial experience. Backtracking, Bush nominated another reliably conservative Appeals Court judge, Samuel Alito of the Third Circuit (Philadelphia), who had also served in the Reagan administration. Roberts was confirmed, 78-22, though even that number of negative votes reflected less unanimity than had historically marked confirmations of well-qualified justices. The more abrasive Alito ran into stronger opposition, finally being confirmed by 58-42, with only four Democrats voting yes. Although no one could legitimately question Alito's qualifications, in the bitter partisan atmosphere of the second Bush presidency, his rigidly conservative judicial philosophy was too much for Senate Democrats to bear. Largely unremarked at the time was the fact that, as Savage points out in *Takeover*, Roberts, Miers, and Alito were all essentially "executive branch lawyer[s] who identified with the test of defending the prerogatives of the president."

The Roberts court soon began to make its mark. With O'Connor's departure, Justice Anthony Kennedy stood as the court's swing vote on most issues. The politically astute Roberts worked from the beginning to craft the kinds of decisions that would keep Kennedy aligned with the four court conservatives, Scalia, Thomas, Alito, and himself, frequently assigning him responsibility for authorship of the majority opinion. As Lou and Carl Cannon observe in *Reagan's Disciple*,

> By the time the Roberts Court ended its first full term on June 28, 2007, its direction was no longer in doubt. A series of rulings, all by 5-4 margins, had made it more difficult for workers alleging job discrimination to sue their employers, had declared unconstitutional on free speech grounds a section of the 2002 McCain-Feingold campaign finance law that had restricted political advertising, and had limited the power of school boards to use race as a tool for maintaining or achieving diversity.

In this shift, they point out, Justice Kennedy's role was critical—so critical, in fact, that the court was sometimes referred to as the "Kennedy court."

The seeming rightward drift in American politics, allowing the Republicans to win the presidency by paper-thin margins in 2000 and 2004, when conditions favored the Democrats, fostered a virtual cottage industry of political analysis. Books such as Thomas Edsall's *Building Red America*, Tom Frank's *What's the Matter with Kansas? How Conservatives Won the Heart of America*, and Jacob S. Hacker and Paul Pierson's *Off Center: The Republican Revolution and the Erosion of American Democracy* all tried to illuminate how the GOP had taken over. The party's secret, in Edsall's words, lay "in accessing and manipulating concealed biases against minorities and homosexuals to persuade middle- and working-class whites to vote against their own economic interests." Citing the GOP's reliance on "an interlocking alliance of muscular conservative 'values' organizations and churches," Edsall predicted that the situation would likely continue unless the Democrats substantially revised their message.

In addition to the fact that it is notoriously difficult to predict future political trends, the presumption of such analysts that the electoral trends of the early 2000s were likely to continue into the future missed a central point: not only political campaigning, but actual conduct of government, shapes voter attitudes. In misreading the tea leaves after his re-election in 2004 and focusing on Social Security "reform," George W. Bush revealed a disconnect between GOP orthodoxy and the interests of the largely white, middle-class, older voter base responsible for his victory. "The narrow election victory supplied no real mandate," writes Bush's former press secretary, Scott McClellan of the 2004 results in *What Happened: Inside the Bush White House and Washington's Culture of Deception*. "There was only division and polarization, and none of us in the president's inner circle seemed to realize how problematic it was at the time." Moreover, the administration's bumbling after Katrina and the worsening of the Iraq war gave evidence of ineptitude that quickly began to unravel at least the outer layers of the supposedly solid Republic base. "The Bush years," writes Kabaservice, "demonstrated anew that conservatives were skilled at politics but deficient at governing and that a Republican Party without moderates was like a heavily muscled body without a head."

Though George W. Bush campaigned on the agenda of the hard right—especially in 2004—there is evidence in certain of his statements near the end of his presidency and in his memoir that he never departed altogether from the bipartisan spirit and "compassionate conservatism" that initially motivated him to seek the White House (perhaps along with a spirit of retribution for the way his father's presidency ended). Kabaservice cites one of Bush's final interviews as president, in which he warned that Republicans needed to avoid the straitjacket of ideological conservatism. In his 2010 memoir, Bush also lamented the way in which state-level gerrymandering had contributed to political gridlock in Washington, creating too many "safely" electable candidates from the extreme wings of both parties. "Our government would be more productive and our politics more civilized," he wrote, "if congressional districts were drawn by panels of nonpartisan elders." If this is the real George W. Bush, it is regrettable that he was unable or unwilling to speak out in these ways while in the White House. Instead, by acting on an imagined mandate to move the nation to the right, he contributed to a hardening of the partisan deadlock that had been so clearly reflected in the disputed election of 2000.

The Politics of Certitude

In his 2007 study, *A Divider, Not a Uniter*, Gary Jacobson focused more on Bush's conduct of the war on terrorism and the Iraq war as truly divisive events than on Bush's not-so-successful domestic policy agenda. From 9/11 on, egged on by Vice President Cheney and Secretary of Defense Rumsfeld, Bush conducted foreign and national security policy as if he had a free hand. This strategy worked for a time, while the nation, including the political opposition, worried more about the possible next attack on the

Figure 7.2 George W. Bush relied inordinately on his influential advisors, Vice President Dick Cheney and Secretary of Defense Donald Rumsfeld, and—to a lesser extent—his second secretary of state, Condoleezza Rice. Here, Rice, Cheney, and Rumsfeld are shown participating in a video conference with Bush while he was in Iraq in June 2006. © Jason Reed/Reuters/CORBIS

United States than about reining in an out-of-control executive branch. Even before the end of Bush's first term, however, public and congressional support had begun to unravel. Not only the administration's conduct of the war, but also its handling of "detainees" (a term carefully used in preference to "prisoners") came in for increasing criticism both in the 2004 election campaign and throughout Bush's second term.

As soon as he was re-elected, Bush shook up his national security team, moving National Security Advisor Condoleezza Rice to the State Department to replace the increasingly uncomfortable Colin Powell and promoting Rice's deputy, Stephen Hadley, to the national security post. An additional change with potential impact on the administration's conduct of the war on terrorism was the replacement of the prickly John Ashcroft with Bush's loyal Texas friend, Alberto Gonzalez. The new team was clearly all-Bush. With Powell's departure, Cheney's influence was greater than ever. The vice president exercised his control largely through craft and misdirection, but also through sheer persistence. Speaking about her unsuccessful jousts with Cheney over environmental issues, Bush's first Environmental Protection Agency (EPA) head, Christine Todd Whitman, described Cheney's *modus operandi* to Barton Gellman (in *Angler*): in meetings with Bush and Cheney (who monitored all important interactions with the president), said Whitman, a Cabinet member would present the best case possible, hoping to have convinced the president, but "you leave and the vice president's still there. So together, they would then shape policy."

Although the military situation in Iraq continued virtually unchanged during the first months of 2005, an important development occurred early in that year, as U.S. forces quietly stopped searching for the elusive WMDs. As Bush's approval ratings began a steady slide downward, he effected a shift in rhetoric, if not policy, taking more personal responsibility for the invasion of Iraq and conceding that not everything had worked just as planned. In Draper's words, "humility was slowly ratcheted up and triumphalism slowly ratcheted down." In December, the president finally acknowledged publicly the failure to find weapons of mass destruction, but he expressed no regret for his decision to go into Iraq. He also began to acknowledge responsibility for the extensive domestic surveillance program that had grown up since 9/11, about which relatively little had been known till the *New York Times* blew its cover in a December story.

Another growing political liability for the administration was the festering question of how to handle the detainees captured during the war on terrorism—most of whom were being held at the U.S. military prison in Guantanamo Bay, Cuba, but some of whom—the most "high-value," as the CIA described them—were incarcerated at secret locations abroad. There they were systematically subjected to extreme punishment (many called it torture outright) such as the technique known as water-boarding, during which the subject feels as if he or she is drowning. The details of the "extreme rendition" of detainees to these black sites and the

264

torturous measures used to obtain information and force admissions of guilt were not fully known till much later, but suspicions abounded, creating an ever more difficult political climate for Bush—even in his own party. In summer 2005, Republican senators John McCain, John Warner, and Lindsey Graham took the lead in drafting a measure to rein in administration excesses against terror suspects. Undeterred by strong White House opposition and heavy lobbying by Cheney, in December both houses passed the Detainee Treatment Act as an amendment to the 2006 Defense Department's appropriation bill; the margins were overwhelming: 90-9 in the Senate and 308-122 in the House (with 107 Republicans in favor). Essentially, the measure provided that "Geneva principles" on prisoners of war must govern the treatment of those captured in the war on terrorism. Cheney pretended to acknowledge defeat, conceding to the *Wall Street Journal*, "I don't win all the battles," and Bush made a show of White House support in a joint appearance with McCain after the bill's passage. In truth, however, the administration had no intention of abiding by the restrictions imposed by the language of the Detainee Treatment Act. Signing the bill into law at the end of December, Bush inserted a statement into the Federal Register to the effect that he would interpret it "in a manner consistent with the constitutional authority of the President to supervise the unitary executive branch and as Commander in Chief." The implications of the president's statement were stunning. As Savage observes, "[t]he entire year's fight in Congress had been irrelevant, the White House had declared, because Congress lacked the constitutional authority to pass a law that tied the commander-in-chief's hands."

Within months, even the conservative-dominated Supreme Court tried to block the administration's increasingly arbitrary handling of the detainee issue. In a landmark June 2006 decision, *Hamdan v. Rumsfeld*, a 5-3 majority ruled that the president did not have the authority to try alleged terrorists before military tribunals. Moreover, the decision continued, fair trials were necessary because they were guaranteed by the Geneva Conventions—suggesting, at least implicitly, that Bush was not free to authorize interrogation techniques that went beyond those permitted by those accords. Major conflict was clearly brewing over handling of the detainees, but Bush and Cheney stayed the course. Three months after *Hamdan*, they succeeded in pressuring the GOP-controlled Congress to pass the Military Commissions Act, in effect voiding the court's decision by granting to the president the right to decide whether particular techniques violated the list of coercive methods in the Conventions.

Chances for military success in the Iraq war depended heavily on the viability of the new government that was installed in Baghdad in December 2005. Bush counted on the regime's achieving stability. Speaking to the American public immediately after the Iraqi National Assembly elections, he aggressively challenged his domestic political foes: "Defeatism may have its partisan uses, but it is not justified by the facts," he declared. "To retreat before victory would be an act of recklessness and dishonor, and I will not allow it." Neither the war on the ground nor the settling-in of the new government went well in the first months of 2006, however. As suicide attacks increased in both frequency and magnitude, the new U.S.-backed prime minister of Iraq, Nouri al-Maliki, seemed powerless to quell the sectarian violence. Through May and June, the number of attacks on Iraqi regular forces averaged between 800 and 1000 per week—all this, Woodward observed in his 2006 volume, *State of Denial: Bush at War Part III*, despite the huge American investment in "training, equipping, and funding 263,000 Iraqi soldiers and police."

In the face of this deteriorating situation, Bush and Cheney went into overdrive, spinning and re-selling the war to the American public. They divided the labor. While the president took a "regular guy" approach, "asking for trust, visiting the wounded, even acknowledging trouble now and then," writes Gellman, his vice president hammered home the message that victory was inevitable, facts notwithstanding. "Cheney fought gravity, trying to slow the descent" of public opinion, Gellman continues, believing that "[i]mplacable certainty might stave off consensus against the war." No matter how hard the two tried to shore up the nation's confidence in the mission, however, public doubts about the ability of the United States to control the situation in Iraq grew steadily. Criticism in the media increased accordingly.

Already having enough trouble with the GOP-controlled 109th Congress, Bush worried about the impact of Iraq war-weariness on the 2006 mid-term elections. His concern was justified. In an election in which the main force at work was the president's unpopularity, the Democrats delivered a knockout blow, picking up thirty-one House seats to reverse the thirty-seat GOP majority in that chamber, and changing the balance in the Senate from a 55-44 GOP majority to a 49-49 split, with the upper house's two independents joining the Democrats to form the majority. It was clearly an overwhelmingly anti-Bush tide. The Democratic take-over in the House resulted in the election of the first woman Speaker in the history of the nation, California's Nancy Pelosi. "It was Iraq, it was scandal, it was fatigue," writes Draper in *Dead Certain*. "But it was decisive. Matthew Dowd's extinct swing voters had resurrected and swung the other way." Bush stubbornly chose to draw a mixed verdict from the outcome, observing in his first post-election press conference, "Look, it was a close election. If you look at [it] race by race, it was close. The cumulative effect, however, was not too close. It was a thumpin'."

That the president was undeterred by the "thumpin'," however, was obvious in his actions. In December, the bipartisan Iraq Study Group, chaired by former secretary of state James Baker and former Democratic congressman Lee Hamilton, submitted its long-awaited report, pronouncing the Iraq war a "grave and deteriorating" situation and urging the president to shift to a training mission only, while holding al-Maliki accountable to improve the situation on a fixed timetable. Instead of accepting the Study Group's recommendations, Bush decided to double down, committing to a "surge" of additional U.S. forces to try to turn the military tide. The troop surge was a major gamble. As Baker reports in *Days of Fire*, Secretary of State Rice, while promising the president her support for the strategy—told him "I'm there and I'll do everything I can do to support it. But, Mr. President, this is your last card. It had better work." On January 10, 2007, Bush announced to the nation his intent to deploy an additional 21,500 U.S. troops to Iraq. A Gallup poll conducted after the announcement showed less than 40 percent of Americans in favor of the surge strategy.

An unmistakable sign that Bush had heard the electorate at least partially, however, was his removal of the unpopular Rumsfeld as secretary of defense. Although he said nothing to indicate displeasure with Rumsfeld's performance, the first actions of the new defense secretary, Robert Gates, indicated that the president was seeking new directions. Marine Corps general Peter Pace was replaced as chairman of the joint chiefs of staff by Admiral Mike Mullen, who, in his confirmation testimony, acknowledged a number of errors in the conduct of the Iraq war. To oversee the surge, Gates announced the selection of General David Petraeus, who had made a positive impression by achieving a degree of stability in Mosul as American commander there. Petraeus, after declaring his unqualified support for the president's surge strategy, won unanimous Senate confirmation, 81-0. This was tribute more to the man than the strategy, however. Within a week of the general's arrival in Iraq, the Democratic-controlled House adopted a resolution declaring: "Congress disapproves of the decision of President George W. Bush announced on January 16, 2007, to deploy more than 20,000 additional United States combat troops to Iraq."

Though largely unremarked at the time, the surge marked an important turning point. The decision, according to Peter Baker, "was the first and perhaps only time on a major issue in the second term when Cheney came out on the winning side while Rice was on the losing side." While the president and his vice president continued to appear publicly to be in step, Bush was becoming more the "decider" than he had been. "Cheney was not the driving force behind the surge, the way he had been behind the initial invasion in 2003," continues Baker; he was "a secondary player fortifying the president, not the author of the action." One important force that contributed to the erosion of the vice president's stock—with the public and perhaps with

Bush himself—was the opening of the federal trial of his former chief of staff, Scooter Libby, for having outed Valerie Plame as a CIA operative in 2003.

While the surge deployment steadily continued—with an estimated completion date of October or November—the new Democratic Congress became more vocal in its criticism. In mid-February, Speaker Pelosi secured victory for a non-binding House resolution opposing the strategy, 246-182. Three months later, both houses passed a $95 billion defense spending bill, also calling for troop withdrawal by March 2008, as the Iraq Study Group had proposed. Bush vetoed the measure, knowing there were not enough votes to override. Within weeks, Congress returned a bill fully funding the war without the withdrawal deadline. The president was worried, however, as was clear in his allowing a rumor to leak to the *Washington Post* that the administration was beginning to formulate a "post-surge" mission of training and advising Iraqi troops only. Throughout the summer, congressional support continued to erode, as even leading Republicans began to indicate they might not be able to continue to support the effort in Iraq much longer. Gambling that full deployment by September would change the course of the war and turn the tide of congressional and public opinion, Bush sent Cheney to Capitol Hill to shore up support, especially among crucially important Senate Republicans. With the House again having passed a resolution demanding a pullout by spring 2008, the upper chamber was the administration's last hope. When Petraeus and Ambassador Ryan Crocker came home in September to testify on the war, however, they encountered strong cynicism in both houses of Congress. Acceptance of their reports of lower numbers of civilian deaths and IED bombings, one senator remarked, required "the willing suspension of disbelief." Nevertheless, Crocker and Petraeus were sufficiently steady and impressive in their testimony that, as Baker observes, "it quickly became clear they had bought Bush more time."

Public opinion had definitely turned against the war, even though a majority of Americans still believed it would be a mistake to leave Iraq precipitately. It seemed not to matter that the surge was slowly improving the security situation on the ground, as U.S. troop fatalities fell to an average of below fifty per month—much lower than figures of a year earlier. Both Bush and Petraeus predicted that thousands of American troops would be able to return home by mid-2008, bringing the number of U.S. military in Iraq down to pre-surge levels, but the president's political credibility on the issue had evaporated. In late November, in an effort to suggest an endgame beyond the surge, he got al-Maliki to sign a "declaration of principles" committing the two leaders to negotiate a future strategic agreement that would reduce the U.S. role going forward. When al-Maliki continued to founder through the winter, at least in part because of his harsh policies toward the minority Sunni population, an impatient Bush sent Rice to Baghdad to give the prime minister a dressing-down. As quoted by Baker, the secretary of state told al-Maliki he was "a terrible prime minister" who would be "hanging from a lamppost" if he did not begin to show progress in improving the political situation in Iraq.

With the Iraq war not yet approaching resolution, the situation in Afghanistan had also taken a nasty turn, despite steady American support for the regime of Hamid Karzai following his 2002 election as president. By 2006, Taliban attacks on government forces and suicide bombings in civilian centers were increasing sharply, requiring a significant buildup of U.S. training forces. Late that year, Bush increased American troop levels from 20,000 to just over 30,000—still primarily in a training capacity. The Afghan situation was greatly complicated by hostile relations between Karzai and President Pervez Musharraf of neighboring Pakistan, who showed little willingness to crack down on the Taliban training sites within his country from which many of the attacks in Afghanistan were launched. Bush eventually succeeded in pressuring Musharraf to call elections, which were marred by the assassination of opposition leader Benazir Bhutto; in early 2008, Bhutto's widower, Asif Ali Zardari, was elected to the presidency, ensuring at least a friendlier, if not particularly reliable regime in Lahore. Despite the political change in Pakistan, Taliban infiltration from there into Afghanistan continued, with the latter remaining in turmoil as the insurgents concentrated their strength in the southeastern quadrant and continued to foment violence and unrest throughout the nation. The worsening of the situation in Afghanistan added to the vitriol of attacks on the administration by congressional Democrats. The war on terrorism and the ground wars in Iraq and Afghanistan had become the defining issues of Bush's presidency—and seemed likely to be the main points of contention in the 2008 election.

The all-consuming nature of the war on terrorism and Operation Iraqi Freedom also kept Bush from addressing other pressing foreign policy matters during his administration. He had little patience for the kind of personal interventions in which Clinton had engaged, in any case, preferring bold, dramatic strokes to lesser involvements. "The job of the president … is to think strategically, so that you can accomplish big objectives" he told Draper in late 2006. "As opposed to mini-ball. You can't play mini-ball with the influence we have and expect there to be peace. You've gotta think, think BIG." After 9/11, however, Bush seemed to concentrate his strategic thinking, big and small, almost exclusively on Iraq and, to a lesser extent, Afghanistan. Otherwise, he counted on a commonality of interests among the major powers in the war on terrorism to make traditional diplomacy unnecessary. Where this might prove insufficient, power seemed a viable substitute. "As a hedge against the resurgence of tensions between Washington and major powers such as China, Russia, or India," writes Brands in *From Berlin to Baghdad*, "the nation would maintain 'military strengths beyond challenge.'" The influence of Cheney and his neocon allies was obvious in the administration's stance.

This approach found expression in Bush's relations with Russia's emerging strongman, Vladimir Putin. Within three months of 9/11, over the objections of Secretary of State Powell, the president served the required six-month notice on Putin that the United States intended to abrogate the ABM Treaty. Cheney explained the administration's reasoning in his memoir, *In My Time*, observing that not only was the treaty, which barred the development of defensive missiles, "of advantage to the Soviets," but "[t]he number of nations with ballistic missile technology was growing and among them were rogue regimes. ... We had to be able to build systems that could intercept incoming missiles." Still hoping for Russian support in the war on terrorism, however, Bush continued to work with Putin toward longer-term arms reductions. In May 2002, the two signed the Moscow Treaty, calling for significant reductions in both nations' warheads by 2012.

Bush's handling of Putin was compromised from the outset, at least in the eyes of his detractors, by his naive comment upon first meeting the Russian leader that he "had looked the man in the eye" and "was able to get a sense of his soul." His adding that he found Putin "to be very straightforward and trustworthy" only increased the public derision that greeted his observation. Bush's statements looked even worse later, when the Russian leader failed to back the invasion of Iraq, slipping back into what Brands describes as an "antihegemonic stance," and especially in 2008 when Russian tanks rolled across the borders of pro-Western Georgia to take control of two provinces with large populations of ethnic Russians. Bush's putative soulmate had disappointed badly; in a massive understatement he concluded in his memoir that "Russia stands out as a disappointment in the freedom agenda."

Another major casualty of George W. Bush's war on terrorism was American attention to the knotty Israeli–Palestinian problem. Parallel to—and perhaps in conjunction with—the rise of al-Qaeda's aggressions elsewhere in the Middle East, Palestinian terrorist bombings in Israel increased sharply in the months after 9/11, eliciting a predictable Israeli military response. In a vain attempt to quell the violence, Bush dispatched Powell to the region to broker negotiations. Unfortunately, Powell decided on his own to suggest publicly the convening of an international conference. When Bush pressured his secretary of state to disavow the idea, the credibility of the United States as an arbiter in the conflict dried up. Moreover, as Cheney recorded in his memoir, it produced "a watershed moment in relations between [Powell] and the White House," as the secretary took Bush's reaction as "a personal affront." The situation in Palestine deteriorated further when Hamas, categorized as a full-fledged terrorist organization by the Bush administration, triumphed overwhelmingly in Palestine's 2006 elections. With this, the administration's involvement in the traditional politics of the Middle East all but ceased. "Bush decided that he could no longer afford the type of intensive involvement demanded by the peace process," writes Brands. "Nor could he consort with a leader with ties to Hamas and other Palestinian groups that were deemed terrorist organizations." The Israeli–Palestinian conflict thus was placed on a back burner.

The increasingly complicated calculus of the Middle East after 9/11 also led Bush to consider attempting to forge a new relationship with Iran, which had been on the U.S. blacklist for a quarter-century—since the overthrow of the shah. The administration's tentative overtures "came to naught," however, as Brands writes, and Iran, too, "ended up an enemy in Bush's war on terror." The June 2005 election of Islamic extremist Mahmoud Ahmadinejad as Iran's president made matters even worse for U.S.–Iranian relations—yet another unresolved problem as Bush's second term drew to a close.

As the clock wound down on that second term, and with victory nowhere in sight in Iraq, Bush saw an opportunity to establish a legacy of sorts by bringing at least one of his identified "rogue regimes" to heel: Kim Jong-il's North Korea. Relations between the two nations had been rocky since Bush had shifted to a more confrontational tack after 9/11. Given that he had spoken publicly of the "morally abhorrent" aspects of Kim's regime, it is hard to imagine any way that he could have achieved a diplomatic breakthrough and persuaded the erratic North Korean ruler to dismantle his nation's nuclear program. When unilateral economic pressure on Pyongyang proved inadequate, Bush pushed for direct diplomatic engagement of the regional Asian powers. In summer 2003, the so-called six-party talks—including China, Japan, Russia, South and North Korea, and the United States—opened in Beijing. Following two years of on-again, off-again negotiations, in September 2005 Kim seemed to agree to end the North Korean nuclear program—only to withdraw his assent a day later.

Within a year, Pyongyang upped the ante for an eventual settlement by conducting its first-ever test of a nuclear bomb. Bush was almost contemptuous of the resulting display ("Is this the best they can do?" he reputedly asked aides when the details of the test were known), but Kim Jong-il had given his response to those who wanted to deny his government the right to nuclear weapons. Nonetheless, the president continued to work through the six-party talks, which produced another deal in fall 2007 whereby Kim would disable his nation's nuclear facilities in return for generous shipments of heavy fuel. With American forces struggling in Iraq, Bush felt he had little choice but to embrace this optimistic course, hoping that the deal would hold. "If [he] could salvage Iraq and rid North Korea of its nuclear weapons in his final stretch in office," writes Baker, "it would go a long way toward shaping a more positive legacy."

As Bush entered his last year in the White House, however, it seemed unlikely that he would leave a positive legacy. Both in domestic and foreign policy, the impact of his presidency had been divisive rather than in any way unifying or restorative. Although the surge seemed to be improving the military situation in Iraq, the administration received little credit for that improvement. Instead, a war-weary public and an aggressive political opposition were intent on moving beyond the seemingly endless engagement. Years of strong-arming friends and foes alike in Congress had taken a toll. As Bush's approval ratings wallowed way below 50 percent, he took flak from both right and left. Ironically, this was the way in which he had finally become a uniter of sorts. "A spate of anti-Bush conservative books appeared in bookstores alongside the anti-Bush liberal reading list," write Lou and Carl Cannon in *Reagan's Disciple*, "and the 2008 Republican presidential candidates sounded as if they were trying to succeed Ronald Reagan instead of George W. Bush."

Bush's Texas-sized pugnacity was a major reason that his popularity fell so sharply in his final years in the White House. The brashness and sense of certainty that he exuded from start to finish of his eight years in office did not wear well as the crisis environment of 9/11 faded. Although he was more thoughtful than his demeanor suggested, his image as one who shot first and thought afterward undermined public confidence that he took complexities sufficiently into account when making decisions. In fact, most of those who worked closely with him saw greater thoughtfulness at work than was on public display. "[W]hen the moment called for it," writes Draper, "Bush could be quite deliberative," though "the decisions he came to ... tended to be unsurprising." Even Brinkley, who does not go easy on the president for his insensitivity at the time of Katrina, suggests that Bush "often waited before being decisive. He was a practitioner of the long pause. It was as if his certitude was learned—not inherent in his makeup." Whether he made up his mind quickly or took more time in making a particular decision, however, Bush was definitely never given to self-doubt or introspection after the fact. What supporters saw as steadiness and perseverance, critics saw as blind stubbornness. Thus, his dogged commitment to the surge strategy in 2007–2008 gained him little credit with any but the most conservative, pro-GOP media, even though it may have been the right decision at the time.

The obviousness of Cheney's influence and his arrogant, bullying approach in pressing for administration goals hurt Bush with Republicans and Democrats alike. It had been well understood that Bush had picked the seasoned Cheney as his running-mate in 2000 to bolster the GOP ticket's foreign policy credibility, but the free rein enjoyed by the vice president after 9/11 took most by surprise and suggested that Bush was more puppet than puppeteer in the conduct of the war on terrorism. In his study focused on the expansion of executive power under Bush, Charlie Savage consistently uses the term "Bush-Cheney administration" to emphasize the vice president's dominant influence. Gellman agrees, but only to a point. "The history of the Bush administration cannot be written without close attention to the moments when Cheney took the helm," he writes in *Angler*, "sometimes at Bush's direction, sometimes with his tacit consent, and sometimes without the president's apparent awareness." Yet, Gellman continues, "this was decidedly not a Cheney administration. Had there been such a thing, it would have looked very different. Almost certainly it would have self-destructed." This conclusion seems on point.

Although the 9/11 attacks transformed Bush instantly into a unifying and powerful "war-time" president, he clearly failed to capitalize on the opportunity to pull the nation together. Instead, the military morass in Iraq that he and Cheney chose to make the central strategy of the war on terrorism, coupled with the administration's secrecy and its tolerance of the brutal interrogation and treatment of detainees, eroded whatever positive legacy he might have hoped for. Typically, Bush never second-guessed his overall strategy, seeming comfortable accepting whatever the verdict of history might be. "The nature of history," he wrote in *Decision Points*, "is that we know the consequences only of the action we took. But inaction would have had consequences too."

8

The Politics of Red and Blue, since 2008

The election of a new president normally elicits renewed hope that things will get better and, somehow, a frustrating and log-jammed system will work more smoothly for the good of the people. The mood surrounding first-term Senator Barack Obama's landslide victory in 2008 transcended even the usual such optimism. The "Politics of Hope," as Obama had labeled his campaign, was widely hailed as ushering in a wholly different America. Magically, the election of the nation's first mixed-race chief executive by a coalition younger and more diverse than in any previous presidential contest would produce a post-partisan system free of the gridlock that had prevailed for decades, a generous, post-racial society, and a consciously global approach to foreign policy less self-interested than that of any previous administration.

Belying this widespread optimism, Obama encountered an immediate avalanche of opposition in Washington. From day one, both Senate and House GOP leaders resolved to block the new president whenever possible, hoping to ensure that he would have only one term in the White House. Notwithstanding this

Deadlock and Disillusionment: American Politics since 1968, First Edition.
Gary W. Reichard.
© 2016 John Wiley & Sons, Inc. Published 2016 by John Wiley & Sons, Inc.

Figure 8.1 At the 2004 Democratic National Convention, keynote speaker Barack Obama, at that time a candidate for U.S. senator, galvanized the convention with a moving speech emphasizing the need for national unity. "There's not a liberal America and a conservative America," he declared, "there's the United States of America." © Ron Sachs/CNP/CORBIS

fierce resolve on the part of the opposition, Obama managed to achieve significant policy victories in his first two years—most notably and remarkably, a national health-care program that had been blocked by the GOP for more than six decades. These victories were achieved on nearly straight party-line votes, however, while the Democrats controlled both houses of Congress: so much for post-partisan politics. By 2010, GOP anger at the young president and his achievements—reflected in the rapid rise of the so-called Tea Party movement—created a treacherous playing field for Democrats looking toward the mid-term elections. When the Republicans predictably won control of the House in the fall and sharply reduced the Democratic majority in the Senate, gridlock returned with a vengeance.

Obama and his supporters truly believed that his election had signaled the emergence of a new majority. In fact, however, the wave of young, diverse voters responsible for his election receded dramatically in 2010. When he was re-elected in 2012 with surprising ease, propelled by much the same coalition as four years earlier, the shape of the "new" electorate and the nation's likely political trajectory once again seemed completely unpredictable. One thing remained constant, however: the prospect and practice of bipartisan cooperation had completely disappeared. In 2014, after two years of total, nasty gridlock—despite poll findings consistently reflecting public disgust with the unproductive standoff that had passed for politics in the Bush and Obama years—the voters ensured more of the same by returning Republican majorities to both houses of Congress. No reduction of angry, stubborn interparty warfare seemed to be on the horizon before the next presidential election, when a new Politics of Hope might arise— likely to be supplanted by yet another round of deadlock and disillusionment.

The Politics of Hope

Rarely does the out-party have as overwhelming an early favorite for its presidential nomination as the Democrats did with Hillary Rodham Clinton a year before the 2008 election. Only Illinois's freshman senator, Barack Obama, who in February 2007 had made a splash with his passionate declaration of candidacy in the Lincolnian setting of Springfield, Illinois, seemed capable of mounting a meaningful challenge for the party's nomination. Yet even he made little headway through the first half of 2007. By fall, polls indicated that Clinton would breeze through the primaries. Fresh off a resounding re-election victory as junior senator from New York, she had worked hard to establish leadership credentials independent of her husband. So inevitable did her nomination appear in the early fall—and so familiar were the Clintons to the American public—that it was easy to overlook the historic aspect of her nomination, which would represent the first time a woman would head a major-party ticket for the presidency.

In these circumstances, as political scientist Liette Gidlow observes in her edited volume, *Obama, Clinton, Palin: Making History in Election 2008*, "[i]t was deeply ironic that in her contest with Obama, Hillary Clinton got tagged the 'Establishment' candidate." Her outreach to Republicans in the Senate had included co-sponsorship of nearly fifty bills with colleagues across the aisle. Though this had made her an effective legislator, it held potentially negative repercussions for her in her own party. "As wary as she was of being stereotyped as a conventional liberal," write John Heilemann and Mark Halperin in *Game Change: Obama and the Clintons, McCain and Palin, and the Race of a Lifetime*, Clinton "didn't fully apprehend that her split-the-difference stance was reviving an equally damaging narrative" that "she was a calculating, expedient schemer wedded to no great principle other than her own advancement." That perception among a significant body of Democratic primary voters ultimately began to erode her lead—that, and the unprecedented organizing capabilities of the Obama campaign machine.

What the youthful, fresh-faced Obama especially had going for him was the climate of disgust with Washington at the end of the Bush presidency. Just as Clinton's gender seemed to be more asset than liability, so, too, Obama's mixed-race lineage was an appealing characteristic whose time had seemingly come for the Democrats. Twice in a row the party had nominated safe, white alternatives to run against the quintessential party of safe, white voters. Two-thousand-eight called for something different: it seemed time to turn the clock ahead—finally—in American politics. A strong force moving the Democratic party in such a direction was the nation's changing racial demographic, with the electorate rapidly becoming more non-white; another was the outlook of the young, idealistic millennial generation, which polls showed to be particularly disaffected from the cultural battles and gridlocked politics of the preceding decade. In a year when "change from Bush" was likely to be the winning approach, it was Obama, rather than Clinton or any of the traditional white male Democratic politicians seeking the White House, Joe Biden, Chris Dodd, or John Edwards, who promised to have the greatest appeal for these untapped voting blocs. His embrace of a politics of hope, beginning with a triumphal 2006 book tour hawking his best-selling autobiography, *Dreams from My Father*, cemented that appeal.

The 2008 party nomination contests began in earnest more than a year before the election. The winnowing of candidates in both parties started with an unprecedented series of nearly weekly televised debates among the declared hopefuls. "The 2007 preprimary campaign was one of the oddest reality shows in presidential campaign history," wrote Chuck Todd and Sheldon Gawiser in their post-election analysis, *How Barack Obama Won: A State-by-State Guide to the Historic 2008 Presidential Election*. "It seemed a week didn't go by without one of the two major parties participating in a debate. These debates turned into must-see TV for many, as the ratings kept going up as Iowa got closer." Clinton did passably well in these confrontations, but despite her front-runner status failed to pull away from the field. Although Obama was not the sharpest debater among the Democratic aspirants (it was generally acknowledged that Biden was), by at least holding his own against his much more experienced rivals, he steadily built his gravitas and credibility. Not yet fully on display were his charisma on the stump and the almost scarily efficient money-raising and ground operations that his operatives were putting together nationwide. For Obama, Iowa—traditionally the beginning of the primary trail—represented an opportunity to sweep the field of all opposition except Clinton, after which he could take her on *mano a mano*. As unlikely as it had seemed just months before, if he could then take New Hampshire, a distinct possibility given its history of supporting upstart candidates, he might be able to force her out of the race as well.

It was not to be that simple. By winning the Iowa caucuses over Edwards, who had banked on winning there in order to jump-start his own faltering candidacy, Obama moved to the front of the field, as all of the other Democratic candidates except Clinton either dropped out or were on obvious life-support. At this point, however, whether by design or out of exhaustion, Clinton showed a heretofore hidden emotional side that galvanized her heavily female voter base, speaking from the heart in a New Hampshire diner about her travails on the campaign trail and the depth of her commitment to build a better America. It was a Hillary that had not previously been on display, and the "unguarded" tearful moment worked miracles for her candidacy. When the votes were counted, she had edged out Obama by 3 percentage points. "The momentum out of Iowa that was supposed to carry Obama to the nomination," write Heilemann and Halperin, "had been stopped in its tracks, just five days later. With one win of her own, Hillary had changed the game again."

The primary race that followed was the most remarkable in memory, extending the "reality TV" syndrome through the spring. The two candidates slugged it out almost evenly, with Obama winning the key state of South Carolina, performing well throughout the South, and winning small state after small state, many of them winner-take-all primaries. Along the way, the young challenger helped himself immeasurably with much of the moderate white electorate (not only within the Democratic party) by delivering an insightful, disarmingly forthright disquisition on race in American politics, in response to vicious attacks from the right on his association with his controversial Chicago pastor, the Reverend Jeremiah Wright. Clinton, increasingly relying on the white, working-class vote, managed to win many of the largest states, but was unable to forge ahead in the delegate race due to the proportional voting rules that prevailed in most of the states where she won. When her "must-win" victories in Texas and Ohio left her still short of Obama's delegate count, the race was effectively over. The nomination was ultimately decided by the 200-some "super-delegates" to the convention, mostly office-holders who foresaw the clear advantage Obama's star-power and organizing advantages could bring in the November election. The Democratic contest ended quietly in June, as seemingly every undeclared super-delegate came over to the Obama camp.

The Democratic primary season "probably lasted longer than it should have," Todd and Gawiser wrote shortly after the election, "because of the media fascination with the Clintons." Hillary Clinton's stubbornness—and her (as well as her husband's) unceasing belief that she was the better qualified of the two candidates to occupy the White House—was also responsible for the race extending to the last possible moment. The contest had seen the party break along consistent fault lines. Blacks, college-educated whites, and particularly young voters of all races had supported Obama in droves; in the Clinton camp were women (except for African Americans), white working-class voters, and—to a surprising extent—Hispanics. Clinton's concession speech in June went a long way toward healing rifts that might have crippled the Democrats in the fall. "Although we weren't able to shatter that hardest, highest glass ceiling this time," she reassured the millions of women who had supported her, "the light is shining through like never before, filling us all with the hope and the sure knowledge that the path will be a little easier next time." Heaping praise on Obama and making clear her support for him in the coming campaign, she was visibly laying a foundation for another possible presidential run. The nominee, meanwhile, had cemented his image as a "transformative" candidate. As Todd and Gawiser observed, the tortuous primary campaign "did more to help Obama than hurt him. He became a better debater... . He became a candidate who could speak a bit more from the heart than the head... . And of course, without Clinton, he never would have had to run campaigns in all 50 states." The latter fact, of course, would make it possible for him to put states into play for the Democrats that had not, in memory, gone blue in a presidential election.

The media had anointed an early favorite in the Republican party, too. Because it seemed now to be his turn, but also because he had emerged as perhaps the strongest defender of administration policy in Iraq, Arizona Senator John McCain led in most GOP preference polls. McCain's campaign apparatus, however, was a mess. By September, even as he was making one of his top challengers, Mitt Romney, look bad on Iraq, his war chest was nearing empty. After weighing the possibility of dropping out, the Arizonan instead plunged full speed ahead, scrambling for dollars and betting once again, as he had in 2000, on New Hampshire as the key to the nomination. Romney, who as governor of Massachusetts had proudly signed into law a sweeping state-supported health-care program, almost certainly would have fared better if he had run a centrist campaign. Instead, cowed by the presence in the race of McCain, who had honed a reputation as a party renegade and moderate (however undeserved by this time), and the socially liberal former mayor of New York City, Rudy Giuliani, Romney instead chose to "out-extreme" the GOP candidates on the right, including most notably former governor Mike Huckabee of Arkansas. In light of Huckabee's evangelical credentials and conservative record, there was never a way this outflanking strategy could work. Romney was also plagued by "the Mormon thing," as he himself called it, but refused to confront the question of his religion in a way that might reduce anxieties that some Americans still held about the somewhat mysterious and secretive faith.

The Iowa caucuses were Romney's undoing, as they had been for so many others in past primary seasons. When Huckabee won in Iowa, Romney could only limp back to his home territory with the hope of besting McCain in New Hampshire. In truth, he hardly stood to benefit no matter what the outcome there, since as former governor of a neighboring state, he was expected to win. The outcome was worse than expected, however, as McCain, repeating his successful town hall strategy of 2000, easily defeated his Massachusetts rival. When the Arizona senator also eked out a narrow victory in South Carolina. Romney was finished, though he stayed in the race and chalked up uninspiring totals in a number of other southern states. Meanwhile, McCain's campaign looked to be on a positive course. When he blew away Giuliani in Florida, his path to the nomination was clear. He clinched the nomination on March 4. Republicans, who should have been elated at having their battles behind them while Clinton and Obama were still tearing into each other on the other side, were uneasy nonetheless. Their "greatest concern," write Heilemann and Halperin, was that "the party had chosen Bob Dole all over again." Instead of running the risk of becoming stale news, McCain chose to withdraw from the field for a while, allowing the Democratic bloodletting to occupy the nation's front pages. In retrospect, this was a huge tactical error. Instead of defining himself for the American electorate, he waited for the successful Democratic candidate to do it for him—not with a good result.

Moving toward the party conventions in late summer, the only big stories concerned the candidates' respective selections of running mates. Obama, recognizing the value of choosing someone older and more experienced—especially in foreign policy—made a universally applauded choice in selecting Joe Biden. Though gaffe-prone, Biden had put in many years on the Senate Foreign Relations Committee, including most recently as chair, and held strong appeal for the working-class constituencies that had favored Clinton in the primaries. McCain, lacking an obvious choice to strengthen the GOP ticket, briefly toyed with selecting former Democratic vice-presidential candidate and now-independent Joe Lieberman, but the Connecticut senator's pro-choice sentiments threatened to provoke a floor fight if his name were to come before the convention. On the day after Obama's acceptance speech at the Democratic convention at the end of August, McCain scored a media coup by choosing the untested, largely unknown governor of Alaska, Sarah Palin, as his running mate. "Untested" was the operative word—a fact that soon redounded to the discredit of McCain in the eyes of media and public alike. In the short run, however, the arrival onstage of the striking, telegenic 44-year-old "soccer mom" created a feeding frenzy among conservative Republicans, who could not get enough of her. "Palin-mania," the media labeled it.

While McCain's surprise vice-presidential choice momentarily stopped Obama's momentum, denying him much of a bounce from the elaborately staged Democratic convention in Denver, the gain was short-lived. Palin continued to delight the most partisan of Republicans with her folksy "red-meat" speeches, but her political illiteracy—especially where foreign policy was concerned—soon proved to be a major detriment for the GOP ticket with moderate and independent voters. By mid-September, Obama was again picking up steam.

Aside from their ages and personalities, the two presidential candidates were in some ways alike—especially in their strong disdain for "politics as usual" in Washington. One issue on which they differed very sharply was Iraq—and in particular, the surge. If that issue had proved decisive in the election, it might have been enough to elect Obama. In mid-September, however, the dynamic of the campaign was permanently altered, as the war issue was pushed to the margins by a full-scale economic crisis. The economy had been a moderately serious concern for Republicans all along, with real-estate prices steadily declining and the federal deficit once again growing apace, largely due to the administration's unwillingness to raise revenues to pay for the war. The bottom fell out altogether in the second half of September when first the prestigious Lehman Brothers investment house and then several other financial firms and banks collapsed like a house of cards. As the stock market plummeted and commentators across the political spectrum fretted about the worst crash since the Great Depression, McCain destroyed his credibility by first insisting, "The fundamentals of our economy are strong," and then reversing himself the following day by declaring the situation "a total crisis." As Obama quietly worked with his economic advisers to get on top of the facts of the situation, McCain pressured Bush to help him launch a "hail Mary" pass by hosting an emergency White House conference; Bush had barely consented before McCain was on television announcing the suspension of his campaign so that he could return to Washington to devise a solution to the crisis. Obama reluctantly agreed to do the same.

The prospect of the two major party candidates suspending the political wars in order to devise effective public policy in the face of crisis was appealing in the abstract. The problem, however, was that there was no attractive—certainly, no immediate—solution in sight. At the White House conference, McCain embarrassed both himself and Republican congressional leaders by displaying neither understanding nor initiative in the face of the crisis. His apparent confusion was in sharp contrast to Obama's cool and thoughtful demeanor, remarked on by virtually everyone present, and later even by Bush in his memoir. The president, seeing the political writing on the wall as far as the outcome of the November election was concerned, followed the advice of Treasury Secretary Hank Paulson and—with solid support from Obama and congressional Democrats—pushed through over GOP objections a most un-Republican bailout of the sinking financial sector. The Troubled Asset Relief Program, or TARP, initially authorized $700 billion in relief to banks and other financial entities bogged down by portfolios filled with disastrously depreciated mortgage loans; the total would later be reduced to just under $450 billion. The turnaround was not immediate, but within days the stock market began to recover.

The size of the federal bailout shocked the public and would later be grist for those who wished to demagogue the issue, but it was helpful to Obama and the Democrats. The contrasting images of the two candidates in the face of the crisis were indelible, as the youthful Obama was now viewed as the steady hand—presidential in every way. His lead steadily widened in the last couple of weeks, buttressed by his cool and confident performance in the televised presidential debates. To the great surprise of most of the media, after a series of embarrassing mistakes in interviews early in the campaign, Palin managed somehow to hold her own against Biden in the lone vice-presidential debate. But by then the race was over—hard as it was for oft-disappointed Democrats to believe.

On election night, Obama's victory exceeded even his campaign's optimistic projections. The outlines of Blue America were still essentially those that had been developing since 2000, but Obama also carried the two states that had been Democratic bugaboos in 2000 and 2004, Florida and Ohio, respectively, as well as the important swing states of Iowa and Colorado, and three others that had not initially been considered to be in play: Indiana,

North Carolina, and Virginia. The relentless ground organizations and massive funding that had vanquished Hillary Clinton in those states were widely credited for these impressive triumphs. The victor's 7-percentage-point popular vote victory and 365 electoral votes were the highest totals for any Democrat since Lyndon Johnson's rout of Barry Goldwater in 1964. Significantly, Obama's coattails also helped solidify Democratic control of both houses of Congress. A pickup of eight Senate seats gave the party a solid 57-41 margin in that chamber (which, together with the two reliable independents, left them only one vote short of the coveted filibuster-proof sixty), while a net gain of twenty-four seats produced a strong 257-178 majority in the House.

Not only the size of Obama's victory, but its shape, gave the Democrats great hope for the future. He had predictably carried African American voters by 95 percent, but had also won the steadily increasing Hispanic vote by 66 to 32 percent, and—most encouraging of all—young voters of all races by the same margin. Although, like Gore and Kerry before him, Obama lost the overall white vote, his share among whites age 18 to 29 was a remarkable 68 percent. Equally telling was the Democratic candidate's 60 to 38 percent victory over McCain in the segment of the electorate with a family income below $50,000 a year. The question was whether these results were the product of unique circumstances coupled with a unique, fresh candidate, or portended a momentous shift in American electoral politics that would play itself out as the losing coalition aged and left the political stage.

Even many who had not voted for Obama were caught up in the drama and enthusiasm of his victory, which seemed to signal the dawning of a new, post-racial America. Despite the sizable negative blip on the radar screen represented by California's passage of Proposition Eight, a state constitutional amendment banning same-sex marriage (fueled by Mormon money and passed due to a higher-than-usual turnout of socially conservative African American voters), moderate and liberal voters were hopeful that the three-decades-old culture wars were coming to an end. Amazingly, the Iraq and Afghanistan conflicts, so divisive months earlier, proved unimportant in the final results, as just

10 percent of voters considered war to be the most important election issue. Perhaps—just perhaps—the future would be characterized by a more functional political system than had prevailed since the early years of Bill Clinton's presidency.

Amidst leaks to reporters that Obama had devoured Doris Kearns Goodwin's *Team of Rivals*, a best-selling book about Lincoln's cabinet composed of former political foes, the new president set about constructing a modern-day facsimile. His most important catch was Hillary Rodham Clinton as secretary of state. Reeling in his primary campaign nemesis produced a partnership stronger than any had foreseen and one that would prove advantageous to both over the long haul. Almost as significant, if not as dramatic, was his success in persuading Bush's highly respected secretary of defense, Robert Gates, to remain at his post. A third important appointee, New York Fed chairman Timothy Geithner as treasury secretary, represented another nod to bipartisanship, since Geithner was respected as much by Republicans as by Democrats. In shaping the rest of his cabinet, Obama experienced one severe disappointment: having to give up on the candidacy of former Senate majority leader Tom Daschle, whom he had wanted to appoint as both secretary of health and human services and White House czar for health-care reform. When Daschle's tax difficulties did him in, Obama settled on another important early supporter, Kansas governor Kathleen Sebelius, for the HHS post. She proved loyal and steady, but possessed neither the political acumen nor the coalition-building skills of Daschle.

Commentators argued from the beginning about the wisdom of Obama's approach once in the White House. Even though enjoying the advantage of strong Democratic majorities in both houses of Congress, he committed to a "post-partisan" strategy of attempting to craft negotiated approaches to achieve the ambitious objectives he had laid out in his campaign—including health-care and immigration reform. Admirers saw this as proof of his consistency and principled commitment to civil governance. "Breaking Washington's addiction to partisanship," writes Chuck Todd in *The Stranger: Barack Obama in the White House*, "was one of the basic promises of Obama's first campaign, and he meant to keep it." Similarly, James Kloppenberg observes in *Reading Obama: Dreams, Hope, and the American Political Tradition,* "Obama has long been a moderate Democrat, a master of mediation drawn toward deliberation rather than drawing lines in the sand." His strategy also drew fire, however, especially from the left. Representative of this line of criticism is Ian Haney López, who writes in *Dog Whistle Politics: How Coded Racial Appeals Have Reinvented Racism and Wrecked the Middle Class,* that Obama "squandered" an opportunity in 2009. "The moment was right for Obama to offer the country a new narrative," he observes. "But almost immediately, with his inaugural address, [he] pivoted from a campaign that had preached 'change' to a presidency that promised compromise." Adds Haney López: "The right did not initially fetter Obama. Instead, Obama's decision not to offer the country a renewed liberal narrative contributed to conservative counter-mobilization."

Obama's initial approach is probably best explained by the fact the problems he faced were immense, and he knew Republican hostility following his election ran deep. TARP had dealt with only the most extreme symptoms of the economic crisis. The near-total collapse of the banking system during the fall had produced cascading negative impacts, sending consumer confidence to the basement, producing frighteningly high and rising unemployment figures, and seeming to imperil the American economic system itself. Recovery clearly required further government intervention, which was anathema to Republicans— especially if the president and his party might receive the credit for saving the economy. White House courtship of GOP leaders in the first days of the new administration proved completely fruitless, however, a pattern that would prevail throughout Obama's presidency. The administration's economic stimulus measure, the American Recovery and Reinvestment Act (ARRA), received almost no support from congressional Republicans. In the House, where the GOP's so-called "Young Guns"—Eric Cantor (whip), Kevin McCarthy (deputy whip), and Paul Ryan (ranking Republican on the Budget Committee)—had taken a near-blood oath to obstruct whatever the White House might offer, the $775 billion relief package passed without a single Republican vote in favor. In the Senate, only three reliably moderate Republicans—Maine's Olympia Snowe and Susan Collins and Arlen Spector of Pennsylvania—supported the White House measure.

Obama experienced no greater success with Republicans on any other administration-sponsored legislation between his inauguration and the 2010 mid-term elections. Unfortunately for the president, except for the eleven months when the Democrats had a filibuster-proof sixty-vote majority between March 2009 (with Specter's surprising switch to the Democratic party) and the following February (when Republican Scott Brown was sworn in after winning the Massachusetts Senate seat vacated by Ted Kennedy's August 2009 death), White House-sponsored legislation could succeed only with some GOP support. The only instances where the necessary cooperation was forthcoming were the Lilly Ledbetter Fair Pay Act, which did away with the statute of limitations where pay discrimination complaints were concerned, and the 2009 Omnibus Appropriations Act. In the case of the Ledbetter Act, which primarily benefited women, all four Republican women senators voted with the united Democrats.

The key test of the administration's "cooperationist" strategy came with its health-care reform bill, the Patient Protection and Affordable Care Act (shorthanded as ACA). Speaker Pelosi's firm control of the House Democratic caucus allowed Obama to focus his conversion efforts on the Senate. It was a daunting task, since not only was the GOP unified in opposition but even some Democrats were negatively disposed. After a prolonged unsuccessful effort to win the support of GOP senator Chuck Grassley (Iowa), the administration turned its charms on the more persuadable Olympia Snowe of Maine. Snowe voted for the measure in the Finance Committee, but efforts to win her vote on final passage foundered because Democrats on the Health, Education, Labor and Pensions Committee added nearly 1000 pages to the bill at the last minute. Giving up on obtaining any GOP support at all, Obama instead concentrated on ensuring the votes of two Red State Senate Democrats whose constituencies strongly opposed federal intervention in health care, Louisiana's Mary Landrieu

291

and Nebraska's Ben Nelson. Though the sweeteners provided to the two recalcitrant Democrats ultimately had to be stripped from the bill, the strictly partisan strategy worked; on Christmas Eve, the bill passed by a straight party-line vote of 60-39—during the short window of time when appointed Democrat Paul Kirk, occupying Kennedy's seat until the February special election, could provide the crucial sixtieth vote to block a filibuster.

Since the House and Senate versions of the health-care reform bill differed, however, formal reconciliation of the two bills was necessary. This task was immensely complicated by Scott Brown's arrival in the Senate, which broke the Democrats' supermajority. Pelosi and Senate majority leader Harry Reid now became creative, working out a deal whereby certain House amendments could be accepted by the Senate as part of a budget reconciliation bill, on which filibusters were not permitted. The bill finally passed in late March, with not a single Republican vote having been cast in support of the measure on any roll call in either house.

The provisions of the Affordable Care Act, which would become the GOP's prime target in subsequent campaign seasons, included mandatory health-insurance coverage for all individuals not already insured, creation of government-established insurance exchanges with federal subsidies for low-income clients, minimum insurance plan requirements, a ban on denial of coverage based on pre-existing conditions, and allowance for inclusion of children up to age 26 on their parents' health-insurance plans. While Obama's critics portrayed the new law as "socialism lite" (or even not-so-lite), the accusation was a stretch. Political scientist Ruth O'Brien offers a more nuanced and compelling characterization in *Out of Many, One: Obama and the Third American Political Tradition*. "What [was] important" to Obama in the bill, she writes, was "not that the state provide health care, nor that the state make health care private, but that the individual must buy into health care and that health insurance companies must reform their actual practices." Under Obama's approach, she observes, "the state mediates and facilitates, moderating proprietary capitalism through consumer reform."

The final significant piece of administration-sponsored legislation to pass before the 2010 elections, the Dodd–Frank Wall Street Reform and Consumer Protection Act, was designed to avert a repeat of the kind of financial malfeasance that had led to the 2008 crash. Dodd–Frank—which provided for consolidation of regulatory agencies, comprehensive regulation of financial markets (including so-called "derivative" investments that had been responsible for so much of the problem), establishment of a new consumer protection agency, and prohibition of proprietary trading by depository banks—passed the House 223-202 and the Senate 59-39, once again with zero GOP votes in support. Obama signed the bill into law on July 21, 2010. Left for dead as the session closed was the administration's proposal for cap-and-trade legislation to limit pollution and incentivize industry to adopt renewable energy sources, for which not even enough Democratic votes were available to produce victory.

Against steep odds, the administration had achieved much. "The scope and substance of the legislative policy initiatives enacted during the 111th Congress [were] considerable," writes political scientist Stephen Wayne in James Thurber's edited volume, *Rivals for Power: Presidential-Congressional Relations*, "approaching that of the first two years of the Johnson administration." The president had not accomplished things in the way he had hoped, however. Post-partisanship never had a chance.

Fortunately for Obama, his first opportunities to appoint new members to the Supreme Court came during the two years when he enjoyed a Democratic-controlled Congress. What was not so fortunate, however, was that the two vacancies he was able to fill resulted from the retirements of two of the court's most reliably liberal justices, David Souter and John Paul Stevens. Almost immediately after Souter announced his retirement in May 2009, Obama nominated Sonia Sotomayor, a Clinton appointee to the Second District Court of Appeals in New York. She was confirmed after fairly tough hearings by a mostly party-line vote, 66-31; many Republicans were convinced that she would be unable to approach cases neutrally, based on her frequent allusions to the value of her experiences as a Latina. A year after Sotomayor's confirmation, the court's senior and most liberal member, John Paul Stevens, announced that he was stepping down. Obama nominated a second woman (who would become the third on the court, which had never occurred before), Elena Kagan, who had left her position as Harvard's first female Law School dean to serve as his solicitor general. After more than a month of hearings, Kagan, too, was confirmed by an essentially party-line vote, 63-37. Partisan treatment of Supreme Court nominees had apparently become the norm.

Even though the great recession and health-care reform largely preoccupied Obama during his first two years in office, he also had to sort out the ongoing military involvements in Iraq and Afghanistan. During the 2008 campaign, he had frequently distinguished between the "war of choice" in Iraq and the "war of necessity" in Afghanistan. He began a draw-down in Iraq almost immediately after coming to the White House; in late February, with 130,000 U.S. troops still in the field, he promised a withdrawal of all combat troops by August 2010, with the remainder of American personnel to be gone by the end of 2011. "This early action," writes James Mann in *The Obamians: The Struggle Inside the White House to Redefine American Power*, "effectively removed Iraq as the most contentious issue in American life." The best way forward in Afghanistan was not so clear, however. In Obama's view, Bush had neglected the theater of operations that represented the real base of terrorism, and the one in which Osama bin Laden was probably still in hiding. The public was weary of war, however. Within the administration, Vice President Biden argued for restraint in ground military operations, believing a military solution to be unrealistic, while Secretary of State Clinton supported greater military pressure in Afghanistan. Obama leaned to the latter view; at the same time as he presented his plan for withdrawal from Iraq, he announced that 17,000 more American troops would be deployed to Afghanistan, calling the action "necessary to stabilize a deteriorating situation ... which has not received the strategic attention, direction and resources it urgently requires." By May, he had replaced the commander in the field, whom he thought insufficiently grounded in the techniques of counter-insurgency, with a favorite of Iraq-front hero General David Petraeus. The new commander, General Stanley McChrystal, a Green Beret, took his charge seriously. In September, he pressed the administration for 40,000 additional troops—while, quite inappropriately, going public with his views of the necessity for such a deployment. After mulling over the options, Obama gave McChrystal almost all he had requested, announcing in mid-December an additional 30,000-troop deployment but promising at the same time that a gradual withdrawal would begin in July 2011.

Administration critics complained, not without reason, that it was counter-productive to announce a planned withdrawal simultaneously with the additional deployment. But even while increasing the U.S. presence in Afghanistan, Obama was drawing new limits. As then-CIA director Leon Panetta later wrote in his memoir, *Worthy Fights*, with this decision the president "mov[ed] away from a notion that our primary goal was to destroy or eliminate the Taliban. Rather, he adopted the formula that our mission was to 'disrupt, dismantle, and defeat' al Qaeda." The revised strategy included a sharper focus on capturing or killing bin Laden. The president had now taken ownership of the war in Afghanistan "It's His War Now," trumpeted the cover of *Time* magazine's December 14 issue.

General McChrystal did not last long in Afghanistan. By spring 2010, it had become clear that the additional 30,000 troops were insufficient to accomplish the objectives of taking Marja and Kandahar, and then moving on to secure Kabul. While the failure could arguably have been due to strategic shortcomings, the main problem was that McChrystal made the ill-advised choice to criticize administration policy in Afghanistan in a June *Rolling Stone* interview. He was gone within weeks—the second general to be cashiered by Obama in the space of eighteen months. Recognizing the need to make an unassailable appointment to replace him, the president prevailed upon Petraeus to take what amounted to a demotion and leave his Central Command post to take leadership of the U.S. and NATO forces in Afghanistan. "Obama ...

rolled the dice on Petraeus," write Marvin and Deborah Kalb in *Haunting Legacy*; "his political fortunes were in the general's hands." Fortunately for the White House, Petraeus's magic held—at least with Congress, where criticism of Obama's handling of the war quieted after the general's appointment. Moreover, U.S. and NATO troops finally seemed to be making progress against both al-Qaeda and the Taliban. The American public was growing more impatient with the war in Afghanistan, however, just as it had soured on the conflict in Iraq. According to a December 2010 poll, only 44 percent thought the United States should remain in Afghanistan until "stability" there was achieved.

In its first two years, the administration had delivered on its promises in important ways, including injecting needed resources into the faltering U.S. economy, enacting the Affordable Care Act and significant financial reforms, and shifting the emphasis in a war on terrorism gone bad. Partisan warfare had only grown more intense, however, as Republicans were locked in a blood feud with the Democratic president. "[T]he paradox of Obama's first two years," observes O'Brien, was that "while legislatively he accomplished so much, politically he achieved little." Looking toward the 2010 mid-term elections, there was every reason to expect the situation to deteriorate further.

Government by Dysfunction

Obama was the target of vituperative attacks from the moment he entered the White House. The barrage of negative commentary included diatribes with such titles as *The Amateur*, *The Communist*, *The Great Destroyer*, and *The Manchurian President*, as well as persistent malicious rumors that he had been born outside the United States and was thus illegally in the White House. From the beginning, too, Obama was the target of "racial reactions," as Haney López observes in *Dog Whistle Politics*. Race-tinged criticism took a number of forms. For example, writes Haney López, "the confluence of liberalism and race made the subliminal message behind 'Obamacare' [as the administration's health-care program was immediately labeled] especially damaging: *here comes a black man to get government involved raising taxes on you in order to find even more giveaways to minorities.*" So palpable was the racial subtext in criticisms of the president that Republican national chairman Michael Steele—himself an African American—worried that they could undermine his party's efforts to recover from its 2008 defeat. Acknowledging that the GOP had been "essentially defined by race" since Nixon's invention of the southern strategy, Steele implicitly promised that his party would do better going forward. This appeared unlikely, however, since, as O'Brien writes, Obama's election seemed to many Americans to give permission to ignore race issues, based on the belief, against significant evidence to the contrary, "that racism is less of a problem in the United States today than it was in times past."

The most direct early challenge to the new president came from an angry grass-roots movement that erupted without warning within a month of his inauguration. Growing out of a CNBC correspondent's public rant against the administration's programs to assist homeowners who either had defaulted on their mortgages or were at risk of doing so, the so-called Tea Party movement attracted activists who equated White House intervention with favoritism for those undeserving of assistance. There was more than a hint of racial subtext in this line of attack, as well; as O'Brien notes, many Tea Party adherents tended to view Obama as a threat to "white privilege and supremacy, or simply whiteness." Media coverage focused on the anti-politics thrust of the movement, but in fact much of its leadership came from the ranks of longtime conservative activists, just as its funding tended to come from extreme-right sources. Ironically, while the Tea Party was rooted in the angst of the extreme right, as journalist Jonathan Alter writes in *The Center Holds: Obama and His Enemies*, it "was propelled by the same forces that had brought Obama to power: disgust with government and a bad economy."

The drama of the Tea Party movement, including its bitter denunciations of Obama and his policies, dominated the media throughout 2010—especially Fox News, the editorial pages of the *Wall Street Journal*, and the ubiquitous right-leaning radio talk shows. This messaging had a huge impact on political discourse leading up to the mid-term elections. "[M]edia coverage for Tea Party complaints about 'big government' spending and bailouts helped Republicans and conservatives to reset national agendas of debate," write Theda Skocpol and Vanessa Williamson in *The Tea Party and the Remaking of Republican Conservatism*. "People stopped talking about Obama and 'change we can believe in' and started talking about government tyranny."

While posing a strong challenge to Obama and Democrats in the 2010 mid-terms, the Tea Party also represented an implicit threat to many Republicans. Scott Brown's success in winning with Tea Party support in deep-blue Massachusetts left an indelible imprint that the new movement was clearly a force to be reckoned with—and satisfied—for any GOP candidate in the 2010 elections. For doubters, the fate suffered by popular, long-term Republican congressman Mike Castle in the Delaware Senate primary was a lesson; having never lost a statewide election, Castle was upset by an unknown Tea Party favorite, Christine O'Donnell (whose general election campaign was ultimately undone by innumerable problems, including her having dabbled in witchcraft). "Anytime Republicans thought of trying to be even a smidgen more moderate," writes Alter, "they worried about being *primaried*."

The 2010 mid-term campaign was the most circus-like in memory. The potency of the Tea Party produced not only unpredictable, unknown candidates and extreme rhetoric in the GOP, but also absurdist political theater. Easily the most bizarre event was the "Rally to Restore Sanity and/or Fear," an event co-sponsored by the Comedy Central cable TV channel's popular satirical newscaster team Jon Stewart and Stephen Colbert that drew an estimated 215,000 to the National Mall on the eve of the elections. For all the hyperbole, however, the mid-term elections boiled down to a simple referendum on the administration. The Republicans swept the board, picking up sixty-three House seats to take control of that chamber and gaining six in the Senate, sharply reducing the Democratic margin in the upper house. The massive House gains marked the largest GOP victory since the first mid-term elections of Truman's presidency, sixty-two years earlier. Though the Republicans tried to focus on Obamacare, the verdict was more general. Of the thirty House Democrats who had opposed health-care reform, seventeen were defeated. "In the end," observed the *New York Times* in its post-election analysis, "it may have mattered less whether vulnerable Democratic incumbents voted for or against the health care law than that they simply had a D by their names." Notable GOP freshmen elected to the Senate included rising stars Rand Paul of Kentucky and Marco Rubio of Florida, both with strong Tea Party backing. Alarmingly for Democrats—especially just two years after they had supposedly constructed a new majority—GOP candidates secured a majority of women's votes for the first time since 1982; only under-30 years of age, black, Hispanic, and gay and lesbian voters seemed to continue to back Democrats strongly, but their respective shares of the total vote declined sharply from 2008.

The Republicans' sweeping victory changed the political task for Obama from challenging to almost impossible. Knowing life would only get harder when the new Congress convened in January, Obama worked to accomplish as much as possible before the lame-duck Congress left town. The six weeks after the election proved extraordinarily productive, as he surprisingly managed to win sufficient GOP support to achieve two major goals.

The president focused first on getting the lame-duck Senate to ratify the START 2 Treaty, the expired arms reduction treaty left over from the George H. W. Bush presidency. Hoping to "re-set" relations with Russia, Obama had negotiated the agreement with Putin's successor (and soon-to-be predecessor), Dmitri Medvedev, in April 2010. Its specific terms required the two nations to reduce their respective stockpiles of nuclear warheads by one-fourth, but Obama had in mind more than mutual arms reduction. "On the surface, the new START treaty was merely another arms control agreement between Washington and Moscow," writes James Mann in *The Obamians*, but the START 2 Treaty was "part of a broader effort to stop the development of nuclear weapons in other countries." Suspecting Obama's larger agenda, most conservative GOP senators were firmly opposed. With hard-won support from John McCain and backing from some of the few remaining moderate Republicans including Richard Lugar, Lamar Alexander, Susan Collins, and Olympia Snowe, the administration secured the necessary two-thirds margin, even though Republicans voted 13-26 against. Vice President Biden was widely credited for putting the necessary coalition together.

The second major White House victory in the lame-duck session came only after Obama made a concession roundly criticized by many liberals. Convinced that a grueling fight over extension of the Bush-era tax cuts would be inevitable in the new Congress, he decided to trade two-year renewal of the cuts for a thirteen-month extension of unemployment insurance for the chronically out-of-work and a one-year continuation of the payroll tax holiday. So many Democrats objected to this deal that the president had to deputize Bill Clinton to help sell it to his party colleagues. The tax-cut concession proved to be a good bargain, however, as it also paved the way for Obama to deliver on his campaign promise to the gay and lesbian community to get rid of the discriminatory "Don't Ask, Don't Tell" policy in the armed forces. With polls showing steadily growing tolerance on gay and lesbian issues, the administration had worked assiduously with the joint chiefs since early 2009 to build momentum for the change. Most important, a survey of 115,000 active-duty military found that over 80 percent of service members reported good or neutral experiences with gays and lesbians in their ranks, and only 30 percent worried about any potential difficulties should DADT be repealed. The repeal bill passed 250-175 in the House and 65-31 in the Senate, with small numbers of moderate Republicans in each chamber breaking from their caucuses to support it. Still cautious about outrunning public opinion on the matter, Obama delayed the official dismantling of the policy until the joint chiefs could guarantee a peaceful transition in their respective branches. "Don't Ask, Don't Tell" finally came to an end more than six months later. In early 2011, the president announced that the administration would no longer enforce the Defense of Marriage Act (DOMA) against same-sex couples legally married in states that allowed such unions, further solidifying his position with gay and lesbian voters.

Only one item on Obama's to-do list for the lame-duck Congress was blocked: a proposed bill to permit a path to citizenship for young undocumented aliens who had been brought to the United States by their parents but had since either graduated from college or served in the military. Having initially yoked this so-called DREAM Act with repeal of "Don't Ask, Don't Tell" for strategic reasons, Obama ultimately yielded to pressure from the leading gay and lesbian rights organization, the Human Rights Campaign, to separate the two measures. Cut adrift, the DREAM Act fell five votes short of cloture in the Senate. Immigration reform remained the proverbial third rail for a majority of the members of Congress.

When the new Congress hit town in January 2011, it was clear that Obama had been wise to get as much as he could from its predecessor. With Senate Democrats now far short of the votes needed to end GOP filibusters and the aggressive "Young Guns" holding GOP colleagues (and the more pragmatic Speaker, John Boehner) hostage in the House, there was virtually no hope of cooperation between the administration and the new Congress. Hoping to find a way to deal with the new, more hostile environ-ment, Obama added Reagan White House veteran David Gergen to his staff and let his aides leak that he was reading Lou Cannon's *President Reagan: The Role of a Lifetime.* None of this helped. "The single most important thing we want to achieve," GOP Senate minority leader Mitch McConnell announced, "is for President Obama to be a one-term president."

The GOP's strategy was evident in one confrontation after another. Within weeks, Budget Committee chair Paul Ryan unveiled a draconian spending plan that proposed repeal of the Affordable Care Act, virtual elimination of Medicaid, and other severe cuts in spending that would disproportionately affect the poor—in Alter's words, "the most radical policy blueprint to come out of official Washington in a generation." If the Republicans' plan were enacted, Obama told an audience at George Washington University, it "would lead to a fundamentally different America than the one we've known." Although the budget proposal gained no traction, the House kept up its frontal assault, voting on more than thirty different occasions to repeal the health-care measure. As long as Obama held the veto pen and Democrats controlled the Senate, however, such votes were symbolic only. Meanwhile, the Republican House leadership allowed the government to approach a dangerous fiscal cliff by refusing to take up a bill to raise the debt limit until agreement could be reached on the reductions necessary to bring the deficit back to the currently approved level. "[T]he fractious, backbiting, finger-pointing, polarizing, partisan, kick-the-can-down-the-road brinksmanship of Washington politics these days is, let's face it, the reality of American governance in the modern era," wrote *New York Times* columnist Peter Baker in June 2011.

Concerned that his party could be recreating the scenario that had blown up in the faces of Newt Gingrich and his intransigent colleagues two decades earlier, Speaker Boehner struggled to convince his true-believing troops that compromise was necessary. Obama was working hard to strike a "Grand Bargain" that would couple a debt ceiling increase with a combination of targeted spending reductions and enhanced revenues. After White House–congressional talks appeared to have fallen completely apart, the two sides managed to reach a deal of sorts in the first days of August, with bipartisan majorities in both houses passing a $2.5 trillion debt increase. The White House paid a steep price for the agreement, as Republicans exacted a promise of $1 trillion in cuts over the next ten years. The compromise bill also established a bipartisan "Super-committee" to design the deficit-reduction plan, ensuring that the budget would remain political theater for the several months leading up to the presidential election. If the committee's efforts were unsuccessful, the result would be automatic sequestration of funds across all federal departments by the end of 2012. Once again, most of the president's liberal allies were critical of the deal he had struck, believing—as Alter writes—"[t]he Republicans had taken America's full faith and credit hostage and Obama had paid them ransom."

As the 112th Congress settled in on a path toward being one of the least productive Congresses in memory, Obama began to build his case for re-election. In September 2011, with great fanfare, he rolled out a largely symbolic plan he labeled the American Jobs Act, knowing that it could not pass. Three months later, conspicuously evoking the symbolism of Teddy Roosevelt's "New Nationalism" of a century earlier, he delivered a bristling, populist-flavored speech in Osawatomie, Kansas, making the case for government intervention in support of those millions of Americans who had never recovered from the financial meltdown of 2008–2009, having lost their savings, the equity they had enjoyed in their homes, and, in numberless cases, the homes themselves. "This is a make-or-break moment for the middle class and all those who are fighting to get into the middle class" he asserted, trying out an appeal that he would repeat throughout his re-election campaign. The Osawatomie speech was also a direct response to a second grass-roots movement every bit as hostile to Washington wheeling-and-dealing—but also to the excesses and sloppy practices of Wall Street—as was the Tea Party, but from the opposite ideological pole. "Occupy Wall Street," with its tens of thousands of mostly young adherents engaging in massive sit-ins to protest the victimization of the "ninety-nine percent" at the hands of the "one percent" of extremely wealthy Americans who had not been hurt by the Great Recession, emerged full-blown in September 2011. A vivid manifestation of disappointment with the lack of change that Obama's election had produced, the movement provided the president with yet another reason to strengthen his earlier appeals to the powerless.

While the administration's war of attrition with Congress ground along depressingly through 2011, at least the news from Afghanistan was not all bad. Under Petraeus, American forces finally seemed to be making material strides in their policing and training efforts, even though the corruption and intransigence of the Karzai regime posed a continuing political challenge. The war on al-Qaeda took a major positive turn at the beginning of May, moreover, when Obama surprised the nation by announcing that Osama bin Laden had been tracked down and killed in a Navy

SEAL raid on a compound in Abbottabad, Pakistan. The top-secret raid, which strained relations with Pakistan because of unannounced violation of its airspace, was a huge political coup for the president. "Absent a major crisis," writes Alter, "the killing of bin Laden stripped the Republicans of a weapon, that Democrats are weak on national security."

Not all the news from the Islamic world was helpful to Obama going into his campaign for re-election, however. In January 2011, events began to unfold throughout the Middle East that quickly grew into a region-wide revolution labeled "Arab Spring." Though the causes of rebellion differed from one country to the next, the common theme was a desire to be rid of long-term authoritarian regimes with a history of persecuting religious minorities. The unrest threatened governments both friendly and unfriendly to the United States, posing a diplomatic dilemma for the administration as to how to react and which factions to support. The first ruler to fall was Tunisia's Zine El Abidine Ben Ali in January, an event that the U.S. government let pass without major response. This reluctance to become involved was consistent with the aloof posture Obama had taken in the face of the ultimately unsuccessful "Green Revolution" in Iran in the first year of his presidency; by the time of the Arab Spring, as Mann notes, that Iranian rebel movement "had been eviscerated."

As chaos gripped Egypt in February 2011, threatening the ouster of longtime U.S. ally Hosni Mubarak, Obama could no longer avoid taking a stand. In a much-heralded speech delivered in Cairo in June 2009, the young president had broken new policy ground by recognizing the damaging impact of colonialism and the Cold War on Muslim peoples and implying a need to respect aspirations for self-rule in the region. In his speech accepting the Nobel Peace Prize six months later, he struck a similar theme, stating his belief "that peace is unstable where citizens are denied the right to speak freely or worship as they please, choose their own leaders, or assemble without fear." Now, in the face of the challenge to the pro-Western Mubarak, he weighed in on the side of Egypt's young, secular revolutionary movement and called for Mubarak's resignation. Deserted by his strongest allies, the

Egyptian leader stepped down. To the consternation of the United States and other Western powers, however, the months following saw the gradual rise to power of the quasi-radical Muslim Brotherhood, rather than the secularists who had fomented the initial uprising. These developments, ultimately culminating in the election of the anti-Western Mohamed Morsi as Egypt's ruler in June 2012, left Obama open to critics on the right who believed his failure to back Mubarak had increased Western vulnerability throughout the Middle East. Morsi himself was overthrown by a military coup a year later, to be replaced by a regime in many ways similar to Mubarak's.

The fate of a third Arab strongman targeted by revolutionaries, Libyan tyrant Muammar Qaddafi, was of less concern to Obama's domestic political critics, but the administration's response to that uprising, too, evoked strong criticism from congressional Republicans. As Qaddafi's troops fought a rearguard action against Libya's Islamist rebels, Obama cooperated with UN allies to tilt the conflict in favor of the latter. Hoping to avoid military involvement on yet another front while trying to find a way out of Afghanistan, the president authorized American participation in air strikes on Qaddafi's forces, but stated that the United States would "lead from behind." With the aid of this air cover, Libyan rebels eventually defeated and killed Qaddafi in October, but Obama's infelicitous phrase would live on during the 2012 campaign, allowing the GOP again to portray him as irresolute in the face of international conflict and threats to U.S. security.

With Obama's approval ratings consistently below 50 percent in the year leading up to the 2012 election, the Republican nomination seemed a prize worth winning. Tea Party influence had been enormous after the mid-term elections, but was clearly on the wane by mid-2011. Yet the Washington political environment was still overheated and moderation did not seem to be a viable option for those seeking to head the GOP ticket. The early favorite was Mitt Romney, who was back for a second run. Other much-talked-about possibilities either stayed out of the race altogether or withdrew early, including longshot media personalities Donald Trump and (since signing on to Fox News) Sarah Palin, former GOP national chairman Haley Barbour of Mississippi, and several governors and former governors: Florida's Jeb Bush, brother of George W.; Mitch Daniels (Indiana); Chris Christie (New Jersey), and Mike Huckabee (Arkansas).

Those who committed to the race squared off in a series of unforgiving debates beginning months before the first primary voters went to the polls. The main challenge for the participants was to win over the fervently conservative party base. "The debates were mostly held before Tea Party crowds that hooted down questions from moderators and cheered only the most right-wing pronouncements," writes Alter. "None of the candidates tried to moderate his or her views with an eye to the general election." The problem, however, was that in the end the winner would have to present a credible alternative to the president in the general election. The nearly weekly debates produced a revolving door of front-runners, but Romney remained the likely eventual nominee in the opinion of most. Tea Party favorite and Minnesota congresswoman Michelle Bachmann quickly plummeted in popularity once she demonstrated the limitations of her knowledge in confrontations with the other candidates. Texas governor Rick Perry then briefly reigned as the favorite of the right, before flaming out in a memorably bad debate performance.

Even in this less-than-inspiring field, Romney evoked so little enthusiasm that the door was left perpetually open for someone—anyone—else to claim the Republican nomination. One problem was the heavy baggage he carried from his 2009 *New York Times* op-ed piece criticizing the government bailout of General Motors, which the editors had gratuitously titled "Let Detroit Go Bankrupt." Together with his record as CEO of Bain Capital, an equity company that had presided over the closing down of numerous companies, the op-ed branded Romney as what one of his rivals gleefully labeled a "vulture capitalist." In the quest for anyone but Romney, a particularly fascinating candidate briefly came to the fore: Herman Cain, a successful African American pizza company executive who focused his campaign on implementation of a flat tax. Unfortunately for Cain, however, past indiscretions with female subordinates came to light in late October, pushing him out of the race.

Most improbably, the race seemed to boil down to a choice between Romney and—of all people—Newt Gingrich, who had arisen from the political ashes in vintage bomb-throwing form. With his typical lack of humility, the former Speaker asserted in a December ABC News interview, "I am going to be the nominee." At this point, freed of the worrisome Perry and with Cain permanently sidelined, Romney's endlessly rich political action committee (PAC), Restore Our Future, poured virtually everything it had into destroying Gingrich's chances. Heading into the all-important Iowa caucuses, the Romney–Gingrich slugfest held the attention of the media, while two remaining longshot candidates—former Pennsylvania senator Rick Santorum and libertarian candidate Ron Paul (father of Rand)—labored quietly to try to pull off an upset.

The Iowa caucuses outdid themselves as a candidate-sorting mechanism in 2012. Perry and Bachmann, finishing fifth and sixth, respectively, were officially out. Gingrich, having barely survived the savaging by the Romney forces, appeared grievously wounded. Romney, who finished in a virtual tie for first with the unlikely Santorum, remained alive, and could now move onto friendly ground in New Hampshire. Choosing to ignore Santorum, Romney and Gingrich bludgeoned each other in the next two critical contests, with Romney prevailing in New Hampshire and Gingrich taking South Carolina. Meanwhile, Santorum hung on, hoping for a miracle. The massive dollars behind Romney eventually prevailed. When he overwhelmed Gingrich and Santorum in the Florida primary, both were effectively finished. The trail ended in early April with Romney's victory in the Wisconsin primary.

Though the identity of the nominee was clear, dark clouds hovered over the GOP. The Republican primaries had been marked by a demonstrable enthusiasm gap, with turnout especially low in states considered key battlegrounds in the general election. Moreover, Romney had been mauled by his GOP rivals on the Bain Capital issue and his numbers against Obama in a one-on-one faceoff had actually declined as he closed in on the nomination; by March he trailed the president in head-to-head polls by 43 to 51 percent. A successful party convention was essential, but not much went right at the GOP's Tampa conclave at the end of August. After Hurricane Isaac forced cancellation of the entire first night's schedule, keynoter Chris Christie disappointed Romney forces by focusing his remarks on his own accomplishments in New Jersey. Ann Romney's warm, personal speech humanized her husband, but a long, mystifying soliloquy by octogenarian actor Clint Eastwood immediately prior to Romney's acceptance speech seemed to undo any good that had preceded it. The nominee's choice of the youthful Paul Ryan as his running-mate pleased party conservatives but did not bode well for making inroads with independents in the general campaign. The GOP's image was not helped, either, by the fact that only slightly more than 1 percent of the delegates to the convention were black.

In contrast to the GOP's near-debacle in Tampa, the Democrats' convention a week afterward was a positive, well-orchestrated affair. From John Kerry's evocation of Obama's most dramatic success in the war on terror ("Ask Osama bin Laden if he's better off now than he was four years ago!" Kerry thundered to tumultuous applause) to former president Clinton's virtuoso explanation of the economic recovery that had marked the preceding four years ("No president, not me, not any of my predecessors could have fixed in four years the economy that Obama had inherited."), the convention proceeded almost flawlessly in building the case for the incumbent's re-election. Post-convention polls showed a bounce of five points for the president.

Like his two predecessors in the White House, Obama had faced no primary opposition and thus was able to concentrate his campaign resources on defining his opponent negatively as soon as it became clear who that opponent would be. His forces eagerly seized the opportunity, launching a summer-long media campaign that branded Romney with an elitist, non-empathetic image. This strategy proved to be a masterstroke, as the GOP candidate could not undo the damage the ads had created. Ryan's presence on the ticket was welcomed by the Democrats, as well, since the president had opened his re-election campaign in early April by lambasting the Wisconsinite's budget plan. In addition to running to the left on economic issues, Obama found other ways, as well, to shore up important parts of his base. In May, following a premature public signal from Vice President Biden that the administration's position was about to change on the issue, the president announced on ABC's *Good Morning America* that he now fully supported same-sex marriage. The president's public statement was ground-breaking; while winning him huge points with younger supporters, as well as gays and lesbians, the pronouncement cost him little with either blacks or Latinos. Wrote openly gay Andrew Sullivan in *Newsweek*: "He shifted the mainstream in one interview." When a month later the First Circuit Court of Appeals ruled key provisions of DOMA unconstitutional, Obama's position with gays and lesbians was further enhanced. The president received an unexpected gift from the Supreme Court, as well. In June 2011, in a surprise ruling authored by Chief Justice Roberts, the court declared the "individual mandate" provision of the Affordable Care Act constitutional based on the federal government's power to tax. The decision did not remove Obamacare as a major Republican issue in the 2012 election, but the president was now free—temporarily, at least—of charges that his signature health-care plan was unconstitutional.

The hardening lines of division between Red and Blue America promised a bitter general election campaign, but Obama began as the favorite. X-factors that could upset predictions were numerous. World events, especially in such a volatile time, could intrude at any point. Just such an event occurred within a week of the Democratic convention, in the form of an attack on the U.S. diplomatic compound in Benghazi, Libya, in which four Americans were killed, including Ambassador Christopher Stevens. The attack and murders probably would have inflicted serious political damage on the administration, but for Romney's inept response. By issuing a premature statement to the press that mischaracterized Obama's reaction upon learning of the attack, the GOP candidate appeared petty and overly partisan when a more appropriate response would have been to honor the fallen Americans first and attempt to sort out the damage later. Although Republicans in Congress would later continue to try to embarrass the administration—both Obama and Secretary of State Hillary Clinton—by conducting years-long investigations into its handling of Benghazi and trying, as had become a pattern, to label the whole incident a scandal, the episode caused no real damage to the president's re-election campaign.

As Obama worked successfully to re-energize his 2008 base, Romney and Ryan struggled to convince voters that further tax cuts and budget reductions (especially in entitlement programs) would bring economic recovery. Unfortunately for the Republican ticket, many of their economic arguments could be seen as targeting the poorest Americans, especially persons of color who depended disproportionately on the social welfare programs under attack, including Obamacare. Romney's image suffered further damage when, in mid-September, a videotape surfaced that had recorded him telling wealthy donors at a pricy fundraising event that he knew *a priori* that he could never win over 47 percent of the electorate because they did not contribute to the economy and would never agree to shake their dependency on government programs. The polls remained generally close, but the projected distribution of votes suggested that the president would win enough of the battleground states to prevail in the Electoral College, especially if voter turnout were high.

Obama still had to make his way through three presidential debates, however—any one of which could elevate his opponent in some unexpected way. The danger of this happening was all the greater, given the president's deep contempt for Romney, which led him to underestimate such a possibility. On October 3, disaster struck, as a well-prepared Romney knocked an obviously dismissive, disengaged Obama for a loop in the first debate. The president's biggest mistake was in letting his rival glibly slip away from the extreme positions he had embraced throughout the primaries and general election campaign. The trouncing Obama suffered changed his approach. For the next two debates—and for the rest of the campaign—the president conducted himself much more like the candidate of four years earlier, with an aggressive edge, as he hammered away at Romney. "If I give up a couple of points of likability and come across as snarky, so be it," the *New York Times* reported the president telling his aides. By consensus he won the remaining two debates, leading most pollsters to predict his re-election. The final blow to Romney came as the damaging effects and aftereffects of Super Storm Sandy intruded into the campaign in its final week. Following the administration's quick and empa-thetic response to the victims of Sandy's devastation of large swaths of Staten Island and coastal New Jersey, the irrepressible Governor Christie engaged in a public show of affection and respect for Obama that burnished not only his own bipartisan cre-dentials, but the president's, as well. Bill Clinton's energetic partic-ipation in the campaign during that last week, as Obama focused on trying to help the many victims of the storm's devastation, provided the *coup de grâce* for the president.

The election results were lopsided in Obama's favor. Winning the popular vote by 51 to 47 percent, the president took all of the battleground states except Indiana and North Carolina and rolled up an Electoral College margin of 332-206—not much below the totals from his resounding victory four years earlier. To the Republicans' surprise and dismay, both black and Hispanic voters turned out in greater numbers than in 2008, with Obama winning an even higher percentage of the latter vote (71 percent) the second time around. Even self-identified moderates went for the president by a 15 percent margin. Most encouraging of all to the Democrats, the youth vote (voters aged 18 to 29) again broke overwhelmingly for Obama, 60 to 37 percent. Though the gay and lesbian vote was harder to track, the president's work on behalf of that population clearly paid off; the election produced a number of victories for state-level same-sex marriage measures, as well as the election of the nation's first openly gay U.S. senator, Tammy Baldwin in Wisconsin. Obama's coattails proved to be longer than predicted. In the House, the strong GOP majority produced by redistricting after the 2010 census shrank, though by only eight seats, leaving the party in control by 234-201. The results in the Senate produced an even more positive outcome for the president and his party. Although the Democrats had to

2000

WINNER:

☐ **George W. Bush, Republican**
Running Mate: Dick Cheney
Popular Vote: 50,455, 156
Electoral Votes: 271

☐ **Al Gore, Democratic**
Running Mate: Joe Lieberman
Popular Vote: 50,992,335
Electoral Votes: 266

RI
CT
DE
DC

2012

WINNER:

☐ **Barack Obama, Democratic**
Running Mate: Joe Biden
Popular Vote: 62,346,445
Electoral Votes: 332

☐ **Mitt Romney, Republican**
Running Mate: Paul Ryan
Popular Vote: 58,976,480
Electoral Votes: 206

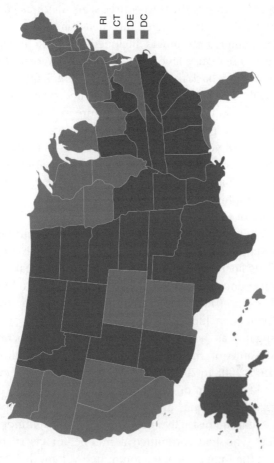

RI
CT
DE
DC

Figure 8.2 Barack Obama's re-election in 2012 built on voting trends that had begun to harden by 2000. The Democrats dominated the increasingly dependable "blue states" on both coasts and in the populous Great Lakes region, while the broad swath of Republican "red states" in the South and interior Midwest seemed an expansion and solidification of trends resulting from Nixon's 1968 Southern strategy. http://www.archives.gov/federal-register/electoral-college/map/historic.html#2000. http://www.archives.gov/federal-register/electoral-college/map/historic.html#2012

defend twenty-three of the thirty-three seats up for election, they made a net gain of two, increasing their majority to fifty-five. Prominent Senate newcomers included Texas Republican Ted Cruz, a strong Tea Party favorite, and liberal Democrat Elizabeth Warren, who took back the Kennedy seat from Scott Brown.

In the wake of Obama's re-election, Democrats again had high hopes that they were the party of the future in American politics. Not only had the president succeeded once again in mobilizing huge numbers of young and non-white voters—clearly the electorate of tomorrow—but even in losing the House, Democrats had outpolled Republicans by more than a million votes. The Obama campaign's sophisticated get-out-the-vote operation, demonstrably superior to the GOP's efforts, provided part of the explanation for the outpouring of such voters, effectively countering the efforts in Republican-controlled states to roll back what the party saw as overly liberal voting laws that encouraged illegal voting. As Haney López documents, thirty-eight states had introduced new election laws in 2011 designed to impede participation by "questionable" voters, including requiring specific voter ID cards. Such laws (castigated as "voter suppression" by the Democrats) may have had some of their intended impact, as overall turnout declined from 2008 to 2012. There was strong anecdotal evidence, however—in the form of long lines of patient voters in many of the nation's largest cities and in other heavily minority voting precincts—that the restrictive measures had only a minor impact.

Romney, who had committed a number of verbal blunders throughout the long campaign, committed yet another as he dissected the results in a post-election conference call with supporters. The problem, a *Los Angeles Times* article reported the defeated candidate saying, was that the Obama campaign had given "a lot of stuff to groups they hoped they could get to vote for them," specifically singling out African Americans and Hispanics. Like his unfortunate "47 percent" comments early in the campaign, such a characterization could only hurt the GOP looking to the longer term. It seemed clear that if the party were to have a better chance in subsequent presidential elections, it would need to change its image where its attitude to such voters was concerned.

On the other hand, the new rules of political finance seemed favorable for the Republicans going forward. The Supreme Court decision in the 2010 case, *Citizens United v. Federal Election Commission*, had completely altered the playing field for political fund-raising and spending, eliminating most of the controls that had been constructed in the years since Watergate. Declaring corporations the legal equivalent of "individuals," the court made it possible for them (as well as for unions, although the latter were no longer the political force they had once been) to spend unlimited funds for political purposes. An even more significant result of *Citizens United* was the uncapping of political spending by so-called independent expenditure groups with no identification of individual donors required. This change contributed to the exercise of unprecedented influence in the 2012 presidential campaign by supposedly "unaffiliated" PACs that in reality closely orchestrated their activities with their respective candidates of choice. The GOP benefited disproportionately. Given the astronomical spending levels of 2012, it was difficult to know where this would end.

By any measure, the election of 2012 was a watershed in modern American politics. "The substantive stakes of the race were huge," write Mark Halperin and John Heilemann in *Double Down: Game Change 2012*:

> If Obama had lost, much of what he had accomplished, starting with health care reform, would have been reversed by Romney and the GOP Congress. But the personal stakes were equally vast.... Had he fallen short in his quest for re-election, his story would have changed overnight, with his presidency recast from a heroic landmark to a failed one-term accident. In victory, he secured his legacy as a transformative figure.

The Politics of Trench Warfare

Obama's re-election rekindled hopes for the change that he had promised four years earlier. His second inaugural address was a ringing affirmation of equal rights for all, as he paid homage to the heroes of past civil rights movements, surprising many by including reference to Stonewall, the symbol of gay and lesbian rights, alongside Selma and Seneca Falls, symbolic of African Americans' and women's rights, respectively. Taking a jab at Republican "voter suppression," he added, "Our journey is not complete until no citizen is forced to wait hours to exercise the right to vote." In *The Center Holds*, penned just months after the speech, Jonathan Alter captured the popular sense that, with Obama re-elected, things were somehow going to be different. "[T]he conservative agenda of dramatically shrinking government that seemed achievable in 2011 and 2012 was now little more than a fantasy," he wrote. "A set of values that had been part of the American consensus since at least the New Deal would remain in place."

Reality did not reflect such a settled verdict; Obama's second term would prove to be the most polarized period yet, in what had become a full generation of bitterness and division in American politics. The title of a 2012 book by political scientists James Mann and Norman Ornstein, *It's Even Worse Than It Looks*, sums up the utter ugliness of politics during the later Obama presidency—with no sign of improvement on the horizon. The mandate that Republicans appeared to read into the election results was that American voters had purposely chosen divided government, and were counting on House Republicans to thwart the Democratic president.

Compelling evidence of the hopelessness of Obama's situation vis-à-vis Congress came just weeks after his re-election. In a horrific attack in Newtown, Connecticut, a deranged young gunman wielding a semi-automatic rifle shot and killed twenty first-grade students and six teachers at Sandy Hook Elementary School, as well as his mother and himself. In the wake of this national tragedy, and with public opinion overwhelmingly on his side, Obama sought meaningful gun-control legislation, including renewal of the expired ban on assault weapons and expansion of background checks to include guns sold at firearms shows. Optimistically, in the wake of the slaughter at Sandy Hook, he once again dispatched his reliable vice president to Capitol Hill to round up the votes for passage. As the National Rifle Association cranked up its time-tested pressure tactics, however, hope for significant Republican support for this latest gun-control proposal evaporated. When the bill finally came up for a vote in the Senate in mid-April, it was killed by filibuster, with only two Republicans (Pennsylvania's Pat Toomey and Mark Kirk of Illinois) voting with the administration. By this time, it hardly mattered, since Speaker Boehner had already declared that the bill would not be brought up for a vote in the GOP-controlled House in any case. That over 80 percent of the voters supported the measure made no difference. The parties were at war; the only winner, deadlock.

As Todd observes, the futile four-month struggle over gun control at the start of Obama's second term virtually guaranteed a lost year ahead. Not surprisingly, within two months of his defeat on the gun measure, the president hit the wall again with his immigration reform proposal. This time, the administration bill made it through the Senate when the White House conceded a massive buildup of the border patrol in exchange for a pathway to citizenship for most of the country's millions of undocumented immigrants. Once again, however, the measure died in the GOP-controlled House. The needed one hundred or so GOP votes were lacking, writes Todd in *The Stranger*, as many Tea Party-conditioned members viewed the vote in terms of their own survival, rather than "the overall political health of the national party."

With the odds already hopelessly stacked against Obama's achieving any of his objectives in the year after his re-election, stunning revelations by a young NSA contractor, Edward Snowden, concerning NSA and FBI wire-tapping of American citizens ensured total political paralysis. When the story had been completely told after weeks of increasingly alarming revelations, it was clear that billions of pieces of information on U.S. citizens had been gathered, and that the communications of foreign leaders, notably including German chancellor Angela Merkel, had also been tapped. The Snowden leaks provided a field day for congressional Republicans, who raked the administration over the coals for months thereafter. The reports also damaged Obama with some of his strongest supporters. "Domestically," writes Todd, "the revelations contributed to a growing disillusionment with the president, both among his politically active young liberal base and among a burgeoning libertarian strain that is beginning to influence both parties." Once again, as was true in the case of Benghazi and the alleged administration "cover-up" of what had happened there, the White House found itself sidetracked from its agenda by the need to answer questions about the extra-legal intelligence-gathering that Snowden had exposed. Meanwhile, Snowden himself found somewhat uncomfortable exile in Russia, with his legal status in the United States remaining an open question.

In contrast to the total gridlock between the White House and Congress throughout 2013, the Supreme Court was productive. Three decisions, in particular, made clear what had been suggested by the verdict on the Affordable Care Act a year earlier: the Roberts court was not going to shy away from political controversy nor was it going to be predictable. Indeed, in some ways John Roberts was proving to be the most politically skilled chief justice since Earl Warren, demonstrating an ability to lead his fellow justices—even on highly controversial issues—in directions consistent with public opinion. Most notable in this regard were three major decisions handed down in the final week of June. The first was a direct slap at the administration. In a 5-4 decision in *Shelby County v. Holder*, the court took a step that had been feared by civil rights organizations since the Reagan years, declaring the crucial "pre-clearance" provision (Section 4(b) of the 1965 Voting Rights Act) unconstitutional. Because the formula used to determine which states were required to seek pre-clearance to change their voting laws had not been revised in nearly fifty years, the court reasoned, the provision subjected those states to disparate treatment on arbitrary grounds. Although the decision left open the possibility of restoring selective pre-clearance if the formula were updated, the makeup of Congress suggested that the issue would not be taken up any time soon.

In contrast to the conservative cast of the *Shelby County* decision, the court's two other blockbuster decisions during the last week in June 2013 finally put the two largest outstanding civil rights issues for gays and lesbians on a path to resolution—and in a way consistent with the Obama administration's position. A day after its Voting Rights decision, the court announced its decisions in *United States v. Windsor* and *Hollingsworth v. Perry*, which dealt, respectively, with the impact of DOMA on the legal rights of same-sex spouses and the constitutionality of California's Proposition Eight, which had banned same-sex marriage in that state. In both cases, the court came down on the side of advancing the rights of same-sex couples. In *Windsor*, a 5-4 majority ruled that DOMA's limitation of the word "spouse" to heterosexual marriages was unconstitutional under the "due process" clause. By the same margin, the court ruled in *Hollingsworth* that California's state officials could legitimately refuse to represent the state in appealing the Circuit Court of Appeals decision striking down Proposition Eight, and that private citizens who had attempted to appeal the ruling had no legal standing to do so. Though taking the narrowest path available in the case before it, the court thus signaled its potential willingness to uphold a universal right to same-sex marriage throughout the country.

If 2013 was a lost year for Obama, in most ways the next year was worse. After a two-and-a-half-year delay, the administration formally launched the federal health exchange promised in the Affordable Care Act. The rollout, as Todd writes, was "rocky, to put it charitably; disastrous, to be more realistic," threatening "to undermine Obama's central promise and the governing philosophy that underpinned his party." An even larger political problem for the president, however, was that, contrary to his reassurances dating from the initial debate over the legislation that no one would have to give up a health plan with which they were satisfied, thousands of such cases were being reported across the nation. As the mess dragged on for nearly six months, and the numbers of enrollees in Obamacare lagged behind administration predictions, Republicans stepped up their attacks. Finally, Obama replaced overwhelmed Health and Human Services Secretary Sebelius with Sylvia Mathews Burwell, a deputy who better understood the process and its problems, but the damage had been done. Enrollment numbers climbed steadily thereafter— and in a neutral environment, it could even be said that the plan was delivering much of what Obama had promised—but the rocky start could not easily be overcome. It was clear that Obamacare would remain *the* defining issue for Republicans until its architect was gone from the White House.

Obama also continued to face foreign policy conundrums in 2013 and 2014, even beyond the problem of finding the right pacing for the decided-upon drawdown of U.S. troops in Afghanistan. The echoes of the Arab Spring presented confounding challenges—especially in Syria, where the government of President Bashar Hafez al-Assad had managed to hang on despite early reverses and the nation's civil war had metastasized into almost a free-for-all among several difficult-to-categorize, brutal, and dangerous extremist branches. The most dangerous—and heinous—of all of these was ISIL or ISIS (Islamic State of Iraq and the Levant, or Islamic State of Iraq and Syria, depending on the acronym used), a group that took anti-Western terrorism to new depths, initially specializing in media-publicized beheadings of its chosen enemies. The lives of several Americans were publicly extinguished in this egregiously inhuman way. As ISIS's viciousness spread into neighboring lands in the Middle East, victims included not only rival religious factions, but journalists and humanitarian workers, as well as hundreds of thousands of innocent civilians.

Obama's vulnerability to partisan criticism for his seeming paralysis in the face of the Syrian civil war and the inhumanity of ISIS was heightened by the fact that in August 2012 he had drawn a "red line," implying direct U.S. response, if it were found that the Assad regime had employed chemical weapons against its own people. When American intelligence turned up reliable evidence several months later that this had indeed occurred, Obama was forced to respond, but he did so very slowly. By late August, almost exactly a year after drawing his red line, the president resolved to act in concert with Britain and began to make his case to the American public. His plans were derailed, however, when the British Parliament turned down Prime Minister David Cameron's request for a resolution supporting military action in Syria. Obama thereupon decided, with little advance preparation, to seek congressional authorization to take unilateral action, at the same time working within the UN to put together a broad anti-Assad coalition. Since polls showed the American public even less willing than Congress to support another military venture in the Middle East, the authorization measure seemed to be doomed. Understanding that he would likely face defeat, Obama chose to accept a brokered solution that had been offered by—of all nations—Russia, whereby Assad agreed to place his chemical weapons under international control. The president's red line had amounted to nothing. Another American intervention in the troubled Islamic world had been averted, but Obama's credibility both at home and abroad took a serious hit.

That Russia provided the diplomatic escape valve enabling Obama to extricate himself from the dilemma over Syria in early 2014 was amazing in the light of simultaneous events in the Ukraine that caused a severe worsening of U.S.–Russian relations. Once again an apparently local uprising became an international crisis when a militant pro-Western rebel group drove Ukraine's Russian-backed president from power in February 2014. As the United States and other Western powers gave lip-service support to the budding revolution, Russian president Vladimir Putin (who had "rotated" back into the presidency in 2012 after Medvedev's caretaker term) intervened decisively. Putin shocked the West by seizing and annexing the Crimea, a part of Ukraine since the 1960s, and—even more controversially—supplying war materiel and condoning participation in the "civil war" by Russian-supplied forces, including even some Russian regulars. Lacking the stomach for a renewed Cold War or worse, Obama and other Western leaders limited their response to imposing heavy economic sanctions and attempting to isolate Putin's government. Whether or not that would be possible was an open question, as the Ukrainian conflict ground on month after month. If these events reflected a re-set in U.S.–Russian relations, it was certainly not the kind of re-set Obama had sought. In fact, the frustrations of the White House in dealing with the Ukraine crisis began more and more to mirror its seeming irresolution in the face of factional conflict in the Middle East.

In *The Stranger*, Chuck Todd aptly sums up the seemingly insoluble world realities that faced Obama: "the changing world order is threatening America's place, and there isn't much Obama or any other president can do about it."

Given the chronically low public approval ratings experienced by both Obama and congressional Republicans in the first two years of his second term, there was zero reason to hope that the 2014 mid-terms would produce improvement in the negative political climate. In fact, the elections only made matters worse in terms of dysfunction and inaction. For the first time in Obama's presidency, Republicans won control of both houses of Congress. With a pickup of thirteen seats in the House, the GOP majority swelled to 247-188. In the Senate, the results were even more dismal for the Democrats. With a net gain of nine seats, the Republicans almost exactly reversed the pre-election balance, coming out with a 54-44 majority (independents Bernie Sanders of Vermont and Angus King of Maine continued to caucus with the Democrats). Mitch McConnell, who had remained intransigent toward the White House since his vow to ensure that Obama would be a one-term president, was now majority leader. Conservative columnist David Brooks, in a post-election *New York Times* column, wrote optimistically that "Republicans won this election in part because they re-established their party's traditional personality." In fact, however, even though GOP candidates had avoided the sort of foot-in-mouth disease that had cost the party and Romney so dearly two years earlier, echoes of the Tea Party and extreme social conservatism had marked the campaigns of many victorious Republicans. Despite post-election promises like Missouri senator Roy Blunt's assurance that his party would now prove it could "be a governing party rather than a complaining party," there was no basis to hope that anything would change in Washington during Obama's final two years in office.

It should have surprised no one that in the wake of the elections, Obama resolved to achieve what he could through the exercise of his executive powers, rather than continue to try to work with an obstructionist Congress. His most dramatic exercise of unilateral power was his announcement in December 2014 that, following negotiations so secret that they had not even been rumored in the media, he would re-establish diplomatic ties with Cuba, reversing a half-century-old policy of U.S sanctions and isolation—and bringing into question the future of the Cold War-spawned immigration preference that had been granted to Cubans fleeing the Castro regime. "I do not believe we can keep doing the same thing for over five decades and expect a different result," Obama explained in announcing the move. While Cuban American senator Marco Rubio of Florida, a possible candidate for the 2016 GOP nomination, excoriated the president for the move, along with several other Republican leaders, the lack of public outcry at the diplomatic coup discouraged any unified response from the GOP. Over the next few months, negotiations moved forward concerning the exchange of Cuban and American ambassadors, which finally occurred in July 2015.

Obama's second bold move via executive order did not fare as well. In an effort to circumvent Congress's repeated failure to act on his immigration reform proposals and citing the executive branch's "prosecutorial discretion," he issued an order to protect from deportation and to grant work permits to some four million undocumented immigrants. With the order scheduled to take effect in early 2015, House Republicans initially tried to blackmail the president by threatening not to re-fund the Department of Homeland Security unless it was rescinded. The Senate GOP leadership forced House leaders to back down, but Obama was thwarted anyway when the courts intervened and stayed his order. In July 2015, the Fifth Circuit Court of Appeals upheld the stay, with prospects dim that the Supreme Court would hear the case soon—or ever. The fate of the four million souls involved remained up in the air. To a fascinating and unprecedented degree, the year 2015 saw the federal courts—and in particular, the Supreme Court—fill the policy vacuum created by the utter failure of the two "governing" branches to make any progress in resolving major issues confronting the nation. The end of the 2014–2015 session produced two High Court decisions that seemed to bring final resolution to issues of immense political importance. Both represented vindication for the beleaguered Obama administration. In a much-anticipated ruling in *King v. Burwell*, by a vote of 6-3 the court upheld the provision of the Affordable Care Act permitting federal subsidies to participants in the federally-run health exchanges. Had the court gone the other way, approximately six million newly insured Americans would have lost their subsidies and, likely, their insurance, with the future of Obamacare plunged into chaos. Republican leaders publicly criticized the decision, but they might secretly have been relieved, since they had developed no clear alternative to the health-care reform that had now been in place for more than two years. Although further court challenges remained possible, it was more and more likely that Obama's legacy would, after all, include the historic health-care reform act.

The second landmark court decision announced in June 2015 settled, finally, the issue of whether or not states could deny same-sex couples the right to marry. In *Obergefell v. Hodges*—yet another 5-4 decision written by Justice Anthony Kennedy—the High Court affirmed marriage as a constitutional right of all Americans. "No longer may this liberty be denied" anywhere in the nation, Kennedy wrote. For same-sex marriage activists, it seemed that the affirmation of this basic right had taken forever, but viewed in the context of other broad social changes, the movement of both public opinion and constitutional law had been almost breathtaking. In just two decades after "Don't Ask, Don't Tell" and passage of DOMA, the most important elements of the LGBT agenda had been achieved.

For all of the promise of hope and change that had greeted Barack Obama's entrance into the White House in January 2009, his legislative achievements were almost nil. Even those he attained in his first two years, as Todd writes, may arguably have "resulted simply because Republicans on Capitol Hill took their visceral hatred of the president too far." Undoubtedly, a large part of Obama's problem with Congress was his distaste for the kind of camaraderie that had come so naturally to the likes of Lyndon Johnson, Ronald Reagan, and Bill Clinton. Nor did he seem to be able to establish a consistent strategy with respect to his Republican congressional foes, at first trying to go "beyond partisanship" and then, belatedly, trying to play hardball. In fairness, there was probably no way he could have created a cooperative political environment, so sour had the political climate become by the time he came to the White House. The Republicans had decided from the outset to block him at every turn. "Such obduracy," wrote Elizabeth Drew in the *New York Review of Books* in February 2010, "was without precedent in modern times."

Clearly, Barack Obama was not able to deliver on the Politics of Hope he had promised in 2008, but his administration represented much more than a holding action. Midway through his second term, there were faint signs that his persistence and focus could be beginning to pay off. In addition to victories in the courts that upheld important administration priorities, he managed the rare feat in June 2015 of securing passage for a key administration bill, the Trans-Pacific Partnership (TPP), with more support from Republicans than from Democrats. The TPP granted Obama and his successor in the White House over a six-year period authority to negotiate trade agreements with eleven other nations, including those of the Pacific Rim, with Congress having only a yes-no vote. As had been the case with NAFTA, many liberal Democrats opposed the measure as likely to undermine protections for American workers, while some in both parties worried about Congress's abdication of authority to amend such agreements in the future. Although Vice President Biden was unable this time to work his magic on a majority of congressional Democrats, the bill passed 62-37 in the Senate and 218-208 in the House, with ample GOP support. Viewed by the media as a major part of Obama's likely legacy in foreign policy, passage of TPP suggested to the hopeful that total deadlock might not be inevitable for the remaining period of his presidency.

Another major accomplishment for Obama in mid-2015, on the other hand, promised to be far more divisive. As early as his first inaugural, he had signaled to Iran his desire to break the thirty-year standoff dating from the hostage crisis under Carter, promising to "extend a hand if you are willing to unclench your fist." His intended endgame was to trade a reduction or end to economic sanctions on Iran in exchange for Iran's agreement to cease development of nuclear weapons capability. In July 2015, after over eighteen long months of negotiations involving five additional powers (Britain, China, France, Germany, and Russia), he announced such a settlement had been reached. Congressional Republicans, and even some Democrats, were adamantly opposed to approving U.S. participation in the agreement (they could do nothing about the agreement of the other powers and Iran) and threatened to pass a resolution to kill the pact. Obama, Biden, and Secretary of State Kerry pulled out all the stops to rally just enough Democratic support in the Senate to ensure a filibuster to block a vote that surely would have gone against the administration. By September, GOP critics had to give up, and the deal was safe—another "legacy-defining victory" for the administration, the *New York Times* noted.

Despite the continuing partisan standoff, there were a few positives to note as Obama's second term was winding down. Remarkably, in an era marked by the deepest public cynicism and inter-party dysfunction in generations—perhaps ever—Obama had managed personally to stay above the fray, and was almost sure to leave office with his honor intact. More important for the country, despite his acknowledged shortcomings as a politician, Obama would likely leave the presidency no weaker than he found it—a major achievement, given the constant attacks on him and the office from the time of his first inauguration.

Looking toward the election of 2016, more than fifteen aspiring Republicans were in the field several months before the first primaries, virtually all of them running far to the right and critical of nearly everything Obama and the Democrats stood for, including—still—the Affordable Care Act. Early on, GOP voters seemed most interested in candidates with no government experience, including Donald Trump and retired surgeon Ben Carson. Moving toward the 2016 primary season, it was unclear whether this anti-establishment strain would prevail in the end. In the Democratic party, Hillary Clinton once again seemed the one to beat. This time around, however, pressed on the left by independent Bernie Sanders and with the specter of other progressive Democrats as possible rivals, she tacked left early, stressing a more populist approach on economic policy than had characterized her 2008 run.

Even though it was too early to predict how the 2016 race would shape up, all signs pointed to another very polarizing election. As primary season approached, the intractability of violence in the Middle East–and especially the spread of seemingly random terrorist attacks in Europe and the United States– threatened to increase both volatility and extremism in the electorate. The institutions of government would likely emerge intact from the Obama years, but it would be up to the people to restore a semblance of harmony and hope to the American political system as a whole.

Conclusion: Deadlock and Disillusionment

Scholars of recent American politics have tended to see the 1980 election as the beginning of an era dominated by the political right. Reagan's election, this thesis goes, marked the ascendancy of a politically and socially conservative agenda that lasted into the early twenty-first century. Examples of scholarly studies advancing this thesis are Michael Schaller and George Rising, *The Republican Ascendancy: American Politics, 1968–2001*; Donald Critchlow, *The Conservative Ascendancy: How the GOP Right Made Political History*; Sean Wilentz, *The Age of Reagan: A History, 1974–2008*; and Dean Baker, *The United States Since 1980*. Such an interpretation always had weaknesses, but it seemed to work as well as any other until the deepening party discord and dysfunction leading to and accompanying the election and re-election of Barack Obama made clear that the picture is far more complex.

If 1980 did not mark the onset of a new political era, however, in what historical context can contemporary U.S. politics best be understood? This book argues 1968 is the best point of departure to make sense of American politics today The convulsive three-cornered presidential contest that put Richard Nixon in the White

Deadlock and Disillusionment: American Politics since 1968, First Edition.
Gary W. Reichard.
© 2016 John Wiley & Sons, Inc. Published 2016 by John Wiley & Sons, Inc.

House definitely represented a turning point, in that the Democratic coalition that had dominated and defined the New Deal era was never again victorious thereafter. When Democrats Jimmy Carter and Bill Clinton won the presidency in 1976 and 1992, respectively, their coalitions clearly differed from the liberal coalition that had dominated in the New Deal political era—and from each other's, as well. The same was true of Barack Obama's initial victory in 2008. In none of these cases, moreover, did victory in the general election reflect the return of a lasting Democratic majority. In fact, no election since 1968—including that of 1980—has begun a run of single-party control for any significant length of time.

If the period since 1968 has not been characterized by the dominance of one party or the ineluctable forward march of a single ideology, then what are the characteristics that can be said to define this political "era"? It is true that conservatism has sharpened its edges during these decades, but so has the liberal impulse intensified on issues of the day such as reproductive rights, same-sex equality, immigration, and inequity of wealth. It is the growth of partisan intensity on both sides of such questions—creating increasingly deep division—not the strength of a single ideological pole that has been the most significant defining characteristic of the post-1968 political era. As political scientists and historians who have written about the period agree, such polarization has been manifested in various ways. In his 2008 study, *Party Polarization in Congress*, political scientist Sean Theriault provides solid statistical analysis and cites works by several other scholars to support this point. Steadily increasing polarization in the years since 1968 "can be demonstrated with any number of interest group ratings, ideology scores, or roll call summaries," writes Theriault. "Different scholars using different methods and different data all show the same basic divergence between Democrats and Republicans in the halls of Congress." James Thurber makes the same point in *Rivals for Power: Presidential-Congressional Relations*, tracing the growth in party unity scores in both parties' congressional caucuses from decade to decade and showing that both were consistently over

90 percent by the 2000s. What these trends reflect, Thurber adds, "is the disappearance of the moderates or what some call the vital center in Congress." The same point is made explicitly by Geoffrey Kabaservice in *Rule and Ruin* and Gary Jacobson in *A Divider, Not a Uniter: George W. Bush and the American People*, and is implicit in a number of other works on the period.

The behavior of recent presidents has naturally been affected by the increasing partisanship in Congress, with the result that their conduct, too, has been increasingly partisan. As his book's title makes plain, this is Jacobson's major argument in his study of George W. Bush's presidency. Chuck Todd extends the argument to cover Bush's predecessor and successor, as well. "When Obama leaves office," he writes in *The Stranger*, "it'll be 24 straight years of polarizing presidents, all three of whom were elected, in part, to help end some of the acrimony." Though Todd may underestimate Bill Clinton's skills at overcoming the partisan divide he faced, especially after his re-election, but as the histories of the second Bush and Obama presidencies demonstrate, his statement rings true for those two most recent chief executives—whatever their original intent.

Perhaps the most shocking manifestation of partisanship in contemporary American public life is that it has even characterized the Supreme Court. Although the Roberts court has been less predictable than many expected, the way the justices have lined up on the spectrum of cases the court has considered in recent years reveals a historically unique pattern. Analyzing decisions delivered in its 2011–2012 session, the *New York Times* presented a fascinating visual, demonstrating that for the first time in modern history, the court had developed a partisan configuration wherein the five justices appointed by GOP presidents from Nixon through George W. Bush were all to the ideological right of the four that were appointed by Democrats Carter and Clinton. According to the *Times*, never before had this been the case. Such politicization of the court, if continued into the future, could gravely harm the nation's political system as a whole. "The perception that partisan politics has infected the court's work," the *Times* observed, could "do lasting damage to its prestige and authority and to Americans' faith in the rule of law." The court's maintenance of its reputation for ideological neutrality is especially important as it has seemed to be the only branch of government willing to try to resolve the most divisive issues of the day.

All of these elements have worked together in recent decades—notwithstanding Barack Obama's hopeful pronouncement of "a single America" in his 2004 Democratic convention keynote speech—to maintain the divided political map of our time: Red America and Blue America.

The increasingly partisan nature of the American news media has been a powerful factor in the increase of political polarization. This is a common observation in works that discuss the breakdown of bipartisan cooperation in recent decades. "Beyond [the] Beltway-based causes of rigid partisanship, the rise of overtly partisan media on television, radio, and the Internet have promoted ideological division," Ronald Formisano writes in his essay in Liette Gidlow's volume on the 2008 election. "Even the so-called mainstream media tend to undermine bipartisanship by their preference for covering or even encouraging conflict." Such partisanship in the news media has been especially aggressive and effective on the right. The Clinton presidency, in particular, energized Fox News and legions of like-minded radio talk show hosts to whip up grass-roots opposition and hostility. Continuing their campaign to discredit critics of George W. Bush's war on terrorism, they criticized Obama vituperatively from the moment he entered the White House. Skocpol and Williamson, in their study of the origins of the Tea Party, emphasize the prominent role of these right-wing media outlets in stimulating and sustaining that movement's influence. In addition to permitting Americans to reinforce their biases without the inconvenience of confronting opposing viewpoints, another pernicious effect of the slanted presentation of news—whether on the right or on the left—is that it has caused huge numbers of voters to turn off altogether from news sources. Ignorance, of course, is the enemy of democracy, as political scientist Markus Prior observes in his 2007 book, *Post-Broadcast Democracy*.

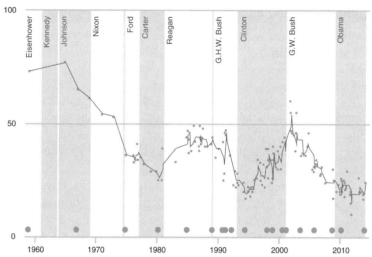

Figure C.1 In February 2014, the Pew Research Center published a graph showing survey results on public trust in government from 1958 to 2014. Despite obvious "rally points" related to Reagan's election, the triumphant Gulf War, the booming economy of the late 1990s, and the aftermath of 9/11, the long-term trajectory in public trust has clearly been downward. Given the bitterness of partisan conflict in the second decade of the new century, it is hard to see how trust in government can easily be restored. Public Trust in Government: 1958–2014 http://www.people-press.org/2014/11/13/public-trust-in-government/. Pew Research Center

Increased partisanship and polarization in the years since 1968 have produced two other negative effects in the contemporary political era: growing disillusionment, verging on disgust, with government as a whole, particularly on the part of moderates and independents; and a resulting tendency for the electorate, in its impatience, to opt for divided government (at least one House of Congress controlled by the opposition party) whenever the pace of hoped-for change from the party in power seems too slow. In November 2014, *New York Times* columnist Frank Bruni aptly described this syndrome. "[I]n almost every election during [the past decade], the party in control of the White House, the Senate or the House of Representatives has changed," he wrote. "It's been a nearly constant seesaw, with a sustained message from voters: What we have isn't working. Give us different." This trend has been clear for at least two decades. The best recent examples are the mid-term elections of 1994, 2006, and 2010, all of which represented overwhelming rejection of an administration for which the electorate had entertained hope just two years before. But the trend was in evidence much earlier. "One of the most fundamental characteristics of the regime order that has emerged out of the critical realignment of the late 1960s," asserted political scientist Walter Dean Burnham in Pomper's volume on the 1992 election, "has been divided government as a normal rather than an exceptional state of affairs." This tendency has only grown stronger since Burnham offered his observation.

The inevitable result of all of these trends has been chronic policy deadlock. Such deadlock, in turn, further exacerbates the very alienation that produces the situation in the first place. There is an irony at work here, as Jacobson points out. "Although ordinary Americans took part in the trend toward greater partisan and ideological polarization in national politics during the final decades of the twentieth century," he writes, "they did not like its manifestations."

Taken together, the political trends discussed here have led to an almost total disintegration of the comity that once character- ized Washington and to the disappearance of any semblance of bipartisan commitment to the public welfare. This sorry state of affairs first became noticeable near the end of the Reagan administration, when Democrats sensed an opening due to the Iran-Contra revelations. There has been little remission since. Political scientist Eric Uslaner identified this malady more than twenty years ago in *The Decline of Comity in Congress*, in which he likened the two houses of Congress to "day care centers in which colicky babies get their way by screaming at the top of their lungs." It is worth quoting Uslaner's thoughtful explication of the importance of this precious commodity to the health of democratic government:

Serious discord demands that we *exchange* views with adversaries and give them the respect that we demand of our own ideas. It also requires keeping our sense of humor, often an important element in rhetoric. Comity permits reasoned debate over policy. It makes give-and-take possible and inhibits the acceptance of nonnegotiable demands. Comity is not the end product; policy based on civil debate is.

The unrelenting partisan attacks on Clinton, Bush, and Obama in turn, and perhaps most of all, the impact on American political discourse growing out of the Tea Party movement, provide powerful reinforcement of Uslaner's observations.

American politics in the years since 1968 has thus not been a story of the triumph of the right—nor of splintering on the left—as many scholars contended for so long, but rather one of a growing political paralysis arising from increasingly bitter partisan discord and deepening public disillusionment. That disillusionment has been both cause and effect of policy paralysis. The way forward is not clear, but it will need to be found if the United States is to survive as an effective democracy—let alone exercise anything like leadership in today's rapidly changing world.

Bibliographical Essay

The literature on post-1968 American politics is enormous, and seems to have grown exponentially over the past decade or so. Scholarly studies by historians and political scientists and works by journalists make up a substantial part—but by no means all—of this literature. Memoirs of presidents, Cabinet members, and members of Congress active during the period are also numerous. The "literature" that has grown in greatest profusion in recent years, however, is a genre of slanted, critical screeds, most of which are the product of extremist voices in the media. This essay will not discuss these patently one-sided works, but rather will focus on the more balanced and responsible sources that have been useful in the production of this book.

There are no previous scholarly studies of American politics that cover the entire time period of the present volume. The few existing studies covering U.S. political life in the years since 1968 (most of which end well before Obama's election) generally argue that the era was marked by the rise and primacy of the political right. The two best-known such works are Michael Schaller, *The Republican Ascendancy: American Politics, 1968–2001* (2002)

Deadlock and Disillusionment: American Politics since 1968, First Edition.
Gary W. Reichard.
© 2016 John Wiley & Sons, Inc. Published 2016 by John Wiley & Sons, Inc.

and Sean Wilentz, *The Age of Reagan: A History, 1974–2008* (2009). Another solid overview of recent politics, which begins at a later date and also advances the thesis that Reagan's election marked the beginning of the contemporary political era, is Dean Baker, *The United States Since 1980* (2007). Since incorporating the Obama years into these studies would make it impossible to sustain the thesis that we have been living in a Reagan-determined conservative political era, it seems unlikely that any of these three works could be simply "updated" without significant revision. A general political history that takes a different approach, but ends its coverage in the 1990s, is Iwan Morgan, *Beyond the Liberal Consensus: A Political History of the United States since 1965* (1994). Another relevant and useful study, which focuses on the conservative movement itself rather than American politics as a whole, is Donald Critchlow, *The Conservative Ascendancy: How the GOP Right Made Political History* (2007). Perhaps the strongest study of the modern right, taking a very different perspective that is revealed in its title, is Geoffrey Kabaservice, *Rule and Ruin: The Downfall of Moderation and the Destruction of the Republican Party, from Eisenhower to the Tea Party* (2012). Two useful works on the Democratic party during large portions of the time frame of this study—almost complementary in their foci—are Ronald Radosh, *Divided They Fell: The Demise of the Democratic Party, 1964–1996* (1996) and Kenneth S. Baer, *Reinventing Democrats: The Politics of Liberalism from Reagan to Clinton* (2000). Julian Zelizer, *Arsenal of Democracy: The Politics of National Security—From World War II to the War on Terrorism* (2010), provides an excellent overview of political conflict over security issues throughout the period covered by the present volume. A broader social history of the era, tying cultural developments to political change, is Robert O. Self, *All in the Family: The Realignment of American Democracy since the 1960s* (2012).

Informative works by political scientists that shed light on the themes of this book, including electoral politics and presidential–legislative relations in the modern period, include Marty Cohen et al., *The Party Decides: Presidential Nominations Before and After Reform* (2008); Richard S. Conley, *The Presidency, Congress, and Divided Government: A Postwar Assessment* (2003); Geoffrey Layman, *The Great Divide: Religious and Cultural Conflict in American Party Politics* (2001); Francis E. Lee, *Beyond Ideology: Politics, Principles, and Partisanship in the U.S. Senate* (2009); David R. Mayhew, *Divided We Govern: Party Control, Lawmaking, and Investigations, 1946–2002* (2nd ed., 2005); Sean M. Theriault, *Party Polarization in Congress* (2008); and Eric M. Uslaner, *The Decline of Comity in Congress* (1993).

Several studies have been published on political themes in the years covered by this volume, as well. On foreign policy and politics, two of the best are Julian E. Zelizer, *Arsenal of Democracy: The Politics of National Security—From World War II to the War on Terrorism* (2010) and Marvin Kalb and Deborah Kalb, *Haunting Legacy: Vietnam and the American Presidency from Ford to Obama* (2011). Other books on foreign policy and politics since the middle of the twentieth century include Derek Leebaert, *The Fifty-year Wound: How America's Cold War Victory Shaped Our World* (2002) and Richard Melanson, *Reconstructing Consensus: American Foreign Policy since the Vietnam War* (1991). Kenneth O'Reilly examines the civil rights policies and politics of several recent presidents (as well as many earlier ones) in *Nixon's Piano: Presidents and Racial Politics from Washington to Clinton* (1995). Ian Haney López, *Dog Whistle Politics: How Coded Racial Appeals Have Reinvented Racism and Wrecked the Middle Class* (2014), is a strong indictment of the use of race-baiting, subtle and not so subtle, in presidential campaigns and politics generally in the past several decades. Two strong recent studies of politics and race issues, generally, are Matthew D. Lassiter, *The Silent Majority: Suburban Politics in the Sunbelt South* (2006), which covers the period between 1960 and 2000, and James T. Patterson, *Freedom Is Not Enough: The Moynihan Report and America's Struggle over Black Family Life—From LBJ to Obama* (2010). Manning Marable, *Race, Reform, and Rebellion: The Second Reconstruction in Black America, 1945–1990* (3rd ed., 2007), provides a highly critical perspective on the politics of race relations from a leftist perspective.

Of the general histories of Nixon's presidency, one of the most recent, Tim Weiner's Pulitzer Prize-winning *One Man Against the*

World: The Tragedy of Richard Nixon (2015), draws the sharpest _ portrait of the president's secretiveness and paranoia. Also reliable and highly informative are Stephen E. Ambrose, *Nixon: The Triumph of a Politician, 1962–1972* (1989); Richard Reeves, *President Nixon: Alone in the White House* (2001); Herbert S. Parmet, *Richard Nixon and His America* (1990); and Tom Wicker, *One of Us: Richard Nixon and the American Dream* (1991). All of these works, while reliable, tend to be strictly chronological, rather than thematic, in their treatments. More focused thematic studies, also solidly based, are Melvin Small, *The Presidency of Richard Nixon* (1999), and Rick Perlstein, *Nixonland: The Rise of a President and the Fracturing of America* (2008). David Greenberg, *Nixon's Shadow: The History of an Image* (2003), is a fascinating, well-researched study of Nixon both in reality and in the public imagination, emphasizing the thirty-seventh president's ability to profit from image manipulation. Joan Hoff, *Nixon Reconsidered* (1994), as the title suggests, is an early revisionist work that—while not forgiving Nixon for his Watergate sins—portrays him as an important agent of change in the areas of welfare, civil rights, economic policy, environmental policy, and government reorganization. A broad study of the 1960s and early 1970s that includes insightful discussion of the Nixon presidency (as well as Ford's) is James Morton Blum, *Years of Discord: American Politics and Society, 1961–1974* (1991). Useful monographs on specific aspects of the Nixon presidency are Allen J. Matusow, *Nixon's Economy: Booms, Busts, Dollars, & Votes* (1998); Stephen Hess, *The Professor and the President: Daniel Patrick Moynihan in the Nixon White House* (2014); and Richard P. Nathan, *The Plot That Failed: Nixon and the Administrative Presidency* (1975).

The story of the 1968 presidential election is well told in Lewis Gould, *1968: The Election That Changed America* (1993); Lewis Chester, Geoffrey Hodgson, and Bruce Page, *An American Melodrama: The Presidential Campaign of 1968* (1969); and, most recently, in Michael Nelson, *Resilient America: Electing Nixon in 1968—Channeling Dissent, and Dividing Government* (2014). Nixon's strategy for winning the election is deftly described by Kevin Phillips, *The Emerging Republican Majority* (1969). See also Jules

Witcover, *Very Strange Bedfellows: The Short and Unhappy Marriage of Richard Nixon and Spiro Agnew* (2007), which covers the Nixon–Agnew story through Agnew's forced resignation. An excellent, thematic history of the election is Walter LaFeber, *The Deadly Bet: LBJ, Vietnam, and the 1968 Election* (1968). Another interesting monograph, which as its title suggests covers events after the election as well, is Ken Hughes, *Chasing Shadows: The Nixon Tapes, the Chennault Affair, and the Origins of Watergate* (2014).

Nixon, his Secretary of State Henry Kissinger, and their forays into world affairs have been the subjects of numerous books. Among the strongest sources on the Nixon–Kissinger relationship and the policies they developed are: Frederick Logevall and Andrew Preston, eds., *Nixon in the World: American Foreign Relations, 1969–1977* and Robert Dallek, *Nixon and Kissinger: Partners in Power* (2007). Kissinger's memoir, *The White House Years* (1979), while self-serving, is valuable.

The literature on Nixon and the Vietnam War is large and still growing. Here it will suffice to list several titles that are especially informative. George C. Herring, *America's Longest War: The United States and Vietnam, 1960–1975* (4th ed., 2002), remains the standard work, if one can be identified, and has some coverage of domestic politics. Another solid study is Robert Schulzinger, *A Time for War: The United States and Vietnam, 1941–1975*. Studies with a stronger focus on the politics of the war include Melvin Small, *Antiwarriors: The Vietnam War and the Battle for America's Hearts and Minds* (2002), and, by the same author, *At the Water's Edge: American Politics and the Vietnam War* (2005); Andrew Johns, *Vietnam's Second Front: Domestic Politics, the Republican Party, and the War* (2010); Jeffrey Kimball, *Nixon's Vietnam War* (1998); and Larry Berman, *No Peace, No Honor: Nixon, Kissinger, and Betrayal in Vietnam* (2001). Still the best study of the draft and its end during the Vietnam War is Lawrence Baskir and William Strauss, *Chance and Circumstance: The Draft, the War and the Vietnam Generation* (1978).

Studies of Watergate, including works by historians, journalists, and administration figures, have also abounded. Easily the best scholarly treatments are Stanley Kutler, *The Wars of Watergate: The Last Crisis of Richard Nixon* (1990), and Keith Olson, *Watergate: The*

Presidential Scandal That Shook America (2003). A second study by Kutler, *Abuse of Power: The New Nixon Tapes* (1997), is also a useful source. Carl Bernstein and Bob Woodward, *All the President's Men* (1974), is, of course, the classic record of the "breaking" of the story by the *Washington Post*, and still an excellent read. Of the many memoirs by Watergate principals, the most valuable as historical sources are H. R. Haldeman, *The Haldeman Diaries: Inside the Nixon White House* (1994); John D. Ehrlichman, *Witness to Power: The Nixon Years* (1982), and John Dean, *Blind Ambition: The White House Years* (1976). Michael Schudson, *Watergate in American Memory: How We Remember, Forget and Reconstruct the Past* (1992), is an interesting examination of the many "meanings" of Watergate. The only substantial study of the 1972 election, which provided the political context for the crimes leading to the Watergate scandal, is Bruce Miroff, *The Liberals' Moment: The McGovern Insurgency and the Identity Crisis of the Democratic Party* (2007).

The decade of the 1970s as a political era is very well covered by Laura Kalman in *Right Star Rising: A New Politics, 1974–1980* (2010). A second excellent treatment of the years from Nixon to Reagan is Rick Perlstein, *The Invisible Bridge: The Fall of Nixon and the Rise of Reagan* (2014). More general treatments of society and politics in the 1970s, which remains a subject of fascination for scholars, include Peter Carroll, *It Seemed Like Nothing Happened: The Tragedy and Promise of America in the 1970s* (1982); Edward Berkowitz, *Something Happened: A Political and Cultural Overview of the Seventies* (2006); Philip Jenkins, *Decade of Nightmares: The End of the Sixties and the Making of Eighties America* (2006); and two volumes by Bruce Schulman: *The Seventies: The Great Shift in American, Culture, Society, and Politics* (2001) and *Rightward Bound: Making America Conservative in the 1970s* (2008). Judith Stein's *Pivotal Decade: How the United States Traded Factories for Finance in the Seventies* (2010) focuses on the very significant economic transformations of the decade as causes of political change.

The literature on the two-year presidency of Gerald Ford itself is understandably scant. John Robert Greene's *The Presidency of Gerald R. Ford* (1995), while recognizing Ford's decency, emphasizes his lack of vision. Similarly, Richard Reeves, *A Ford, Not a Lincoln*

(1975), is a very critical appraisal of Ford's rise to the presidency and his first hundred-plus days in the White House. In contrast, Yanek Mieczkowski, in *Gerald Ford and the Challenges of the 1970s* (2005), portrays Ford more positively, as successfully confronting the challenging crises of the era. A brief and balanced treatment is Douglas Brinkley, *Gerald R. Ford* (2007), a volume in the *Times* Books series edited by Arthur Schlesinger. Useful monographs on particular aspects of Ford's presidency are Christopher Lamb, *Belief Systems and Decision Making in the Mayaguez Crisis* (1989); Loch Johnson, *A Season of Inquiry: The Senate Intelligence Investigation* (1985); Frank J. Smist, Jr., *Congress Oversees the United States Intelligence Community, 1947–1989* (1990); Martin Shefter, *Political Crisis/Fiscal Crisis: The Collapse and Revival of New York City* (1985); and Ronald Formisano, *Boston Against Busing: Race, Class, and Ethnicity in the 1960s and 1970s* (1991). Thomas DeFrank, *Write It When I'm Gone: Remarkable Off-the-Record Conversations with Gerald Ford* (2007), is—as the title suggests—a fascinating look into the post-presidential mind of Nixon's unelected successor.

Despite the general consensus that Jimmy Carter's presidency was a failure, it has been the subject of several solid studies. The first full-length treatment was political scientist Betty Glad's *Jimmy Carter: In Search of the Great White House* (1980), a critical account that alleged Carter failed to understand power. In 1988, two more positive studies appeared that drew on the newly available oral histories of the Carter presidency collected by the Miller Center for Presidential Studies: Erwin Hargrove, *Jimmy Carter as President: Leadership and the Politics of the Public Good*, and Charles O. Jones, *The Trusteeship Presidency: Jimmy Carter and the United States Congress*. More recent, balanced accounts of Carter's presidency are Burton I. Kaufman and Scott Kaufman, *The Presidency of James Earl Carter* (rev. ed., 1993) and Julian Zelizer, *Jimmy Carter* (2010). Gary Fink and Hugh D. Graham, eds., *The Carter Presidency: Policy Choices in the Post-New Deal Era* (1998), is a collection of scholarly papers on various policy aspects of Carter's presidency that were presented at a conference at the Carter Center. Three additional informative monographs are Mark Rozell, *The Press and the Carter Presidency* (1988); N. Carl Biven, *Jimmy Carter's Economy: Policy in an Age of*

Limits (2002); Kevin Mattson, *"What the Heck Are You Up To, Mr. President?": Jimmy Carter, America's "Malaise," and the Speech That Should Have Changed America* (2009); and J. Brooks Flippen, *Jimmy Carter, the Politics of Family, and the Rise of the Religious Right* (2011). Among the several books written by Carter after his presidency, his memoir, *Keeping Faith: Memoirs of a President* (1982), is most useful for historians.

Several scholars have written about Carter's foreign policies, beginning with Gaddis Smith's largely admiring *Morality, Reason and Power: American Diplomacy in the Carter Years* (1986). Recent, more critical studies that focus on the inconsistencies of Carter's policies due to the competition between Secretary of State Cyrus Vance and National Security Advisor Zbigniew Brzezinski are Scott Kaufman, *Plans Unraveled: The Foreign Policy of the Carter Administration* (2008), and Betty Glad, *An Outsider in the White House: Jimmy Carter, His Advisors, and the Making of American Foreign Policy* (2009). Monographs on various aspects of Carter's foreign policies include Strobe Talbott, *Endgame: The Inside Story of SALT II* (1979); Joshua Muravchik, *The Uncertain Crusade: Jimmy Carter and the Dilemmas of Human Rights Policy* (1986); David Forsythe, *Human Rights and U.S. Foreign Policy: Congress Reconsidered* (1988); Michael Hogan, *The Panama Canal in American Politics: Domestic Advocacy and the Evolution of Policy* (1986); David Farber, *Taken Hostage: The Iran Hostage Crisis and America's First Encounter with Radical Islam* (2005); and Nicholas E. Sarantakes, *Dropping the Torch: Jimmy Carter, the Olympic Boycott, and the Cold War* (2011).

Not surprisingly, given the widespread propensity to interpret recent American politics as dominated by Ronald Reagan and his policies, the 1980 election has received more scholarly attention than other recent presidential contests. The best general study is Andrew Busch, *Reagan's Victory: The Presidential Election of 1980 and the Rise of the Right* (2005), but Gerald Pomper's contemporaneous edited collection of essays by fellow political scientists, *The Election of 1980: Reports and Interpretations* (1981), is still valuable for its close analysis of the election's results. Two solid monographs on important aspects of the election are Timothy Stanley,

Kennedy vs. Carter: The 1980 Battle for the Democratic Party's Soul (2010), and Gary Sick, *October Surprise: America's Hostages in Iran and the Election of Ronald Reagan* (1991). As their titles suggest, Thomas Ferguson and Joel Rogers, *Right Turn: The Decline of the Democrats and the Future of American Politics* (1986); William C. Berman, *America's Right Turn: From Nixon to Bush* (1994); and Michael Schaller, *Right Turn: American Life in the Reagan-Bush Era, 1980–1992*, all treat the 1980 election as the beginning of a new conservative political era. In addition, some of the books cited at the beginning of this essay take the same approach. The only study of Reagan's re-election victory in 1984 is Jane Mayer and Doyle McManus, *Landslide: The Unmaking of the President, 1984–1988* (1988).

An early definitive history of Ronald Reagan's presidency was Lou Cannon's *President Reagan: The Role of a Lifetime* (1991). Cannon, a journalist who followed Reagan from the years of his governorship of California, had earlier written a strong study of Reagan's first two years in the White House entitled *Reagan* (1982). Michael Schaller, *Reckoning with Reagan: America and Its President in the 1980s* (1992), was the first study of the entire administration by a historian, although Robert Dallek had published a brief study on Reagan's first three years, *Ronald Reagan: The Politics of Symbolism*, in 1984 (revised and published again with an afterword in 1999). Since the mid-1990s, several additional strong volumes on Reagan's presidency have appeared, based to varying degrees on materials at the Reagan Library. Most have been generally favorable. Richard Reeves, *President Reagan: The Triumph of Imagination* (2005), portrays Reagan as more politically astute than some critics have credited, while Gil Troy, *Morning in America: How Ronald Reagan Invented the 1980s* (2005), though recognizing Reagan's "mixed legacy," sees him as defining his political era. Other reliable works include William Pemberton, *Exit with Honor: The Life and Presidency of Ronald Reagan* (1998); Robert M. Collins, *Transforming America: Politics and Culture During the Reagan Years* (2007); and John Patrick Diggins, *Ronald Reagan: Fate, Freedom, and the Making of History* (2007). Of these authors, the conservative historian

Diggins is the most admiring, exalting Reagan as an "Emersonian libertarian" and the "liberator" of Eastern Europe from communism. Kevin Phillips, *The Politics of Rich and Poor: Wealth and the American Electorate in the Reagan Aftermath* (1990) is a critical examination of the impact of Reaganomics on wealth distribution in the United States, while Daniel K. Williams, *God's Own Party: The Making of the Christian Right* (2010), provides a useful account of the Christian conservative movement that formed an important part of the "Reagan revolution" base. Reagan's post-presidential autobiography, *An American Life* (1990), is valuable for anecdotes and for a sense of the man's character. Two useful memoirs from administration insiders are Martin Anderson, *Revolution* (1988), and C. Everett Koop, *Koop: The Memoirs of America's Family Doctor* (1991).

Most monographs on Reagan's presidency focus on aspects of his foreign policy, especially relating to the end of the Cold War. The most useful of these are James Mann, *The Rebellion of Ronald Reagan: A History of the End of the Cold War* (2009), and James Graham Wilson, *The Triumph of Improvisation: Gorbachev's Adaptability, Reagan's Engagement, and the End of the Cold War* (2014), both of which are based on deep archival research. Three studies that focus on Reagan's quest to end the nuclear arms race are Frances FitzGerald, *Way Out There in the Blue: Reagan, Star Wars and the End of the Cold War* (2000); Paul Lettow, *Ronald Reagan and His Quest to Abolish Nuclear Weapons* (2005); and Martin Anderson and Annelise Anderson, *Reagan's Secret War: The Untold Story of His Fight to Save the World from Nuclear Disaster* (2007). Will Bunch, in *Tear Down This Myth: How the Reagan Legacy Has Distorted Our Politics and Haunts Our Future* (2009), takes a decidedly more negative tack, contending that Reagan's record has been whitewashed as a result of "myth-making" since the time of his death in 2004. Malcolm Byrne, *Iran-Contra: Reagan's Scandal and the Unchecked Abuse of Presidential Power* (2014), presents a highly critical account of high-level administration involvement in the defining crisis of Reagan's final years in the White House. The only monograph on the Reagan presidency to date that focuses on domestic policy is Robert Detlefsen, *Civil Rights Under Reagan* (1991).

There are two generally informative journalistic accounts of the 1988 election: Jack Germond and Jules Witcover, *Whose Broad Stripes and Bright Stars? The Trivial Pursuit of the Presidency 1988* (1989), and Peter Goldman, Tom Mathews, and the *Newsweek* Special Election Team, *Quest for the Presidency: The 1988 Campaign* (1989). Martin Wattenberg, *The Rise of Candidate-Centered Politics: Presidential Elections of the 1980s* (1991), takes a unique approach to the politics of the 1980s, expanding on the theory of "dealignment" and the weakening of partisan loyalties during the decade, contending that the electorate did not become more conservative despite three straight elections favoring the GOP.

Most of the literature on the first Bush presidency has been sympathetic, emphasizing his strength in foreign policy at the same time as acknowledging his administration's limited domestic achievements. Three overviews of his administration have appeared to date: John Robert Greene, *The Presidency of George Bush* (2000); Herbert S. Parmet, *George Bush: The Life of a Lone Star Yankee* (2001); and Timothy Naftali, *George H. W. Bush* (2007)—another of the short interpretive volumes in the *Times* presidential series. Parmet's volume is the only full-scale biography; although not formally "authorized," it is based on full access to Bush's then-unpublished diaries. There have been two strong collections on various aspects of the first Bush's presidency, in which most of the essays are by political scientists: Colin Campbell and Bert A. Rockman, eds., *The Bush Presidency: First Appraisals* (1991), which appeared midway through Bush's term, and the more recent *41: Inside the Presidency of the first Bush*, edited by Michael Nelson and Barbara Perry (2014). The latter includes a number of strong essays on Bush's achievements in the context of events since his presidency. An early study that sees Bush as working "around" Congress is Charles Tiefer, *The Semi-Sovereign Presidency: The Bush Administration's Strategy for Governing Without Congress* (1994). Bush's memoir, *All the Best, George Bush: My Life in Letters and Other Writings* (2013), provides insights into his character but even more useful is Jon Meacham's Destiny and Power: The American Odyssey of George Herbert Walker Bush (2015).

On Bush's foreign policy, a highly useful source is the memoir he co-authored with his national security advisor, Brent Scowcroft, *A World Transformed* (1998). Similarly informative is James Baker's memoir, *The Politics of Diplomacy: Revolution, War & Peace, 1989–1992* (1995). Christopher Maynard, *Out of the Shadow: George H. W. Bush and the End of the Cold War* (2008), is also useful, though its focus is mostly on events related to the end of the Cold War as opposed to being a definitive history of Bush's foreign policies. The most thorough treatment of the first Bush administration's responses to world events can be found in Hal Brands's more encompassing work covering the Clinton and second Bush administrations as well, *From Berlin to Baghdad: America's Search for Purpose in the Post-Cold War World* (2008). Micah Sefry and Christopher Carl, eds., *The Gulf War: History, Documents, Opinions* (1991), is a useful collection on the military conflict that defined much of Bush's presidency.

Journalist and political commentator E. J. Dionne's aptly titled *Why Americans Hate Politics* (1991) provides insightful analysis of the collective psyche of the American voting public at the end of the Reagan–Bush years that led to the three-cornered race of 1992. On election itself, see Gerald M. Pomper, ed., *The Election of 1992* (1993), and Peter Goldman et al., *Quest for the Presidency* (1992). Clinton's re-election campaign is well covered in Stephen J. Wayne, *The Road to the White House, 1996: The Politics of Presidential Elections* (1996); Bob Woodward, *The Choice: How Bill Clinton Won* (1996); and Pomper et al., *The Election of 1996: Reports and Investigations* (1997). Richard Reeves, *Running in Place: How Bill Clinton Disappointed America* (1996), is an election-year analysis of Clinton's first term, the thesis of which is clear from the title. Dick Morris presents a first-hand account of Clinton's "triangulation" strategy leading into the 1996 campaign in *Behind the Oval Office: Winning the Presidency in the Nineties* (1997).

Clinton's presidency has drawn substantial attention from journalists and historians alike; this literature is likely to continue to grow as materials at the Clinton Library become more widely available and the political career of Hillary Clinton continues to unfold. Probably the best and most balanced study of his presidency to date is John Harris, *The Survivor: Bill Clinton in the White House* (2005). Perhaps not surprisingly, given Clinton's penchant for self-revelatory comment, his White House memoir, *My Life* (2004), is a highly useful source of inside information. Similarly, George Stephanopoulos, *All Too Human: A Political Education* (1999), is more than usually informative for its genre, although it covers only the years till Stephanopoulos left the Clinton administration. Two perceptive "insider" studies of the early years of Clinton's presidency by journalists are Elizabeth Drew, *On the Edge: The Clinton Presidency* (1994), and Bob Woodward, *The Agenda: Inside the Clinton White House* (1994). Other studies that provide insight into Clinton's fascinating character as well as political events during his administration, are: James MacGregor Burns and Georgia Sorenson, *Dead Center: Clinton-Gore Leadership and the Perils of Moderation* (1999); William C. Berman, *From the Center to the Edge: The Politics & Policies of the Clinton Presidency* (2001); Joe Klein, *The Natural: The Misunderstood Presidency of Bill Clinton* (2002); and David Bennett, *Bill Clinton: Building a Bridge to the New Millennium* (2014). Steven Schier's edited volume, *The Postmodern Presidency: Bill Clinton's Legacy in U.S. Politics* (2000), is a collection of solid essays by political scientists that illuminate his redefinition of the office of the presidency and "unprecedented courtship of public opinion." Two interesting works that draw on oral reminiscences are Michael Takiff, *A Complicated Man: Bill Clinton's Life as Told by Those Who Know Him* (2010), and Taylor Branch, *The Clinton Tapes: Wrestling History with the President* (2009); the latter is a quasi-authorized work in that the author draws on his recollections from approximately eighty conversations with Clinton during the course of his presidency. Steven Gillon's *The Pact: Bill Clinton, Newt Gingrich, and the Rivalry that Defined a Generation* (2008) is a well-documented historical account of the unlikely political alliance that developed between those two principals after Clinton outfoxed the Speaker in the government shutdown episode. Theda Skocpol's *Boomerang: Health Care Reform and the Turn Against Government* (1997) tells the story of the failed Health Security effort of 1993–1994.

The two major studies of Clinton's foreign policy that have appeared to date take opposing views of the forty-second president.

William G. Hyland, in *Clinton's World: Remaking American Foreign Policy* (1999), contends that by failing to identify an overall strategy, Clinton missed an opportunity to reshape post-Cold War American policies and global relationships. *Clinton's Secret Wars: The Evolution of a Commander in Chief,* a 2009 work by Pulitzer Prize-winning journalist Richard Sale, offers a more positive interpretation of Clinton's "underestimated achievements," contending that he developed into a tough world leader. Most useful of the memoirs focusing on the administration's foreign policy are Madeleine Albright (with Bill Woodward), *Madam Secretary: A Memoir* (2003); Warren Christopher, *Chances of a Lifetime: A Memoir* (2001); and Strobe Talbott, *The Russia Hand: A Memoir of Presidential Diplomacy* (2002).

In addition to a spate of polemics published by conservatives eager to discredit Clinton and his policies, three informative books have been published that explore the constitutional implications of his presidency. In *An Affair of State: The Investigation, Impeachment, and Trial of President Clinton* (1999), federal judge Richard Posner presents a learned and detailed analysis of the Lewinsky scandal in the courts and impeachment struggle, concluding that the president was undeniably guilty as charged in a technical sense but that, given popular support for his continuation in office, the impeachment and trial were no more than a "political circus." Two general treatments of constitutional issues raised during Clinton's term in office are David Gray Adler and Michael Genovese, eds., *The Presidency & the Law: The Clinton Legacy* (2002), and Ryan Hendrickson, *The Clinton Wars: The Constitution, Congress, and War Powers* (2002). Pro-Clinton studies describing the relentless investigative attacks that marked his years in office are Sidney Blumenthal, *The Clinton Wars* (2003) and Jeffrey Toobin, *A Vast Conspiracy: The Real Story of the Sex Scandal That Nearly Brought Down a President* (1999).

The unique power relationship formed by Bill and Hillary Clinton has been a source of fascination since his first presidential campaign in 1992. Roger Morris, *Partners in Power: The Clintons and Their America* (1996), is a scathing contemporary account of the Clintons' rise to power. Especially useful and informative is

William Chafe, *Bill and Hillary: The Politics of the Personal* (2012), an account of the ways in which the couple's unique political partnership grew out of Clinton's extramarital exploits, which obligated him to empower the First Lady in important ways. Two reliable studies of Hillary Clinton as First Lady are Gil Troy, *Hillary Rodham Clinton: Polarizing First Lady* (2006), and Carl Bernstein, *A Woman in Charge* (2007). Her own post-White House memoir, *Living History* (2003), while interesting, provides only limited insight into the first couple's relationship and tribulations during Bill Clinton's years in office—as might be expected from "memoirs" published by a very much still-in-the-game politician.

The strong rightward shift at work in American politics that helped explain George W. Bush's strong showing in 2000 despite a booming economy under Clinton is the focus of at least three useful books: Thomas Frank's widely read *What's the Matter with Kansas? How Conservatives Won the Heart of America* (2004); Thomas Edsall, *Building Red America: The New Conservative Coalition and the Drive for Permanent Power* (2006); and Andrew Gelman, *Red State, Blue State, Rich State, Poor State: Why Americans Vote the Way They Do* (2008).

Assessments of the George W. Bush presidency must begin, of course, with the contested 2000 election and its denouement in the U.S. Supreme Court. Easily the most useful and informative analysis of the legal battles that led to the court's decision in favor of Bush is Bruce Ackerman's edited volume, *Bush v. Gore: The Question of Legitimacy* (2002), which includes essays by more than a dozen legal scholars most of whom concur that the court should not have intervened as early as it did, even though it might eventually have had to act. Charles Zelden, *Bush v. Gore: Exposing the Hidden Crisis in American Democracy* (2008), is a nonpartisan analysis of the legal opinions in the various legal cases along the way, while Jeffrey Toobin's *Too Close to Call: The Thirty-six-Day Battle to Decide the 2000 Election* (2001) provides a valuable account of events from election day to court decision. The best analysis of voting results in the election is Gerald M. Pomper et al., *The Election of 2000* (2001).

No fewer than five solid studies of George W. Bush's presidency have already appeared, though three of them were produced before the end of his second term. An excellent analysis that emphasizes the divisiveness of Bush's tactics and policies is Gary Jacobson, *A Divider, Not a Uniter: George W. Bush and the American People* (2007). Two other insightful early studies are Robert Draper, *Dead Certain: The Presidency of George W. Bush* (2007), and Lou Cannon and Carl Cannon, *Reagan's Disciple: George W. Bush's Troubled Quest for a Presidential Legacy* (2008). Julian Zelizer, ed., *The Presidency of George W. Bush: A First Historical Assessment* (2010), includes a number of strong essays on varied aspects of Bush's presidency. Peter Baker, *Days of Fire: Bush and Cheney in the White House* (2013) presents a compelling case for a view consistently held by Bush's Democratic foes: that his presidency was, in fact, nearly a co-presidency, with the vice president a dominant force in both foreign and national security policy. On Hurricane Katrina, which played such an important role in Bush's undoing in his second term, see Douglas Brinkley *The Great Deluge: Hurricane Katrina, New Orleans, and the Mississippi Gulf Coast* (2006).

The unprecedented volume of post-administration literature on Bush's vice president underscores Cheney's inordinately influential role. The two best Cheney books, both essentially sharing Baker's thesis, are Barton Gellman, *Angler: The Cheney Vice Presidency* (2008), and Charlie Savage, *Takeover: The Return of the Imperial Presidency and the Subversion of American Democracy* (2008). An earlier study of the same stripe is Lou Dubose and Jake Bernstein, *Vice: Dick Cheney and the Hijacking of the American Presidency* (2006). Cheney's memoir, *In My Time: A Personal and Political Memoir* (2011), offers little that is new or surprising, but reinforces the same general impression through its tone of certainty about decisions made, especially in the war on terrorism. The influence of another hard-line ally, Secretary of Defense Rumsfeld, is detailed in Bradley Graham, *By His Own Rules: The Ambitions, Successes, and Ultimate Failures of Donald Rumsfeld* (2009). Rumsfeld's *Known and Unknown: A Memoir* (2011) offers a self-assessment as uncritical as Cheney's. Tellingly, no book has appeared that focuses on Condoleezza Rice's influence in the

Bush administration, though she chronicles her contributions in her own memoir, *No Higher Honor: A Memoir of My Years in Washington* (2011). An insightful study of Cheney, Rumsfeld, and "neocon" influence in the Bush years, even though it was published only a few years into his first term, is James Mann, *Rise of the Vulcans: The History of Bush's War Cabinet* (2004).

Every study of George W. Bush's administration, of course, focuses on 9/11 and the war on terrorism. A starting point for those interested in this specific subject is, of course, *The 9/11 Commission Report: Final Report of the National Commission on Terrorist Attacks upon the United States* (2004). Valuable perspectives on both the events of 9/11 and the administration's tactics in responding to those events can be found in: Bob Graham (with Jeff Nussbaum), *Intelligence Matters: The CIA, the FBI, Saudi Arabia, and the Failure of America's War on Terror* (2004); Thomas Kean and Lee Hamilton (with Benjamin Rhodes), *Without Precedent: The Inside Story of the 9/11 Commission* (2006); and Louis Fisher, *The Constitution and 9/11: Recurring Threats to America's Freedoms* (2008). Richard Clarke's memoir, *Against All Enemies: Inside America's War on Terror* (2004), provides insights into the politics of combating terrorism in both the Clinton and George W. Bush administrations. Richard Hass, *War of Necessity, War of Choice: A Memoir of Two Iraq Wars* (2009), is also useful, as are the four detailed volumes on Bush's handling of the war by Bob Woodward: *Bush at War* (2002); *Plan of Attack* (2004); *State of Denial: Bush at War, Part III* (2006); and *The War Within: A Secret History, 2006–2008* (2008). Robert M. Gates, *Duty: Memoirs of a Secretary of War* (2014), is informative about both the Bush and Obama administrations' conduct of the wars after 9/11. Another memoir, Colin Powell's *My American Journey* (1995), provides valuable insights into the administrations of both presidents George H. W. and George W. Bush.

The considerable influence of Karl Rove on Bush's campaign strategies and policies is the subject of Carl Cannon, Lou Dubose, and Jan Reed, *Boy Genius: Karl Rove, the Architect of George W. Bush's Remarkable Political Triumphs* (2005). Rove tells the story from his perspective in *Courage and Consequence: My Life as a Conservative in the Fight* (2010). His key role is also discussed in the only treatment to appear so far on Bush's successful re-election campaign, *Election 2004: How Bush Won and What You Can Expect in the Future* (2004), by Evan Thomas and the staff of *Newsweek*.

The election of Barack Obama, America's first mixed-race president, was truly historic. It was so well chronicled in John Heilemann and Mark Halperin, *Game Change: Obama and the Clintons, McCain and Palin, and the Race of a Lifetime* (2010), which drew on hundreds of interviews, that the work is likely to remain the standard account. Liette Gidlow's edited volume, *Obama, Clinton, Palin: Making History in Election 2008* (2011), is an excellent complement, including a number of incisive essays on race and gender issues related to the campaign and its outcome. In *How Barack Obama Won: A State-by-State Guide to the Historic 2008 Presidential Election* (2009), Chuck Todd and Sheldon Gawiser present a detailed and informative breakdown of electoral behaviors both nationally and on a state-by-state basis.

Since Obama's presidency has not yet been completed as this book is being written, the literature on it is still very much in development. Insofar as *in medias res* analyses can be considered standard works, two stand out: Chuck Todd, *The Stranger: Barack Obama in the White House* (2014), and Morton Keller, *Obama's Time: A History* (2015). Jonathan Alter, *The Center Holds: Obama and His Enemies* (2013), has as its primary focus Obama's successful come-from-behind 2012 re-election victory. Alter's *The Promise: President Obama, Year One* (2010), is also an informative source on Obama's beliefs and tactics, despite its limited chronological focus. James Thurber, ed., *Rivals for Power: Presidential–Congressional Relations* (2013), belying its general-sounding title, contains a number of very strong essays focused on Obama's interactions, successes, and failures with Congress—a subject that will be important to historians in assessing his presidency. The first broad study of Obama's foreign policy is Colin Dueck, *The Obama Doctrine: American Grand Strategy Today* (2015).

Several first- and second-hand accounts of various political battles during the Obama presidency have already appeared. On the great recession of 2007–2009 and the government's response, the most informative accounts are the memoir of Obama's first secretary of the treasury, Timothy Geithner, *Stress Test: Reflections on Financial Crises* (2014); Andrew Sorkin, *Too Big to Fail: The Inside Story of How Wall Street and Washington Fought to Save the Financial System—and Themselves* (2010); and Michael Grunwald, *The New New Deal: The Hidden Story of Change in the Obama Era* (2012). On the battle over health-care reform and its aftermath, see Tom Daschle (with David Nather), *Getting It Done: How Obama and Congress Finally Broke the Stalemate to Make Way for Health Care Reform* (2010), and Lawrence Jacobs and Theda Skocpol, *Health Care Reform and American Politics: What Everyone Needs to Know* (2012). Race politics during Obama's presidency is also the subject of two works: Thomas Sugrue, *Not Even Past: Barack Obama and the Burden of Race* (2010), and Frederick Harris, *The Price of the Ticket: Barack Obama and the Rise and Decline of Black Politics* (2012). The most informative works on Obama's foreign policy to date are James Mann, *The Obamians: The Struggle Inside the White House to Redefine American Power* (2012), and two memoirs,; Hillary Clinton, *Hard Choices* (2014) and Leon Panetta's *Worthy Fights* (2014).

The two grass-roots movements that grew up during the Obama presidency are important manifestations of the political era and have drawn deserved attention. Relevant works on the Tea Party movement are Theda Skocpol and Vanessa Williamson, *The Tea Party and the Remaking of Republican Conservatism* (2013), and Ronald Formisano, *The Tea Party* (2012). Todd Gitlin's *Occupy Nation: The Roots, the Spirit, and the Promise of Occupy Wall Street* (2012) is most informative on the origins and meaning of that movement. Mark Halperin and John Heilemann, in their sequel to *Game Change* focusing on the 2012 election, *Double Down: Game Change 2012* (2013), chronicle the Obama re-election campaign's successful neutralization of these movements, at least for the moment.

Obama will undoubtedly be the subject of numerous political analyses after he leaves the White House. To date, two interesting attempts to "categorize" him have appeared: James Kloppenberg, *Reading Obama: Dreams, Hope, and the American Political Tradition* (2011), and Ruth O'Brien, *Out of Many, One: Obama and the Third American Political Tradition* (2013), which characterizes Obama as a "deliberative democrat," different from both advocates of minimalist government and those favoring a strong welfare state. Time will tell, of course, where the forty-fourth president will fit within the recent American political tradition.

It is certain that additional works will appear that discuss the dysfunctional nature of the contemporary American political system (and that perhaps propose solutions). Inevitably, of course, many of those will be of a highly partisan nature. Two informative and largely objective such studies that have been published to date are Ronald Brownstein, *The Second Civil War: How Extreme Partisanship Has Paralyzed Washington and Polarized America* (2007), and Thomas Mann and Norman Ornstein's very aptly titled *It's Even Worse Than It Looks: How the American Constitutional System Collided with the New Politics of Extremism* (2012). It can only be hoped that, sometime in the not-too-distant future, there will be reason for studies that will describe how the American political system has righted itself and civil, productive politics and government have been restored.

Index

Deadlock and Disillusionment: American Politics since 1968, First Edition.
Gary W. Reichard.
© 2016 John Wiley & Sons, Inc. Published 2016 by John Wiley & Sons, Inc.